P9-DCN-753

Who are you indeed who would talk
   or sing to America?
Have you studied out the land,
   its idioms and men?

(Walt Whitman, from *Leaves of Grass*)

THE TWISTED

Capitalist Development in the United States

DREAM

Since 1776

Douglas F. Dowd

California State University at San Jose
University of California at Santa Cruz

Winthrop Publishers, Inc.
Cambridge, Massachusetts

Library of Congress Cataloging in Publication Data

Dowd, Douglas Fitzgerald
    The twisted dream: capitalist development in the United States since
1776.

    Includes bibliographical references.
    1. United States — Economic conditions. I. Title.
HC103.D75   330.9'73   73-16418
ISBN 0-87626-882-3
ISBN 0-87626-881-5 (pbk.)

Copyright © 1974 by Winthrop Publishers, Inc.
    17 Dunster Street, Cambridge, Massachusetts 02138

All rights reserved. No part of this book may be reproduced in any form
or by any means without permission in writing from the publisher.
Printed in the United States of America.
10 9 8 7 6 5 4 3 2.

To Muh for some beliefs;
to M. M. for some skepticism.

Contents

Figures, Tables, and Charts

Preface

The United States is in the midst of a developing social crisis, at once economic, political, and moral, simultaneously domestic and international. *The Twisted Dream* seeks to identify and explain the nature of and the reasons for this crisis.

The complexity of society and the rapidity of social change in the United States are kaleidoscopic in their appearance and bewildering in their effects. Underlying both the complexity and the change is a coherent pattern that establishes the limits and the possibilities of social change, a set of fundamental institutions that may and must be understood as a *system*. The United States is an advanced industrial *capitalist* system, and the leading nation of the world capitalist system.

The very notion of a social system implies that all facets of social existence—economic life, politics, social behavior and attitudes, education and culture—continually interact upon each other through the system of which they are a part. Rapid change and intermittent conflict are inherent to the functioning of modern capitalist systems. When substantial conflicts persist or become irreconcilable, the system is losing its ability to absorb or resist efforts to share its benefits in new ways. It then moves toward crisis.

Today's emerging crisis, which is one of American and therefore also of world capitalism, is resulting from the renewal and strengthening of dynamically related conflicts within and between the United States and the other powerful capitalist nations, and between all of them and the rest of the world. This is by no means the first crisis of capitalist society and probably not its last, just yet.

Capitalism was born in what is now seen as the European crisis of 1560–1660. Two centuries or so later, the capitalist world was once more rocked by abortive revolutions and (in the U.S. and France) by civil war. The ensuing decades were marked by explosive industrialization and imperialist expansion. The major powers enjoyed relative social stability, for a while. The twentieth century's first pervasive crisis was a direct outcome of the earlier industrialization and imperialism. The resulting stresses and conflicts produced World War I, the first major anti-capitalist revolution, and then a breakdown of the world capitalist system. Out of that breakdown came fascism, the world's most serious depression ever, and World War II.

The two world wars and the social upheavals connecting them in the interwar period pounded the major powers to their knees, exposing both internal and external weakness—for all but the United States. Our global economic and military strength grew as others' declined. From 1940 on, the rising power of the United States was inextricably interwoven with war and Cold War, enormous and continuing military expenditures, and the expansion of our overseas influence and power. But for our system, as for so many others in the past, the diet that gave us our strength was also the source of our growing troubles.

The hot center from which the troubles of the United States seemed to have emerged was our prolonged involvement and attenuated defeat in Indochina. The appearance is based on more than illusion, but confuses effects with causes. Indochina was a vortex pulling the United States in deeper year after year, from the Truman Administration on. That the United States for so long could find no way either to give up on the area or to overcome the Indochinese peoples was not a result of particular personalities, mistakes, or accidents. The United States, as the leader of the world capitalist system, explicably and inexorably played out its role, in Indochina as elsewhere. The burdens were heavy; but so were the gains. All empires meet their limits; ours were found in part in Indochina, and in larger part in the relationships within the Rich Man's Club of the capitalist world.

What made for the gains of empire began, by the mid-1960's, to make for serious strains, in the form of increasing international competition, domestic unrest and economic imbalance, and looming national and international instability. The Indochina war hastened these developments, but was itself part of a larger development: the onset of world capitalism's latest crisis.

These are heady assertions, neither to be accepted nor rejected without systematic inquiry and analysis. Most Americans have had little or no exposure to such analysis; even worse, the "best-educated" in social analysis have been trained much as the feet of Chinese women used to be: bound from childhood, resulting in a crippled elegance.

If we do face a social crisis, and if it is a crisis of capitalist society, the manner in which society moves through time, and why, must be comprehended. We must learn to think in analytical terms that are historical *and* that bridge the gulfs now separating the social sciences from each other, and all of them from history. And if the system that requires this study and this understanding is a capitalist system, then we must learn the imperatives and the modes of capitalist development.

Conventional, or mainstream, social science is utterly weak in the face of this challenge. Its typically narrow, segmented, and static (that is, non-historical) analyses are doubtless useful and necessary for a broad range of purposes; for today's purposes we need something more than that, more (in Stephen Spender's image) than "lectures on navigation while the ship is going down."

The public has every right to expect that those who have studied and taught in the areas of economics, political science, sociology, and history would be well-equipped to understand the system within which and because of which the present crisis stirs, every right to assume that courses at all levels of formal education and an accompanying literature would clarify the nature of our system and how it has come to this pass. Such expectations are vain, as so many students and teachers have discovered in recent years. One can go through high school, college, and graduate school in the social sciences and history without either the obligation or the opportunity to engage in serious discussion let alone systematic analysis of the nature and development of American capitalism, or its place in the larger world capitalist system.

In economics, the subject matter is the functioning of an effectually hypothetical "market economy," with the institutions and the life processes of capitalist economy and society ignored, assumed away as not requiring more than casual comment or, more usually, given a quick and approving glance and taken as permanent and beyond question. Economists must study theory and usually study facts, but the selection of *which* facts to study—concerning, say, product or labor markets, matters of employment, foreign trade and investment, and the like—is determined by the questions arising out of the theory. That theory is carried out on such a high and wrong-headed level of abstraction that the matters most crucial for contemporary understanding are blurred and flattened, much as the great heights of modern air travel make it virtually impossible to distinguish between a plateau and a valley, one city or even one nation from another. Chapter One seeks to show how and why this lamentable state of affairs came to be in economics (and, by extension, in the other areas of social inquiry). I have sought to make this failure understandable both to those who have and those who have not studied economics, a study that should be exciting and informative but which is typically boring and obfuscating.

The problems of abstraction in studying economics apply to the other social sciences as well: while students of economics fail to study the connections of "economic" with vital and interdependent "non-economic" relationships and processes of their capitalist society, political scientists and sociologists abstract from the economic setting of capitalist society; historians, meanwhile, generally pursuing what J. H. Hexter has called "tunnel history," burrow through one branch or another of a history (political, diplomatic, military, etc.), walled off from each other and in abstraction from the socio-economic system that gives the historical process its particular dynamics. There are, of course, exceptions—some books, some teachers—but only rarely do they enter the curriculum of even the most serious students of our society.

In the past few years, efforts at change have mounted. Many teachers, especially the younger ones, now seek to remedy the grave defects of social study, for themselves and with their students. The task they face is formidable. This book is an attempt to make it somewhat less so. If this seems an arrogance on my part, it may be softened somewhat by adding that what I have written is cast as nothing more than a general perspective, a treatment of the main paths along which further inquiry might and should move. Numerous suggestions for further reading are scattered throughout the text and at the ends of chapters to aid the student.* This book can be read by any person of any age or prior education, assuming only a serious concern with society.

The theme that ties the book together is the perception of the United States as a capitalist society, and of capitalism as a system that requires, offers, and imposes two principal conditions on society: expansion and exploitation. It is a work of synthesis, combining what I believe to be valuable from Marx, Veblen, and Keynes with recent works in economics, history, and other social studies. It sees the achievements, the problems, and the tragedies of American history as stemming from the needs and the ability of American capitalism to expand and to exploit in ever changing ways.

This is a critical analysis based on my own system of values and perceptions, which I should make explicit at the outset. Although I have lived what I consider to be a privileged existence, since adolescence I have been horrified by the unnecessary cruelties and deprivations of American (and world) society. Very early I came to the conclusion that although human beings as such need not live badly or at each others' throats, they must continue to do so for so long as they live under capitalist institutions. Capitalism's claims to fame have rested on its presumed ability to enhance production and freedom. But the production it enhances has been achieved at the cost of terrible distortions to the human spirit and to nature, and its products are as unevenly and unjustly distributed as its freedoms. When the choice has arisen between maintaining capitalist power or reducing human freedoms—and the choice has arisen many times—freedom has given way to power; it is doing so today, as these words are written. Oppression did not begin with capitalist societies, nor is it confined to them now, but the entire world has moved within a system of capitalist power and standards for

---

*An asterisk following the title of the works cited indicates that the book is available in paperback.

the past few centuries. The most powerful set the tune to which others dance.

The American people have both the need and the opportunity to throw off the incubus of capitalist relationships. For reasons which I hope will become apparent in this book, the time is long past when any reasonable calculus of advantages from American capitalism can be seen as exceeding its costs to ourselves and others. If the United States emerges from the oncoming crisis as still a capitalist society, it will be necessary for it to become more centralized, more militarized, more oppressive, at home and abroad; already we have gone much too far in all these directions. The human spirit, like our air and water, has been heavily poisoned, and cannot last forever as things now go.

We can and must begin to find ways to free ourselves from the deadly weight of acquisitiveness and combativeness, begin to see our lives, our fellow human beings, and our environment as requiring and enabling cooperation and peace, equality, and genuine economic and political democracy. Whatever else may be necessary to move along such new lines toward what I believe must be a democratic socialist society, understanding and political participation based on understanding head the list of priorities.

If this book contributes to those possibilities, it is in no small measure due to the substantial help I have been given by many friends with whom I have been associated professionally and politically for a few or for many years. The opportunity for me to thank them here is most welcome.

Bruce Dancis, David Danning, and Michael Rotkin read all of the manuscript more than once, and their comments and the standards they sought to have me reach have been of great importance. The knowledge, commitment, and energy displayed by these critics, all students in their twenties, well-represent to me the substantial hope for a new and better society; in *my* twenties, if there were such people around I never had the pleasure of meeting them. Lennie and Marilyn Power Goldberg, John Judis, John Roehmer, Chip Marshall, David de Hart, Kathy and Len Gilbert, Lee Polony, and my son Jeff all made useful suggestions for one or more chapters. Richard Davison, whom I first knew as a graduate student some years ago, is a little-known but most astute scholar in history and economic thought, and his careful and lengthy comments were very valuable to me, as were those of Barbara Wiget Davison.

To my great gratification, I have found the faculty and students at California State University at San Jose to be the liveliest and most congenial in my teaching experience. Many of the teaching staff read parts of early drafts: Rob McBride, David Landes, Marty Davis, Gayle Southworth, and Marvin Lee. Their comments were very helpful. James

O'Connor, also at San Jose, influenced my thoughts on the State, the subject of Chapter Eight, through his critical comments and his own recent book, to which I shall refer frequently.

Honora Moore did what she could to render my language into clear English, as did Nancy Benjamin, my excellent editor at Winthrop. Both she and the others at Winthrop—Paul O'Connell, Michael Meehan, Muriel Harman, and William Sernett—showed that a capitalist enterprise can be efficient, congenial, and sensitive, but perhaps only if it is as small as theirs.

My old friend and colleague from Cornell University, Chandler Morse, who fully represents what is best about both the United States and the university, worked hard through more than one draft. I have incorporated many of his extensive comments almost verbatim, so much so that he is almost a co-author. I am most grateful to him. In a different sense, these remarks may also be applied to Paul Sweezy. I refer not to the time he spent in criticizing this work in draft form, which was substantial, but to his own writings, to those of his late co-workers, Leo Huberman and Paul Baran, and his co-editor at *Monthly Review,* Harry Magdoff. For several decades, Sweezy and his close associates helped to sustain and to create a critical and radical position in America. In my view, they have done more than any others in this country, throughout many years of difficulty and confusion; they are owed a great debt by the Left as well as by many who do not consider themselves so.

Finally, Kay Dowd put up with more and contributed more than any other. She listened to or read through all the variations, contributing wisdom, clarity, and cheerful endurance. And that's not all.

Acknowledgments

Floyce Alexander, "Los Angeles," is reprinted with permission of the author.

Kay Boyle, "O This Is Not Spring" from *Collected Poems* is reprinted with permission of the author.

Robert Creeley, "I Know A Man," from *For Love,* reprinted by permission of Charles Scribner's Sons. Copyright © 1962 by Robert Creeley.

Robinson Jeffers, "Eagle Valor, Chicken Brain," by permission of Jeffers Literary Properties. "Shine, Perishing Republic" from *Selected Poems* by Robinson Jeffers. Copyright 1925 and renewed 1953 by Robinson Jeffers. Reprinted by permission of Random House, Inc.

Pare Lorenz, "The River," from *A New Anthology of Modern Poetry,* Selden Rodman, ed. Reprinted by permission of Stackpole Books.

William Vaugn Moody, "An Ode in Time of Hesitation." From his *Poems and Plays.* Reprinted by permission of Houghton Mifflin, Inc.

Diane di Prima, "Revolutionary Letter #10." Copyright © 1971 by Diane di Prima. Reprinted by permission of City Lights Books.

Lola Ridge, "The Legion of Iron" from *The Ghetto and Other Poems.* Published by B. W. Huebsch. Reprinted by permission of David Lawson.

Carl Sandburg, "Who Can Make a Poem of the Depths of Weariness." From *The People, Yes* by Carl Sandburg, copyright 1936 by Harcourt Brace Jovanovich, Inc.; renewed 1964 by Carl Sandburg. Reprinted by permission of the publisher.

chapter one

Economics and Economies,
Past and Present

O this is not spring but in me
  there is a murmuring of new things.
This is the time of a dark winter in the heart
  but in me are green traitors. . . .

(Kay Boyle, *O This Is Not Spring*)

The American dream has always been complex, never single-minded. Both in its nature and in the struggles fought over its realization, the dream has encompassed a broad range of economic, political, and social aspirations. Still, what stands out most prominently in our history, what has most persistently and effectively absorbed the energies of Americans, is without question the individual and national aim of economic advancement. Sitting at the center of Americans' personal and national self-esteem has been the pride of material achievement; the frame of reference for national policy has had its limits and its directions set mostly by what is compatible with economic criteria. What has most frequently moved us to political excitement have been economic hopes and fears—until, perhaps, yesterday.

America has been the business society, par excellence. If, nowadays, support for business standards is on the wane, is it not because rising numbers of Americans have begun to believe that a business society at its best is none too good? Be that as it may, those now concerned to rid America of the ugly and threatening dynamics which are seen as transforming dream into nightmare are also reversing a long-standing assumption about the American process. An ingrained American belief has been that personal and national *economic* improvement would eliminate or facilitate the resolution of *non-economic* problems. Today, by contrast, the suspicion grows that our very means of achieving economic success have created or exacerbated that long and tragic list of problems now dominating American society: racial and sex discrimination and oppression; poverty; the spread of coercion and militarization in our domestic and foreign policies, along with a growing dependence on

1

military production; cities plagued by intractable fiscal, environmental, and social crises; widespread drug addiction, cutting through all segments of society and reaching down even into early adolescence; petty and large-scale crime and corruption in both private and public life that far outdistances what was thought scandalous only a generation ago; a failure of nerve, of imagination, and of morale in the entire educational system; the disaffection of large segments of the young; and a pattern of centralized and concentrated power, both private and governmental, which, taken together with the secrecy and manipulation that such a pattern requires, presides over all. Watergate has come to serve as both illustration and symbol of a goodly portion of these patterns.

Hidden within that melancholic dirge are of course some cheerier notes; not least of them is that millions of Americans seek to set aright what has gone so badly askew. But nothing will be set aright without understanding why it is wrong. The question *why*, when asked of social problems, is always *historical;* whatever else is also necessary, understanding of a social present requires understanding of how it came to be.

The American dream that now seems so twisted became so over time, beginning with the conception of the dream itself. For our purposes, the conception of the dream can be related to two events of the year 1776. The first was a set of ideas—Adam Smith's *Wealth of Nations;* the second was a set of actions—the American Declaration of Independence. These two events had considerably more in common, in origin, intent, and consequences, than is usually supposed. In the intervening centuries the spirit that motivated both events has been transfigured. What became economics and what became the United States have moved in directions neither expected nor intended by their originators.

To understand why is to understand the dynamics of capitalist development, which in turn requires understanding how very much a capitalist economy requires of its associated social and political framework. The defining characteristics of a capitalist economy are that the means of production—mines, mills, factories, land, etc.—are privately-owned, and operated for the profit of the owners. Such an economy has existed for only a brief fraction of human history, the past few centuries. Special circumstances, in a process of violent change, were required to bring capitalism into existence; its continuation has depended upon a precariously balanced set of social institutions and economic processes: power must be held by the relatively few who own productive property, or by others who move in harmony with the needs of capitalism, in order to allow the *exploitation* intrinsic to capitalist development; and the economy must continually *expand,* both in its production and in its geographic sway. The interaction of these imperatives over time weaves together the economic, political, and social relationships that give capitalism its life, its strength, its dynamics, its virtues and its defects.

Adam Smith (1723–1790) and the Founding Fathers were sophisticated thinkers, aware of the complex web of relationships and processes required and enhanced by capitalist development. But, we may say, they viewed these matters through rose-colored lenses. Their optimism, and their social values, led them to emphasize the gains to be had from capitalist development. They minimized the social costs; or, they assumed that the material successes of capitalism would render such costs negligible. Quite the opposite has transpired. One way of viewing our lives today is to see the social costs of capitalism as having overtaken and passed its material achievements. Too many are exploited, in too many ways, for too little; economic expansion has become too costly to human beings and to the rest of nature.

The historical and analytical support for these assertions constitute the heart of this book. Suppose for a moment the assertions are valid. To understand their whys and wherefores is it necessary to understand what is now called *economics?* No, but it is necessary to develop an analytical perspective on the American *economy.* It is both fortunate and unfortunate that mastery of economics is not equivalent to gaining the needed perspective, or necessary in order to do so. Quite apart from an ideological basis that accepts the status quo, conventional economics (as distinct from critical or radical economics) is neither broad enough in its reach nor deep enough in its penetration to suit today's analytical needs. This is not to deny the existence of valuable elements within conventional economics which, happily, can and must be incorporated into a more appropriate framework. But thinking and working solely within the framework of conventional economics does more to obstruct than to provide the possibilities of understanding the American economy.

Much the same can be said of the analytical state of affairs in the other social sciences and in history. What is needed badly is not further refinements of existing conventional economics and of the other social sciences, but the development of a dynamic social science that starts with our world, our needs, our possibilities. Central in that development must be a dynamic new *political economy:* one that allows us to integrate current with historical developments.

This book is an economic historian's attempt to take a small but important step along that long and difficult path, a step which, if successful, will provide a general perspective that will assist in the development of more specific and more theoretical inquiries. Now some clarification of terms is necessary.

CLASSICAL AND NEOCLASSICAL ECONOMICS

When the term "economics" is used here or, generally, by contemporary economists, the reference is to conventional ("mainstream") *eco-*

nomic theory and its applications. Today's economics is an outgrowth and modification of classical economics; as such, it is called *neo*classical economics. The usage of these classifications is by no means standardized. Marx, for example, saw classical economics ending in the early 19th century and Keynes viewed all economists up to himself as classicists. Here, classical economics will be seen as having its first great thinker in Adam Smith, and its last in John Stuart Mill (1806–1873). Neoclassical economics will be viewed as having begun to take hold in the 1870's, with its most influential thinkers being Alfred Marshall (1842–1924) and John Maynard Keynes (1883–1946). Karl Marx (1818–1883) and Thorstein Veblen (1857–1929), unlike the classical and neoclassical economists, were profound critics of capitalism and of the economists of their own time; their ideas and their social values provide the critical guiding framework for this book's analysis.

All these thinkers were unusually sensitive to the nature, the needs, and the possibilities of their times; all were theorists; all were critics, reformers, or revolutionaries. Most decisive of all, and what made them great, was that the values, analyses, and purposes they expressed coincided with significant social interests in their day, and were thus reflected in practice. They not only studied society; in some measure they changed it. All were concerned with capitalism—lovingly, worriedly, or angrily.

Adam Smith (a Scot) was the first to be so concerned in a fully systematic manner, and the first theoretician of capitalism as a *system.* He laid the groundwork of what became the methodology of classical economics, altered but basically retained by neoclassical economists, transformed and transcended by Marx and Veblen.

All theory, social or physical, works from and within a *methodological* framework, which guides the theorist in what is examined, what ignored, what emphasized, what relegated to secondary consideration, what taken as "given" and what taken as the "variables" to be analyzed. For social theorists, methodology is developed in accord with basic social values, with their conception of human nature and of society, with their initial conception of what problems most require analysis and resolution.

The classical economists, who are also called political economists, had much the same set of social values as their successors the neoclassicists. But the needs of early capitalism were different from those of the ensuing century. The classical economists were concerned with establishing the conditions within which capitalism and industrialism could successfully emerge from the confines still lingering from a precapitalist tradition; the neoclassicists were working with an already well-established industrial capitalist society. As will be seen, Smith and David Ricardo (1772–1823) theorized in order that political constraints holding back development could be understood as doing just that; J. S. Mill, writing some decades later, synthesized classical thought while at the same time seeking to puzzle through some of the consequences of the successes facilitated by the contributions of Smith and Ricardo. These classical economists all constructed analyses that encompassed developments over time, and all related economic to political and social relationships; it was this that made their economics *political economy*. The absence of these characteristics is the most relevant factor in identifying neoclassical economics up through Keynes. The narrowness of neoclassical economics gave it what strength it has possessed; its present grave inadequacies are owed to that analytical narrowness also. Neoclassical economics retains important uses for contemporary purposes, but these uses do not include adding to the possibility of comprehending the dynamics of capitalism. But those dynamics must be understood by both the supporters and the critics of capitalism. Let us now proceed to examine what Adam Smith and the American revolutionaries had in common.

MERCANTILISM, CAPITALISM, AND POLITICAL ECONOMY

Both Smith and the revolutionaries were fighting against British mercantilism, Smith to get it off the back of British capitalism, the Americans to get it off their own backs. Smith correctly saw that mercantilistic restrictions were holding back the dynamic potential of the British economy; the Americans correctly saw that the same system as applied to the colonies not only held back but skimmed the cream from American economic development. Smith had to undertake a full analysis of how capitalism works; much to their surprise, the Americans had to set off a national revolution.

Interestingly enough, although Smith did not anticipate the American revolution—nor did more than a handful of Americans until about 1775—his analysis of British capitalism led him to conclude his book with a critique of British colonial practice that supported the American position:

> The rulers of Great Britain have, for more than a century past, amused the people with the imagination that they possessed a great empire on the west side of the Atlantic. This empire, however, has hitherto existed in imagination only. It has hitherto been, not an empire, but the project of an empire; not a gold mine, but the project of a gold mine; a project which has cost, which continues to cost, and which if pursued in the same way as it has been hitherto, is likely to cost, immense expense, without being likely to bring any profit; for the effects of the monopoly of the colonial

trade, it has been shown, are, to the great body of the people, mere loss instead of profit.[1]

It was Smith who invented the concept "mercantilism," or what he called "the mercantile system." Its importance in his argument and his day requires examination of the term; the fact that much of what capitalist economies practice today is called "neomercantilist" increases the importance of doing so. First, it will be fitting to examine the times in which mercantilism came into being, and seek to extract the essence of those times in order to understand not only the term but its continuation in practice today.

The "mercantilist period" is generally seen as extending from the 16th century through the 18th century. The societies involved directly were the new nation-states of Western Europe. Although each of these societies practiced mercantilism in different ways and over different stretches of time during the three centuries, all were faced with the same general set of conditions, and all held two aims in common: profit and power. As the new nation-states struggled for power, territory, and gain all over the globe, they created an epoch of constant warfare. In the 17th century, when the mercantilist period was at its peak, there were at most four years not marked by international war.

The mercantilist period opened with the expansion of Europe into the Americas, Africa, and the Far East. Maritime trade and navies were essential and dangerous, costly and profitable. Piracy and warfare were inseparable from trade; plunder and slavery were its handmaidens. National economic strength was inseparable from national military strength. Not to win was to lose; national autonomy required national aggressiveness. It was the birth of the modern world, whose defects are thus congenital. If we owe much to those earlier centuries, in our cultural, political, and technological advance, they also set us on the paths of modern nationalism, militarism, imperialism, and capitalism. Then as now, all these were tightly intertwined.

Trade and control over resources in the overseas areas were highly interdependent: spices, sugar, tea and coffee, gold and silver, and slaves obsessed the economic, political, and military figures of that era. Private fortunes and national strength waxed and waned as rivalry and wars for domination of the sea lanes and the lands they connected saw first the Spanish, then the Dutch and, by the 18th century, the French and British struggle for leadership. The 17th century was dominated by the Dutch; the 19th by the British. The Dutch had wrested control from the Spanish; the British from the French. The decisive element in both cases

---

[1] Adam Smith, *An Inquiry into the Nature and Causes of the Wealth of Nations,** McCulloch edition (London, 1869), p. 760.

was the ability to devise an appropriate blend of private and public institutions to enhance the profit and power necessary to national strength.

The Dutch depended upon their genius in making the most of water resources, beginning with fishing, to shipbuilding and shipping, to a complex pattern of overseas trade, pre-modern industry, and finance. The British, slowly coming from behind, took advantage of their agricultural and mineral resources and location (fronting on both Europe and the Atlantic) to put all that together into the first modern industrial society. The energetic development of capitalist institutions and impulses was both cause and consequence of the successes of the Dutch and the British; the complicated failure to break the crust of medieval and dynastic molds largely explains the undoing of the Spanish and the French.

Adam Smith sought a laissez-faire State for Great Britain; that is, a State that would serve as a "night watchman" over economic life rather than as a fussing and intrusive parent. He saw the latter role as characterizing the mercantilist State.[2]

More specifically, there was virtually no area of economic life untouched by State controls, subsidies, or regulations. Overseas trade was carried on through numerous Crown-chartered trading monopolies, only the most famous of which was the East India Company. Industries deemed critical by the State were similarly vested with monopolies of production, although key industries such as arms found themselves on a list which also included whiskey. The supply of labor, the conditions under which labor worked, and its possibilities of geographic movement were subject to intricate regulations. The manner in which the land was farmed was unregulated, but the conditions of land tenure (affecting the control and the sale of land) were subject to non-market constraints. Finance was dominated by a thick web of taxation and, at the end of the 17th century, the Bank of England was chartered so as to gain a virtual monopoly over banking. The French cry of *laissez-faire, laissez-passer!* symbolized Smith's position: freedom of enterprise and movement.

Smith was a good historian and knew that the mercantilist network of private-public privilege and power had served a vital role in earlier periods. He knew that the military and economic risks of the early modern period required the protection and subsidization by the State; that the State's security required a strong economy and access to overseas colonies which would give it the strength to preserve itself. But he

---

[2]"State" is capitalized here, to distinguish it from the American usage that almost always refers to the separate "states." This narrow question and the much more complicated set of matters concerning the State are discussed in Chapter Eight.

saw that what was positive in one historical setting had become negative later, precisely because the success of mercantilist policies had made them unnecessary.[3]

What was negative about mercantilism? In ways that very much suggest current conditions, the intimate cooperation between the State and its private economic favorites had created a locus of power that ultimately and inexorably mixed corruption with economic stultification. Access to the favors of the Crown was the key determinant of private economic activity. Although the activities thus encouraged strengthened some of the muscles of Britain's economy, others remained undeveloped. Trade, industry, and finance by Smith's time required freedom more than parental protection; the laws and customs surrounding labor and the land held back their "rational" utilization. For Smith, not the State but the "law of supply and demand," the free market, was the best determinant of what should be produced, who should produce it, how it should be produced, and how the production should be distributed. This meant the elimination of *all* Crown-granted monopolies, *all* restrictions on trade, and the transformation of land and labor into commodities. The only State activities deemed worthwhile by Smith were those that private business could not—or should not— undertake: defense, justice, and "certain public works."

World trade had expanded enormously in the 18th century. The sea lanes were for England and its powerful navy becoming safe enough to allow a sharp distinction between mercantile and naval voyages: this had been quite impossible in the 17th century. Trading opportunities multiplied, but trade monopolies continued in the ruts of the past. The "industrial revolution" was growling beneath the surface while Smith wrote; industrial monopolies granted by the Crown impeded the possibilities. Surplus labor was bottled up in parishes where work was unavailable; the new factories would need that labor in the growing cities. And so on. *Laissez-faire!*

Smith was unquestionably correct in arguing that the mercantilist policies of the State were hampering private enterprise. In seeking to bring about an unhampered capitalist economy, he was of course seeking also to bring about a society in which the possession and use of private property in the means of production would determine both the qualitative and the quantitative aspects of social existence. Smith believed that by replacing State power with *market competition* as the domi-

---

[3]A misleadingly calm but comprehensive survey of the mercantilist period at its height throughout Europe is given by G. N. Clark, *The Seventeenth Century** (London: Oxford University Press, 1950). A series of analyses emphasizing the change and conflict of the period is Trevor Aston, ed., *Crisis in Europe, 1560–1660** (London: Routledge, 1965). An excellent study of England for the period stretching from 1530 to 1780 is Christopher Hill, *Reformation to Industrial Revolution* (New York: Pantheon, 1968).

nant force in the economy that power itself would be dispersed. He, and those who still follow his belief, failed to see how very strong and effective the impulses would become to replace what we may call "*state* mercantilism," with "*private* mercantilism." Instead of the State granting privileges from the top down, private economic power created its own monopolies, while also using the relatively weak State to protect it or lend a hand.

COMPETITION, POWER, AND PROPERTY

Smith relied upon market competition, what he called the "invisible hand," to transform individual self-seeking into social well-being. He was a wise, observant, and humane person, and in no way innocent concerning the proclivities of businessmen, "an order of men," he said, "whose interest is never exactly the same with that of the public, who have generally an interest to deceive and even to oppress the public, and who accordingly have, upon many occasions, both deceived and oppressed it." [4]

His analytical enemy was the State, the Crown, what we would call the government. That was appropriate enough in his era. Monopoly in Smith's day was not privately achieved, but publicly granted. The truly private enterpriser did not and could not gain pervasive market power, which technology did not then allow. Thus it was reasonable for Smith, distrustful though he was of businessmen, to believe that distortions of economic life *and* of public life had their origins at the top of the society —in the State. He knew that businesses would do what they could to avoid market competition in what they sold for the very reasons that competition is deemed socially valuable: it keeps down prices and profits. He also knew that those same businesses would value competition among those from whom they bought, for the same reasons. What he failed to take into account was how very effective businesses would be in combining their *political* activities with their *economic* activities. The combination was made all the more effective as the development of modern industrial technology rendered small-scale production and therefore competitive market structures less tenable, while access to political power by the larger business firms became both easier and more necessary. Smith's shortcomings on this account are more comprehensible than those of subsequent economists. It is one thing not to foresee the future, and quite another to ignore the facts of everyday life.

One important source of Smith's optimism concerning the consequences of laissez-faire capitalism was a certain myopia regarding the

---

[4]Smith, *The Wealth of Nations,* p. 215.

relationship between property and power, and the decisive relationship between that relationship and capitalist development. Smith was not blind on this matter; far from it:

> Whenever there is great property, there is great inequality. For one very rich man, there must be at least five hundred poor, and the affluence of the few supposes the indigence of the many. The affluence of the rich excites the indignation of the poor, who are often both driven by want and prompted by envy to invade his possessions. It is only under the shelter of the civil magistrate that the owner of that valuable property, which is acquired by the labour of many years, or perhaps of many successive generations, can sleep a single night in security. . . . The acquisition of valuable and extensive property, therefore, necessarily requires the establishment of civil government.[5]

Thus, Smith was not blind at all; but myopic if, as was true, the aim of his analysis was to benefit the society as a whole rather than the few most privileged within it. The last sentence of the foregoing quotation, at least in substance, could have been written by Karl Marx, who saw the State, Smith's "civil government," as "the executive committee of the ruling class." But Smith did not perceive the private owners of productive property as a "ruling class." There is a difference between Smith's belief that property must be protected from the propertyless, and Marx's belief that the existence of a small class of property owners and a large population of the propertyless would set the tone and direction of social development. Smith believed that property had to be protected by the State; he also believed that society would be protected from property by the forces of market competition. That was not to be.[6]

The guiding theme around which the analysis of this book revolves, and that will be emphasized and elaborated upon time and again, is that capitalism thrives not only by *expansion,* which Smith advocated and facilitated, but as well by *exploitation,* which he did not advocate but for which, through his argument for the systematic elimination of social constraints, he provided, although doubtless unintentionally, a basic rationale. The exploitation of labor was intense long before Smith wrote and he fully recognized it as it existed in his own day; the means he proposed for increasing "the wealth of the nation" had as their ultimate end the improvement of the lot of the common people.[7] But the im-

---

[5]Ibid., p. 561.

[6]Problems surrounding Smith's position in this and related areas will be explored again in Chapter Two, pp. 42–5. The data on property and income in the United States will be the subject of Chapter Five.

[7]A readable presentation of Smith's main argument, and one which also centers in upon Smith's humanitarian and communitarian purposes, is Eli Ginzberg, *The House of Adam Smith* (New York: Octagon Books, 1964).

plantation of the Smithian social framework meant that his own social hopes would be brutally swept aside, and that human exploitation would be intensified in ways and to a degree unimagined by Smith.

Writing a century and a half after *The Wealth of Nations,* and thus with the benefit of hindsight, R. H. Tawney (1881–1966) attacked laissez-faire economics by contrasting it with medieval social thought, in these scathing words:

> . . . to found a science of society upon the assumption that the appetite for economic gain is a constant and measurable force, to be accepted, like other natural forces, as an inevitable and self-evident *datum* would have appeared to the medieval thinker as hardly less irrational or less immoral than to make the premise of social philosophy the unrestrained operation of such necessary human attributes as pugnacity or the sexual instinct.[8]

CLASSICAL ECONOMICS AND INDUSTRIAL REVOLUTION

The impact of Smith's *magnum opus* was triggered more by his times than by the ideas themselves. At a critical moment, he had put together existing ideas into a new and compelling whole. His basic argument was not universally accepted, either ideologically or economically; the tendencies energized by the industrial revolution accomplished in fact what his persuasiveness had failed to do. Smith was the broadest in vision and highest in optimism of the classicists. David Ricardo narrowed the scope of argument in his *Principles of Political Economy and Taxation* (1817). In his *Essay on Population* (1798) and his *Principles of Political Economy* (1820) the Reverend Thomas Malthus (1766–1834) substituted apprehension for optimism. Because Malthus' arguments, whether or not attributed to him, have gained a relatively wide audience today, it will be worthwhile to pause a moment to examine them.

Malthus was a pessimist. Economics came to be called "the dismal science" in part because of the gloominess of his anticipations. His gloom centered on two probabilities, both of them imperfectly but vividly argued for: 1) the prospect of population growth outrunning resources, and 2) the likelihood of what we would call stagnation or depression, and which he called "gluts of production." As a parson whose attachments were to the rural virtues, Malthus did not share the enthusiasms of Smith or Ricardo regarding capitalist development. This enabled him to peer more critically at its prospects, albeit quite literally as a reactionary. Taken seriously in his own time, especially by his noted

---

[8]In *Religion and the Rise of Capitalism** (New York: Mentor, 1950), p. 35. Published first in 1926.

theoretical antagonist Ricardo, Malthus came to be scorned by economists over the next century. In more recent years, the laughter has subsided.

This is not to say that Malthus was correct for all times and conditions, although for the functioning of *industrial capitalism* he may well have been. He is best known for his argument that the limits of development are set by the fact that population increases geometrically (1, 2, 4, 8, 16 . . .) but that subsistence (that is, production, especially of food) increases only arithmetically (1, 2, 3, 4, 5 . . .). He was subsequently laughed at because technological development appeared to have intervened to allow subsistence to increase more dynamically than he foresaw, at the same time that industrial development appeared to reduce the rate at which population increased. By the end of the 19th century, economists believed that optimism had a solid grounding in fact: bourgeois economists didn't foresee what imperialist expansion would do to upset the presumably benign relationships then apparent, and Marxists believed that the problems foreseen by Malthus were the problems of *capitalism,* not of economic development as such. When international capitalism moved into the processes of imperialism over the past century—processes considerably more powerful in their impact than the earlier waves of geographic expansion—one consequence was to *increase* population growth rates in the imperialized areas while simultaneously engendering in them a process of retrogressive development (or underdevelopment). The technological developments that relieved population pressures in the advanced countries exacerbated those pressures in the rest of the world—to say nothing of the depletion of resources and environmental problems created by the same processes. Industrialization proceeding under capitalist auspices could benefit a fraction of the world's population, but only at the expense of the rest; ultimately, it appears, only at the expense of all. (Chapters Six and Seven explore these and related questions more fully.)

In his other major argument, Malthus anticipated both Marx and Keynes in their theories of capital accumulation and the determination of the causes of depression. Here we may point to the simple contours of the argument. Production takes place for profit in a capitalist economy. Profit depends upon sales in generally buoyant, that is, sellers', markets. The level of "effective demand" (a concept also used by Marx and Keynes) is the measure of total sales. That level is determined by the combination of sales to businesses (for equipment, etc.) and consumers. The former sales depend upon the actual and expected state of business. The latter depend upon the purchasing power of consumers. Since the state of business is partially and importantly dependent upon consumers' purchasing power, and since the mass of consumers are poor, the economy will periodically or even persistently be faced with gluts—that is, with inadequate levels of effective demand. Malthus therefore saw the need for what he called "unproductive consumption," anticipating Marx and Keynes in their conviction that private prosperity would come to depend upon public spending. The conclusions of Malthusian analyses had some validity, but not in his own time. The decades after he wrote were marked by rapid technological improvement and worldwide economic expansion. He was wrong, but only for a while.

David Ricardo was the most illustrious successor to Smith, both in his effective contributions to political change and to political economy. Ricardo developed "the principle of diminishing returns," which says that increases in the use of one factor of production (e.g., labor) in combination with another *fixed* factor (e.g., land) will mean increasing *inefficiency* after some level of production has been reached. Ricardo used that principle to carry forward Smith's aim of freeing the economy from political restrictions; in this case the restrictions were in the form of protective tariffs on imported grain (called "corn" in England). The Corn Laws made the price of bread unnecessarily high in England; the price of bread was a key determinant of wages; and wages were the strategic factor in manufacturers' costs. Therefore, the Corn Laws provided an unearned income to the better-off landowners but reduced the profits of manufacturers. Industrial development was held back by protective tariffs on grain; Ricardo argued the necessity to abolish the Corn Laws. They were, in 1846.

Ricardo's analytical focus was considerably narrower than Smith's; he used history less and logic more. The analytical procedures of subsequent economists were considerably more affected by Ricardian than by Smithian modes of analysis, although perhaps Ricardo would be unsettled by what he helped to bring about. His great work, *The Principles of Political Economy and Taxation,* was written after he had retired from a successful career in the London stock exchange, and was seen at the time as the highest development of economic science. It was the work of a man who was in close touch with the world he analyzed, combining close reasoning with observable fact and a clear emphasis on policy. Later economists who adopted his logical reasoning all too often tended to neglect the observable facts of their own, different times in favor of seeking more elegant and abstract theorems.

The decade of the 1840's saw the full triumph of Free Trade for Great Britain, both at home and in its foreign economic relationships. In that same decade John Stuart Mill composed the great synthesis of classical economics, his *Principles of Political Economy* (1848). Meanwhile, efforts to reintroduce protections for labor in the market were underway, in the form of Factory Laws, which sought to limit the working hours and conditions of women and children. 1848 was also the year of *The Com-*

munist Manifesto. We shall begin to touch on Marxian ideas shortly; here the continuity and change in the development of conventional economics remains our focus.

John Stuart Mill, writing seventy years or so after Smith, could look back on an economy and an economics that Smith had helped to create. Both the economy and economics were of course very different from what Smith himself had proposed or developed. Mill lived at a time when the human suffering as well as the economic achievements of capitalism were both evident. Furthermore, the problems facing the society were those not of a struggling new capitalism but rather of one beginning to generate the problems of age. Or so it seemed to Mill, for he did not foresee the renewed explosion of economic growth that lay ahead: industrialization spreading all over Europe, North America and Japan; a new wave of technological advance giving vitality to capitalism, through the cheapness of its metals, its fuels, its transportation and communications, its foodstuffs and raw materials; or, making all that possible, the completion and deepening of the imperialist conquest of the entire world by the major powers.

In 1848, Mill believed that the period of major vitality and expansion was drawing to a close. He pondered the probability and the implications of a "stationary state" (i.e., a non-expanding economy), which he, like many today, saw as desirable. He believed that the long hours of work from dawn to dusk were unnecessary, and the conditions of work in mine and mill inhumane; he saw the need for at least mild forms of social intervention. The increase of production had occupied the thoughts of Smith and Ricardo; for Mill the main problem was one of income distribution. He was an urbane and humane believer in capitalism, believing still in 1848 that political liberty and human decency were compatible with capitalist institutions. He was anything but rigid in his attachments, however, as revealed by this passage from his *Principles:*

> If, therefore, the choice were to be made between Communism with all its chances, and the present state of society with all its sufferings and injustices; if the institution of private property necessarily carried with it as a consequence, that the produce of labour should be apportioned as we now see it, almost in an inverse ratio to the labour—the largest portions to those who have never worked at all, the next largest to those whose work is almost nominal, and so in a descending scale, the remuneration dwindling as the work grows harder and more disagreeable, until the most fatiguing and exhausting bodily labour cannot count with certainty on being able to earn even the necessaries of life; if this, or Communism, were the alternative, all the difficulties, great or small, of Communism would be but as dust in the balance.[9]

---

[9](New York: People's Edition, 1872), p. 128. When he wrote, "Communism" and "Socialism" were words used interchangeably.

It is generally believed that by the time he died in 1873, Mill had become a socialist. The development of British socialism in the late 19th and early 20th centuries, it is worth noting, depended considerably more upon Mill than Marx, both in its analysis and its politics.

INDUSTRIAL CAPITALISM AND NEOCLASSICAL ECONOMICS

Classical political economy may be viewed as an attack on and critique of the dying remnants of the feudal and mercantilist epochs. It was an economics of *development*. Development is a process extending over time, taking on its pace, direction, and forms because of the connections *within* the economy and *between* the economy and larger society.

Neoclassical economics came into being at a time when industrial capitalism was established, most especially in Great Britain. In the hands of some, neoclassical economics served as an apologia for capitalism, as a sustained argument showing why Marx was wrong, or why even moderate social intervention in economic life would harm the society. Of equal or greater significance, however, was its function in meeting the positive needs of the business economy. Those needs were not for institutional change, for the abolition of political constraints, and the like. That had been accomplished in Great Britain in the century or more preceding the 1870's, when neoclassical economics began to take the form it carried into the 20th century. Neoclassical economics took the political setting for granted, and made political economy into economics; economics became the science of economizing. It became, in the words of one of its modern spokesmen, "the science which studies human behavior as a relationship between ends and scarce means which have alternative uses."[10]

A "science" of scarcity, of economizing, of maximizing, is *quantitative* in its focus. *Qualitative* relationships can be taken as "given," that is, left unexamined. Not being concerned with development, but with making the most of a good thing, neoclassical economics could ignore historical (that is, real) time; its analysis was static, not dynamic. Social and political institutions, technological change, technology itself, the structures and functions of wealth and power—all this and more could quite logically be taken as given. Those who developed neoclassical economics decided upon these "givens" deliberately and in keeping with those analytical problems they chose to emphasize. Some of their less self-conscious descendants often seem not to know what is even on the list of what is being ignored; as one wag has put it, some students and their teachers may now believe that "society," far from being the subject matter of the social sciences, is merely a synonym for "parameters."

---

[10]Lionel Robbins, *The Nature and Significance of Economic Science* (London: Macmillan, 1932), p. 16.

In short, neoclassical economics works from a methodology that places both process and social relationships outside its ken, except insofar as posited abstractly for purposes of the argument. This is so for the works of all neoclassical economists, including the two greatest, Marshall and Keynes, and despite the quite different questions they confronted.

Economic theory today divides into two major sectors, *microeconomics* and *macroeconomics*. The fundamentals of the former are found in Marshall's *Principles of Economics* (1890) and of the latter in Keynes's *General Theory of Employment, Interest, and Money* (1936). Marshall was the great synthesizer of neoclassical economics; Keynes, finding it necessary in the midst of the disastrous depression of the 1930's to alter a key assumption of that economics, may very well have opened a floodgate in his attempt to plug a hole in the dam.[11]

The classicists, to repeat, were concerned with bringing about change, and the changes were both controversial and substantial. The differences between their focus and that of the neoclassicists is aptly suggested by the epigram on Marshall's title page: *Natura non facit saltum* —nature makes no leaps. It was not the intent of neoclassical economists to provide an analysis that would rationalize such leaps; quite the contrary. Theirs was an explicable response to the needs and interests of business in the latter part of the 19th century, especially and perhaps solely for Great Britain: efficiency and profit.

Marshall saw nature and society as ruled by the "principle of continuity." Change was at the edges of life, slow, incremental, "marginal." In a world characterized by scarcity—of resources, of skilled labor, of capital—because caught up in a pervasive process of industrialization, the problem became one of making the most of what was available: the problem was economizing, or, what is saying the same thing, maximizing. Increased efficiency, enabled and enhanced by economic rationality, was the means to that end. Economics thus focused on the units where efficiency presumably would be achieved. On the supply side that was the individual firm, using materials, equipment, and labor in the most efficient combinations. The economy would be getting the most for the least when all firms produced where their costs and outputs were in quantitative *balance* with prices and purchases, with consumers maximizing "utility"—a subjective and empirically unknowable state. Obvi-

---

[11]Neoclassical economics subdivides more numerously than into two parts: welfare theory, capital theory, wage theory, general equilibrium theory, trade theory, monetary theory; or, in some versions, distribution theory, the theory of markets, and the like. For present purposes micro and macro will suffice. For a penetrating critique of neoclassical welfare economics, see Herbert Gintis, "Neoclassical Welfare Economics and Individual Development," *Occasional Paper No. 3* of the Union for Radical Political Economics (July, 1970). (Hereafter, URPE.)

ously, the laws of supply and demand are a more complicated matter than this. More important, however, is the conception of human nature and society that the classical economists handed down to the neoclassicists, and the latter's modifications of that conception. A digression on this matter is essential.

HUMAN NATURE AND CONDUCT

All competent social theorists begin with a working conception of "human nature" and the ways in which that presumed nature contributes and responds to social relationships and processes. Most of us merely inherit these ideas which lead us unknowingly to accept or reject social ideas and proposals. But the meaning and the validity of any social theory rests upon its view of the raw materials of that theory: the nature of our species and of the process of social change. The most profound differences between those who have accepted capitalism and those who have not are thus to be found in this area of analysis; the other differences follow.

Smith was a philosopher of high esteem before he turned his talents to economic affairs. He believed in an inherent "natural order" superior to anything humans might create, and that the wisest form of social organization is that which allows people to act as nearly as possible in harmony with the dictates of that "natural order." Those dictates, if not interfered with by human and especially governmental meddling—such as those of mercantilism—would lead to an "obvious and simple system of natural liberty." According to Smith, human beings are actuated by six motives: self-love, sympathy, the desire to be free, a sense of propriety, a habit of labor, and "the propensity to truck, barter, and exchange." Let them be, said Smith, and the beneficence of Providence will provide that social order which, though not perfect, is the best to be had. There is little we can do that will be anything but harmful except to let the natural order realize itself. This in turn meant allowing the self-interest which characterizes us to assert itself. Practically, this meant ridding society of the State's meddling and allowing a laissez-faire society to emerge. "Each for himself," as someone has put it, "and God for all." The subsequent development of capitalism led to an added phrase: "As the elephant said, while he danced among the chickens."

If Smith's conception of human nature was narrow—by comparison with Marx, Veblen, and John Dewey, for example—it was narrowed even further by the neoclassical economists (although broadened somewhat by John Stuart Mill who thought education could play a role allowing people to expand social possibilities). For Smith's six human attributes, the neoclassical economists substituted *homo economicus,* compressing human nature into a mold of rational economic maximization, ignoring "sympathy," and seeing labor as something humans seek to avoid. They worked with the now discredited conception of "man as hedonist"—that is, one who seeks to maximize pleasure (especially by consumption) and minimize pain (by minimizing work). Thorstein Veblen, the most penetrating American critic of neoclassical economics and of American society, disposed of their notions of human nature in a brilliantly sardonic passage:

> The hedonistic conception of man is that of a lightning calculator of pleasures and pains, who oscillates like a homogeneous globule of desire of happiness under the impulse of stimuli that shift him about the area, but leave him intact. He has neither antecedent nor consequent. He is an isolated, definitive human datum, in stable equilibrium except for the buffets of the impinging forces that displace him in one direction or another. Self-imposed in elemental space, he spins symmetrically about his own spiritual axis until the parallelogram of forces bears down upon him, whereupon he follows the line of the resultant. When the force of the impact is spent, he comes to rest, a self-contained globule of desire as before.[12]

Marx and Veblen viewed the classical and neoclassical conceptions of both human nature and society as culture-bound and ahistorical, although they might disagree about other fundamental questions. Both saw the human species as a part of nature, rather than a species set apart from or against nature; more important, they saw human beings as transforming nature and (most clearly in Marx) as thereby being transformed as part of nature. Both also perceived human nature as being distorted—Marx used the term "alienated"—by the social conditions of capitalism. As for society, given this conception of the relationship between humans and nature, it followed that *no* form of social organization was "natural": all societies are in a process of continuous change, all are transitory, all are historically dynamic, all give rise to processes and relationships which displace them. The difference between Marx and Veblen on this latter score was not on the question of permanence or change, but on the question of how the process of change works out, and the directions in which it moves. Marx was optimistic, Veblen gloomy.

In addition to these differences between the classical–neoclassical economists and Marx and Veblen, there is one striking difference regarding labor. For Marx, the main motive forces of history revolved

---

[12]In *The Place of Science in Modern Civilization* (New York: B. W. Huebsch, 1919; and Russell & Russell, 1961), pp. 73–74. This book contains the bulk of Veblen's methodological essays, including a critically friendly analysis of Marxism.

around the production and reproduction of life. For Marx, an animal's life—and people are animals—is its *activity,* what it does; first and foremost what humans do is produce and reproduce the stuff of life. Work is not only natural, but fulfilling. Under capitalist conditions, however, people do not labor for themselves. They labor for others, for those who own and control the means of production, who decide what will be produced and why—for profit—it will be produced, and by whom the workers, because they are propertyless and thus powerless, are exploited. Under such conditions, Marx said, the worker is *alienated.*

> First, . . . the work is *external* to the worker, . . . it is not part of his nature;
> . . . consequently, he does not fulfil himself in his work but denies himself, has a feeling of misery rather than well-being, does not develop freely his mental and physical energies but is physically exhausted and mentally debased. The worker, therefore, feels himself at home only during his leisure time, whereas at work he feels homeless. His work is not voluntary but imposed, *forced labour.* It is not the satisfaction of a need, but only a *means* for satisfying other needs. Its alien character is clearly shown by the fact that as soon as there is no physical or other compulsion it is avoided like the plague.[13]

Because the productive life of people under capitalism is necessarily alienating, Marx saw workers as therefore alienated from nature, from themselves, from other human beings, and from their essential and distinctive nature (which Marx called "species-being"). For the conventional economists' mechanical view of humans, Marx substituted a dynamic view, where human beings, nature, and society moved in a process of continuous interaction. Fundamentally, Veblen agreed.

Veblen put forth his views in *The Instinct of Workmanship* (1914). Before examining those views, it is necessary to show how he uses the term "instinct," for many of the criticisms leveled at Veblen have sought to dismiss him as being "unscientific" for merely using the word. After stating that "instinct" is a concept "of too lax and shifty a definition to meet the demands of exact biological science," Veblen goes on to say the following:

> A genetic inquiry into institutions will address itself to the growth of habits and conventions, as conditioned by the material environment and by the innate and persistent propensities of human nature; and for these

---

[13] *Karl Marx; Early Writings,* * translated and edited by T. B. Bottomore (New York: McGraw-Hill, 1963), pp. 124–25. This book contains the so-called "Economic and Philosophic Manuscripts" of 1844, where Marx's theory of alienation, which lies at the base of much of his later thinking, was first expressed. These manuscripts were unpublished until 1932. Although Veblen, who died in 1929, could not have known of these ideas directly, his own views are strikingly similar.

propensities, as they take effect in the give and take of cultural growth, no better designation than the time-worn "instinct" is available. . . . "Instinct," as contradistinguished from tropismatic action, involves consciousness and adaptation to an end aimed at . . ., the conscious pursuit of an objective end which the instinct in question makes worth while. . . . The ends of life, then, the purposes to be achieved, are assigned by man's instinctive proclivities; but the ways and means of accomplishing those things which the instinctive proclivities so make worth while are a matter of intelligence. . . . Men take thought, but the human spirit . . . decides what they shall take thought of, and how and to what effect.[14]

Veblen's "instinct of workmanship" virtually equates with Marx's notion of work as the life activity of human beings, in the sense that workmanship and what Veblen calls "the parental bent" refer to the production and reproduction of life. The sense of workmanship has for Veblen a "sub-instinct," that of "idle curiosity." It is this that accounts for the growth of technology, science, and culture, and that makes human beings into transformers of nature and not merely a part of it. For Veblen, as for Marx, what he calls "the regime of private property" leads people to shirk labor and to become reduced as human beings. Another "instinct" of Veblen's is worth noting: "the instinct of sportsmanship" is his ironic way of referring to the combative, warlike, and ultimately self-destructive penchants recorded in history. If Veblen is gloomier than Marx, part of the reason is that he sees workmanship and sportsmanship as running a sort of race between life- and death-giving activities, with little reason to believe that a society controlled by "force and fraud" would allow the race to be won by life. We will have occasion to return to these questions later. Now we turn our attention back to the nature and evolution of neoclassical economics.

TRANSFORMATION AND FAILURE OF THE MARKET ECONOMY

The narrow and mechanical view of human nature and the view of the basic outlines of 19th century British society as the representation of an essentially unchanging "natural order" verge on the ludicrous today. Even as the basic analytical framework of neoclassical economics was being constructed, it was being consigned to irrelevance. The market economics of Marshall assumed a competitive and small-scale economic structure; otherwise it made no sense. But in the very period in which he wrote, monopolies were moving toward center stage; today all the major industrial capitalist powers are characterized by monopolistic

---

[14] *The Instinct of Workmanship** (New York: Macmillan, 1914), pp. 2–6.

(technically, "oligopolistic") structures of ownership and control. (See Chapter Three.) Marshall assumed and advocated an unobstrusive, though not an unimportant, State; all modern States are interventionist, and obviously so. The world of Marshall was seen as one of market scarcity; although a desperate scarcity of needed goods exists for most of the people of the world today, *market* scarcity is not a major problem for the people of the industrial powers. Their problems, instead, revolve around questions of distribution, direction, and quality; their political economies are indeed the major cause of scarcity for the rest of the world. In Marshall's world, one power was pre-eminent: Great Britain. Today, there are non- and anti-capitalist powers of great and lesser strength, and capitalist rivals for the once unchallenged strength of Britain and, now, of the United States. An "economics of choice" in such a world becomes something worse than a bad joke; it is positively dangerous to the degree that it is taken as a basis for thinking about *economies.*

One might think that the extraordinary turbulence of the period that began in the 1890's, that encompassed World War I, the Soviet Revolution, a decade of economic stagnation in Great Britain (in the 1920's), and the emergence of fascism in Italy and Germany, would have caused mainstream economists to re-evaluate their theories. But it took the Great Depression of the 1930's to even begin that process; then, as will be seen, the changes brought about were theoretically peripheral, if also of great practical importance.

DEPRESSION, KEYNES, AND WAR

The central importance of economic expansion for the maintenance of capitalism is so great that we shall devote much of two chapters (Four and Seven) to explaining why that is so, and under what conditions the need has and has not been met. Here our attention will be confined to the alteration of economics induced by the *failure* of expansion after World War I. Great Britain was economically stagnant throughout the twenties, suffering from an average of 10 percent unemployment for the decade. The entire capitalist world collapsed in 1929, and the collapse was most devastating in the two most highly-industrialized nations, the United States and Germany.

The enormity of that depression is suggested by the fact that industrial production in the United States and Germany fell by 50 percent. Since World War II, by way of contrast, it has never dropped more than a few percentage points, and then for very brief periods. Neoclassical economics was caught off guard by the Depression. The facts were plain, but the theory could not handle such facts. Neoclassical theory, until it was revised in 1936, taught that when unemployment occurred it was "voluntary"; that is, it was because workers were demanding excessive wages. When unemployment rose to 25 percent of the labor force (1933) and long bread and soup lines were a daily sight in all cities, it became difficult to believe that unrealistic expectations concerning wages had placed the unemployed on those lines. There were no jobs to be had at *any* wages for them.

The theoretical sticking-point for the economists was "Say's Law." Jean-Baptiste Say (1767–1832), who sought to implant Smith's ideas in France, had shown the theoretical impossibility of depression in arguing that "supply creates its own demand." That is, everything produced would be sold, either to consumers or to businesses, because 1) the value of production created money incomes of an equivalent value, and 2) that portion of incomes not spent on consumer goods but saved would be offset by business purchases of investment goods. The key notion allowing this conclusion was that consumers would reduce their expenditures to save *only* because the rate of interest on savings would induce them to do so; the rate of interest was determined by the demand for funds created by those investors. In short, consumption and investment were reciprocally motivated; if consumption declined it was *because* investment rose to the same degree. Thus, supply creates its own demand. Of course if workers irrationally chose to demand wages higher than they were worth, they were choosing to place themselves out of the labor market.

Keynes's *The General Theory of Employment, Interest, and Money* jiggled one assumption in that theory and came out with opposite conclusions. It showed that consumption and investment are *not* reciprocally motivated; that savings are related more to changes in money income than to the rate of interest. Not only could depression and high unemployment occur, but in the normal and rational functioning of industrial capitalism they were downright likely, and, without government intervention, the economy could get stuck in them with no tendency to escape. Up to the time of the *General Theory*, classical–neoclassical economics had served to show why governmental intervention was both unnecessary and undesirable. Keynes, though himself a neoclassical economist of the highest order, showed why intervention was necessary in order to save capitalism itself. Capitalism had matured; it had to take care.

Like all the great thinkers who had preceded him, Keynes was not so much a creator of new ideas as one who integrated others' ideas *and* at a time when events compelled attention. Swedish economists had for several years been developing the basic ideas presented by Keynes, and Keynes was directly and indirectly assisted by a small group of young and brilliant economists such as R. F. Kahn, Joan Robinson, and Michael Kalecki.[15]

Depression or no, resistance to the new ideas in the economics profession was strong and lasting, as Keynes had anticipated. "The difficulty," Keynes wrote in the Preface to *The General Theory,* "lies, not in the new ideas, but in escaping from the old ones, which ramify, for those brought up as most of us have been, into every corner of our minds."[16] If anything, the opposition to Keynesian ideas was even greater among practical "men of affairs" who did not relish being told that thrift was not necessarily a virtue, and that not only government spending but *deficit* spending (that is, an excess of government expenditures over taxes) and perhaps even socialized consumption and investment had become at least intermittently necessary. For American businessmen and politicians, the blocks to understanding were all the higher, given the British citizenship and aristocratic mien of the theorist, theorists being suspect enough in any case.

President Franklin Roosevelt and Congress responded noticeably but ineffectually to the prescriptions of the "New Economics," but widespread acceptance came only after the practical experience of World War II and the Cold War taught both economists and businessmen that the ideas worked and that the policies were profitable when applied. The first textbook to incorporate Keynesian ideas was Paul Samuelson's *Economics* (1947), banned in several states as being "communistic"; the first administration after World War II to absorb and apply the ideas seriously was that of John F. Kennedy; by 1970, even the arch conservative Richard Nixon had announced "I am a Keynesian." Keynes died in 1946. It is doubtful that he would have been pleased with the narrowing and the application of his ideas which allowed their acceptance even in the farther reaches of American conservatism.

Such an evolution requires explanation of what Keynesian theory accomplished and what it left undone. Only its bare bones have survived; not only policy-makers but most economists are unaware of the body surrounding those bones in Keynes's original presentation and in his subsequent arguments. He caused neoclassicists to examine a few of their premises; the main machinery of their economics survived and has gone on to spin even finer webs of counter-factual analysis.

Keynesian theory is often called "the theory of effective demand." It places the cause of depression in inadequate levels of aggregate demand

---

[15]Joan Robinson, herself a noted neoclassical economist at the time, has subsequently done much to reintegrate Marxian theory into what is valuable in conventional theory. Kalecki was even then a brilliant Marxist; he did much to enrich theory before his death in 1970. See his *The Last Phase in the Transformation of Capitalism.** (New York: Monthly Review Press, 1972), a collection of essays.

[16] *The General Theory,** p. viii.

for goods and services, the key component of which is the demand of businesses for investment goods (plant, equipment, etc.). Such expenditures take place both to maintain existing productive capacity, and to expand productive capacity. The latter is called *net investment,* and is the source of economic expansion. Net investment takes place only when investment is expected to yield a satisfactory profit. In a business society, this sounds like common sense. It is a way of saying that the key economic *decisions* are made by businessmen, even though the largest share of all *expenditures* is made by consumers. When profit expectations are inadequate, investment will be inadequate to maintain adequate levels of production, employment, and income. The critical problem then becomes one of understanding what determines the state of profit expectations, thus of the volume of investment, thus of the degree to which the economy will or will not expand. That is the analytical problem; the real-world problem is that increases in production, employment, and income, far from providing the basis for their maintenance—as Say's Law proposed—guarantee instead that at some point investment will fall, and bring everything else down with it. Consequently, for Keynes, a source of demand other than private consumption and private investment must stand in readiness to fill in the gap: government spending.[17]

What was wrong with Say's Law? It did not recognize that as the national income rises so do savings. Consumer expenditures of course rise with income; but they rise at a declining rate. That is, savings rise at an increasing rate. Therefore, the volume of investment must rise as income rises. But money income has risen because production and productive capacity have risen (setting aside inflation). Thus the need for investment *increases* just when the likelihood rises that *excess* productive capacity, profitless productive capacity, will emerge. Expansion is brought to an end by its very successes. (Marx and Veblen came close to the same kind of argument.) Why is *deficit* government spending necessary at that stage? Because the government must spend, and if it were to do so while also raising taxes it would take with one hand what it is giving with the other. It may be added that when the economy is facing unduly rising price levels, Keynesian analysis applies equally well, but turned around: monetary and fiscal policies should aim to curb private spending, raise interest rates to discourage such spending, and also tax more than the government spends. All capitalist governments have put these notions into practice in one setting or another and to one degree or another in the recent past.[18]

---

[17]Also, in times of slack demand, monetary policy (exercised by the Federal Reserve System) should seek to reduce interest rates to lower the *obstacles* to investment.

[18]For useful discussions of American and European practices since World War II, see Andrew Shonfield, *Modern Capitalism** (New York: Oxford University Press, 1965). The details of the American experience will be traced in Chapter Four, below.

Keynesian economics constituted a significant improvement over what preceded it, but at least three things have rendered its meaning inadequate for the present. First, as suggested above, its acceptance was only partial. Although Keynes both in and subsequent to the *General Theory* showed that he understood the need for structural changes in the economy—in production, consumption, income distribution—today's Keynesians continue to analyze and prescribe in terms of marginal adjustments and aggregative policies. Their effect is to maintain rather than to change structures, at best. Second, Keynes developed a theory for an economy whose dynamics were national, or domestic; the internationalization of the American economy requires a substantial theoretical alteration, not merely an "adjustment," to handle those dynamics. Third, the theory Keynes developed was meant to apply to a fundamentally private economy, with government activities brought in to alter troublesome developments. Today's economy is privately dominated, but the structure of the economy is heavily and permanently infused with government as spender, taxer, employer, etc. In different words, Keynesian theory pounded cracks in the wall of neoclassical laissez-faire philosophy and capitalist practice; in doing so, it necessitated a different theory, one that would incorporate an imperialist State into its analysis. Mainstream economics shows no inclination—nor did Keynes —to move along those lines; its principal tendencies in recent years have been to mathematize and refine the micro and macro economics of the past. At the edges of the mainstream, however, some attempts are underway, in economics and in the other areas of social analysis.

TOWARD A NEW POLITICAL ECONOMY

The attempts now underway to change the various aspects of social analysis are a response to a society that is changing rapidly and under great stress, whose major characteristics interact in such a way as to threaten what has not already been damaged or destroyed. All the economists we have looked at were responding to the needs of their times for changes, large or small; except for Marx and Veblen, the changes they sought were designed to strengthen or to preserve industrial capitalism. The search for a new society, not the shoring up of the status quo, underlies today's search for a new social analysis.

This chapter opened with the observation that a long and tragic list of social problems, from racism to centralized power, is now seen as having a close or significant connection with the successful functioning of American capitalism. No single one of those "problems" owes its existence to economic relationships alone, if by economic we mean what conventional economists mean—namely, supply and demand relationships. Even with that narrow definition of economics, however, it may be asserted that none of these problems exists except that in some way or in some degree its origins and persistence connect with the economic relationships of American capitalism. What degree? What ways? Why? How? Since when? With what prospects for improvement or worsening?

Conventional economists cannot, as such, be expected to answer such broad and complicated questions adequately; as *economics* is refined into ever more specialized compartments and techniques, it is reasonable to expect that conventional economists' understanding of the *economy* will decline further.

A capitalist economy rests upon and promotes private ownership of the means of production, and production for profit, the main breeding grounds of power in our society. It moves through time, and changes as it moves; it is dynamic and it requires a compatible social and political framework, one that appears to be incompatible with the needs and potentials of a large portion of its population.

As citizens, some conventional economists have found ways to understand some or all of these matters. When they do so, it is as reasonably informed and wise individuals. As economists (that is, as people working within and applying a body of economic theory), almost all of what now concerns the American people and themselves as citizens has been deliberately and in principle excluded from the reach of their theory. Conventional economic theory does not raise the appropriate questions; when conventional economists do raise such questions they do so without the guidance of their theory. If untrained people knew more of this they might understand why economists seem as mystified as the person in the street by problems such as simultaneous inflation and recession and world monetary crisis. And they might conclude, as many younger economists have concluded, that still another New Economics is needed.

The strong criticisms of conventional economics running through this chapter should not be construed to suggest that economics—let alone theory as such—is useless. Neoclassical economics, or "marginalism," is a theory of minor adjustments within a given social and economic framework. It makes no pretense of providing understanding of socio-economic structures and processes, or of when and why it might be necessary to seek structural changes in production, consumption, trade, income distribution, investment, or, say, in the structure of power. Minor adjustments to achieve improved efficiency are always called for, in *any* economy; marginalism of the micro or the macro variety will be useful so long as that is so.

But at a time when structural changes are badly needed and loudly called for, society has the right to expect something more than marginalist theory from its economists. Economists are not but should be servants of all the people, not just of those presently in power. "The people" is of course an over-general abstraction. There are conflicting groups of all sorts among "the people." Economics claims to serve everyone and no one, and to do so in the name of objectivity. But of course the profession contains within it economists who do in fact, well or badly, serve one or another of those groups, whether the economist is in a university, the government, a trade union, or a corporation. Mostly they serve those closest to the maintenance of the status quo.

Under these circumstances objectivity becomes a pretense; it is also a state of confusion. Objectivity means writing, thinking, and teaching with scrupulous and fearless regard for evidence, logic, and honesty. That is what it means. If, however, one means by *objectivity* what most social scientists seem to mean—namely, social *neutrality*—the matter is transformed. Nobody should be neutral, and probably nobody can be, except by self-delusion. Everybody should be objective and everybody can be. Those who know where their sympathies lie on the omnipresent range of human controversies can be objective *and* they can consciously distinguish between objectivity and neutrality. Those who make no such distinction and who confuse the two are neither objective nor neutral. They mislead themselves and cannot help but confuse and mislead those with whom they communicate. It may be said that the classical economists did not work under such confusion; the confusion became rampant with the presumed scientism of neoclassical economics, whose training has encouraged it. This is one of the reasons why so many conventional economists today are taken aback by the politically candid, self-styled "radical economists," whom they criticize for *being* political. But everyone is political, those who wish to preserve things as much as those who wish to change them. Everyone cares; save us, especially in the social sciences, from those who don't.

Caring is not enough, of course. We need an appropriate framework of analysis. Whatever else it must be, this framework must be informed by history. What is changing cannot be understood except as part of a process that leads to change. To study historically is to study in terms of *connections;* it is to take fewer matters as *given.* Conventional economics shies away from such modes of inquiry; political economy in the past did not. The political economy of the present and the future cannot. We need not start from scratch. Not only Marx and Veblen, but others less well-known and less critical, have studied so. The analyses they constructed remain inadequate for our time and place, but they are still a place to begin an examination of political economy.

The range of Marx's inquiries was as broad as society itself, although he bore down most heavily on economic analysis, in *Capital.* Almost all conventional social scientists, and not least the economists among them, have rejected the possibility of Marx having said anything of use to those living in capitalist society—and most of those have done so with the confidence that comes from not having bothered to read Marx. Veblen is a name that is now virtually unknown in professional circles, except perhaps as that quaint man who coined the term "conspicuous consumption" so long ago.

The indifference and scorn meted out to these two intellectual giants is something made comprehensible by their own analyses; that is, their analyses explained the manner in which critical theories are deflected by an intellectual status quo, as well as by those in practical life. Both also help us to understand why basic impulses toward change in economics and in the society have taken this long to appear. It is a matter of staying power, and of the enormous difficulties attaching to both intellectual and social change. Those out of power have little to work with and much to oppose; those in power have much to work with and little to oppose. Until, that is, the society finds itself in a crisis.

It appears that American society, and economics as well, is now in the first stages of a profound crisis. As the crisis deepens, the social consciousness of all is enhanced, and those with power find it more necessary and more difficult to keep their hold on things.

Since the 1930's, conventional economics has been in a process of transformation as it has attempted to cope with a whole new range of pressing questions: depression, endemic inflation, business monopolies and trade unions, modern public finance, economic growth and development, poverty, ecology, and a series of complicated international developments. But when those efforts have been informed by theory, the theory has remained neoclassical theory. If theory may be thought of as a compass, it may be said that a bad compass is likely to be worse than none at all: errors become systematic and cumulative. This cannot be taken as an argument for substituting hunches and intuition for inadequate theory; we need to develop a new theory.

Whatever else might characterize that theory, it must come to terms with history. In a time of rapid and troubling change, the minimum basis for understanding is that we know how we got to where we are, and why; in a time when change cuts through all quarters of social existence, we must know how the various aspects of social existence connect and interact. The specialization of social inquiry that has given us "economics," "sociology," and "political science," and innumerable specializations within each of those, has led to analytical compartments hermetically-sealed off from each other. The social analysis our times require must take society for what it is, an organic and dynamic whole. Were such an analysis to develop, many of the specialized efforts of conventional social scientists could take on a new and positive meaning.

Attempts are being made to move in these directions in all the social sciences. In economics the most noteworthy development has been the emergence of the Union for Radical Political Economics (URPE). Begun in the late 1960's, amidst a certain hilarity from the better-established members of the profession, URPE is now a growing and increasingly respected organization. Its journal, the *Review of Radical Political Economics (RRPE)*, has provided an outlet for numerous searching inquiries and critiques of conventional economics and of the American economy. We shall have reference to many of these contributions in this book.

Neither the tasks set by URPE for itself, nor those set by their counterparts in the other social sciences, will be easily or quickly fulfilled, anymore than a decent and safe society will be easily or quickly created. Among the matters on the agenda, one that compels immediate attention is the attempt to comprehend the whys and wherefores of capitalism as a social system, and the manner in which that system has worked itself out in the United States.

READING SUGGESTIONS

In this and succeeding chapters we shall list books that will facilitate the serious reader's ability to push beyond the very general perspective offered here. Countless references could be listed; the criterion guiding these is some combination of accessibility, readability, breadth and depth.

Robert L. Heilbroner, *The Worldly Philosophers** (New York: Simon and Schuster, 1953) is a lively introduction to the lives and works of the major figures in the development of economic thought. If it is occasionally too breezy, that quality is perhaps an inevitable accompaniment of the author's most readable style. Eric Roll, *A History of Economic Thought** (Englewood Cliffs, N.J.: Prentice-Hall, 1946—subsequent editions should be avoided) is by no means lively, but it does penetrate more deeply than Heilbroner, and is especially useful in relating the classical and neoclassical economists to each other and in placing Marx with respect to them. Leo Rogin, *The Meaning and Validity of Economic Theory: A Historical Approach* (New York: Harper's, 1956) is the most incisive and insightful analysis of how and why economic theory developed, up through Keynes. Unfortunately, the author died before he completed this work, and parts of the text reflect this. Nonetheless, it is a superb analysis.

The shortcomings of conventional analysis can be studied from various standpoints. Joan Robinson, *Economic Philosophy** (Chicago: Aldine, 1962) is a cheerful but slashing critique of conventional theory by one who has made substantial contributions both to it and to Marxian theory. Benjamin Ward, in his *What's Wrong with Economics?* (New York: Basic Books, 1972), laments the methodological inconsistencies and inadequacies of conventional economic theory in a detached but devastating analysis. Sidney Schoeffler, *The Failures of Economics: A Diagnostic Study* (Cambridge, Mass.: Harvard University Press, 1955) is an earlier technical critique of economic theory from a coolly logical standpoint, an attempt to reform from within that has been studiously ignored by the profession since its publication. A book concerned with the development of theory in the natural sciences, Thomas Kuhn, *The Structure of Scientific Revolutions* (Chicago: University of Chicago Press, 1962), which sought to show how and why the hard core of scientific theory—what Kuhn calls their "paradigms"—undergoes development and displacement, has stimulated controversy on the degree to which his analysis applies to *social* thought. URPE, in its *RRPE*, vol. 3, no. 2 (July, 1971), devoted an issue to that controversy: "Special Issue on Radical Paradigms in Economics." Responding to the Nixon policies of late 1971 and to the current state of macroeconomics, the *RRPE* devoted another issue to "On the New Economic Policy: The New Economics and the Contradictions of Keynesianism," Special Issue, vol. 4, no. 4 (August, 1972), perhaps best read after Chapter Four below. James Weaver, ed., *Modern Political Economy: Radical and Orthodox Views on Crucial Issues** (Boston: Allyn & Bacon, 1973), provides a useful series of contrasting views. Many of the criticisms of economics made here have their counterpart for sociology in C. Wright Mills, *The Sociological Imagination** (New York: Oxford Univeristy Press, 1967).

The best introduction to Marxian *economic* theory is Paul M. Sweezy, *The Theory of Capitalist Development** (New York: Monthly Review Press, 1968; originally published in 1942), although it is somewhat dated in some of its contemporary judgments. I have sought to do something of the same thing in my *Thorstein Veblen** (New York: Washington Square Press, 1964) for Veblen's entire range of social analysis. Dudley Dillard, *The Economics of John Maynard Keynes** (Englewood Cliffs, N.J.: Prentice-Hall, 1948) does for Keynes what Sweezy did for Marx, for those who wish to "do" Keynesian theory.

I have stressed the importance of history and in the following chapters will take this advice, at the same time incorporating the ideas of Marx and Veblen, both historical in their approaches. William Appleman Williams, one of the very best American historians, in his *The Great Evasion** (New York: Quadrangle, 1964), argues that American scholars and citizens have been badly crippled in their ability to understand their country by their assumption that Marxism is irrelevant to American development. Others of Williams' books will be cited later.

A Marxian view of American and of world history may be found in two books of Leo Huberman: *We, the People** and *Man's Worldly Goods,** both available in paperback from Monthly Review Press. Both these books were written in the 1930's by a humane and brilliant man who was a lifelong socialist. Both can now be seen as having serious errors of omission and commission—regarding racism, sexism, and what now appears as an uncritical view of the Soviet Union. That so fine and learned a man as Huberman could make such "mistakes" is instructive. Thus, although we might hope that no decent white person would write of Native Americans today as Huberman did in his *We, the People,* we may be quite sure that virtually all whites did then. Regarding the Soviet Union, a different point must be made: in the 1930's to join in the general attacks on the Soviet Union was to join a reactionary crusade, setting aside entirely the difficulty of having access to reliable information. Young and old are still making "mistakes," and doing so honorably. Louis M. Hacker, *The Triumph of American Capitalism* (New York: Columbia University Press, 1940), puts forth a somewhat crude Marxian analysis through the 19th century, and departs entirely from that view for the 20th century.

Two other books, quite different from each other, are worth noting here. One shows that realism in economics has not always required radicalism in viewpoint. J. M. Clark, *Studies in the Economics of Overhead Costs* (Chicago: University of Chicago Press, 1923), sought to integrate "micro" and "macro" materials into a dynamic whole, connected to the facts of modern industrial life in the United States. Clark's father was perhaps the most eminent of American neoclassical economists; J. M. Clark himself was much influenced by Veblen's down-to-earth approach, although not by his social outlook. In any case, the economics profession has taken little or no advantage of Clark's major contribution. We have said a bit about alienation in this chapter, and will have reason to bring the matter to the fore again. A convenient and broad collection of fictional and non-fictional essays in the general area is Eric and Mary Josephson, eds., *Man Alone: Alienation in Modern Society** (New York: Dell, 1962).

Note: Many of the works cited throughout this book are available in relatively inexpensive paperback editions. Such editions are identified here by an asterisk following the title of the work (whether or not the reference pertains to the original work or to the paperback reprint).

chapter two
Capitalism

Unhappy, eagle wings and beak, chicken brain
Weep (it is frequent in human affairs) weep for the terrible
  magnificence of the means
The ridiculous incompetence of the reasons, the bloody and
  shabby
Pathos of the result.

(Robinson Jeffers, *Eagle Valor, Chicken Brain*)

Capitalism is a world economic system with a global division of labor.
Its emergence and development over the past several centuries has been
the dominant force of world history. Capitalist nations have certain
basic characteristics in common; each capitalist nation also has defining
characteristics that set it apart from and often in conflict with the others.
For certain analytical purposes, the defining national adjective—American, British, German—is critical; for other purposes the noun capitalism
is decisive. For our purposes it is essential to grasp and integrate the
meaning of both. As Maurice Dobb has put it,

> Capitalism is not a system that is cut to a certain pattern and remains the
> same for all time. Product of a complex process of historical development,
> capitalism is itself continually subject to historical development. It
> changes from one decade to the next, it is different in many respects in
> one country from what it is in another country, according to the specific
> features of that country and according to the peculiarities of that coun-
> try's history. . . . But that does not mean that it is not valuable to pick out
> and to study certain *general features* of capitalism—to isolate and analyze
> certain relationships that are typical of capitalism in all its varied forms
> and manifestations. In fact it is essential to do this as a *preliminary* to a
> more detailed study, if we are to see the wood for the trees—if we are to
> grasp the general lie of the land as well as be acquainted with each
> separate bit of it.[1]

---

[1]Maurice Dobb, *Economics of Private Enterprise** (Sydney: Current Book Distributors,
1944), p. 3.

Our concern is with American capitalism. The latter part of this chapter will examine its beginnings and some of its general features; the rest of the book will analyze its development up to the present. But first we must focus upon the nature and imperatives of capitalism in general.

Where capitalism has emerged, it has always been in a specific historical context, within a particular culture. The ways in which, say, British capitalism evolved are owed to the specific temporal, spatial, historical, and cultural characteristics of Great Britain. But all these characteristics in turn were strengthened, weakened, shaped and distorted over time by the driving general forces of a developing worldwide capitalist system.

As a given society moves through time it never totally loses all traces of its cultural characteristics, whether under the impact of feudalism, capitalism, or socialism. However, the special power of capitalism as a system of production has been due to its ability—indeed, its need—to subordinate all social relationships to its dynamism. Marx and Engels put it vividly in the *Communist Manifesto:*

> The bourgeoisie [i.e., capitalists] cannot exist without constantly revolutionizing the instruments of production, and thereby the relations of production, and with them the whole relations of society. Conservation of the old modes of production in unaltered form was, on the contrary, the first condition of existence for all earlier industrial classes. Constant revolutionizing of production, uninterrupted disturbance of all social conditions, ever-lasting uncertainty and agitation distinguish the bourgeois epoch from all earlier ones. All fixed, fast-frozen relations, with their train of ancient and venerable prejudices and opinions, are swept away, all new-formed ones become antiquated before they can ossify. All that is solid melts into air, all that is holy is profaned, and man is at last compelled to face with sober senses his real conditions of life and his relations with his kind.

What is it about capitalism that gives it such power? What needs does such a system have, what imperatives must it satisfy, that drive it so forcefully through time and space and tradition?

THE HEART OF THE MATTER: EXPANSION AND EXPLOITATION

First and foremost, a capitalist economy lives through expansion; its heartbeat is the process called capital accumulation. When mainstream economists and politicians today speak to the needs of economic growth, it is this process to which they refer. It sounds simple enough.[2]

---

[2]Those who call for a cessation or slowing of economic growth, on grounds of ecological threats, must—but seldom, if ever, do—contend with the fact that they are thereby calling for a new socio-economic system, not just the ecological de-fanging of the present one. Of this, more in Chapter Six.

But what makes expansion necessary, even compulsive? What makes it happen? What gives the process its push, its direction, its rate, its quality, its consequences? To answer those questions requires careful inspection of the socio-economic relations within a given capitalist society and of the relationships between it and other societies.[3] Whatever else such relationships entail—and they entail very much indeed—their unwavering requirement is exploitation. Also, feeding and being fed by the interaction of expansion and exploitation is a dynamic system of economic, political, and social power that buttresses, feeds upon, and guides the process of development.

Because expansion and exploitation are fundamental to the process of capitalist development, an inquiry into their causes and consequences necessarily carries deep into the nature and dynamics of capitalism. Here we shall make a brief and abstract foray into that territory; subsequent chapters will take up the American specifics.[4]

Expansion is a process; *exploitation* is a set of relationships. Both are necessary for capitalist development, and neither functions effectively without the other. Their interaction is decisive—the process moving within the relationships, changing them and being changed by them. The means and ends of business behavior require and lead to expansion; these means and ends and the powerlessness of workers produce exploitation. To support these generalizations it is essential to explain 1) the nature of capitalist production, and 2) the conditions of labor and what brought them to be. Let us take them up in turn, understanding that they came into existence historically as an interacting, mutually deter-

---

[3]Expansion is essential to capitalist health for a variety of interacting, interdependent reasons. For purposes of convenience, we may list the most important here, with the understanding that fuller explanation and discussions of their meaning will occur in one way or another throughout the book: 1) expansion is the ongoing source of generalized market *scarcity*, which is to say the ability of sellers to maintain relative power over buyers, and thus to exact a tribute; 2) competition among firms within an economy and between different national economies requires expansion if its effects are not to be mutually destructive; 3) technological innovation (in products and productive techniques), a natural and accelerating process under conditions of industrial capitalism, requires market expansion if the increased production and productivity that makes technological change profitable is to occur; 4) the capital goods industries (e.g., machinery, metallurgy, mining) depend upon expansion in the rest of the economy (and in their own sector) if they are not to suffer losses through excess capacity; 5) the highly unequal distribution of income of capitalism, which generates a high volume of savings, requires an ongoing high volume of net investment expenditure—which *means* expansion—to absorb those savings; 6) the unequal distribution of income, of power, of status and prestige in capitalist societies is rendered less explosive to the degree that the actuality and the hope of rising real incomes persists; in turn this requires continuous economic expansion. Once more, it is the interaction of these needs, not each taken singly, that is at stake.

[4]Arthur MacEwan, "Capitalist Expansion, Ideology, and Intervention," *RRPE* (Winter, 1972), is a useful general introduction that relates the abstract discussion to contemporary developments.

mining and dynamic development. First let us examine the principles of business behavior under the conditions of classic capitalist competition.

The direct aim of the capitalist business is to make a profit; when it fails to do so, it goes under. Except for brief and exceptional periods, profits cannot be made unless businesses function within a process of economic expansion, as manifested in the growth of commodity markets—that is, expansion of the markets in which commodities are sold. This is so whether or not business is able successfully to exploit its labor force, the prime condition surrounding the *production* of commodities. Conversely, even in expanding markets profits cannot be made unless production is carried on in an exploitive context. The competitive conditions of the 19th century meant that only direct labor exploitation would allow profits, given expanding market conditions. A full understanding of contemporary American capitalism will show that the combination of monopolistic structures, modern advertising, our overseas relationships, and the taxing and spending activities of the modern capitalist State makes for additional avenues of exploitation. The dependence upon expansion and exploitation does not decrease as capitalism moves from a competitive to a monopolistic structure; what changes is the nature and determinants of the expansion process and the burden and the forms of exploitation. As later discussions will show, the alterations are manifested both in domestic and overseas developments.

BIGGER IS BETTER; MORE IS NOT ENOUGH

To understand the compulsive quality of expansion under capitalism, we must begin with business competition and rivalry, the relationships between capitalists; to understand the profitability accompanying expansion we must begin with the class structure of society, the relationships between the powerful and the powerless. Engels put it in a nutshell:

> Competition is the most complete expression of the battle of all against all which rules in modern civil society. This battle, a battle for life, for existence . . . , is fought not between the different classes of society only, but also between the individual members of these classes. Each is in the way of the other, and each seeks to crowd out all who are in his way, and to put himself in their place. The workers are in constant competition among themselves as the members of the bourgeoisie among themselves.[5]

---

[5]Frederick Engels, *The Condition of the Working-Class in England in 1844** (London: Allen & Unwin, 1950), p. 75. Published originally in 1845.

It is fairly easy to see how and why workers would compete among themselves for jobs; nor is it difficult to imagine business competition. But why does the competition require and lead to expansion?

Capitalism emerged full-blown only when the traditions and restrictions of earlier times had been swept away. It was also a time of rapid geographic expansion and the ever-swifter growth of technology and science. The expanding production sought by Smith took place in a context of increasing productivity, brought about by technological improvement. Once set loose, the rate of technological change became increasingly rapid and pervasive in its impact. A competitive capitalist economy is one where the only protection a given firm has is its own strength. That strength finally depends upon its profitability. In the modern world, this means that each firm must adopt the latest in technology, for both defensive and offensive reasons. With all or most firms in a given industry doing so, both production and productivity increase. The market must expand to absorb the increased production. In the normal course of such processes, some firms succeed and others fall by the wayside. The surviving firms continue to expand, in themselves and by gobbling up others. The result is large-scale production, large-scale ownership, and large-scale control: a tendency toward monopoly. Along with economic expansion, both facilitating it and required by it, is geographic expansion—expansion of foreign markets, access to increasingly-needed foodstuffs and raw materials, and profitable foreign investments. Again, the *Communist Manifesto:*

> The need of a constantly expanding market for its products chases the bourgeoisie over the whole surface of the globe. It must nestle everywhere, settle everywhere, establish connections everywhere.

But there is more involved. The aim of profit under capitalist conditions, as earlier in the mercantilist period, sets up a corollary aim: *power.* Control over productive property is the *sine qua non* of profits; property and profits *are* private power, and private power has access to State power; such access allows protection and enhancement of an already privileged position. Smith, it will be recalled, knew that State power was essential to protect the unequal division of property in society, the division that has capitalists on one side and propertyless workers on the other. Power inheres in property ownership, and power begets power both at home and abroad, as powerlessness begets powerlessness.

The emergence of laissez-faire capitalism depended upon the abolition of State mercantilism. What Smith had correctly viewed as obstacles to the full increase of productive powers was also a system of protections and privileges. Labor was obliged to work, but it had also had the right to work and in principle the right not to starve. Capital, to the degree that it had the favor of the State, was likewise insulated from the market. Laissez-faire capitalism left individuals' and enterprises' fates in the hands of impersonal market forces, forces which changed swiftly and at times violently. In the absence of built-in social constraints on the free operations of the markets for labor power and goods, protection and privilege had to be gained through private efforts.

Ownership of the means of production, that is, property ownership, in such a society was the prime source of advantage. The means of enhancing that advantage for both offensive and defensive purposes was to move toward monopoly—the control over supply. For those whose incomes come from their work rather than from property, means of controlling *their* supply were even more indispensable. This is what trade unions, professional associations, licensing, and the like achieve. Both for business and for labor, the seeking and the achievement of such ends require access to or the protection of State power. In 19th century American and British capitalism, property, business, and power were simply and clearly linked; in the more complicated world leading to the present, the basic relationships continue, but in a more intricate pattern. The nature of those relationships is suggested when economists refer to monopoly as "control over supply." They appear more clearly when we view control over supply in its monopolistic forms as being the monopolization of property and of skills. Property retains the advantage, for labor power must combine with property to become productive.

Businessmen agree that production is for profit, and that expansion is good and necessary. Neither they nor most social scientists, however, agree that exploitation is an actual, let alone a necessary, accompaniment of business success. Conventional social analysis leads few to think in terms such as these; it fails even to raise questions that might lead us to check a concept like exploitation against social reality. Yet how is one to comprehend a situation in which incomes are distributed "almost in an inverse ratio to the labour," as J. S. Mill said, unless one recognizes that some are being exploited by others and that that relationship can persist, as Smith said, "only under the shelter of the civil magistrate"?

Such assertions and such questions require explanation, all the more essential because the existence of systematic and persistent exploitation is rejected or treated aloofly in conventional social analysis. The requisite analysis is necessarily historical: how did a small number of people gain the power to exploit the majority of the population?

EXPLOITATION AND CAPITALISM

Workers as such are propertyless. To produce they must work with materials and equipment owned by capitalists; to survive, they must produce. As Marx put it, ". . . the labourer purchases the right to work for his own livelihood only by paying for it in surplus-labour. . . ."[6] By "surplus-labour" Marx meant unpaid labor—that is, exploited labor. Exploitation as a concept leads directly to power as a reality.

The power of the employer derives from his position in the scale of income and wealth, his control over the means of production, and his related political and social prestige and power. All these are inextricably linked. Conventional economics starts and ends with the capitalist producing for profit; it ignores the fact that what makes the process possible is the control over property exercised by the capitalist and the power preceding and accompanying the achievement of that control. Having ignored the relationship, conventional analysis is therefore under no obligation to explain its existence.

How did modern property relationships come to be? Has it always been thus? Why and how does it persist? We need not posit some golden idyll of a dim past to answer that as capitalism came into being it did so on the wreckage of medieval property relationships. In the medieval world, private property as we understand the term did not exist. Neither land nor labor were commodities; neither could be bought or sold. The fundamental form of wealth was land.

Land was *held,* not "owned," within a set of concomitant obligations. The rights to the land, for lord or serf, were the rights of "usufruct": rights to the produce of the land. The holding of land was consequent upon a feudal "contract," in which those granted land were obliged to provide "aid and counsel" to their lord. Aid and counsel took the form of military, political and religious service. The serf and his family were required to work the lands and to provide other forms of necessary labor for their lord. The serfs were attached to the land hereditarily, generation after generation on the same estate. The various strata of lords— knights at the lowest level, emperors at the highest—found their status within each generation. They were "free" to form their contracts. Free meant "honorable." They were the gentlemen and ladies of the medieval world. The serfs worked three to four days a week for their lord, farming his land, repairing paths and bridges, and the like; the rest of the week they worked for themselves. The work they did for their lord was surplus labor; it was the degree of their exploitation. It was, in its day, their taxes, paid in labor power. Custom and force in varying measure held the serfs to their tasks and the land on which they performed them. That simplicity gave way as the medieval world gave way to the modern, altering economic, political, and social structures and processes.

The medieval structure began to give way around the 12th and 13th centuries in an irregular pattern, depending very much upon specific

---

[6]Karl Marx, *Capital** (New York: International Publishers, 1967), vol. I, p. 515. Originally published in 1867.

location and circumstances.[7] The more or less constant warfare of early medieval Europe had moderated by then, because of the success of feudalism in bringing relative peace—while also undermining the reasons for its own continuance as a social system. Peace allowed improvements in agricultural production, trade, and commerce. Serfs began to commute their labor services into money payments called "quitrents," an early version of what we call rent. In England, serfs became "copyholders." They were free in themselves and also free to use and sell the entire produce of their lands. Farming practices remained unchanged, but the holding of land was no longer medieval—nor was it yet a commodity. The copyholders are the "sturdy yeomanry" of renaissance literature. Their conditions were transformed and displaced as full commercialization took over.

The improvement in the conditions of life that began as serfdom and feudalism declined led to increased population as well as to increased trade and production; towns and cities grew; new and powerful nation-states emerged; technology improved; global expansion became the hallmark of the 16th and 17th centuries.

Alongside that set of changes, becoming disturbing in England in the 16th century, substantial in the 17th, and a landslide in the 18th, was the so-called "enclosure movement"—a movement that enclosed with a hedge or fence a whole estate, with its many "open" fields, into one "enclosed," unified farm, displacing many holders by one owner. That process, impelled by the gains to be made by a larger-scale and increasingly commercial agriculture producing wool and grains, entailed the transformation of a once populous and free peasantry, farming its own lands, into a propertyless and "free" working class. They, together with the increasing population that was already landless, became the modern working class, with nothing to sell but their labor power and with no way to stay alive without doing so.

The enclosure movement was a many-sided process. Its early beginnings were in 13th century England, a time of prosperity and rising commercialism connected with the expanding wool trade and the rise of towns. The key period in terms of establishing precedents was in the 16th century, the century of the Reformation, of the disposition of Church lands on the market, and the creation of English mercantilist

---

[7]The diversity of the pattern in various parts of Europe, and the forces at work, are analyzed at their best in *The Cambridge Economic History of Europe, Vol. I: The Agrarian Life of the Middle Ages* (Cambridge: Cambridge University Press, 1942), edited by J. H. Clapham and Eileen Power. In the *Encyclopaedia of the Social Sciences*—an invaluable fifteen-volume work—under the entry "Feudalism," Marc Bloch provides a succinct and illuminating analysis of European feudalism and its decline. His own *Feudal Society** (Chicago: University of Chicago Press, Phoenix Books, 1964) 2 vols., is the classic study, rich in wisdom and detail.

policies. The precedents established then led to rising enclosures in the 17th century; the statistical tidal wave took place in the latter part of the 18th century. By 1820 or so, almost all the agricultural land of England had been enclosed; by the close of the 19th century a few thousand families owned almost all of it. The means utilized to enclose lands—that is, to ease or force the peasantry or yeomanry from their lands—included force as well as law. The legalities were accomplished through the "Justices of the Peace" and through Parliament—by men who were generally of the enclosing class.[8]

The changes of the 16th through the 18th centuries in England were the social equivalent of an earthquake. The power of the Roman Catholic Church was broken in the 16th century, to give way to the "divine right of kings," which in the 17th century gave way to what later became the "divine right of capital." Land tenure and land utilization ceased to be determined by tradition, as commercialism and finally the making of land into a commodity transformed all of rural life. In the opening years of the 19th century, labor itself became a commodity, no less and no more than any other article of commerce, free from obligations and free of protection. All this seems natural to us today, but it was a process fought over every step along the way by those to whom it seemed unnatural and immoral. Neither land nor labor had been viewed as means to solely commercial ends in the earlier centuries; now they were. Only today is the view spreading in America that commercial considerations should not be dominant for either land or labor. Engels observed the connections between the two in 1843: "To make earth an object of huckstering—the earth which is our one and all, the first condition of our existence—was the last step toward making oneself an object of huckstering. It was and is to this very day an immorality surpassed only by the immorality of self-alienation."[9]

Earlier, we referred to Marx's conception of human nature and society. Marx saw alienation as intense under capitalist conditions, and evermore intense with the development of industrial capitalism. The propertylessness of the worker, displaced from the land and without the tools of work, meant the loss of control over what is produced, or how, or why, or when. The natural relationship of people to production for

---

[8]See R. H. Tawney, *The Agrarian Problem in 16th Century England** (New York: Burt Franklin Publishers, 1959), for a profound analysis of the critical breakdown of agricultural traditions. (Originally published in 1912.) For the nature and consequences of the later period see the definitive work on the period in all its respects, Paul Mantoux, *The Industrial Revolution in the Eighteenth Century** (London: Cape, 1928), esp. Ch. 3. (Originally published in 1906.)

[9]From his *Outlines of a Critique of Political Economy,** quoted in Istvan Meszaros, *Marx's Theory of Alienation** (New York: Harper Torchbooks, 1970), pp. 314–15. This is an excellent analysis of the whole matter of alienation.

use is mediated by the necessity to work for a wage, producing commodities for the market—for someone else's profit, and under harsh working conditions. The development of modern industry and the increased specialization accompanying it increases alienation but does not cause it; the cause lies in the separation of the worker from control over his work. Workers are alienated from each other, as they compete for jobs; from nature, from which they become separated; from their work; and from their own basic nature. The problem is not work, which is natural and fulfilling to man; nor is it property, which is necessary for the work to be done. The problem is the conditions within which work takes place, and who controls the property. "Wages," Marx said, "are like the oil which is applied to a wheel to keep it running."[10] Like the commodities they produce, workers in industrial capitalism become things.

FAITH, HOPE, AND COMPETITION

Something else, perhaps most momentous of all, happened as the medieval gave way to the modern world. One of England's most searching political philosophers put it this way:

> The movement from feudalism to capitalism is a movement from a world in which individual well-being is regarded as the outcome of action socially controlled to one in which social well-being is regarded as the outcome of action individually controlled.[11]

That was the change given its fullest rationale by Adam Smith: the fate of society, and of the individuals in it, was entrusted to the outcome of a no-holds-barred economic contest. The only rules were those protecting property; all else was in the laps of the gods. No doubt, in the setting of the 18th and 19th centuries, such an economy would grow and change at rates that were, by previous standards, extraordinarily high, as dramatically portrayed in the *Communist Manifesto*:

> The bourgeoisie, during its rule of scarce one hundred years, has created more massive and more colossal productive forces than all preceding generations together. Subjection of nature's forces to man, machinery, application of chemistry to industry and agriculture, steam-navigation, railways, electric telegraphs, clearing of whole continents for cultivation, canalization of rivers, whole populations conjured out of the ground— what earlier century had even a presentiment that such productive forces slumbered in the lap of social labor?

---

[10]Bottomore, *Karl Marx: Early Writings*, p. 138.
[11]Harold J. Laski, *The Rise of European Liberalism* (London: Allen & Unwin, 1936), p. 28.

Smith had been correct in anticipating that the abolition of social constraints upon the economy would enhance the "wealth of the nation." What he did not foresee was that the very competitive economy he posited, and the market competition that would transform individual self-seeking into social well-being, would be pushed aside. Nor did he see that the concentrated State power against which he railed successfully would be surpassed by an even more powerful private-State pattern of power. The latter was all the more substantial because, unlike explicit State power, it was difficult to identify and harder to control. Those who had to be controlled were in fact in control.

What emerged in the century after Smith wrote belied his intentions. Where had he gone wrong? We have noted some points earlier, but there are others. Smith did not anticipate that technology would develop in such a way that the forms of business organization that became both possible and necessary would be incompatible with small-scale industry, which was the basis of a competitive economy. Smith was not naïve. He assumed that businessmen would be unable to resist the temptation to monopolize when he noted, in a famous observation, that "people of the same trade seldom meet together, even for merriment and diversion, but the conversation ends in a conspiracy against the public, or in some contrivance to raise prices."[12] However, his fears on that score were neutralized by his key assumption that a highly decentralized market structure would block such natural inclinations. With the technology of his day, his view made sense. But the very success of the economy in subsequent decades also meant the failure of the "invisible hand."

Smith tripped over another matter of greater weight: the distribution of income and wealth, and the ways in which those patterns affect both the process of expansion and the possibilities of exploitation. For this shortcoming, Smith had less excuse than for his failure to anticipate technological development adequately. The distribution of income and wealth when Smith lived was already highly unequal, and becoming more so. They were the days of high turmoil associated with the enclosure movement, a process which impoverished many while placing more wealth in fewer hands. It was a contemporary of Smith's, after all, whose epic poem "The Deserted Village" has done so much to tell us —if romantically and sentimentally—what was lost when efficient agriculture was gained:

Ill fares the land, to hastening ills a prey,
Where wealth accumulates, and men decay:
Princes and lords may flourish, or may fade;

---

[12] *The Wealth of Nations,* p. 130.

A breath can make them, as a breath has made;
But a bold peasantry, their country's pride,
When once destroyed, can never be supplied.[13]

England had ceased to need "a bold peasantry" while Goldsmith wrote; to further its economic growth it needed a docile and powerless labor force that would work under wretched conditions in mine, mill, and factory. England got what it needed largely through the enclosure movement; other capitalist nations found both similar and different ways to create or to import a powerless working force. The conditions of Irish workers brought into England were even worse than those of the English; the great British historian Macaulay found those of German workers worse still, leading to his characterization of them as "degenerate dwarfs." That he was not entirely off the mark, setting aside his ugly language, is suggested by this observation concerning Germany: "In 1828 General von Horn warned the Prussian Government that these [Prussian] districts could not supply their quota of army recruits since the health of young factory workers was being undermined."[14]

What Smith failed to anticipate regarding technology, private economic power, and intensive human exploitation is less egregious as a defect for a moral philosopher than his failure to grasp what would become of a society loosed of all social constraints but those of the market. Recall Tawney's analogy concerning giving sex and pugnacity free reign and the central role in social organization. Then imagine how degraded and empty sexual relationships would become in a society knowing or caring little of ethics or love; how violent a society would be in which sheer physical strength dominated the relationships between people. Tawney knew that such a society would not be wished by anyone; the point is simply that allowing economic self-interest to function without constraint is equally destructive of human needs and possibilities.

Smith was right in believing that the abolition of social constraints would allow the capitalist economy to grow apace; indeed, the prime reason for the economic power of capitalism is that it is unconstrained. But the results were not benign, as Smith had hoped they would be.

---

[13]Oliver Goldsmith (1728–1774) was Irish, but the setting of the poem was England. This is but a fragment of a very long poem. The 16th century enclosures prompted Sir Thomas More to observe that "shepe are eating men," as those enclosures converted arable into pasture lands.

[14]W. O. Henderson, *The Industrial Revolution in Europe, 1815–1914** (Chicago: Quadrangle, 1968), p. 23. This book is a useful source on developments in Europe, to balance our emphasis on England and the United States. It is dry, but informative. See Thorstein Veblen, *Imperial Germany and the Industrial Revolution* (New York: Viking, 1946) for a searching and witty comparison and analysis of British and German developments, accompanied by many general insights. Originally published in 1915.

Rapid economic growth taken alone is neither desirable nor undesirable. It must be judged in terms of its larger meanings to human beings and to natural resources; in what it elicits and what it deflects or suppresses in human beings; in what it does to the nature of human relationships; how it serves human needs; how it encourages human possibilities. In establishing competition as the ruling principle of social existence, a capitalist society makes combative relationships necessary for all. If there are quantitative rewards for those who are victorious, there are human losses for all. This is so even after the reintroduction of social constraints, for the basic processes remain competitive and combative. Human inclinations other than naked self-interest narrowly defined are pushed into the realm of the impractical, the "idealistic." As Tawney says,

> It is obvious, indeed, that no change of system or machinery can avert those causes of social *malaise* which consist in the egotism, greed, or quarrelsomeness of human nature. What it can do is to create an environment in which those are not the qualities which are encouraged. It cannot secure that men live up to their principles. What it can do is to establish their social order upon principles to which, if they please, they can live up and not live down.[15]

To which may be contrasted, as Tawney points out, "the compound of economic optimism and moral bankruptcy which led a 19th-century economist to say: 'Greed is held in check by greed, and the desire for gain sets limits to itself.' " (Ibid., p. 27)

Smith, Ricardo, and Marx all analyzed *competitive* capitalism. Neither Smith nor Ricardo foresaw the harshness of competition let loose; neither foresaw its leading to monopoly. But these were starting-points for, Marx. Marx saw competitive capitalism as an inhumane and dehumanizing social system, dependent upon greed for its energy and exploitation for its fuel. He took for granted that it would increase production and productivity over time; given its dynamics he also took for granted that monopoly would replace competition. Even after a century or more of evidence confirming Marx's judgment, conventional analysis continues without substantial recognition or analysis of these two major characteristics of capitalist development. What Marx took for granted is seen analytically as aberrant, or not seen at all.

The transition from competitive to monopoly capitalism was facilitated by but not *due* to technological change. It was the increasing scale and complexity of production *combined with* the major business impulses of those who controlled the means of production that led to monopoly.

---

[15]R. H. Tawney, *The Acquisitive Society** (New York: Harcourt Brace Jovanovich, 1920), p. 180.

The concentration and centralization of capital that is characteristic of all industrial capitalist societies today arises out of, not despite, competitive capitalism. It is the way the system moves through time.

Those who survive capitalist rivalry do so by absorbing or by destroying the lesser firms. Capitalism is a predatory form of economic organization. For Smith's optimism to have been well-founded, limits would have had to have been set on the size of the bigger fish. Set by whom, the bigger fish? In the absence of any explicit institutions designed to control such a process—and Smith's laissez-faire capitalism excluded any such—the bigger fish become more and more immune to any constraints on their behavior or further growth. They are best able to respond effectively to changing technology, and are best able to survive intermittent blasts of depression. The history of the United States, most capitalistic of all capitalist nations, reveals these processes most clearly.

THE AMERICAN SETTING: CAPITALIST PARADISE

A generalization that will be agreed upon by both the critics and the supporters of our system is that both capitalism and industrialism have pushed further ahead in the United States than elsewhere. How and why this came to be can be explained by all those matters that contribute to industrialism and to capitalist development, by the manner in which they interacted in our past. Let us note first the most obvious of these contributing factors—our geographic advantages—and place them in the American social context.

Everything and anything that might facilitate the emergence of capitalist institutions and the progress of industry was available to America. All that was lacking was control over our own destiny; that was achieved in our War for Independence. Most obvious and striking of American advantages has been our physical setting.

No nation has matched the quantitative or qualitative abundance of natural resources of this country, whether the reference is to climate, terrain, soils, coasts, bays, rivers, lakes, forests, and minerals or to the convenient locations of each of these with respect to each other. Nor can the vast oceans that give us almost total security from invasion be ignored as a developmental advantage. All these are obvious. But there were other and less obvious advantages, institutional and historical, which were of great importance in our evolution as a capitalist society.

The temporal and social conditions under which colonial America and the United States came into being were most auspicious. America as such had no medieval past, and thus no tradition of social controls to deny or to destroy. On this continent, all that had to be destroyed were the Native American and Mexican communities standing in the way.

The settlement and development of America, as a colony of the British, represented the leading edge of British development, rather than the British past. In the 17th century, and even more in the 18th century, that meant a Britain moving rapidly toward capitalism.

Attempts to implant traditional agricultural forms (e.g., manorialism in upstate New York) or stringent social codes (e.g., theocratic attempts in Massachusetts) were made; the strong winds of commercialism and the extraordinary opportunities of the period combined to blow away such social structures. There were few people in America in comparison with the rich resources of the land. Labor was short in supply; workers were wanted in shipping, trade, fishing, petty industry, and agriculture. This was an especially severe problem for those who wished to exploit the valuable agricultural possibilities of the southern colonies. Serfdom was impossible; slavery was not.

Commercial slavery began well before significant settlement of the North American colonies. The African slave trade was well-established in the 16th century; slaves were widely-used in South America and in the Caribbean, especially for sugar cultivation. As the American South began to grow tobacco for the market, but even more so when rice, indigo and especially cotton plantations grew in number and importance, North America became the prime user of African slaves. Estimates of the numbers of Africans enslaved and carried to the Americas range from fifteen to twenty millions; it is estimated that from 50 to 85 percent of these died en route.[16]

The non-slave labor force of the colonies was made up of immigrants, many coming as "indentured servants," which meant working three to seven years to pay for passage. Arriving largely as adults, immigrants were a boon to the young economy, for their childhood, their unproductive years, had been "paid for" in their home countries. This remained an advantageous characteristic of the expanding American labor force up to World War I. Apart from slaves, by that time well over thirty million had emigrated here.

In addition to the "social cheapness" of the American labor force over time, another feature should be noted: those who came voluntarily to this country, whether propelled or drawn by religious, political, or economic considerations, were clearly desirous of or suited to the non-traditional shape of American society. Their characteristics facilitated the growth of such a society.

From its first days, and setting aside those enslaved, America was a land of enterprisers—small or large farmers, artisans or petty manufac-

---

[16]J. W. Schulte Nordholt, *The People That Walk in Darkness** (New York: Ballantine, 1970) is an excellent and comprehensive treatment of the slave trade from its beginnings. It has a useful bibliography for further study.

turers, domestic or foreign traders, low or high financiers. It was a capitalist society from birth; or, if not quite then, as soon as it could crawl. By the mid-18th century, America had the ability to walk, but was increasingly held back by British capital and British power. What mercantilism had been to British capitalism in Great Britain, both in its positive and its negative aspects, British regulations were to the Americans, as Smith had noted.

Few indeed were the Americans who foresaw either the need or the possibility of revolution against Britain, until the mid-1770's. Once war broke out, the ability of the Americans to fight successfully was enhanced not only by the ocean between but also by the diverse interests and rivalries distracting the British from a sole preoccupation with the North American colonies; for instance, the Caribbean sugar colonies were seen as more important economically at the time. And, of course, Britain had to contend with its European rivals, particularly the French, who aided the Americans directly and indirectly.

Of great importance to the Americans before and after the Revolution were the expansive trends beginning to take hold in the world with the coming of the 19th century. The old structures of power were cracking up in Europe, and new waves of economic and geographic expansion were transforming the world. In that setting, the United States found new and growing sources of trade, of technological innovation, of capital, and of immigrants. Added to our already substantial advantages in resources, attitudes, and labor supply, this dynamic new world context propelled American economic development along its path toward industrialism with an unmatchable set of advantages; the relative ease of our economic development did much to obscure and to suppress the social conflicts associated with capitalist development.

Next we should characterize the role of the State in our history. In rebelling against the British, Americans were also rebelling against the role of centralized State power. Consequently, even though the War brought Americans to a pitch of patriotism and nationalism which would still be considered intense by world standards, an affection for a strong *central* government did not result. But this did not mean a distaste for governmental assistance when it was necessary and useful. Thus, our first decades as a nation saw a minimal role for the *federal* government and a vital role for the separate *state* governments. The federal government presided over a unified foreign trade policy, a uniform currency, and a national policy for absorbing and conquering the lands to the west. The state governments played the decisive role in developing transportation (roads, canals, and railways), banking, and, among other economic matters, business and labor laws.

The upshot, for the first half-century of our existence as a nation, was far from the laissez-faire society proposed by Smith. That came later, in its American form. We may note very briefly three different periods regarding the role of the State in American economic life. The first period was American mercantilism, described above. The second period, replacing mercantilism after Jackson's presidency, occurred as American laissez-faire capitalism began to flourish. It came to its roaring climax in the decades after the Civil War, called by Mark Twain the "Gilded Age," and by Vernon Parrington the "Great Barbecue." The third phase leads up to the present, and was a response to the instabilities and beckoning possibilities of maturing industrial capitalism. This phase began to develop and to find coherence somewhat before but especially during Wilson's presidency and involved increased centralization of State power in Washington. This was both consequence and cause of the increasing concentration and centralization of economic power in the corporate world of industry and finance, and was accompanied by the first waves of overseas imperialism by the United States. Gabriel Kolko has called this the phase of "political capitalism." In Chapter Eight the background and functioning of this process will be examined intensively.

MIRROR, MIRROR, ON THE WALL ...

Americans tend to view our national history as having made astounding economic achievements with a minimum of the coercive and violent practices associated with other nations' histories, and as having taken place within a political and social context at once humanitarian, egalitarian, and democratic. Such a view requires blindness to certain basic features of our development. The blindness is systematic and pervasive. It neglects the origins and the meaning of slavery as a central determinant of our early economic development, as it neglects in a connected way the other forms of labor exploitation hastening and shaping our economic achievements. It pays only the slightest attention to the connections between our rapid growth and the spoliation of our natural environment that cheapened the direct costs of that growth. In turn, our inability as a people to comprehend our history of human and resource exploitation has made it terribly difficult for us to comprehend or control the consequences of our past. And there is one further blind spot in the ways we view our history, one that has come to haunt us as it finally penetrates our consciousness: it concerns geographic expansion.

Economic expansion was noted earlier as being essential to capitalist health; geographic expansion must now be noted as playing a key role in our process of economic expansion. Capitalism began that way; the settling of the American colonies was itself an instance of geographic expansion for the British. Capitalism seeks to continue that way. Americans are generally critically conscious of the incessant attempts of *other* nations to enlarge their geographic influence and control; we are familiar with notions like British, or French, or German, or Japanese "imperialism." Our own processes of geographic expansion have been the most continuous and successful of all nations. Only rarely, however, do our histories speak of American imperialism; instead, we read of "westward expansion," or of "manifest destiny." We do not view our process of geographic expansion on this continent as imperialism, but as simply a filling of the space up to "our" natural boundaries. We do not see our history as one of exterminating or penning in the Native American population, or of holding back and pushing away the other contenders (French, British, Spanish, Mexican, Russian) for geographic control, but rather as merely securing "our" lands, lands that were in some unexamined sense "ours" to begin with, or "ours" when we could get around to settling and exploiting them.

Given that view of expansion on this continent, it was natural and easy to see our extra-continental expansion—into the Caribbean and Pacific, first, and directly and indirectly over the face of the entire globe, later—as having much the same qualities. If the rest of the globe was not "ours" in the same sense as actual settlement, it was ours to protect, to assist, to shape, to lead, to make "free." As finally became the case with Indochina, it was ours to destroy if necessary, in order to make "free."

A line from Jamestown to Indochina runs through our history. Its importance must be measured first in terms of what it has meant to those we have killed, caged, or shoved aside. But only at our peril can we overlook the importance to our past and our future that the studied innocence of that line has meant in the shaping of American policy and American consciousness, and how it connects with our treatment of human beings and nature here at home.[17]

Ensuing chapters will elaborate upon all the foregoing generalizations about American capitalist development. Here a few summary points may be of use. The United States had the easiest, swiftest, and most successful process of economic achievement of any society in history, whether we measure by the level or composition of production, by productivity, or by per capita real income. Most capitalist of all nations, the United States has had less open and sustained class conflict than

---

[17]Historians did not even begin to pull this history together until very recently. See Richard W. Van Alstyne, *The Rising American Empire** (New York: Oxford University Press, 1960; Chicago: Quadrangle, 1965) and William Appleman Williams, *The Contours of American History** (Chicago: Quadrangle, 1966) for two books that trace our expansionism to its early beginnings. Studies influenced by these initial breakthroughs will be noted and relied upon in Chapter Seven, where our geographic expansion is a central topic.

other capitalist nations. Americans have seen more hope for themselves *within* the system than their counterparts elsewhere; when they have moved to struggle, as in trade union conflicts, they have generally adopted both the means and the ends of their business antagonists.

Having come to be as a nation created in the name of minimal State power, the United States now functions as a highly centralized State at home. As the first society to fight a successful revolution for national independence, the United States now sits in the midst of a complicated web of neocolonial relationships constructed in this century, in the name of what Williams calls "anti-colonial imperialism."

Nor can we fail to note that the land whose Declaration of Independence speaks in inspiring ways of human dignity and freedom has as its most fundamental and unresolved question an intensive form of racism practiced from our first years, and increasingly so after our independence. We continue despite repeated warnings from all quarters that if racism has not already been our undoing, it will one day be so. Much the same is said about our destruction of the environment, the deadly qualities of our air, the poisoning of our water supply.

In short, in creating the world's most powerful economy, the United States has also produced a society teeming with troubles. The troubles are connected in such a way that we must speak not of "social issues" but of a developing social crisis. Racism and imperialism were not invented by Americans. But the development of American capitalism has nourished them in ways and degrees going beyond that of the Europeans. The power of these monsters to create fear, tension and violence cannot be viewed as separable from the power of the economy that has allowed or required them to grow.

American capitalism is the acme and the epitome of capitalism. As such, it departs further and further in time from inherited non-commercial values; in the process, institutions supportive of non-commercial values are vitiated, weaken, and disappear. At the same time, many people become increasingly aware of the essential inhumanity and a-morality of a society dominated by profit-making and wealth-garnering, and the subjection of the human spirit and human activities to machine-like conditions. The tension between these two developments, between the natural course of capitalist development and the increasing resistance of the human spirit, lies at the root of our developing social crisis.

Human beings are inherently moral, possessed of feelings of sympathy, empathy, solidarity with our kind, and the need and ability to live creative and loving lives. These attributes continue to emerge, and manifest themselves, now as in the past, despite the presence of our baser capabilities. One need not be a Marx or a Veblen to see people as something more than creatures of material self-interest; all the major religions, psychiatry, and the landmarks of our literature, art, and music remind us of what we have been and what we can be, as do the numerous struggles fought by so many peoples for dignity throughout history. The crisis awaiting us shows itself first as a crisis of economic and political life; its root is a moral crisis, whose resolution will determine the realization or the destruction of our species' needs and possibilities.

READING SUGGESTIONS

There are many books of selected readings; among the best as an accompaniment to the approach taken in this and subsequent chapters is Richard C. Edwards, Michael Reich, and Thomas E. Weisskopf, eds., *The Capitalist System** (Englewood Cliffs, N. J.: Prentice-Hall, 1972). For a closely-reasoned historical analysis of capitalism by a leading Marxist, see Maurice Dobb, *Studies in the Development of Capitalism** (London: Routledge, 1946). Christopher Hill's excellent study of the early modern period of England's development was cited in Chapter One; the succeeding period is excellently treated in E. J. Hobsbawm, *Industry and Empire* (New York: Pantheon, 1968).

Passages from the *Communist Manifesto* have been quoted several times. The *Manifesto* is available in many forms; a valuable selection of Marxian writings which includes the *Manifesto* is *Karl Marx and Friedrich Engels, Selected Works** (Moscow: Progress Publishers, 1968), also available in other editions. C. Wright Mills was much influenced by as well as honestly critical of Marxism. His views are put forth in *The Marxists** (New York: Dell, 1962). Shlomo Avineri, *The Social and Political Thought of Karl Marx** (Cambridge: Cambridge University Press, 1971) is an excellent and thorough analysis, readable, critical, and sympathetic in treatment.

The difficulties and violence associated with economic development have been studied carefully by Barrington Moore, Jr., *Social Origins of Dictatorship and Democracy** (Boston: Beacon Press, 1966). Chapters on the English Civil War of the 17th century, the French Revolution, and the American Civil War are especially useful. The processes by which land and labor became commodities in England in the 18th and 19th centuries are studied exhaustively—and, for the reader, sometimes exhaustingly—by Karl Polanyi, *The Great Transformation** (New York: Holt, Rinehart and Winston, 1944). The effort to work through Polanyi's strangled prose is repaid. The nature of the medieval world and the manner in which commercialism grew in England are treated brilliantly and in human terms by Eileen Power in her *Medieval People** (New York: Anchor Books, 1956); her *Wool Trade in English Medieval History* (New York: Oxford University Press, 1941) is a superb analysis of the relationships between political and economic developments.

R. H. Tawney is one of the deservedly most influential historians of the rise of capitalism. In addition to works of his previously cited, his subtle and profound analysis of the manner in which religious thought changed in meaning, if not always in words, from the 16th to the 18th centuries is well worth study. It is found in his 175-page introduction to Thomas Wilson, *A Discourse Upon Usury* (London: Bell, 1925), itself the work of a 16th-century divine. E. P. Thompson, *The Making of the English Working Class** (New York: Vintage, 1966) has written that history "from the bottom up," and has very much influenced a new generation of historians. It is an excellent history, as well as an excellent model of historical writing.

Two comprehensive views of capitalist development, both affected by Marx and both differing in important ways from Marx, are Thorstein Veblen, *The Theory of the Leisure Class** (New York: Macmillan, 1899), and Joseph A. Schumpeter, *Capitalism, Socialism, and Democracy** (New York: Harper & Row, 1942).

A systematic and comprehensive introduction to Marxian social analysis, consisting entirely of thoughtfully selected quotations from Marx, Engels, and Lenin, is Howard Selsam, David Goldman, and Harry Martel, eds., *Dynamics of Social Change** (New York: International Publishers, 1970).

The succeeding chapters will be much concerned with aspects of the economic history of the United States. Frequent reference will be had to one or another of the books in a series published over the years by Holt, Rinehart and Winston (New York), entitled *The Economic History of the United States.* The separate volumes are generally valuable in themselves and each has a most useful bibliography. It seems appropriate to list all these books here for handy reference. Lawrence A. Harper, *The Colonial Period to 1775;* Curtis P. Nettels, *The Emergence of a National Economy, 1775–1815;* Paul W. Gates, *The Farmer's Age: Agriculture, 1815–1860;* George R. Taylor, *The Transportation Revolution, 1815–1860;** Fred Shannon, *The Farmer's Last Frontier: Agriculture, 1860–1897;** Edward C. Kirkland, *Industry Comes of Age, 1860–1897;** Harold U. Faulkner, *The Decline of Laissez-Faire, 1897–1917;* George Soule, *Prosperity Decade: From War to Depression, 1917–1929;** Broadus Mitchell, *Depression Decade: From New Era Through New Deal, 1929–1941;* Donald L. Kemmerer, *The U. S. Economy, 1940–1960.*

chapter three

Business as a System
of Power

They pass through the great iron gates—
Men with eyes gravely discerning,
Skilled to appraise the tonnage of cranes
Or split an inch into thousandths—
Men tempered by fire as the ore is
And planned to resistance
Like steel that has cooled in the trough;
Silent of purpose, inflexible, set to fulfilment—
To conquer, withstand, overthrow. . . .
Men mannered to large undertakings,
Knowing force as a brother
And power as something to play with,
Seeing blood as a slip of the iron,
To be wiped from the tools
Lest they rust.

(Lola Ridge, *The Legion of Iron*)

"The business of America," President Coolidge once remarked, "is business." More pointed, while also reflecting the subsequent progress of *big* business, was the famous statement thirty years later of Charles Wilson (of General Motors, and Secretary of Defense under Eisenhower); "What's good for General Motors is good for America." These pithy assertions, and others of their genre—"The public? The public be damned!"—have been much maligned by those with a loftier vision for America. But as matters now stand—that is, in the absence of fundamental institutional change—it is unquestionably true that when business is bad, Americans are badly off; when GM and the other giant corporations are in trouble, so is not only the entire economy, but the entire society.

In short, America is a business society, for better or for worse. It is, indeed, *the* business society, even in comparison with other capitalist societies. Unlike the others, we started that way; we have become even more so with the passage of time. If, in our own day, deep questioning of the performance of American society has become pervasive, is it not because business calculations rather than human needs and possibilities so much dominate the entirety of our lives—not only in industry, but in our foreign policies, our domestic politics, our schools, our health care systems, our environment, and even our culture?

That ours is so fully a business-like society and the most fully-developed of capitalist societies allows two major inferences about the historical development of the United States. First, *all* social activities—the production of all goods and all services from carrots to computers and from mechanics to ministers—have flourished or languished dependent upon the degree to which they have satisfied the finally financial criterion of *marketability*. Indeed, most Americans are unaware that other, essentially qualitative, criteria exist to be taken seriously. From the necessary evaluation of a business firm in terms of its income statement and balance sheet, American society has moved insensibly to evaluating virtually all activities in similarly quantitative and pecuniary terms: What does it cost? How much does he make? Will it sell? Is it profitable? So it is with our ways of speech, with paintings and movie stars, with professors and journalists, even with religious personages. The society has left or created no comfortable resting-place for other means of evaluation.

Second, if business criteria have made their way into all walks of life, the prime reason is that capitalist development has been so successful in its own terms in the United States. No other country has had so long and so impressive a history of expansion, production, and productivity, with over time our levels of per capita real incomes. Capitalism stresses material achievement as its promise. American capitalism has fulfilled that promise. If, in the process, large sections of the population have been shunted aside, exploited, and oppressed, left outside the charmed circle of material well-being drawn by the American Dream, then that is by no means unique to the United States where, in fact or in illusion, the majority has seen itself as blessed to reside in the most blessed of all nations.

To say that American capitalist development has been successful for so long is to point to two other major aspects of our development: the persistent and remarkable profitability, and the easy and comprehensive access to power, prestige, and authority by American businessmen and those who live by their criteria. These two processes have sustained and reinforced each other, and they bear closer examination, which must continue to focus most heavily on the questions of *expansion* and *exploitation*, the alpha and omega of capitalist development.

ONWARD AND UPWARD

Expansion may be thought of as having two directions: upward, the growth of the economy in its productive capacity and its structure of production, and outward, the expansion of the land surface under the control or influence of the national economy.

The temporal and social advantages for capitalism in the United States were noted at the close of Chapter Two; those advantages were facilitated mostly by our *geographic* realities and possibilities. The meaning of the North American colonies to the British was slight by comparison with what could be made of the continent stretching westward from the lands the British had settled on the Eastern Seaboard. Given the limited maritime and military technology of the time, the new United States had virtually a free hand in moving into the wide open and very rich spaces to the west of the original thirteen colonies, and much more was made of the original land space because of that expansion into the West.

Consider briefly what access to the West stimulated and allowed and, more subtly, what it required (most especially, canals and railroads). For the South, the western lands were both a life-saver and a boon—a life-saver because the South's techniques of cultivating tobacco and cotton had depleted the soils; a boon because the new and even richer lands fitted most profitably into rapidly expanding markets in the Old World (most importantly, cotton for England's burgeoning textile mills). The South's movement westward into Alabama, Mississippi, and Louisiana meant, of course, the wholesale destruction of Native Americans and of their remarkable and healthy societies, as well as a vast increase in the numbers of black slaves imported and bred for plantation cultivation.[1]

But the South's geographic and economic expansion was profitable—to the plantation owners, to the merchants and shippers and financiers tied into plantation agriculture. Still more, the entire American economy depended very much upon the dynamism, the foreign exchange, and the internal trade generated by King Cotton in the first half of the 19th century. The importance of the South's economy in the United States

---

[1] See Paul Jacobs, Saul Landau, and Eve Pell, *To Serve the Devil** (New York: Vintage, 1971), in two volumes. Vol. 1, *Natives and Slaves,** traces the early history of our treatment of Native Americans, African slaves, and Chicanos; Vol. 2, *Colonials and Sojourners,** examines the lesser-known histories of Hawaiians, Chinese, Japanese, and Puerto Ricans in the American context. Besides a brief narrative history, the authors have collected valuable documents wherein these peoples speak for themselves; and there is a useful bibliography. An excellent anthology concerning Afro-Americans is Eric Foner, ed., *America's Black Past** (New York: Harper & Row, 1970).

was well-reflected in its power in the federal government. By any measure of population, land, or capital, the South's power was disproportionate, whether referring to the legislative, judicial or executive branch of government. The South's power, not the moral issue of slavery, was the central issue leading to the Civil War; when the South lost, it was because the economic power of northern industry, agriculture, and finance had surpassed it. If we may judge the intentions of warriors by what they do after victory, the organization and functioning of the American federal government during and after the Civil War tells us that northern intentions were to adapt federal power to the needs of industrial, not planter, capitalism.

The North's economic strength rested on the commercial, industrial, and financial activities that had their small beginnings in colonial New England, New York, Pennsylvania, and New Jersey. The beginnings were small because of the less bountiful agricultural possibilities in the North as compared with the South. However, forced to diversify and to improvise, by the 1830's the small beginnings had become a torrent of economic life, with still greater dynamism lying squarely ahead.

Much of the North's early development had depended on the South, for the merchants of the North were heavily involved in the slave trade and in the associated rum and general mercantile trade in a series of "triangular" patterns linking North America with the Caribbean, Africa, and Europe. Veblen had a characteristically insightful and sardonic view of these northern activities:

> The slave trade never was a "nice" occupation or an altogether unexceptionable investment—"balanced on the edge of the permissible." But even though it may have been distasteful to one and another of its New-England men of affairs, and though there always was a suspicion of moral obliquity attached to the slave-trade, yet it had the fortune to be drawn into the service of the greater good. In conjunction with its running-mate, the rum-trade, it laid the foundations of some very reputable fortunes at the focus of commercial enterprise that presently became the center of American culture, and so gave rise to some of the country's Best People. At least so they say.
>
> Perhaps also it was, in some part, in this early pursuit of gain in this moral penumbra that American business enterprise learned how not to let its right hand know what its left hand is doing; and there is always something to be done that is best done with the left hand.[2]

The North's process of economic development soon became the most dynamic industrialization process in the world up to that time; it was

---

[2]Thorstein Veblen, *Absentee Ownership and Business Enterprise** (New York: Huebsch, 1923; Viking, 1954), p. 171.

weaning itself from its heavy southern diet even at the time it was gaining the most from it. Of the several factors that loom large in northern economic development, one whole complex related to westward expansion. It was as vital as it was timely.[3]

THE DREAM UNFOLDS

It is impossible to speculate beyond a certain point on what the United States would have been like had its geographic scope been confined to that of the original colonies. But we need not speculate. For the states north of the Mason-Dixon line, the trans-Appalachian West was not merely a beckoning frontier; it was a seemingly endless expanse of land teeming with excellent soils, waterways, minerals (including gold and silver), and forests. To exploit those lands, the United States had to import rising millions of people,[4] dig canals and build the largest rail network in the world—30,000 miles by 1860, 53,000 by 1870, twice that by 1882, and over 210,000 miles by 1904—import capital, and develop a technology that could master the great spaces and complex needs of such a land. But these needs had another side to them: they offered boundless possibilities to a society dominated and led by people with their eyes on financial gain.

The millions of immigrants contributed not just labor power, but imagination and enterprise and energy. The transportation network required new private and public financial institutions, and it constituted an enormous demand for a whole range of products—most importantly, metals and machinery and coal, the heart of 19th century industrial development. A new technology was required to dig canals, to tame the plains and the mountains with rails and powerful locomotives, and to exploit the surface and subsurface resources of America's varied lands. All this, taken together with a persisting labor shortage, meant that the United States became the first of all industrial nations to develop a

---

[3]The pre-Civil War history is rich in details that we are skirting over or ignoring. See the works of Nettels, Gates, and Taylor suggested at the close of Chapter Two; for the post-Civil War period, Shannon and Kirkland provide support for most of our generalizations.

[4]The important surge that began in the 1840's was much facilitated by the revival of indentured labor during the Civil War, and became a headlong rush from 1861 on. Between 1861 and 1920, over twenty-eight million people came to the United States as immigrants. Movement to the West was principally by the "native-born" Americans, but their rush to take up western lands was reinforced and made possible by the filling up of eastern cities by the newcomers. Toward the close of the century immigration was induced largely to work the mines and the mills spreading over the whole country, and the immigrants were now coming from Eastern and Southeastern Europe, rather than the United Kingdom and Western Europe—with profound social and political results.

comprehensive machine technology for all aspects of production—agricultural, mineral, manufacturing, and transportation.

The resulting high labor productivity, combined with the widespread ownership of land (relative to Europe) yielded a level and a distribution of income that provided the first *domestic* mass market for modern production. By the end of the 19th century, the structure of American production in both consumer and capital goods was broader and deeper than anywhere else in the world; and the process had just begun.

With unprecedented swiftness, the United States filled in its continental boundaries, and in doing so created an economy that dazzled the world. But the unprecedented swiftness was matched by unprecedented rapacity—a heedless exploitation of natural resources, and a pattern of human exploitation whose viciousness was obscured, on the one hand, by the widespread expectation that *everyone* would someday rise in the socio-economic structure and, on the other, by the equally widespread indifference to the conditions of those (especially nonwhites) who in fact had no such prospects.[5]

From all this, a process of economic expansion whose buoyancy and profitability, despite intermittent business panics and crises, transformed the northeastern quadrant of the United States into a businessman's Eldorado. Meanwhile, cities grew like mushrooms over the face of the nation—New York, Philadelphia, and Boston, of course; but also Chicago, Cleveland, Cincinnati, St. Louis, New Orleans, Omaha, and San Francisco. The growth of the cities, like the growth of the economy, was a response to business needs and possibilities; as for anything more complicated, that could wait—or be forgotten.

Survival and success in the expansionist process required passing the test of the market, the test of a fully commercialized society. Those who survived grew in strength, and they garnered the society's power, prestige, and authority. *Power* means the ability to decide, to influence, to control; *prestige,* both a source and a consequence of power, refers to the deference received by those who possess power in society; *authority* resides in those who have the weight of law, of custom, and of society's deepest values vested in them.

---

[5]The position and history of workers in its major aspects will be dealt with in Chapter Five. Meanwhile, serious students of American history will find it illuminating to read any one of several novels that explore the lives of ordinary people. See, for example, Upton Sinclair, *The Jungle* (slaughterhouse workers, turn of the century Chicago), O. E. Rolvaag, *Giants in the Earth* (Dakota farm life, 19th century), T. S. Stribling, *The Store* (southern tenants, post-Civil War), A. Cahan, *The Rise of David Levinsky* (Jewish immigrants, late 19th century), James Farrell, *Studs Lonigan* (slum life, Chicago, early 20th century), and Agnes Smedley, *Daughter of Earth* (autobiographical novel, late 19th-early 20th century). The list could be very long, and very rewarding. Films such as "The Emigrants" (Swedish), which portrays the harsh conditions pushing people toward the United States, and the harsh conditions endured in the process (around 1850), are also good ways to improve one's sense of the past.

In the U.S., already by the close of the 19th century, the strength of the business impulse had swept aside all non-commercial contenders for power, prestige, or authority—except those political figures who knew where the power lay. In practice, this meant a multitude of things; most especially it meant that what business needed, business got. When complications arose, it was almost always when one business group was in contention with another business group—small versus big business, farmers versus railroads, for instance. We now turn to the evolution of American business as "a system of power."[6]

CAPITALISM, AMERICAN-STYLE

Adam Smith's hopes for a benign capitalist order rested squarely on his prescription for a fully competitive economy. In such an economy, all firms would be small; that is, the percentage of a given industry's output produced by one firm (or by a few firms) would be insignificant as a percentage of the whole industry output. Without control over supply, each business would have to function in response to the free market; *with* control over supply, the powerful firm could control the market. Smith's policies were designed to eliminate the control provided by State-granted privileges and monopolies. He did not examine the future dynamics of the kind of private economy he sought. Marx and Veblen did.

The *general* development of capitalism was first analyzed and explained by Marx, who sought to understand "the laws of motion of capitalist society." Marx barely touched upon the American experience. His empirical focus was Great Britain in the mid-19th century. Britain was the leading industrial capitalist society of the time, and Marx was in Great Britain. As a contributing journalist to the *New York Tribune*

---

[6]This perspective is put forth most explicitly by Robert A. Brady. His *Business as a System of Power* (New York: Columbia University Press, 1943) analyzes the patterns of power and the directions of the major capitalist powers—Great Britain, France, Germany, Italy, Japan, and the United States. Though dated in detail, the basic analysis remains very valuable (and largely ignored by almost all economists). Brady was much influenced by Marx and Veblen, and affected the development of this book's viewpoint because of my studies with him at the University of California (Berkeley). The approach to business power in the rest of this chapter will emphasize attempts to control the market directly. The use of power by business to affect the process of economic growth will be taken up in Chapter Four; the relationship of business power to the distribution of income and wealth and the organization of labor will be examined in Chapter Five; Chapter Six will examine the functioning of business power in the cities and as affecting the environment; Chapter Seven, business power in the world; and Chapter Eight, The State, will seek to bring all this together.

in the 1850's and 1860's, Marx had occasion to observe and comment upon American developments; he never did more than that.[7]

It was left to Veblen to initiate the first systematic critique of American capitalism. Born in America almost a half-century after Marx's birth, Veblen was well-situated to study the more advanced and specifically American experience.[8] Veblen did not have to imagine or speculate on the course of capitalist development in America since the time of Marx, let alone that of Smith. He lived and wrote when the full sweep of American business and industrial practices was in evidence. His starting-point was to distinguish between "business" and "industry":

> The industrial arts are a matter of tangible performance directed to work that is designed to be of material use to man. . . . [The] arts of business are arts of bargaining, effrontery, salesmanship, make-believe, and are directed to the gain of the business man at the cost of the community, at large and in detail. Neither tangible performance nor the common good is a business proposition. Any material use which his traffic may serve is quite beside the business man's purpose, except indirectly, in so far as it may serve to influence his clientele to his advantage.[9]

In brief, business is a matter of making money; industry, of making goods.

Veblen was by no means unique in noting the aggressiveness and the "effrontery" of businessmen. But the way in which he combined this widespread view with a larger analysis doomed him to the role of a lonely and scorned prophet. In his *Theory of Business Enterprise* (1904) he foresaw the two leading developments of American capitalism as centering on the drive for monopoly and the steady build-up of the forces of economic depression; in *Absentee Ownership* (1923) he was able to look around him and see his expectations confirmed. Another major probability as he saw it was an "increased unproductive consumption of goods," by which he meant the need to manipulate and persuade the population to buy unnecessary and trivial commodities, and the growth

---

[7] And much of what he did say was without benefit of serious research, understandably. This is especially true regarding his observations on the developing Civil War, the most momentous process at the time in the United States. For astute criticisms of Marx by a Marxist in this respect, see Eugene Genovese, *In Red and Black** (New York: Vintage, 1972), especially Chapter 15.

[8] Lewis Corey, *The Decline of American Capitalism* (New York: Covici-Friede, 1934) is the first systematic Marxian attempt. Brady's book, published in 1943, combines Marx and Veblen. Paul Baran and Paul Sweezy, *Monopoly Capital** (New York: Monthly Review Press, 1966) brings together Marxian, Veblenian, and Keynesian theory with contemporary data in a comprehensive analysis of recent American capitalism. The authors describe their work as only "a brief sketch," but it is much more than that, in that it attempts to provide an up-dated Marxian *theoretical* framework.

[9] *Absentee Ownership*, p. 107.

of arms production, accompanied by what he called "a strenuous foreign policy."

Precisely because the kind of competitive economy desired by Smith would entail effective price competition, Veblen argued, businessmen would energetically move to eliminate the competitive structure that allowed and required it. Their view of price competition was effectively suggested when they described it as "cutthroat competition." Businesses, monopolistic or otherwise, continue to "compete." But the forms taken by modern business rivalry are not such as to reduce costs, prices, and profits to some optimal level, as predicated in the competitive model; quite the contrary. Price competition has been replaced by two major forms of business rivalry: 1) "non-price competition," which takes the form of price-*increasing* advertising, packaging, and other forms of sales promotion; and 2) efforts to gain special privileges at all levels of government—to stabilize prices, to gain privileged contracts, to influence taxing and spending, labor and foreign policies, and the like. To recall an earlier observation, the *State* mercantilism that Smith fought against has been revived and joined by a *private* mercantilism. We can do no better than to refer to Veblen again:

> This decay of the old-fashioned competitive system has consisted in a substitution of competitive selling in the place of that competitive production of goods that is always presumed to be the chief and most serviceable feature of the competitive system. That is to say, it has been a substitution of salesmanship in the place of workmanship; as would be due to happen so soon as business came to take precedence of industry, salesmanship being a matter of business, not of industry; and business being a matter of salesmanship, not of workmanship. . . . Competition as it runs under the rule of this decayed competitive system is chiefly the competition between the business concerns that control production, on the one side, and the consuming public on the other side; the chief expedients in this business-like competition being salesmanship and sabotage. Salesmanship in this connection means little else than prevarication, and sabotage means a business-like curtailment of output.[10]

The hoped-for effects of a competitive economy need not depend upon the existence of textbook forms of "perfect" or "pure" competition. But they do depend upon the existence of pervasive and effective competition which, as data below will show, has little to do with the American reality. A competitive economy is one in which firms respond to the market, rather than setting the terms upon which the market responds to them. In such an economy there might be monopolies, but

---

[10] *Absentee Ownership,* p. 78. This was written in 1923; Veblen makes it clear elsewhere that the process of "decay" began decades earlier. For details, see Faulkner, *Decline of Laissez-Faire,* cited earlier, and Arthur Robert Burns, *The Decline of Competition* (New York: McGraw-Hill, 1936).

they would be under constant scrutiny and regulation, or they would be temporary. In the former case, which economists call "natural monopolies," the monopoly is justified by the technology of the industry; this is typical in utilities, where it is economically foolish to have duplicative large-scale water or gas-works, for example. The aim of the regulatory agency is to combine the advantages of large-scale production with the pricing results of a competitive industry where prices are set so as to attract the necessary amount of capital into the industry, but without the profits of monopoly. (In practice, those who sit on regulatory boards are predominantly from or in sympathy with those industries being "regulated.") Temporary monopolies, on the other hand, are presumed to disappear as soon as the new technology or unusual market circumstances giving rise to them are countered by long-run competitive forces.

What would *not* be, in an effectively competitive economy, is what exists in all the major capitalist countries today: patterns of concentrated power in all of modern industry and increasingly in trade, construction, finance, and in hitherto competitive sectors. To which must be added a State apparatus that, far from restraining private economic power, responds to it, represents it, and paves the way for it. Americans have become familiar with part of the pattern in recent years as they have become conscious of the so-called "military-industrial complex." The relationships exemplified in that pattern are not new; they are merely the latest development in the always close ties between business and government in the United States. These ties will be explored historically and in detail in Chapter Eight.

Returning now to the question of business competition in the American economy, and assuming that the textbook model is neither necessary nor possible, did anything even approximating an effectively competitive economy ever exist in the United States? And if it did, how, why, and by what was it corrupted?

THE INVISIBLE FIST

Of the many points to be noted, perhaps the first is that the capitalist system posits the businessman as its dynamic center. He, the "entrepreneur," is expected to respond to stimuli and to overcome obstacles so as to produce what society needs and wants. But to do this, he must possess one form of power: ownership of productive assets. To the degree that he succeeds, he is likely to gain more economic power, and other forms of power as well.

In practice, the dice are loaded in favor of those who own and control society's productive assets; and they are a tiny percentage of the population. By design and by default, those who are *not* property owners are weak in influence and power. For the competitive system to work well economically and socially in Adam Smith's terms, in short, those who are powerful must be frustrated in what they seek—that is, profits and power. The social rationale for a competitive capitalist economy is thus a curious one: market competition will prevent those who have power in the society from realizing their aims. In reality, competition is eliminated and the benign principles are abandoned, except for their half-lives in textbooks and rhetoric.

The point may be made in another way. Social and economic policies are decided upon and implemented by those with power. The laissez-faire society is one in which all sources of public policy-making over the economy are eliminated on principle. What is left is economic power alone, private economic power, and that resides solely in the hands of those who own and control the means of production. Not, certainly, in the hands of the propertyless wage-earner (who in Smith's time didn't even have the vote); not, of course, in the hands of Church or State, by design. So in a society devoid of social controls other than the market, the capitalist will do what he can to mitigate the one threat to his strength and profitability: he will seek to eliminate competition. There is nothing to stop him, and much—including the political power he picks up along the way—to help him. In 19th and 20th century America, the developing large-scale technology provided such assistance, for the small-scale structure implied by and required for a competitive economy is quite generally incompatible with modern technology, both on business and economic grounds. If a capitalist economy is made socially "safe" only by competition, what then remains of the social rationale for capitalism in the modern world?

Until the years just after the Civil War, the American economy may be said to have been effectively competitive. During that early period, businessmen's desires were no less profit-oriented than after the 1870's; what was different was technology and the extraordinary onrush of events associated with westward expansion. In the last quarter of the century, the westward movement began to stabilize while large-scale technology spread throughout the production process.

In the period before the Civil War (roughly speaking), there were, of course, large as well as small firms. The largest firms tended to be found in transportation, communications, finance, and trade; the occasional large *manufacturing* firm (in textile machinery, for example) had no substantial influence on the economy as a whole, which was changing its structure and growing so rapidly. Once more, however, the impact of the large-scale technology after the Civil War deserves emphasis.

The seller's impulse toward monopolization is a constant in history. (Thales, the ancient Greek philosopher, is known for his attempts to corner the market in olive oil.) That impulse becomes necessary and, when successful, much more profitable when it joins with the economics of modern—that is, large-scale—industry. The productive efficiency associated with modern industry is owed to the scale of production. This in turn entails not only widespread specialization in production, but also much in the way of expensive and long-lasting plant and equipment. The normal ups and downs of capitalist economic expansion and the intermittent glutting of markets combine with large-scale plants to yield destructive ("cutthroat") competition—price competition which entails selling below cost in bad times as a way to minimize losses. When that happens, or in order to prevent it from happening, the number of firms in a given industry shrinks, leaving the giants to endure and to prosper. For if eliminating competitors *diminishes* the prospects of price competition, it also *increases* the possibilities of enhancing profits in both bad and good times through controlling the market. ("Controlling the market" in this respect means controlling—i.e., restricting—supply, something that cannot be accomplished in a competitive market.) Thus the key characteristic of modern business behavior becomes that of dominant firms restricting supply in order to dictate and sell at a desirable price, a process that distorts both the supply and demand sides of the market, and that gives the large firms access to broad power over society as well—in a society that systematically and in principle foregoes locating that power in *non*-economic institutions.

FROM MERGERS TO MONOPOLY: THE GIANTS FEED

Until about 1860, the corporate form of business was largely confined to transportation and finance. With few exceptions, the emergence of corporations in manufacturing awaited the new, large-scale technology that emerged and spread after the Civil War.

From 1873 until the mid-1890's the entire industrial capitalist world underwent what was then called "The Great Depression." Unlike the Great Depression of the 1930's, the most prominent feature of the earlier period was pressure on profits, rather than massive unemployment. That pressure was due to the steady and dramatic lowering of prices through the period, which was in turn the result of great increases in efficiency, combined with the inability to cut off domestic or foreign competition in the context of relatively free trade and relatively competitive market structures.

Consequently, that same period saw the first general attempts to control price competition through one form of business reorganization or another. "Gentlemen's agreements" not to cut prices, profit pools, and trusts (all of which maintained the separate identity of the member corporations) were all tried; but the form which won out was the merger. The process in which mergers occurred is called the "combination movement." By the late 1890's, mergers or combinations (in which many firms were combined under one ownership and identity) became the rule; the years between 1897 and 1905 witnessed their first spectacular rush. During these years, over 5300 industrial firms came under the control, finally, of 318 corporations, the most advanced and powerful firms in the economy.

The turn-of-the-century wave of mergers was seen as spectacular, until subsequent waves surpassed it. As Figure 1 shows, a higher peak was reached in the 1920's; then, after what has been called a "ripple" in the 1940's, the largest wave of all began, which continues with force to this day. Economists have speculated as to what conditions are associated with increasing or decreasing merger activity. The evidence of the past seventy years or so suggests that the only period in which the *rate* of merger activity declines is that of depression; the impulse toward bigness and power is otherwise persistent.

The first waves of mergers were an outcome of the combination of expanding technology and businesses' aims of avoiding competition and of making profits. Technology then led to centralization of production facilities in a given location (for example, steel in Pittsburgh). Since World War II, however, technological development has led to *de*centralization of productive facilities geographically; at the same time the *control* over those facilities has become ever more centralized, spreading not simply over one industry but many different industries. Let us examine the process more closely.

Initially, mergers took place in each industry as it began to employ modern, large-scale technology. Sometimes the process was more like warfare than business in the late 19th century.[11] Mergers spread from transportation to manufacturing, to utilities and finance, to mining and construction and trade; by now mergers are the dynamic mode in all significant business, including entertainment, hotels and even agriculture, long considered the final preserve of effective competition.[12]

The patterns of the merger movements are striking; most striking of all is the tidal wave that began during World War II and reached its historic peak in 1968–1969. Figures 1 and 2 reveal not only the recent upsurge in mergers but the domination of those mergers by the largest 200 corporations and the increasing size of the transactions. As *Fortune* points out, "from 1964 through 1966, there were 293 mergers in which

---

[11]Tactics ranging from outright gun battles (in the fight to control the Erie Railroad, for example) to the most relentless financial "terrorism" (in Rockefeller's successful steps toward monopoly in oil) are related and detailed in Matthew Josephson, *The Robber Barons** (New York: Harcourt Brace Jovanovich, 1934), for the period 1861–1901.

[12]Still most important in controlling the forces of the market in agriculture, however, is governmental policy, which was brought into being under the pressure of farmers beginning over half a century ago. More will be said of these matters in Chapter Six.

Annual number of
mergers and acquisitions

FIGURE 1

Acquisitions of Manufacturing and Mining Companies 1895–1972

15 *Billions of dollars*

Assets obtained through
mergers and acquisitions

Assets acquired by the
200 largest companies

10

207

168

155

5

94

73

101

91

52

98

82

91

41

35

29

38

30

66

70

19

23

0

1963   '64   '65   '66   '67   '68   '69   '70   '71   '72
est.

Figures denote number
of transactions.

FIGURE 2

Big Acquisitions 1963–1972

the acquired companies had assets of more than $10 million; in the final three years of the decade there were 530. The average size of the transactions, $38 million in the first period, rose to $64 million during the second. In the peak year of 1968 the nation's top 200 industrial firms acquired a total of ninety-four large companies, with aggregate assets of more than $8 billion."[13]

Throughout all this merger activity there have been several subprocesses. At first, mergers were in one industry, where all the merging firms produced much the same product. These are called *horizontal* mergers, where competitors in a given industry come under the ownership and control of one company (for example, one steel company buying out another). While those mergers continued, another form, *vertical* mergers, began to appear, especially in the 1920's, in which a company buys out its suppliers and/or its customers (for example, Ford gaining its own steel facilities; U.S. Steel buying out coal mines and a bridge-building company).

Horizontal mergers lead to concentration of power in a given industry, and to *oligopoly:* a few dominant sellers in an industry. Vertical mergers strengthen the hand of already large firms, while also creating higher barriers to entry by new firms. Around forty years ago another form of merger began to attract attention, as it does even more so today: the *conglomerate,* where the firms acquired by a corporation are only distantly related, if at all, to the industry of the acquiring firm. In the vast merger movement since 1950 all these forms—vertical, horizontal, and conglomerate—have been operating, with the conglomerate form taking the prizes for drama. The drama became especially vivid in the 1960's, with "the new conglomerates."

The expansion of the "new conglomerates" was dominated by eight companies: ITT, Gulf & Western, Ling-Temco-Vought, Tenneco, White Consolidated, Teledyne, Occidental Petroleum, and Litton Industries. "Each of these companies made acquisitions during the 1960's totaling more than a half-billion dollars; for six the asset value was over a billion dollars."[14] Of the various important aspects of this movement, one worth noting is that it has sped up the process of bringing traditionally "small business" industries—for instance, food processing, non-electrical machinery, and textiles—under the control of giant corporations.

---

[13] *Fortune,* April, 1973, from which the charts are also derived. A useful and comprehensive analysis of mergers is Samuel Richardson Reid, *Mergers, Managers, and the Economy** (New York: McGraw-Hill, 1968).

[14] John M. Blair, *Economic Concentration: Structure, Behavior and Public Policy* (New York: Harcourt Brace Jovanovich, 1972), p. 285. This is probably the most comprehensive study of the whole question. The author has spent his life working on the problems of big business in the Federal Trade Commission. His data on conglomerates are drawn from Federal Trade Commission, *Economic Report on Corporate Mergers** (Washington, D.C., 1969), the best factual study of the conglomerate movement.

The early merger movements, whether horizontal or vertical in origin, led to the *concentration* of economic power within the affected industries. When we add the conglomerate mergers to the earlier movement we come to an additional characteristic: *centralization*. Furthermore, combined with the concentration and centralization of *private* economic power is the associated concentration and centralization of *public* power. The concentration and centralization of State power shows itself in the enormously enhanced powers of the federal government today as compared with, say, 1900; it is revealed even more pointedly in the extraordinary powers increasingly arrogated by the presidency—and, conversely, the declining powers of Congress and the separate states.[15] The government at all levels represents the interests of many groups in American society, of course—doctors, organized labor, the aged, the poor, et al.—but it represents most and best the interests of the most powerful. The most powerful are unquestionably the most powerful business corporations. Let us examine some representative data suggesting their position in the American economy.

FACTS ARE STUBBORN THINGS

There is no mystery as to the size or the identity of America's giant corporations. *Fortune* annually publishes its "Fortune 500" and "Second 500," showing assets, sales, employees, income, profits, etc., of the largest industrial corporations; their data in turn are derived from a multitude of governmental and private sources, all open to the public eye. Economists are fully aware of these data, but they have yet to alter conventional economic *theory* to fit the data—quite possibly because to do so in any systematic manner would require abandoning the entire structure of the theory. One respected conventional economist, understanding this, has said (in the convoluted language used by economists when they address each other): "To argue that monopolistic deviations can be ignored because of their minor importance is to exhibit ideological bias. To argue that piecemeal antitrust leads to improvement is false. The only bias-free option is the option that leads to a centrally con-

---

[15]This development will be analyzed more fully in Chapter Eight. In recent years, beginning in the Johnson Administration and accelerating under Nixon, the Supreme Court has become subject to crasser political considerations than earlier, as well, which has had the effect of placing more of the power of the judiciary in the White House. A careful and outraged analysis of the process may be found in Louis M. Kohlmeier, Jr., *God Save This Honorable Court* (New York: Scribner's, 1972), whose conclusion it is that "President Nixon's place in history is secure: Nixon politicized the Supreme Court more dramatically than any President in history" (p. 281).

trolled economy. But how many believers in fact are prepared to accept this conclusion?"[16]

Let us now look at some representative facts concerning the concentration and centralization of control over productive assets, sales, profits, employment and the like:[17]

— The 500 largest industrial (manufacturing and mining) corporations in 1972 controlled 65 percent of the *sales* of all industrial companies, 75 percent of their total *profits,* and 75 percent of total industrial *employment.*

— The 1000 largest industrial corporations in 1972 controlled about 72 percent of industrial *sales,* about 80 percent of industrial *profits,* and about 84 percent of industrial *employment;* that is, the "Second 500" account for 6.5 percent of sales, 6 percent of profits and about 9 percent of industrial jobs—a fraction of the business done by *The* 500, and that leaves very little indeed for the remaining hundreds of thousands of industrial companies.

— The industrial corporation with the greatest *assets* is EXXON (formerly Standard Oil of New Jersey); in 1972 its assets were $21.5 *billion.* The company with the smallest assets of the top 500 in 1972 was Varian Associates, with $188 *million.* EXXON's sales in 1972 were $20 *billion;* Varian's, $203 *million.*

— The top 500 industrial companies had *sales* of $558 billion in 1972; GNP—the total money value of all goods and services at their final stage—was $1,152 billion. Total sales of the Second 500 were about $59 billion. The top ten corporations (GM, EXXON, Ford, GE, IBM, Mobil Oil, Chrysler, Texaco, ITT, and Western Electric) had sales of $133 billion. That is, the top 500 corporations controlled just under half of the entire GNP; the top *ten* corporations more than 10 percent of GNP (and about 24 percent of the top 500 and more than twice the sales of the Second 500). The top 50 of the 500 did

---

[16]Andreas G. Papandreou, *Paternalistic Capitalism* (Minneapolis: University of Minnesota Press, 1972), p. 26. Another "bias-free option" leads to a decentralized socialist society, in the minds of many. The author was Chairman of the Department of Economics at the University of California (Berkeley), until he became immersed in Greek politics as an important figure, and was expected to lead the government. The military junta now ruling Greece jailed Papandreou when it seized power; he was freed and exiled after much pressure from outside. Papandreou sees the present dictatorial government as the exact equivalent of the Thieu regime in South Vietnam, up to and including its installation and support by the United States. See pp. 121–34.

[17]The data are familiar, and may be found in many economics textbooks. These are drawn primarily from Blair and Reid, both cited above, from Robert T. Averitt, *The Dual Economy** (New York: Norton, 1968), and from *Fortune,* May, 1971, May, 1972, and May and June, 1973.

47 percent of the business of the 500. In short, the concentration of the economy is continued within the top 500, where the bulk of power is centralized in the hands of a small percentage.

— The *assets* of the top 500 industrial corporations in 1972 were $486 billion; of the second 500, about $46 billion. The assets of the top ten companies were $109 billion, more than twice that of the Second 500.

— In 1972, GM was first in sales of the top 500, with $30.4 billion —2.6 percent of GNP for one company.

— The *profits* of the largest ten corporations (industrial and non-industrial)—AT&T, GM, EXXON, IBM, Texaco, Ford, Gulf Oil, Sears Roebuck, Mobil Oil, and Standard Oil of California —were $10.3 billion *after* taxes, in 1971. The two largest— AT&T and GM—made $2.2 and $1.9 billion, respectively. Total corporate profits in 1971 were just under $50 billion after taxes. That is, the ten top corporations gained over 20 percent of *all* corporate profits in 1971.

— Between 1970 and 1971, the *sales* of the top 500 industrials rose by 8.4 percent. GM, increasing its sales by $9.5 billion that year, by itself accounted for 24 percent of the sales increase of the 500, and it accounted for 76 percent of the net income increase of the 500. Adding in Ford and Chrysler brings the figure up to 89 percent of the net income increase of the top 500. Auto sales and profits increased even more spectacularly in 1972 and 1973, as sales of cars rose to record-breaking levels (about 12 million in 1973).

— Between 1969 and 1972, the top 500 increased their sales by about $113 billion; but they hired 137,000 fewer workers in 1972 than in 1969.

Such are some of the data of a concentrated economy. Economists seek to systematize these kinds of data with what are called concentration measures. Table 1 shows the percentages held by the largest four corporations in a given industry, using various measures.

Averitt's *Dual Economy* was used for some of the foregoing data. In his conclusion, he calls for a new microeconomic theory to build around the concentrated "center" and the weak "periphery." Having provided us with the data and an analysis showing that these describe a permanent feature of the American "dual economy," Averitt comes forth with the surprising conclusion that "we can attain perpetual prosperity while retaining a high level of what the business community calls 'economic freedom.' "[18] His optimism depends upon his hopes for governmental

---

[18]Ibid., p. 200.

"moral suasion," which he takes to be "more effective in highly concentrated industries dominated by center firms than elsewhere" (Ibid.). To have such hopes is to assume that private economic power is one thing and State power something else, something independent of private eco-

TABLE 1
Concentration in Manufacturing Industries

Percentage of Sales, Total Assets,
Net Capital Assets, and Profits after Taxes Accounted for by the
4 Largest Firms in Each Industry for 28 Selected Industry Groups,
4th Quarter, 1962

		Percent of total		
Industry	Sales	Total Assets	Net Capital Assets	Profits
Motor vehicles	80.8	79.7	83.1	89.1
Aircraft	47.3	41.9	32.6	46.6
Other transportation equipment	30.3	44.2	59.9	51.6
Electrical machinery	34.4	35.6	41.5	44.4
Metalworking machinery	14.5	16.3	18.5	19.1
Other machinery	20.6	24.3	31.5	39.6
Primary iron and steel	40.2	48.0	48.8	44.3
Primary nonferrous metals	27.3	41.1	47.7	37.1
Other fabricated metal products	14.7	19.9	30.3	17.7
Stone, clay, and glass products	18.1	19.9	19.8	23.4
Furniture and fixtures	5.2	8.4	9.6	5.3
Lumber and wood products	21.2	31.0	41.5	48.6
Instruments	37.9	41.2	50.2	56.6
Miscellaneous manufacturing	16.3	33.1	34.3	25.2
Dairy products	42.9	48.8	47.4	73.9
Bakery products	33.6	39.6	38.2	52.8
Other food	12.5	13.2	14.9	20.1
Textile mill products	22.0	26.1	25.7	30.5
Apparel	4.9	7.7	11.4	7.4
Paper	20.7	23.2	22.3	35.0
Basic industrial chemicals	42.0	45.5	44.6	64.6
Drugs and medicines	31.0	29.2	33.3	32.6
Other chemicals	28.5	30.0	33.6	35.8
Petroleum refining	50.3	50.1	47.7	54.3
Rubber	48.1	55.0	56.4	51.6
Leather	26.7	32.1	35.4	28.8
Alcoholic beverages	41.4	47.2	30.8	58.3
Tobacco	70.9	72.7	69.8	72.5

SOURCE: Bureau of Economics, Federal Trade Commission.

nomic power.[19] In a capitalist society the shred of truth contained in those hopes is completely out-weighed by the realities of power—a matter to be looked at more closely in Chapter Eight.

The data above have been concerned with the functioning of the domestic economy. The figures show that the corporations involved constitute the hard core of power in the United States. When we look at the latest development of American business power—the *multinational* corporation—we see the emergence of a powerful tendency for the same pattern of concentration and centralization in the capitalist world economy. Multinational corporations' main features are an integral part of the functioning of the American overseas empire; here it is appropriate to examine only the general shape of the development.

WHAT'S GOOD FOR AMERICA . . .

The multinational corporation, as its name suggests, has its origins and its headquarters in one nation, and it buys, invests, produces, and sells in many nations. As Stephen Hymer has pointed out,

> The multinational corporation is in the first instance an American phenomenon. Its precursor is the U.S. *national corporation* created at the end of the 19th century when American capitalism developed a multi-city continent-wide marketing and manufacturing strategy. . . . Though many U.S. corporations began to move to foreign countries almost as soon as they completed their continent-wide integration, the term *multinational* came to prominence only after 1960. . . . National firms think in terms of the national market; multinational firms see the whole world as their oyster and plan manufacturing and marketing on a global scale. . . . The shift in business horizons is closely connected to the aeronautical and electronic revolutions which made global planning possible.[20]

In 1972, about $450 billion (of a total of about three trillions) of the world's production was attributable to multinational corporations. Of that amount, about $200 billion was produced by American multinationals, about $100 billion by foreign-based companies which also operate in the United States (for example, Royal-Dutch Shell), and the rest

---

[19]Six case studies of how private and public power work together and separately to corrupt the presumed functions of both are collected in Robert L. Heilbroner, et al., *In the Name of Profits** (New York: Warner Paperback, 1973). The studies are illustrative of a much larger whole.

[20]Stephen Hymer, "The United States Multinational Corporations and Japanese Competition in the Pacific," an unpublished ms. which the author has kindly allowed me to use here.

by inter-production in other countries. The proportion of world production contributed by multinational corporations is now growing at the rate of about 10 percent per year. Were that rate to continue—and the turbulence and complexities of the world economy make it unlikely—the few hundred multinationals would generate about one-half of world production by the year 2000.

Naturally, almost all of the multinational corporations are among the very largest corporations in their own countries. Also, as might be expected, the emergence of this phenomenon for American corporations coincided with (was both cause and consequence of) our taking up primary status in the world economy from the 1920's on. Its most spectacular period of growth has been the past twenty-five years, the period in which the American economy has become internationalized, and the capitalist world economy Americanized. The dynamic center of any future power struggle in the capitalist world economy will surely find the multinationals taking leading roles.

The increasing proclivity of American corporations to locate their producing plants all over the world has vital consequences for the functioning of the American as well as other economies. Apart from what it means for the multinational corporations, it means a significant redistribution of productive jobs around the globe, and it affects resource flows, foreign policies, economic growth rates and patterns, and the international monetary system (as will be shown in Chapter Seven). Whatever surprises and shocks the future holds, some of them will be due to the growing importance of these giants, as much of what has happened in the recent past has been clothed with their purposes and their needs.

Necessarily, the emergence of the American multinational corporation, like the emergence of the national corporation, has been facilitated by the State, which is much accustomed to responding to business needs and possibilities first, and asking and being asked questions about what it means to society, later—often too late. The internationalization of the American economy and the Americanization of the capitalist world economy could not be accomplished without great changes in our global military posture, by comparison with any earlier period. Thus, there is an additional matter to be stressed in viewing the evolution of American business as a system of power: its relationship with the State and within that the relationships between business and the military. Here only the bare outlines will be suggested, anticipating fuller discussions later.

Among the justifications for capitalism as a system was one that, running contrary to the facts, is still frequently put forward. It claims that a "free enterprise" system minimizes the role of the State, and that it encourages everybody to pursue their rational material interests. One by-product of such a system would be efficiency; another would be material well-being; still another would be a government swayed by rational, meaning material, considerations.

But recently (that is, since about 1930), the United States has found itself confronted with developing needs and possibilities that cannot be resolved by a free market economy. There was the Great Depression of the 1930's, which only World War II resolved. There was the widespread unrest of that same period, taking the form of labor and socialist movements which, if they were never closely threatening, seemed so to the business class. There was the growth of fearsome Communist nations, assumed to be expansive and threatening to American interests, or even to "freedom" in the entire world. There was an already voracious and growing need for industrial raw materials, for markets, and for investment outlets, as well as a need for strategic sites to protect our expanding economic and political interests. Closely related to these developments was the growth of corporations that became usefully, vitally, or fully dependent upon military contracts—contracts typically constructed on a cost-plus (i.e., guaranteed profit) basis.

These developments, taken together with the long-standing cultivation of patriotic attitudes among Americans, combined to produce a military-industrial complex most profitable to a hundred or so very large and thousands of smaller business firms, and a working force that was in fact or in its job fears dependent upon war production. Almost all Americans saw these developments, combining economic, military, political, and ideological needs, possibilities, and appeals, neither as malign nor as unreal; they saw them as responsibilities thrust upon America's economic and moral strength—thrust upon them by hostile, crafty, enigmatic and essentially peculiar foreigners. (Lyndon Baines Johnson once remarked, almost peevishly, "those foreigners weren't reared like us.") Later, we shall have occasion to cast doubt on whether the United States was forced by foreigners and/or hostile events to take up the role of Number One in the world. Here we may say merely that the processes of the past decades had the at least temporary effect, salubrious from the viewpoint of American capitalism, of bringing the majority of the American people closer to traditional conceptions of American virtues, a consequence anticipated by Veblen in 1904:

> The largest and most promising factor of cultural discipline—most promising as a corrective of iconoclastic vagaries—over which business principles rule is national politics. . . . Business interests urge an aggressive national policy and business men direct it. Such a policy is warlike as well as patriotic. The direct cultural value of a warlike business policy is unequivocal. It makes for a conservative animus on the part of the populace . . . [and] directs the popular interest to other, nobler, institutionally less hazardous matters than the unequal distribution of wealth or of creature comforts. . . . There can, indeed, be no serious question but that

a consistent return to the ancient virtues of allegiance, piety, servility, graded dignity, class prerogative, and prescriptive authority would greatly conduce to popular content and to the facile management of affairs. Such is the promise held out by a strenuous national policy.[21]

READING SUGGESTIONS

Walter Adams, ed., *The Structure of the American Industry: Some Case Studies** (New York: Macmillan, 1961) is one of the best of several such books that examine many different industries in terms of their histories, their structures, and their performance. Leonard W. Weiss, *Case Studies in American Industry** (New York: Wiley, 1967) is similar and equally useful. Thurman Arnold, *The Folklore of Capitalism* (Garden City, N.Y.: Blue Ribbon Books, 1941), is a useful and critical study of the leading ideas and institutions of capitalist society. Arnold was at one time in charge of the Antitrust Division of the Justice Department, from which he was "booted upstairs" for being over-zealous. Joe S. Bain, Jr., *Industrial Organization,** rev. ed. (New York: Wiley, 1968) provides a thorough empirical and analytical study of the structure and functioning of American industry. A. A. Berle, *Power Without Property* (New York: Harcourt Brace Jovanovich, 1959) takes up an explosive issue and, characteristically, puts it down again as though it were not. See also his (with Gardiner Means) path-breaking *Modern Corporation and Private Property** (New York: Macmillan, 1932), a path that might have, but did not (either for him or his fellows in economics), lead to disturbing conclusions and a new political economy.

John Kenneth Galbraith has the unusual virtue, for an economist, of writing bearable and even engaging English; this, certainly not any radical tinge to his ideas, is probably what has placed him near or beyond the pale for many in the economics profession. His *American Capitalism,** *The Affluent Society,** and *The New Industrial State** (Boston:

---

[21] *Theory of Business Enterprise,* pp. 391–93. In today's world, where so much of this has already been accomplished, it may be necessary to point out that Veblen's intent is sardonic, and that all his writings were devoted to preventing such developments from occurring. David Halberstam's *Best and the Brightest* (New York: Random House, 1972) provides an extraordinarily detailed account of the personalities and policies of the 1960's, and abundant references back to the Truman and Eisenhower years. The treatment is journalistic rather than analytical, and the writing style is often indigestible, but those reading it will find that the Cold War in general and the Indochina War in particular were the outcome of some combination of private interest and capitalist ideology, rather than the interest of the American or any other nation's people, and that those making policy since (at least) 1945 did so in a continuous state of arrogance, ignorance, confusion, and systematic deception. Watergate's roots go deep.

Houghton Mifflin, 1956, 1958, and 1967 respectively) are worth reading —for information, for witty criticisms of the profession, and for examples of how a fine mind can stumble if it tethers itself in a pitted field. Andrew Hacker, ed., *The Corporation Take-Over** (Garden City, N.Y.: Doubleday, Anchor Books, 1965) is a useful collection of critical essays on various aspects of corporate power. Charles Perrow, ed., *The Radical Attack on Business** (New York: Harcourt Brace Jovanovich, 1972) covers much the same subject matter, from farther to the left. A radical treatment of the role of expansion in capitalist development is provided succinctly by Edwards in *The Capitalist System,* cited earlier, pp. 99 ff.

The basic history and central problems of combination and competition are treated conventionally and thoroughly in George W. Stocking and Myron W. Watkins, *Monopoly and Free Enterprise* (New York: Twentieth Century Fund, 1951). Watkins has written a fine and compressed analysis of the processes that lead to large-scale production, ownership, and control in the article entitled "Large-Scale Production," in *The Encyclopaedia of the Social Sciences.* The entry "Industrialism" by G. D. H. Cole is also praiseworthy in that encyclopaedia.

Those who wish to study one enterprise in depth can do so in many ways; one fine study of that sort is Keith Sward, *The Legend of Henry Ford** (New York: Holt, Rinehart and Winston, 1948). Ford, who once proclaimed "machinery is the new Messiah"—and "History is bunk"— comes out as something of a crank, and as a very lucky, quite ruthless, and not at all bright businessman, taking in profits at rates—$150,000 *a day* in the early 1920's—that economics textbooks neither describe, explain, nor imagine. Those wishing a good analytic account of the development of the giant corporation's organizational form should consult Alfred Chandler, Jr., *Strategy and Structure** (Cambridge: M.I.T. Press, 1962). Finally, the always close relationships between business and the State are examined from quite different perspectives by Bernard D. Nossiter, *The Mythmakers** (Boston: Beacon Press, 1964), and by Walter Adams and Horace M. Gray, *Monopoly in America: The Government as Promoter* (New York: Macmillan, 1955). Nossiter is a liberal journalist; Gray and Adams seek a reduction in the power and size of Big Business and Big Government.

chapter four

Growth and Development, Prosperity and Depression

As I sd to my
friend, because I am
always talking,—John, I

sd, which was not his
name, the darkness sur-
rounds us, what

can we do against
it, or else, shall we &
why not, buy a goddamn big car,

drive, he sd, for
christ's sake, look
out where yr going.

(Robert Creeley, *I Know A Man*)

A capitalist economy cannot stand still. It must *grow* or shrink; it must continually change its patterns of production, consumption, and trade —that is, *develop*—or cease to grow; irrespective of growth and development, it must continually *fluctuate*. At any time and over time, the capitalist economy is marked by unevenness, uncertainty, and instability. Why is all this so? What are the characteristics of, and differences between, fluctuations, growth, and development? How do they relate, separately and in combination, to the defining traits of capitalism—its need to expand and to exploit? Earlier we have touched on some of the relevant explanations; here we will explore them in greater depth.

However much they disagree on other matters, all economists who have studied capitalism—from Smith through Marx, Marshall, and Keynes—agree on the necessity of expansion. Disagreement centers upon what is required for expansion, what is associated with the process, the likelihood of expansion over time, and the consequences of either adequate or inadequate rates of expansion. How these matters are treated distinguishes classical from neoclassical economics and both of those from radical or dissenting economics.

The classical economists, and especially Smith and Ricardo, developed analyses whose aim was to enhance the possibilities of economic growth and development. J. S. Mill's examination of the likelihood and problems of a "stationary" economy ended the period of classical economics; as Mill's life was drawing to a close, neoclassical economics came to the fore. Until the astounding depression of the 1930's, that economics gave little sustained attention to the processes of growth and development. Neoclassical monetary theory, capital theory, and trade theory—all highly abstract—could be said to be *related* to such questions; since such theories generally took buoyant growth for granted, however, they did not systematically examine the life processes of growth. And, as we saw earlier, development—any sort of significant structural change—was neither sought nor discussed in neoclassical economics. Given the kinds of problems business faced in the late 19th century—centering mostly on market scarcities—and given the essential harmony between the viewpoints of business and economics, this was an understandable neglect. All that was rudely upset by the Depression and by the adjustments of neoclassical theory made by Keynes.

Alongside the aloof attitude of neoclassical economics, and developing in the same years (from the 1870's up to about 1930), there *was* a body of analysis that sought to approach questions of growth, fluctuations, and development directly. The significance of these ideas was not to become meaningful, however, until after the depression of the 1930's was well underway; nor did they divert the smooth flow of calm neoclassicism. In the United States, Veblen was unquestionably the most influential thinker in this area, although his influence was not always acknowledged by those he directly or indirectly influenced: J. M. Clark and Wesley Clair Mitchell, directly, and J. A. Schumpeter, indirectly. Economics in general went its merry way, unruffled by any serious concern with the prospect of untoward booms or slumps, while serious business cycle analysts managed to overlook the gloomy expectations of Veblen's analysis, which in turn was indebted to European, including Marxian, contributions.[1]

In the decade or two preceding the Depression, the seriousness of the problems of expansion and contraction was only barely recognized, in short, as revealed by the credibility given to "theories" that explained

---

[1]A comprehensive and very useful study of this area of economics in its historical development and its contemporary state is Robert Aaron Gordon, *Business Fluctuations,** 2nd ed. (New York: Harper & Row, 1961). Gordon provides a thorough integration of Keynesian analysis with historical and current data. Chapters 12 and 13 examine "the variety of business-cycle theories."

aggregative movements in terms of "sunspots," or, in one instance, by an inverse correlation with the length of women's skirts in Australia. It took a disaster to prompt either the economics profession or its audience to pay heed to the relationship between such disaster and the normal functionings of a capitalist economy.

Joseph A. Schumpeter, a conventional and very conservative economist, was one who—like Veblen, Clark, and Mitchell—stood as an exception to those who saw business downturns as temporary aberrations. Schumpeter was one of those rare people who can learn from those with whose purposes he disagrees; he learned a lot from Marx and (though never admitting it) from Veblen as well. Although he accepted much of the neoclassical mode of analysis, Schumpeter could not do so for the vital questions of growth and development. "Analyzing business cycles," he said, "means neither more nor less than analyzing the economic process of the capitalist era. . . . Cycles are not, like tonsils, separable things that might be treated by themselves, but are, like the beat of its heart, at the essence of the organism that displays them."[2] Schumpeter was an ardent supporter of capitalist society; his studies of capitalist development told him that the best one could hope for was the postponement of its disappearance. He developed this position most fully in his *Capitalism, Socialism, and Democracy.* The healthy dynamic of capitalism for Schumpeter was what he called "creative gales of destruction"—gales powered by technological innovation, leading to the elimination of *old* patterns of competition and monopoly by *new* patterns of competition and monopoly. In this view but not in others, he was close to Veblen and Marx, despite his quite different value system. They saw the life and death of capitalism more as undertakers than as doctors.

WOMB TO TOMB

Writing in the heyday of neoclassical economics *and* of rampant American industrialization, Veblen combined a dour analysis of capitalist growth and development with a dim view of the associated economics:

> There are certain saving clauses in common use. . . . Among them are these: "Given the state of the industrial arts"; "Other things remaining

---

[2]Joseph A. Schumpeter, *Business Cycles: A Theoretical, Historical, and Statistical Analysis of the Capitalist Process,* two vols. (New York: McGraw-Hill, 1939), vol. I, p. v. This massive work ranges throughout the capitalist world in the terms of its title. Schumpeter was given the mantle of greatness by his contemporaries, but his approach and his ideas were given short shrift by them. (Gordon, cited above, is an exception.) Schumpeter was an Austrian, and taught at Harvard from 1932 until his death in 1950.

the same"; "In the long run"; "In the absence of disturbing causes." Now, ... the state of the industrial arts has at no time continued unchanged during the modern era; consequently other things have never remained the same; and in the long run the outcome has always been shaped by the disturbing causes. ... The arguments [of the neoclassical economists] have been as good as the premises on which they proceed.[3]

For Veblen, the process of capitalist growth and development hurried through time under the domination of three major trends: a steady increase in monopolization, a continuing increase in technological strength, and a chronic tendency toward depression. Monopoly results from the native impulse of the business man to eliminate competition —"buy cheap and sell dear." Technological advance ". . . has in recent times been going forward at a constantly accelerated rate, and it is still in progress, with no promise of abatement or conclusion."[4] But why should depression be the outcome of monopoly and technological improvement? That takes us back to Veblen's distinction between business and industry. Business is a matter of making money; what business will produce, in what quantities, and when is determined by actual and prospective market conditions. The advance of technology means ever-increasing production and productivity; the combination of consumer and investment expenditures with the ability of monopolistic business to hold back production—Veblen called it "businesslike sabotage"— places steady downward pressure on the economy, relieved only by intermittent stimuli coming from outside the normal functioning of the economy. Thus,

> Since the seventies . . . , the course of affairs in business has apparently taken a permanent change as regards crises and depression. During this recent period, and with increasing persistency, chronic depression has been the rule rather than the exception in business. Seasons of easy times, "ordinary prosperity," during this period are pretty uniformly traceable to specific causes extraneous to the process of industrial business proper; [e.g., in] the one now drawing to a close, it was the Spanish–American War, coupled with the expenditures for stores, munitions, and services incident to placing the country on a war footing, that lifted the depression and brought prosperity to the business community.[5]

The remedy Veblen saw for this tendency toward chronic depression was for "the vested interests" to *create* these stimuli, for them to develop

---

[3] Thorstein Veblen, *The Vested Interests and the Common Man** (New York: Huebsch, 1919; Viking, 1946), pp. 85–86.

[4] *Absentee Ownership*, p. 251.

[5] *Theory of Business Enterprise*, p. 250. Written in 1904.

means of "unproductive consumption," through a "strenuous national policy," and a popular concern for "national integrity." Those who find this view out of keeping with what appears to be a different reality since 1904 may be reminded that the economy was saved from contraction by World War I and an ensuing prosperity, that it sank into deep depression in the 1930's from which it recovered only after our entrance into World War II, and that our prosperity since then has been accompanied by both Cold War and hot war involving the expenditure on military production of about one-and-a-half *trillion* dollars since 1941. These and other characteristics of our developmental process will be traced more fully later in this chapter. Let us look briefly now at Marx's approach to growth and development. There are implicit and explicit differences between his and Veblen's analysis, as well as many common features.

Marx spoke not of economic growth or development, but of the process of "capital accumulation." This was for Marx the rope on which capitalism climbed through time, aided by intermittent knots of expansion and threatened by periodic frayed stretches, which he called crises (and which are now called recessions or depressions). Marx believed also that this was the rope with which capitalism would ultimately hang itself—with the help of the working class, itself a product of capital accumulation. More exactly, both the expanding and the contracting phases of capitalist development are negative as well as positive in their meaning. Expansion means expanded production and profits, *but* only up to the point where it also means overproduction and upward pressure on wages; contraction means decreased production and losses, *but* it also replenishes the "reserve army of the unemployed," ultimately reduces competition through the destruction of weaker firms, and lays the basis for renewed expansion and the tendency toward monopoly.

For Marx, the process of capital accumulation (that is, of expansion) is energized by what each individual capitalist *wishes* to do and what he and all capitalists *must* do: seeking to make profits in competition with others in the context of an ever-changing technology, the surviving capitalists and the economy are driven to "accumulate," or expand. The capitalist

> . . . shares with the miser the passion for wealth as wealth. But that which in the miser is a mere idiosyncrasy, is, in the capitalist, the effect of the social mechanism, of which he is but one of the wheels. Moreover, the development of capitalist production makes it constantly necessary to keep increasing the amount of capital laid out in a given industrial undertaking, and competition makes the immanent laws of capitalist production to be felt by each individual capitalist, as external coercive laws. It compels him to keep constantly extending his capital, in order to preserve it, but extend it he cannot, except by means of progressive accumulation.

Therefore,

> Accumulate, accumulate! That is Moses and the prophets! . . . Accumulation for accumulation's sake, production for production's sake. . . .[6]

A full treatment of Marxian and Veblenian theory along these lines would show that Marx had a more coherent and a more powerful *economic* theory of capitalist development than Veblen. On the other hand, the looseness and the breadth of Veblen's analysis, and the later period in which he wrote, allowed him to bring in the behavior and meaning of modern monopolistic business organization and of the State in ways going beyond Marx.[7] What seems essential is to combine the strengths of Marx, Veblen, and Keynes with contemporary data and social analysis, an effort already begun by Baran and Sweezy in *Monopoly Capital.* Now let us explore what is meant by fluctuations, growth, and development, in general and in the American experience.

FLUCTUATIONS AND INSTABILITY

In proceeding first to explain the pervasiveness and persistence of business fluctuations in a capitalist economy, it should be emphasized that fluctuations and instability are not viewed as *defects* in such an economy. The price of such instability may be high for particular businesses, industries, and workers at any time, but for a capitalist *economy's* health over time such fluctuations are essential. In what is no more than a suggestive analogy, we may think of the role of business fluctuations in a capitalist economy as comparable to the processes of inhaling and exhaling, of hunger and surfeit, of ingestion and digestion, in the human body. Extending the analogy a bit further, we can point out that it is not the processes as such that are harmful, but the quality of the air and the quantity and composition of the diet that make for health or sickness in the body.

Thus, business fluctuations are inherent to a capitalist economy. To rid the economy of them would require ridding it as well of its basic

---

[6]The first passage is from *Capital,* vol. I, p. 592, and the second from p. 595.

[7]"Above all, Veblen was, and remains alone in assigning a decisive role in the development of capitalism to the reciprocating interaction of business principles and national politics. Others have described the economic impact of war, the psychological effects of militarism, the cultural incidence of nationalism; and none can deny that these forces have become increasingly important, if not actually dominant, in the world of the twentieth century. Yet only Veblen has built all these elements into a reasoned and coherent theory." Paul M. Sweezy, "Veblen on American Capitalism," in Douglas F. Dowd, ed., *Thorstein Veblen: A Critical Reappraisal* (Ithaca: Cornell University Press, 1958), p. 195.

institutional characteristics: private ownership of the means of production, and the right and will to use those productive assets to make profits at the decision of the businessman. A capitalist *economy* is in its nature unplanned, however much each *enterprise* may plan. The economy is complex. It becomes more so as industrialization broadens and deepens specialization in all aspects of the economy—in agriculture, trade, industry, finance, and the broad variety of services. Time must pass between the initial decision to invest and produce; that is, decisions made on the basis of one set of market signals are realized either well or badly in markets that exist later. And all this is made infinitely more complex by virtue of the mediating role of money and finance, to say nothing of the impact of foreign trade.[8]

As noted in Chapter Three, competition, taken in its own terms, is essential to the economic and the social health of a capitalist economy; so is instability. However, just as businessmen have acted when they could to mitigate or eliminate competition (through driving out or buying up competitors, for example), they have also done what little they could to mitigate the harmful effects of instability on their own enterprises. But competition is an industry-wide phenomenon; instability is economy-wide. Consequently, no matter how effective steps may be to eliminate market competition when taken by an individual firm or corporation, the substantial amelioration of instability has depended upon economic intervention by the State. Such intervention became neither significant nor persistent until the onset of the Depression of the 1930's. This marked a major change both in the role of the State and in the structure of the economy. What these changes reflected was the necessity for a *developmental* change if adequate growth rates as well as the mitigation of instability were to be achieved.

If capitalism is *inherently* unstable, and if the United States was capitalist from its earliest beginnings, then our economic history should have been characterized by continuous ups and downs, as indeed it was. The following chart indicates the basic economic fluctuations in the U.S. since 1800:

1800–1807	Prosperity	1819	Panic
1808–1809	Depression	1820–1821	Mild depression
1810–1814	Gradual recovery and boom (in 1814)	1822–1824	Prosperity
		1825–1826	Recession
		1827–1836	Growing prosperity
1815	Panic	1837	Panic
1816–1818	Depression	1837–1843	Generally depressed conditions

[8]See Gordon, *Business Fluctuations.* Chapters 1 and 8 provide a good explanation of instability and its causes.

1844–1848	Mild prosperity	1914–1918	War prosperity
1849–1856	Vigorous prosperity	1919	Mild postwar recession
1857	Panic	1919–1920	Prosperity
1858	Depression	1921–1922	Sharp recession
1859–1860	Revival and prosperity	1922–1923	Prosperity
		1924	Recession
1861–1862	Generally depressed conditions	1925–1926	Recovery
		1927	Recession
1862–1865	War prosperity	1928–1929	Boom
1866–1867	Depression	1930's	Deep depression; short-lived "boom" in 1937
1868–1872	Prosperity		
1873	Panic		
1874–1878	General depression	1940's	War and postwar prosperity; recession in 1946, and in 1949
1879	Recovery		
1880–1882	Prosperity		
1883–1885	Mild recession		
1886–1890	Vigorous prosperity	1950's	Recessions in 1953–54, and 1957–58
1891	Minor recession		
1892	Recovery		
1893	Stock market collapse	1960's	Recession, 1960–61; Expansion, 1961–69;
1894–1897	Mostly depressed years	1970's	Slowdown and inflation,
1898–1907	Prosperity		1969–71
1907	Panic		Inflation and
1908	Depression		rapid growth,
1909–1914	Semi-stagnation		1972–73

SOURCE: Douglas F. Dowd, *Modern Economic Problems in Historical Perspective* (Boston: D.C. Heath, 1965), p. 143.

GROWTH AND DEVELOPMENT, 19TH CENTURY

With such a dramatic pattern of see-sawing throughout our history, why is it that nothing in the way of persistent and deliberate counteracting steps were made part of the State's functions until the past generation or so? It is not far-fetched to make an analogy with a young man who gets periodic hangovers, or an occasional broken limb from skiing. Why does he not take more care, place himself under the advice of a doctor?

The 19th century was the American economy's reckless youth, a period of rapid expansion in every which way, as our geographic boundaries and structure of production were both filled in and expanded. It was a period of extraordinary buoyancy. Each panic or crisis was followed by successively higher peaks of economic activity. Optimism was the rule; for those at the top levels of business it was justified. They had neither inclination nor felt need for a "doctor's care."

In the early 20th century, both the American and the European industrial economies reached maturity; business contractions, market instability, and insecurity became more dangerous. The consciousness of this grew in the United States, and especially among the most powerful of American corporate leaders. In turn, this consciousness led to a transformed view of the proper role of the State—away from laissez-faire. Although the State's role in the economy enlarged substantially after 1900, it did not take up any substantial monetary and fiscal functions; the creation of the Federal Reserve System in 1913, however, was a step in that direction. The postponement of the State's vital function may be explained by the deflecting impact of the expansion induced by World War I and the ensuing prosperity—until 1929. A closer examination of these patterns is now in order.[9]

In Chapter Three we dwelt upon the dynamic interaction between economic and westward geographic expansion in the 19th century. Viewed from the perspective of this chapter, we may observe that process as almost chaotic; we may also understand how its individual and social costs were both softened and obscured by the generally rapid quantitative expansion and the developmental changes accompanying it. In addition, prior to the stage of advanced industrialism of the 20th century, troubles in one part of the economy were felt less immediately *and* less seriously in the rest of the economy than became the case in this century.

The advance of productive efficiency is related to an ever more extensive specialization of function or division of labor, in turn implying increasing economic interdependence. Greater efficiency is thus paid for with greater precariousness. The chronological listing of expansions and contractions earlier shows many depressions and "panics." The very term "panic" suggests the spread of trouble over the economy; in some cases in the 19th century they spread like a prairie fire. What was noteworthy about such instances, however, was that their origins were almost always in the loose and speculation dominated *financial* system of the country, which in turn was usually responding to land and railroad speculation. But underneath the turbulent surface was a deep-

---

[9]Intensive examination of the growing and changing role of the State is postponed until Chapter Eight. Those wishing to explore these matters now, however, may do so in Faulkner, *Decline of Laissez-Faire,* and in two major revisions of American history centering upon these developments: Gabriel Kolko, *The Triumph of Conservatism: A Reinterpretation of American History, 1900–1916** (New York: Quadrangle, 1967), and James Weinstein, *The Corporate Ideal in the Liberal State: 1900–1918** (Boston: Beacon Press, 1968).

ening and spreading industrial system, providing ongoing buoyancy to the economy and optimism to its businessmen. There was no felt need for an activist State to set limits to bad times, for the times were not seen as threatening to become or stay bad enough. "Depression," when it occurred in the 19th century does not signify deep—or, if deep, lasting —(recorded or known) unemployment until the massive depression of the 1930's. (However, that kind of unemployment, industrial unemployment, began to be noticed seriously in the 1890's for the first time.) The generally "depressed" years between 1873 and 1897 were years of steadily falling prices, due to the combination of rapid technological improvements and the tying together of world markets, resulting in foreign competition plus intense domestic competition. Both in Europe and in the United States the response to these conditions was a growth of monopolies, trusts, imperialism, cartels, and tariff protection—relatively simple matters by comparison with what developed in the 20th century.

WORLD WAR I AND THE NEW ERA

There are two important matters requiring explanation for the period from 1914 to 1929: first, the sustained quality of its expansion, by comparison with earlier periods; second, the manner in which that long expansion connects with the great collapse after 1929. If the prosperity of the fifteen years preceding 1929 was unusual in our history, it is even more the case that the depression following 1929 was totally unprecedented in its severity, its duration, and its pervasiveness. Something new was going on; it probably began before World War I in the period we have called "semi-stagnation."

When we seek analytically to integrate the prosperity preceding 1929 with the depression following it, we place ourselves in the arena of growth and development analysis, rather than of short-term business cycle theory, let alone the abstract income and employment theory of Keynes's *General Theory*. That takes us into an exceptionally complex area of analysis; here we can only point to the major elements of what such an analysis has to put together.

First we should note that in the years preceding World War I, the United States had reached the limits of economic complexity then allowed by technology, real income, and business conditions. The limits reached were significantly beyond those attained elsewhere, whether the judgment is made in terms of productivity, the balance between consumer and capital goods production, the total of all production, or the scale of plant production. Second, although the years after 1909 are conventionally seen as a period of "recovery" from the panic and depression of 1907–1908, if there was a recovery it was quite uneven and very feeble. The uncertainty and rocky quality of the American economy had its counterpart in what was, if anything, a worse situation in Europe, where what was by then a "North Atlantic economy" was, by 1914, beginning to slip toward major economic troubles. Because each major segment of the capitalist world economy interacted critically with the rest, these developing weaknesses in the two strongpoints of the world system were ominous portents of the collapse that began in 1929.

Much of the talk about the causes of these difficulties in the United States in the decade before 1914 pointed to the inadequacies of our banking and monetary system. Because those inadequacies were quite real, and their consequences so vivid, they took attention away from deeper problems:

> An inefficient and inelastic credit system, however, was by no means the only cause for the unstable condition of American economic life between 1907 and 1914. High finance had overloaded railroads and other corporations with fantastic capital structures; industrial "trusts," as in the case of United States Steel after the panic of 1907, were reluctant to adjust prices to decreasing demand. Wages were barely keeping up with the increased cost of living, whereas unemployment in manufacturing and transportation amounted to 12 percent or over in 1908, 1914, and 1915 ... [Despite] a vigorous speculative advance ... in the early months of 1914 on both the London and New York stock exchanges ... , the world saw no revival in trade and industry. In the United States the recession of 1913 sank into a depression in 1914 with an increase in gold exports, a decline in foreign trade, a weakening of commodity prices, and an increase in unemployment.[10]

What Faulkner portrays as a condition of substantial instability, in the preceding quote, Baran and Sweezy see as the onset of *stagnation*. "Stagnation" is another term for chronic depression where, in the absence of "external stimuli" such as war, the economy tends to limp along with unutilized productive capacity, depressed business, and high unemployment. Pointing to the increasing severity of the contraction phases of the business cycle from 1908 until the War, and to a sharp increase in unemployment in the same period (averaging 6.6 percent, from 1908 to 1915), Baran and Sweezy conclude that the years after 1907 displayed:

---

[10]Harold U. Faulkner, *The Decline of Laissez-Faire, 1897–1917*, pp. 31–32. This book is rich in information concerning all aspects of American economic (and associated political) developments for the period. What is striking, however, is that the author's devastating recital of facts—devastating to a relaxed view of American capitalism—is accompanied by an essentially complacent analysis. Kolko, in *The Triumph of Conservatism*, working from the same facts, takes them to quite different conclusions. Where Faulkner sees the upshot of what he has reported to be a revival of the "reform movement," (p. 382) Kolko concludes his book with a chapter entitled "The Lost Democracy."

the kind of "creeping stagnation" with which we have become familiar in the later 1950's and the early 1960's. If there is any other interpretation of these facts, we are certainly ready to consider it on its merits. But until we know what it is, we shall feel justified in concluding that if the First World War had not come along, the decade 1910–1920 would have gone down in United States history as an extraordinarily depressed one.[11]

The outbreak of war in August of 1914 entirely altered the economic prospects of the American economy. Instead of having to struggle with what might well have been an intractable depression, both national and international, the United States found itself faced with rapidly growing demands from abroad for its production and its capital. Internally this meant that a likely downturn was replaced by a strong upswing in business and jobs, and an even further extension of our already advanced industrial system. It also meant a substantial boost toward the concentration and centralization of economic power, and explicit business-State coordination and planning, when the U.S. entered the war in 1917. A full panoply of new war agencies brought representatives of agriculture, business, and labor into the government, where they were schooled in new ways to gain and to use power.[12]

Out of these war needs the American economy was able to generate rising instead of falling incomes for the whole range of "ordinary people," and both sustained and high profits for the business world (including farmers). This, taken together with the technological developments facilitated by the war, laid the basis for the "New Era" for the United States economy in the twenties. Added to the advanced development of durable *capital* goods was the introduction on a mass basis of a broad range of durable *consumer* goods (such as automobiles and appliances) and a vast boom in residential, commercial, and public construction (of buildings and roads). Similar developments did not take hold in other industrial economies, if at all, until much later (and, on a mass basis, radios excepted, not until after 1950).[13]

---

[11]The authors go on to make clear that they are not saying the depression of the 1930's would have taken place after 1910, for "by 1915, the automobile era was already well under way, and the great shake-up in living patterns and consumption habits which it brought with it would probably have created a boom. . . ." *Monopoly Capital,* p. 234. Their analysis concerning 1907–1915 begins on p. 228.

[12]See George Soule, *Prosperity Decade,* Chapters 1, 2, and 3, for a complete story.

[13]The "mass basis" referred to, for the United States and other economies, is defined economically; that is, in terms not of the "masses" having access to the relevant goods, but of sufficient numbers of buyers existing to allow *mass production.* Thus, a fair estimate is that not more than about a third of the American people were able to buy throughout the range of consumer durables during the twenties, to say nothing of the depressed thirties. An automobile, for example, was something not even dreamed of by the bottom two-thirds of Americans in the twenties. See George Soule, Ibid.

Another outcome of World War I which must be noted is the manner in which the war speeded up and facilitated the emergence of the United States as the supreme power in the world economy—a position signified by the change from our *owing* over $3 billion before the War and being *owed* over $6 billion by other countries after the War. World War II strengthened us even more—much more, for a while. As will be discussed in Chapter Seven, the domestic economic meaning of America's new world role after World War I was not vital to the prosperity of the twenties, both because the postwar upsurge in economic nationalism (protective tariffs and the like) placed stringent limits on American possibilities abroad, and because domestic prosperity reduced Americans' need to look far afield for profitable possibilities. Nevertheless, seen in a long-term perspective, World War I and its aftermath were critical in placing the United States in the forefront of world economic powers; after 1940, the United States was able to take conscious advantage of what had come within reach when the European powers entered upon the suicidal path of World War I.

With all the enormous stimuli provided during and by the War it is not difficult to understand the subsequent "prosperity decade." But what brought it to an end? And, more to the point (for under capitalism expansions always come to an end), why was the depression of the thirties so deep? Why did it last so long? Why, even more, did it require World War II to lift us out of that depression?

One way to begin to answer such questions is to dwell for a moment on the word "prosperity." Like so many other pleasing terms we find to describe our history, it has to be viewed with an eye to who uses it and what they mean by it. Up until very recently, almost all of those who have informed us about our society—as historians, economists, sociologists, journalists, politicians, et al.—have been in or from the upper ranks of society. They have spoken to us from the vantage point of the middle class, and are the comfortable beneficiaries of the society's achievements. As Veblen said, speaking of professors of social science, "their intellectual horizon is bounded by the same limits of commonplace insight and preconceptions as are the prevailing opinions of the conservative middle class."[14]

---

[14] *The Higher Learning in America, A Memorandum on the Conduct of Universities by Businessmen* (New York: B. W. Huebsch, 1918; Sagamore Press, 1957), pp. 135–36. This citation is from the Sagamore paperback, one of many editions. Originally written in 1908, but not published for a decade, Veblen's *Higher Learning* identified the basic elements of university "corruption" that were rebelled against by students (and some faculty) in the 1960's. However, Veblen was not as surprised as many are today that in a business society the universities (among other institutions) would live under business criteria. As a brilliant and confirmed scholar, this was among the most tragic of his conclusions by his own lights.

Thus, to say that the American economy was prosperous in the 1920's, as these words are commonly used (still to this day), is quite compatible with the existence of widespread misery in American society in the same period. It is also compatible with serious economic problems in a whole range or industries. The "system" was doing just fine in the twenties: it was expanding in its production and power, it was yielding all sorts of new and attractive products for a significant fraction of its population, and it was setting new records for returns to owners of productive assets and of securities and real estate. The period was not only one in which millions of Americans were realizing the life-long dream of "getting something for nothing" but it was also one in which much of what was being gotten hadn't even been thought of only a few years before. But railroads had already begun their long decline, and cotton textiles, staple agriculture (wheat, corn, cotton, tobacco) and coal mining were in serious trouble. Therefore those who depended for jobs on those industries were in even more serious trouble.

Unemployment statistics until the 1930's are notoriously unreliable[15] and there is no way now to establish the hard facts. Estimates for the years 1920–1929 range from an average of 5 percent to something over 13 percent unemployed. Even if we accept the conservative lower figure, we are faced with a jobless rate that would suggest something other than "prosperity" for those directly involved and the even larger number of those peripherally involved. What was true of the twenties has become even more pronounced and better understood in the past decade or so, a period in which extraordinary gains in production and profits have been associated with hard-core poverty for tens of millions of people, and unemployment rates of 10 to 40 percent for important segments of the population (blacks, Chicanos, and especially the young men and women among them). Thus, even with the exceptionally rapid expansion of 1973 (at an annual rate of 14 percent, 8 percent of which was seen as "real," the rest as inflation) officially recorded unemployment hovered around 5 percent.

THE DUAL ECONOMY

At this point it seems appropriate to suggest an analysis that will connect the dubious prosperity of the twenties with the mixed prosperi-

---

[15]Since the 1930's they have remained unreliable, but now scandalously, rather than notoriously, so. It was not until the Depression that systematic attempts to gather and analyze aggregative data (concerning income, jobs, investment, etc.) were institutionalized, so the economists for the twenties and earlier may be excused for the shortcomings of their data. That excuse no longer exists; but it is widespread knowledge that the number of jobless is vastly and systematically understated. Of which, more in Chapter Five.

ty-poverty conditions of our own times. The analysis will take the form of positing the development of a "dual economy."[16]

From its first years, the American economy has contained industries that were lively and growing, together with those that were stagnating and depressed; it has always had groups of people making high, medium, and low incomes—and, until the Civil War, millions of slaves without any money income. But, until the years just before World War I, such disparateness did not constitute a firm basis for *duality* in the economy. The term "duality" as used here suggests not only differences as between groups and sectors in the economy, but the evolution of two paths of change, one dynamic and profitable, the other marked by difficulties and stagnation. That bifurcation began to take hold as the American economy "settled in" to its industrial and organizational patterns before 1920.

Students of American development for the past half century will object to the notion of any "settling in" process for the American economy because, after all, that long period has seen an extraordinary amount of change in products, techniques, and patterns of distribution and finance, along with a great increase in real per capita income. All that is, of course, indisputable. The important aspect about that dynamism, however, is that it has been carried by what O'Connor calls the monopolistic sector and the State sector; meanwhile the competitive sector has drifted into something like a backwash—increasingly dependent upon the monopolistic sector and the State for viability or even livelihood, and increasingly resentful of both.

The prosperity of the twenties is attributable to the dynamism of the monopolistic sector: high rates of technological innovation in production, and a whole new spread of expensive durable consumer goods, combined with an associated and enormous expansion in the petroleum (and linked industries, such as oil pipe) and construction industries.[17]

---

[16]Economic duality as a concept solves some puzzles regarding the American economy, but complicates understanding of underdeveloped economies. (See Chapter Seven.) In the forefront of developing these ideas are Professors Barry Bluestone (Boston College) and James O'Connor (California State University at San Jose). Professor Bluestone put forth the concept at the *Hearings* of the Joint Economic Committee on the President's Economic Report of 1972, in Washington, D.C. (February, 1972), and O'Connor's argument, which moves along some of the same lines but with different terminology, will be found in his *Fiscal Crisis of the State** (New York: St. Martin's Press, 1973). Both economists work with URPE.

[17]Economists can rightly point out that the construction industries—building materials, contractors, and the building trades workers—are competitive in structure, with thousands upon thousands of separate firms. However, they might also know that the *organization* of construction in any given locality has been monopolistic through trade associations, building codes, and cooperating trade unions. More recently, giant corporations such as Bechtel have begun also to lessen the competitive *structural* characteristics of the industry.

If one were to locate the hot center of this dynamism in the twenties, it would be in the expansion of the automobile industry, which meant the expansion of industries directly (metals, machinery, paints, leather, rubber and glass) and indirectly (petroleum, highway, residential housing and service station construction, etc.) connected to the automobile. Today the automobile industry claims that one out of six jobs is tied into it, even if they also deny that it is the instance par excellence of a monopolistic and overweening industry, with GM as the virtual symbol of American economic power.[18]

In the twenties, Americans took great pride in their "New Era." Those who wrote about it, whether F. Scott Fitzgerald or the economist Irving Fisher, paid little or no attention to the seamy side; yet Veblen in 1923 had come down hard on the fact of monopoly and the probability of severe depression, and Sinclair Lewis (in *Main Street* and *Babbitt*, especially) had seen the emptiness of middle-class existence accompanying its "success." The seamy side was where most of the people lived, depending for their jobs on the competitive sector and its "sick" industries.[19]

"An economic system based on private investment decisions thus tends to produce a *dual economy* both in the structure of industries and in the structure of the labor force," said Bluestone in his statement to the Joint Economic Committee in 1972. This pattern was well underway already in the twenties; this development also lies at the base of an explanation for the depression of the thirties.[20]

---

[18]See, e.g., Federal Trade Commission, *Report on the Automobile Industry** (Washington, D.C., 1939), Keith Sward, *Legend of Henry Ford*, and the summary chapter on the industry in Walter Adams, *Structure of American Industry*. The incredible power and impact of automobiles and petroleum are discussed lucidly and factually by Barry Weisberg, *Beyond Repair: The Ecology of Capitalism* (Boston: Beacon Press, 1971), Chapter 5. This point will be discussed in Chapter Six, below, when environmental questions are examined.

[19]Thus, productivity rose between 1920 and 1929 such that a given volume of manufactured goods could be produced in 1929 with only 70 percent of the man years of labor required in 1920; employment in manufacturing rose only slightly in the period despite great increases in production, because of that increased productive efficiency. Meanwhile, employment in mining fell by 200,000. Overall employment rose by 16 percent, while the labor force (those working and seeking work) rose by 21 percent. As manufacturing, mining, and agriculture hired fewer people, jobs opened up in distribution, finance, and services—but not enough jobs, as indicated by the gap between them and the labor force. For data of this sort (and much else besides), consult U.S. Bureau of the Census, *Historical Statistics of the United States, Colonial Times to 1957* (U.S.G.P.O., 1960, plus intermittent supplements). The annual *Economic Report of the President** is useful and convenient for a broad range of aggregative data, but its scope is narrower both in subject matter and time.

[20]Because of the importance of the U.S. in the world economy, and vice versa, a complete explanation of the severity of the Depression must give high importance to the weakness of the world economy in the twenties, and its utter collapse in the thirties. But much of that explanation fits well within a "dual economy" framework for the world

In the midst of the prosperity of the twenties, trouble had begun to develop even in the dynamic sector. The impulses of the corporate leaders of that sector, and their power to realize those impulses, disguised the trouble and postponed the collapse. It is quite likely that the collapse was therefore somewhat more severe than it otherwise might have been. The troubles appeared in the two leading industries: automobiles and housing construction.

Let us examine first the automobile industry.[21] There are three kinds of car buyers: new owners, those replacing an old with a new car, and used-car buyers. By 1924 new car buyers were no longer the focus of the auto industry's attention; their numbers had begun to shrink. What was needed was stepped-up replacement, and a large used-car market to support it. In turn, this led to what has since become the hallmark of consumer goods production and distrubution: deliberate product obsolescence, extensive advertising, and consumer finance. General Motors took the lead in all three; advertising, yearly model changes, trade-ins, and living in constant debt were thereby elevated to what many take to be the American way of life. They also postponed the day when the industry would find itself with chronic excess capacity, as in the 1930's. However, as Soule points out,

> installment buying could not obviate the eventual retardation of expansion. There was certain to come a time when all the families who would utilize installment loans were loaded up with all the debt they could carry. In the long run the only possible means of keeping these new industries expanding would have been to augment the cash purchasing power of the consumers through sufficient increases in wages and salaries or through sufficient reduction in retail prices.[22]

economy—with the industrial nations dynamic, and the raw materials-supplying (Third World) nations exploited and depressed. That will become part of the discussion in Chapter Seven. For the twenties, and an explanation of the Depression that depends squarely on the weakening position of the Third World countries, see W. Arthur Lewis, *Economic Survey, 1919–1939* (London: Allen & Unwin, 1949), especially Ch. 12. This small book provides a useful summary of developments in the major industrial nations in the interwar period.

[21] Paul M. Sweezy, "Cars and Cities," *Monthly Review* (April, 1973), provides a succinct historical analysis of the automobile industry in its broader meanings, as well as its impact on the environment, which will be taken up in Chapter Six.

[22] *Prosperity Decade,* p. 288. But, despite great increases in productivity, prices did not decline in the twenties (after 1922). As for wages, they rose 8 percent in manufacturing and railroads, stayed the same for farm laborers, and declined 14 percent for miners. Meanwhile (1923–1929), corporate profits rose 62 percent, while the national income rose by 21 percent; and, tax policies were changed to lower the taxes paid as a percentage of income the higher the income (one percent reduction at $5000, 31 percent reduction for incomes above $1 million.)

The same kinds of problems affected the construction and sale of housing, with variations due to the different nature of the product. Again, Soule:

> Only a fraction of the population was able to buy or rent new houses or new apartments at the prices charged, and the number which could do so provided an upper limit to the market. After a few years of active building, this limit was being approached [by 1926]. There was still an actual need for better housing in large quantities, but this need could not be converted into a market demand unless either the number of those who could afford the housing was increased by sufficient enlargement of income, or the prices of the new housing could be materially decreased. Neither of these developments occurred.[23]

There is a vital difference between the prosperity of the period encompassing the 1920's and the ensuing depression, and the period since World War II. Although there have been six or so recessions in the latter period, they have been relatively minor with none showing signs of becoming a major depression; nor is such a depression anticipated in the foreseeable future. What differentiates the two periods is the changed role of the State. The change is well-symbolized by the data on government expenditures, which do not, however, inform us on the full meaning of expanded State power.

In 1929, the combined expenditures of federal, state, and local governments, as a percent of gross national product (GNP),[24] were about 10 percent; in 1971 they were over 30 percent, and rising. In the earlier year, such expenditures were about *half* of total *private investment* expenditures, whereas by 1971 they were more than 50 percent *greater* than those expenditures. We have here one mark of how the structure of the economy has changed in the interim. If the structure has changed so much, the economic theory that presumes to tell us how the economy functions must change accordingly; but it has not. Keynesian theory still considers private investment as *the* key variable, and the role of government has not been incorporated into the theory—nor can it be, without a theory of the State that will allow such incorporation. Wher-

---

[23]Ibid.

[24]GNP, as noted in Chapter Three, is defined as the dollar value of the total annual output of *final* goods and services (where "final" means that a good is counted only once —e.g., cotton cloth going into shirts is not counted until the shirt is sold at retail, except for what might be inventoried at the end of a year in intermediate stages). GNP only counts marketed goods and services; it takes no account of valuable activities that are not marketed (such as housework), or illegal activities of any sort. But the costs of both gasoline and smog control devices, for instance, are counted, as is napalm and the like.

ever such a theoretical advance might carry us, it would surely carry us toward a new "political economy."

Before resuming our analysis of the movement from prosperity into depression, a further comment on the concept of the dual economy is in order. As we have seen, in the 1920's a duality in the economy had become pronounced. The monopolistic sector, and those benefitting from it, moved dynamically through the 1920's; the competitive sector lagged behind, afflicting those dependent upon it. What was relatively insignificant then, as the discussion above makes clear, was the third sector emphasized by O'Connor: the State sector. Governmental expenditures were small as a percentage, and they were dominated by state and local expenditures (mostly for highways and education) rather than by federal expenditures. States and localities move *with* the direction taken by the economy; the desired role of governmental fiscal policy is to move in the opposite direction (to stimulate a weak economy, and restrain an inflating one). States and localities do not have the fiscal power (or, by their constitutions, the right) to operate in the desired way, and in the twenties no pressures were being placed on the federal government to do so.

COLLAPSE AND DEPRESSION

As seen by contemporaries, the twenties was a period not only of prosperity, but of endless prosperity. Irving Fisher (the Paul Samuelson of the economics profession at the time) proclaimed, only a few months before the Depression began, that the economy had solved the problem of the business cycle and that it was settled on a high plateau of endless prosperity. The well-off believed him, until, within the next year, many were desperate enough to commit suicide from the shock of their losses.

Individual losses for speculators were indeed great, but of more importance was what happened to the economy. The collapse was so substantial as to be virtually incomprehensible to those born since World War II. Between 1929 and 1933, GNP fell from $104 billion to $56 billion; per capita disposable income (after personal taxes) fell from $678 to $360; the income of farm proprietors from $5.7 billion to (in 1932) $1.7 billion; and unemployment rose from 1.5 million to 12.8 million—25 percent of the labor force![25]

The quantitative disasters suggested by those numbers are impressive enough, and they were staggering at the time; but, quantitatively, there was more to the Depression than that and more still when its qualitative

---

[25]Data taken from *Historical Statistics of the United States*, p. 139, and *Economic Report of the President* (1973), pp. 193, 213, 220.

impact is taken into account. The Depression left no sector of the economy standing upright; the entire capitalist world underwent the same collapse (as did the dependent non-industrial countries). Each nation had its own crisis, and each had a share of a worldwide crisis. Then as now, however, the United States was the leading economy, and, as W. Arthur Lewis says,

> It is clear that the center of the depression was the United States of America, in the sense that most of what happened elsewhere has to be explained in terms of the American contraction, while that contraction is hardly explicable in any but internal terms. The slump was also worse in the United States than anywhere else (with the possible exception of Germany, whose severe contraction was a direct result of American events).[26]

A recession or a depression is a process of contraction, which, whatever else it means, implies a progressive under-utilization of the society's productive resources. Unemployment is the most tragic measure of such under-utilization, but as such it does not capture the imagination of business leaders unless it leads to social turbulence. What is of greater moment to those in business is the implication of shrinking markets for the profitable use of their productive assets. Just how far markets contracted in the 1930's is well-signified by figures for capacity utilization. Industrial producers usually find it desirable (depending upon the technology of their industry) to utilize capacity at rates lying between 85 and 95 percent. Already by 1928, the figures had begun to drop below 85 percent; but witness what happened in the thirties:[27]

1930	66%	1935	68%
1931	53%	1936	80%
1932	42%	1937	83%
1933	52%	1938	60%
1934	58%	1939	72%

When business is bad in a capitalist society, everyone is in economic trouble. Therefore, we may find a close correlation between the capacity

---

[26]Lewis, *Economic Survey*, p. 52. Lewis notes that U.S. national income, a narrower figure than GNP, "contracted by 38 percent, and the unemployment figure increased to fifteen millions." The official American statistic for unemployment, used above, was 12.8 million; but that is quite probably an understatement. In 1929, U.S. industrial production was 46 percent of the total industrial production of the twenty-four most important producers in the world. (Lewis, p. 57.)

[27]Donald Streever, *Capacity Utilization and Business Investment*, University of Illinois *Bulletin*, vol. 57, no. 55 (March, 1960), p. 65; quoted in Baran and Sweezy, op. cit., p. 242. From 1969 through 1972, the rate vacillated around 73 percent. The lowest rate in the twenties was 82 percent (1928).

utilization figures and unemployment rates for the corresponding years (remembering that the official rates are, if anything, understated):[28]

1930	8.7%	1935	20.1%
1931	15.9%	1936	16.9%
1932	23.6%	1937	14.3%
1933	24.9%	1938	19.0%
1934	21.7%	1939	17.2%

In 1941, the year the United States entered World War II, unemployment was 10 percent; it was still 4.7 percent in 1942.[29]

The decline in utilized capacity and the rise in unemployment after 1929, and the persistence of bad news on both scores until the U.S. entered the war in 1941, was matched by the performance of the economy as reflected in the following components of GNP listed in Table 2. Note that GNP did not regain its 1929 level until 1937, then fell back, and barely surpassed the 1929 level again in 1939.[30]

In studying Table 2, note first the comparative magnitudes of the several components—consumption, investment, net exports, and government; and note especially how their relationships have changed between 1929 and the present. The one stable relationship in that period is between GNP and personal consumption, with the latter running at about two-thirds of the former (except for the years of World War II). The most volatile component is gross private domestic investment. The one that rises most as a percentage of GNP is government *purchases,* from 1929 to the present. Today, government *expenditures* (including transfers) occupies about one-third of GNP in current dollars.

As might be expected, per capita consumption dropped seriously after 1929. Population increased by about nine million from then until 1938; but personal consumption expenditures were the same for both years,

---

[28]*Economic Report of the President* (USGPO, 1972), p. 220. *Historical Statistics of the U.S.,* op. cit., p. 73.

[29]The rate has gone close to 7 percent twice since then (in 1958 and 1961) and has been under 6 percent in all the other years, hovering between 5 and 6 percent since 1970. For three years (1943–1945) the rate was under 2 percent; for another three years (1951–1953) near 3 percent; for four years (1966–1969) under 4 percent; and all those "good" years were years of hot war, which added substantial military expenditures to already high and ongoing military expenditures. Note also the move from 2, to 3, to 4, to 5 percent, even in war years.

[30]The main components of expenditure are "personal consumption," "gross private domestic investment," "net exports of goods and services," and "government *purchases* of goods and services." "Government purchases" is a lower figure than "government expenditures," which includes "transfers"—social security benefits, welfare payments, and the like, at all levels of government. In 1970, "transfers" were $92.5 billion, only slightly lower than "purchases" by the federal government, which were $99.7 billion (in 1970 prices).

TABLE 2
Selected Categories of Gross National Product or Expenditure
(In Billions of 1958 Dollars, for Selected Years)

	Total GNP	Personal Consumption Expenditures	Gross Private Domestic Investment	Net Exports	Government Purchases of Goods and Services		
					Total	Fed.	State and Local
1929	204	140	40	1.5	22	4	19
1930	184	130	27	1.4	24	4	20
1931	169	126	17	.9	25	4	21
1932	144	115	5	.6	24	5	20
1933	142	113	5	.0	23	6	17
1934	154	118	9	.3	27	8	19
1935	170	126	18	−1.0*	27	8	1y
1936	193	138	24	−1.2	32	12	20
1937	203	143	30	− .7	31	12	19
1938	193	140	17	1.9	34	13	21
1939	209	148	25	1.3	35	13	23
1940	227	156	33	2.1	36	15	21
1941	264	165	42	.4	56	36	20
1942	298	161	21	−2.1	117	99	18
1943	337	166	13	−5.9	164	148	17
1944	361	171	14	−5.8	182	165	16
1945	355	183	20	−3.8	156	140	17
1946	313	204	52	8.4	48	30	18
1950	355	231	69	2.7	53	25	28
1955	438	274	75	3.2	85	51	34
1960	488	316	72	4.3	95	51	44
1965	618	398	99	6.2	115	58	57
1966	658	418	109	4.2	127	65	61
1967	675	430	101	3.6	140	75	66
1970	720	476	102	2.4	139	65	74

SOURCE: Derived from the 1972 *Economic Report of the President*, pp. 196-7. Figures have been rounded off to the nearest whole number (except for net exports); consequently for government the total is occasionally greater or less than the sum of federal plus state and local. All figures are in "1958"–i.e., "constant"–dollars, a procedure aimed at achieving comparable magnitudes by "deflating" for price changes over time. As an example of the difference when "current" dollars are used, GNP for 1929 would be $103 billion, and for 1970, $974 billion.
*The minus sign for net exports signifies an excess of *imports* of goods and services, i.e., net imports.

and of course much lower in most of the intervening decade. Investment almost vanishes in 1932 and 1933; and, in fact, *net* investment did in 1933 (where "net" refers to increasing productive capacity, while "gross" also includes support and maintenance of existing capacity). During that year utilization rates in industry were at about the half mark, and expectations for the future were gloomy at best.[31] Gross private domestic investment does not begin to approach its 1929 proportion to GNP until 1946, after which time, in response to rapidly growing domestic, military, and foreign markets, it rises rapidly.

The government columns are especially notable, given the general understanding—or misunderstanding—most Americans have about the *spending* impact of the New Deal in the 1930's. Until 1940, federal purchases remained consistently lower than state and local purchases, which themselves remained stable through the decade. Between 1940 and 1941—when President Roosevelt was said to have completed the transition from being "Dr. New Deal" to "Dr. Win-the-War"—federal purchases more than doubled, after which they rose to the point where in 1944 they (plus state and local purchases) amounted to *half* of GNP (with only a slight increase in consumption and a drop in private investment in the same years). A further comment on the alteration in federal spending rates is called for and will help to put the New Deal in perspective.

THE NEW DEAL AND WORLD WAR II

The period of the New Deal was intensely controversial and, not for the first or the last time in our history, one in which both supporters and opponents of New Deal policies took positions they would later alter. To understand the period, it is necessary to make several distinctions: one, between the sub-periods of the New Deal, and two, between the two main activities that gave it its name—deficit spending and institutional reform.

First, we should distinguish the "periods" of the New Deal or, more properly, of the Roosevelt Administration. FDR was first elected president in 1932, and died in 1945, at the beginning of his fourth term. The policies of the "first New Deal" extend from 1933 into 1935; the second —or "real" New Deal—goes into 1938. From 1938 on, Roosevelt is generally seen as having become obsessed with the coming world war. Consistent with his electoral campaign, when he first took office Roosevelt stood for little in the way of institutional change; but he was of

---

[31]The low rates of gross *private* domestic investment in the peak war years (of World War II) may be explained by looking at the high rates of federal purchases. The government built and paid for war plants, which were sold off at bargain basement prices to private corporations after the war.

course a new president, faced with our most major depression, already in its fourth and most severe year. Essentially and initially, Roosevelt pursued the policies laid down by his predecessor, Herbert Hoover, but the unforgettable FDR spirit was different. His policies were emergency policies, but they were "conservative." In this respect, FDR was at one with the Democratic Party at the time: in the campaign of 1932, "National Democratic party leaders criticized Hoover not because he had done too little but because he had done too much. [Their] main criticism . . . was that [Hoover] was a profligate spender. In seeking to defeat progressive measures, Republicans in Congress could count on the votes of a majority of Democrats on almost every roll call."[32]

Roosevelt's statement that they "had nothing to fear but fear itself " was doubtless a good tonic to the fallen spirits of American workers, farmers, businessmen, and speculators. However, more than a tonic was necessary for a body as damaged as the American economy. In that respect, the first months of the New Deal were not encouraging: the federal government spent less in FDR's first five months than had been spent by Hoover in the same period of the preceding year.[33]

Like Hoover, Roosevelt was faced with massive unemployment, and an almost total collapse of agricultural, industrial, and financial markets:

Item: The Dow-Jones dollar average per share of sixty-five stocks (different from their index method of today) fell from $125 to $36 between 1929 and 1933. (Mitchell, p. 438)

Item: The average number of bank suspensions in 1928 and 1929 was 566; in 1930, 1931, and 1932 the average number was 1,700. (Ibid., p. 128)

Item: Merchandise exports fell from $5.2 billion to $1.7 billion in 1933. (Ibid., p. 444)

Item: The value of building construction of all sorts was $4 billion in 1925, $3 billion in 1929, and $500 million in 1933. (Ibid., p. 447)

Item: Farm prices (at wholesale) fell by more than half, 1929–1933. (Ibid., p. 448)

---

[32]William E. Leuchtenburg, *Franklin D. Roosevelt and the New Deal** (New York: Harper & Row, 1963), p. 3.

[33]See Broadus Mitchell, *Depression Decade*, cited earlier, p. 40. This is an unexciting but thorough treatment of the economic history of the period; and it has a full bibliography for further work. Taken together with Leuchtenburg's political history and bibliography, it will enable the reader to get a good grip on the depression years, especially if some of the general and fictional works noted in the *Reading Suggestions* at the end of this chapter are read.

As we have noted earlier, at least a quarter of the labor force was unemployed by 1933. In this early period of FDR's presidency he emphasized "relief " and "recovery"; the second New Deal (beginning in 1935) undertook the more controversial "reform." The distinction is somewhat too sharp, as will be seen; the point remains that the "liberal" reforms of the New Deal await 1935, for reasons to be discussed.

The major steps taken by Roosevelt in 1933 were taken in the name of emergency and in a context in which no opposition to the new president was feasible; Roosevelt had what was called a "honeymoon" for his first "Hundred Days." He closed all banks for four days, by proclamation, and embargoed the export of gold; with Congress he created the Agricultural Adjustment Administration, which followed the path laid down by Hoover in 1928 in supporting farm prices (at the 1909–1914 average), and went beyond Hoover by also limiting production. FDR legislated several "emergency relief acts" which provided simple relief (money payments) and work (usually make-work) relief, and which also continued and expanded the Reconstruction Finance Corporation (from Hoover's days), a forerunner of the sort of federal financial assistance given to Lockheed in 1971. To attempt to bring some order out of the shambles in the securities markets—a shambles in no small part due to the assorted malpractices and downright crookedness characterizing the stock and bond markets—the Securities Act of 1933 and the Securities and Exchange Act of 1934 were passed, providing for supervision and regulation of stock and bond markets. The powers of the Federal Reserve System were expanded, deposit insurance was enacted to prevent the recurrence of bank runs, in which panicky depositors lined up to retrieve money that wasn't there for all (nor can be in a fractional reserve system such as exists in all modern economies), and the Home Owners Loan Corporation was created to refinance home mortgages. And much more.

Probably most indicative of the conservative-mindedness of these first years was the National Recovery Administration (NRA); although "right-wing" is a better term than conservative to describe the NRA if right-wing is meant to suggest a design to disrupt and reverse the process of social change to place more power in the hands of the already powerful. The NRA (established by the National Industrial Recovery Act [NIRA] of 1933) deliberately replaced the "free market" as the approved and impersonal arbiter of production and price with hundreds of "code authorities." These usually consisted of the leading representatives of the business trade associations in each industry, associations in which policies were generally established by the most powerful firms. In the name of establishing codes of "fair competition," the code authorities could set prices below which members could not sell; that is, the NRA made price competition illegal and agreements to restrict production (or virtually *any* agreements) common. In effect, the NRA suspended the antitrust laws.

The NIRA also, in its Section 7A, gave labor the right to organize and to bargain collectively but provided no means of enforcement to make those "rights" meaningful. That would await 1935, and the Wagner (National Labor Relations) Act. The NRA was declared unconstitutional in May, 1935, its function in part to be performed thereafter by the "Fair Trade Laws."

Some slight economic recovery had taken place by 1935, but there were still 20 percent or more unemployed. Social unrest had spread over the country in all regions, evoking memories of the 1890's, only more so. After a long period of decline, socialist ideas took on a new life and received increasing attention, and for the first time explicitly fascist groups began to organize successfully. Neither those on the Right or Left had any national electoral significance, but their growing appeal on local and state levels and in workers' circles began to move to the front of the political stage.

The Communist Party of the United States probably had its greatest influence in this period, mostly through its successful organizing activities in trade unions; they also constituted a bloc of only slightly critical support for the New Deal.[34] The Socialist Party revived, and also constituted a supporting bloc for the New Deal, pulling it slightly to the left. Father Coughlin's National Union for Social Justice was the leading fascist-type group, most effective in the Detroit region, serving up a stew combining racial, religious, and class hatred with economic appeals. Both the demogogically appealing and the poisonous sides of Populism ran through these movements of Right and Left, as they did in Huey Long's "Share the Wealth" movement in Louisiana and Upton Sinclair's "End Poverty in California" movement. The turbulence grew and spread.

Roosevelt was repeatedly and pointedly made aware of all this dissatisfaction. The Second New Deal was his response; his overwhelming re-election in 1936 was his reward for moving with the political winds of the day. The period from 1933 into 1935 was not entirely illiberal; nor was the period from 1935 to 1938 entirely liberal. But the change in emphasis was as obvious at the time as it is today. For the aged, especially, the Social Security Act of 1935 was a beginning, if a weak one. The legislation saw to it that the rich would continue *not* to pay for the alleviation of the poor, irrespective of age; but a crack in the wall of social unconcern had been made. By far the most controversial aspect of the New Deal was the Wagner-Connelly Act, which not only

---

[34]See James Weinstein, "The Left, Old and New," in *Socialist Revolution* 2, no. 4 (July-August 1972), pp. 29 ff.

reaffirmed the right of workers to organize and bargain collectively, but spelled out a list of unfair practices by employers and set up a National Labor Relations Board to adjudicate disputes. This "Magna Carta" of labor was a watershed in American history—a watershed whose affirmative meaning labor had to fight for continuously, however, until World War II. The major cause of labor disputes between 1935 and 1941 was union security, presumably *guaranteed* by the Wagner Act. All this, despite the fact that the Supreme Court upheld the constitutionality of the Wagner Act in 1938. As with the Depression itself, it took World War II to bring an at least temporary end to the perennial conflict between labor and business. The war not only enhanced production enormously and in doing so created a shortage of labor—with altogether sixteen millions entering the armed forces—but it also brought cost-plus contracts to assure profits for business, a free hand for labor to organize in war plants, and thus maximum production for the government.[35]

WARFARE, WELFARE, AND ECONOMIC GROWTH

The Roosevelt years had been dubbed "New Deal," so it was probably inevitable that succeeding administrations would be given their own nicknames, as indeed they were. Truman's "Fair Deal" was followed by what Adlai Stevenson called Eisenhower's "Big Deal." Kennedy initiated the "New Frontier" (which in the Johnson Administration's "Great Society" was revealed to have more geographic than institutional meanings) and the Nixon years have been called the "Raw Deal" by some and the "Cruel Deal" by others. The labels tell very little, but the repetition of the term "deal" is not without a meaning of its own. Since the Depression, what Kolko calls "political capitalism" has meant an endless series of deals between various power blocs within the U.S., and also between American and foreign power groups.

The basic techniques of this modern political economy had been discovered, or re-discovered, in the Wilson administration, and especially during World War I. However, the euphoria and dynamism of the twenties caused relaxation for the powerful and helplessness for the rest. The Depression and the Roosevelt years implanted once more, and for the foreseeable future, that process of power-broking.

Neither the institutional reforms nor the deficit spending of the New Deal had substantial effect before World War II. Precedents were estab-

---

[35]The Taft-Hartley Act of 1947 was designed to limit and reduce the strength of unions. Although vetoed by President Truman, it was made into law by a Congress which, in overriding the presidential veto, revealed how very strong the voice of business was in Congress, and how temporary the peace between business and labor. As will be seen in Chapter Eight, the State has been quite successful in more recent years in taming the chiefs of organized labor, mostly with the carrot of job-creating military expenditures.

lished, however, and habits and experience developed. The revelation of just how useful close relationships with the growing State could be for business, labor, and agriculture combined with the massive spending of World War II to place the impact of the New Deal on the years *after* World War II.[36] For purposes of this chapter, that impact can be understood in its effects on the process of economic expansion. (Domestic policies that affected relationships between classes and groups at home, and foreign policies that promoted geographic expansion will be examined in succeeding chapters.)

In aggregative terms, the striking fact is that in the years since World War II began (with the exception of the three years immediately after the end of the war, 1945–1947) GNP has dropped only *once.* That was in 1954 and the drop was about 1 percent (in constant dollars; in current dollars it did not drop at all). Equally or perhaps more revealing is the record of "disposable personal income" (income of persons after federal income taxes and transfers). After 1947, disposable personal income never fell, except for a drop of less than 1 percent in 1949. The key to this process of sustained growth—i.e., the absence of even a serious recession, let alone a depression—is to be found in the record of federal purchases, and in that category, the key factor is purchases geared to the military.[37]

Between 1946 and 1971 federal purchases of goods and services totaled $1.4 *trillion.* Of that, 80 percent, or $1.1 *trillion* were for "defense" expenditures; over 10 percent of the remaining $279 billion was for highway construction. This says nothing about state and local purchases, which rose steadily from about $18 billion in 1946 to $77 billion in 1971. By 1971, in addition, governmental transfers came to about $100 billion annually. When all this is put together with exports of goods and services (which rose one-and-a-half times in the same period) a process also aided substantially by State policies, it becomes easy to understand why the American economy suffered no major relapse from buoyancy after 1946. Naturally, going along with this was a steady increase in private investment and in consumer expenditures with the explosion of suburban housing and commercial developments, and the rapid spread of automobile and consumer durables ownership.

The policies that underlay this expansion were initiated at the top levels of business, government, agriculture, and labor; but they were

---

[36]A suggestion of how minimal the New Deal years were in terms of federal spending is shown by the fact that in no year of the thirties, despite massive unemployment, did the federal deficit rise to $5 billion; and in only one year, 1936 (an election year), did it exceed $4 billion.

[37]Our reference here has been to *federal* activities. Between 1940 and 1970, while personal income (incomes of persons before taxes) rose 926 percent, *all* taxes (federal, state, and local) rose by 1,840 percent—i.e., twice as fast. *Wall Street Journal,* Nov. 13, 1972.

almost universally supported at all levels of society. Consciously and unconsciously, Americans since the Depression have allowed and encouraged the creation of a political economy that, whatever else it means, is designed never to allow a repetition of a severe depression. The United States appears to have forestalled that evil, but in doing so we appear also to have created a society whose achievements become ever more difficult to applaud, and whose problems now link together in what emerges as a social crisis. The culminating development of the United States is to have mastered the craft of quantitative advance, but at the expense of qualitative deterioration. Even worse, except on the part of those most grievously damaged by the society, there has developed a numbness, even an aloofness, toward that deterioration. The poetically inclined might see it all as a Faustian struggle, with Faustian consequences. Nothing lost save honor.

PRESENT CRISIS, FUTURE DEVELOPMENT

The generalization that opened this chapter—a capitalist economy cannot stand still but must grow or fade, develop or cease to grow—is abundantly confirmed by a recapitulation of the past half century. In the twenties, growth was substantial, and was both preceded and accompanied by structural change. Some of such change was in the nature of decaying old industries, some of it in the dynamic emergence of newer industries. Profits and power gained by the principal beneficiaries were used to enhance their situations even more and were guarded jealously. The economy's growth ceased, and the depression that ensued outdid the prosperity out of which it was born.

The New Deal may be viewed as an attempt at structural change. It did not cure the deep economic stagnation of the 1930's, and it provided little relief for the misery of the mass of the people. But it set some institutional precedents which in later years did much to facilitate structural changes that were necessary for the maintenance of the system. The basic reforms of the New Deal would have meant, had they succeeded at the time, a significant improvement in the conditions of the bottom two-thirds of the population. They did not succeed in that; when those same reforms became securely implanted in the years during and after World War II, they added dynamism to the economy. The crucial development allowing failure to become success was the enormous economic stimulus provided by war.

The years since World War II witnessed the longest sustained period of economic growth in our history, with only the mildest of interruptions. But that expansion is utterly unintelligible unless placed against the structural changes of the same period: the changed position of the

U.S. in the world economy; the great growth of governmental, and most of all military, expenditures in the economy; the impact of social security, unemployment compensation, welfare payments, and an active use of monetary and fiscal policies to provide a floor to the fall of purchasing power (so that consumer expenditures have not fallen once since 1946, in current dollars); the relocation of population from country to city, city to city, and city to suburb, with all the construction and other expenditures entailed; and, by no means least in importance, the changed composition of the occupational structure (toward the services and the professions, and away from agriculture and industrial commodity producers).

These structural changes had at their base the internationalization and militarization of the American economy, and the accompanying growth of an ever more powerful State with increasingly centralized controls over the economy. It all added up to sustained growth; but, as Veblen once pointed out, "things tend to have the defects of their virtues." In this case, the meaning of that reflection is that what made the process work would also bring it to an end. We are now quite clearly in the transition period which marks the ending of the postwar era and the beginning of something different—for better or for worse. It is this that gives an air of crisis to our lives.

The lineaments of that crisis will emerge in later pages as we examine class, race, sex, international and political conflicts, and their manifestations in our cities, our environment, and a whole range of domestic and foreign policies. Here our attention belongs still on the overall functioning of the economy: its growth and development processes. In what ways may it be said that an era is ending?

Most dramatically, the signs exist in the political sphere: widespread opposition to the Indochina War (as compared with virtually none regarding the Korean War, which had as little to commend it); growing criticism and suspicion of not only the military but the industrial projects of the military; the increasing resort to secrecy, manipulation, conspiracy, and downright lying in government—a result, of course, of the *need* to do so, to contrive support for the policies enacted; and, among other things, an extraordinary degree of uncertainty and doubt concerning our present and our future, what looks like a "failure of nerve," on the upper levels of economic and political society.[38]

---

[38]In a letter written in 1843, Marx evocatively characterized the turbulence of that time —which was followed shortly by the 1848 revolutionary uprisings—"Even though there is no doubt about the 'whence,' there does prevail all the more confusion about the 'whither.' It is not only the fact that a general anarchy has broken out among the reformers; each one will have to admit to himself that he has no exact idea of what is to happen." Quoted in David McLellan, *Marx Before Marxism** (New York: Harper & Row, 1970), p. 126. This excellent work ends with the Marx of 1844.

Central to this emerging crisis is the economy's loss of the ability to gain easily and clearly from its "warfare state" policies, combined with the weakness of its "welfare state" policies. Both sets of policies appear to be approaching their limits, although for quite different reasons. Briefly, the Cold War policies ran up against the brick wall of Vietnamese resistance, which is still not understood to this day by those who initiated and continued the effort to subdue the people of Indochina. Had the war gone as expected—beginning in the fifties under Truman with his support of the French; or Eisenhower and his support of Diem; or Kennedy and his faith in counter-insurgency; or Johnson with the massive use of American troops and air power; or Nixon with his reliance upon the most massive aerial bombing in the world's history —had the war gone as expected, it would have been done with, and "cheaply" so, long before any domestic opposition could become meaningful. Nor, to return to the economy, would it have involved expenditures which in turn brought us the most serious inflation in our history.

The inflation, which has much weakened our international as well as our domestic functioning, need not have happened, in *economic* terms alone; nor would it have, had it not been for the unpopularity of the war already when, in 1965, President Johnson escalated our involvement and our expenditures. He did not dare ask for increased taxes to control the inevitable inflation until too late. Furthermore, by the time the taxes began to take hold, the economy was weakening to the point where, in 1969, industrial production turned downward and unemployment began to rise—from over 3 percent to, in 1971, over 6 percent. Beginning in early 1969, President Nixon, seeking to bring down the ominous inflationary rate, pursued restrictive monetary policies (centering on high interest rates) which were candidly expected to "allow unemployment to rise to 5 percent" while controlling inflation. Since 1969, interest rates have risen further. Inflation went on unabated after 1971, reaching the highest levels (at this writing) in 1973, while official unemployment rates stayed high.

In pursuing such policies, Nixon was not departing far from recently received economic wisdom. For some years now, economists have accepted the "Phillips Curve" as revealing a basic truth about the relationship between unemployment and inflation: it says that to reduce unemployment requires increasing the rate of inflation. Once more, an economic "law" that pipes a sad tune for a sadder dance, which when begun saw 3 percent as the partners; now, it appears, 5 percent unemployment and 5 percent inflation are the dancing partners. But what is involved in this relationship is not economic law; it is economic and political power, and requires closer examination.

WALTZ OF THE TOREADORS

We noted above that the inflation of the late 1960's need not have happened, for *economic* reasons. World War II placed much more pressure on the economy than any other war in our history: at its high point, economically, *half of GNP* was military production. Yet prices rose very slowly during that war, as a result of increased taxes, successful inducements to the population to purchase "war bonds" (taxes and bonds withdraw purchasing power, of course), extensive wage and price controls, and rationing. The Indochina War took only a fraction of current output by comparison with World War II, yet prices rose at more than twice the rate between 1966 and 1971 than they did between 1941 and 1945.[39] Whether or not there is inflation *or* unemployment is a political question, a result of policies implemented or not implemented. And that is a result of who makes what policies, and why, and when. President Johnson *allowed* inflation after 1966 because he did not wish the American people to comprehend the extent and cost of America's involvement in the Indochina War; of course he thought the war would be won quickly, too. In a particularly crass example of why inflation is a political rather than an economic problem, Johnson withheld from his own economic advisors the true volume of direct expenditures on the war—to the extent of $10 billion in 1966.[40] In 1967, the President went so far as to sell offshore oil lands in California to oil companies to "raise" $7 billion—secretly. (These were the oil operations which resulted in the 1969 Santa Barbara "oil spill.")

But, as just stated, these are crass instances. The politics of inflation are institutionalized. Whether or not inflation begins is one matter, and may be seen as economic in its origins; how and whether it continues is a matter of politics. Inflation can *always* be curtailed and eliminated; the question is finally at whose expense. The Phillips Curve tells us it must be at the expense of those ultimately unemployed. That is true, other things being equal. But those "other things" are essentially a way of referring to the balance of privilege and gain in the society. Tax policies *can* be designed that would curb inflation at the expense of the upper income groups; expenditure policies *can* be curtailed in such a way as to achieve the same result, without damage to those who can bear that damage least. Monetary policies *can* be utilized that will reduce inflationary pressures with a minimum of adverse employment

---

[39]That World War II began with substantial unemployment and unused productive capacity must be taken into account, of course; offsetting that is that sixteen million of the cream of the labor force was drawn into the armed forces in the period.

[40]See the articles by David Halberstam and Robert Lekachman on these and related matters in *Saturday Review: The Society*, December, 1972.

effects. Between the possibility and the reality stands the structure of power that devises and implements policies. Not surprisingly, those who have power are at the top of the economic and political structure of the society; obviously, their natural inclination is to shape policies that hurt themselves least and benefit themselves most.[41] President Nixon's policies since August, 1971, when the first of a number of "Phases" began, well illustrates this inclination; the growth rate and corporate profits both rose substantially in 1972 and 1973; the rate of inflation declined for a brief period in 1972 and began to move to outer space in 1973; unemployment went down during 1972, but stabilized (at best) in 1973 at 5 percent; real wages (money wages adjusted for price increases) began to decline in mid-1973; war expenditures rose while authorized spending for housing, health, education, and job training were impounded.

Since World War II, the American economy has undergone many *structural* changes; it has gone through a developmental process. We have noted these earlier: internationalization, militarization, and the growth of "consumerism." Within those developmental changes one constant in terms of policy orientation has emerged: the continuing search for tax and expenditure policies that will keep the wheels of business turning rapidly and smoothly. Most relevant in this connection are those policies designed explicitly to encourage business investment. Their results have been many; for present purposes their effects in *maintaining* the basic structure of production and control are most important. They have guaranteed that the economy will remain locked in that condition of alternating or combined inflation and unemployment, mixing fever with sluggishness.

More specifically, the period since World War II has seen the rise of policies designed to encourage business investment and profitability when the market signals suggest otherwise. These policies include investment subsidies, taking the form of "investment tax credits," "stepped-up depreciation allowances," and a host of lesser-known tax policies. Some steps along these lines were taken in the Eisenhower years, but their institutionalization began in the Kennedy Administration. Johnson continued the policies, and under Nixon they have been expanded. Their purpose is to induce corporations to invest when the corporations would not normally be inclined to do so. The inducement is provided by tax benefits, a handy way of referring to a governmentally-subsidized increase in the profit rate.

---

[41]A clear explanation of how these relationships work out in economic terms and thus what the conventional political options are is Francis M. Bator, *The Question of Government Spending: Public Needs and Private Wants** (New York: Harper & Row, 1960). We shall have more to say in this area in Chapter Eight.

Investment subsidies have produced investment; that they have done so in periods of substantial existing excess capacity is looked upon as something of a triumph. But is it? Such investment has the effect of increasing productive capacity in lines already characterized by too much capacity; it fattens a structure that is already too fat. Furthermore, because the government largesse finds its way principally into the areas where powerful corporations dwell—the largesse of military expenditures is also directed there—another effect is to add to inflationary pressures, if they already exist.

All this does not come down to an argument against government taxation or spending, of course. There is a great and growing need for both. The *incidence* of taxation (who pays?) and the *direction* of government spending (who benefits?) is at stake. The American economy requires much doctoring in its mature years. But it will not be lifted out of its chronic tendency to stagnate by following the same diet. A real war on poverty, a real war against ignorance, a real war against poor health and housing would stimulate the economy and end unemployment; the continuation of dependence on military expenditures and investment subsidization of the large corporations—on the principle enunciated by President Nixon in 1971: "profits for business mean jobs for the people"—means continuing unemployment, poverty, and inflation.[42]

It is not difficult to see what the economy and society need, as contrasted with what governmental policy has accomplished in recent decades. It is very difficult to comprehend the conditions within which what is necessary and desirable could realistically be expected to occur, without a fundamental change in the structure of power relationships. Policies imply politics, and politics emanate from power. But is it true that the American economy needs much doctoring? Is *stagnation* a plausible characterization of the American economy? The best way to approach such questions is to examine the perplexing question of *unemployment:* what it is, how much deeper it is than official estimates suggest, and how much worse than that it would be in the absence of the enormous role of the military.

BROTHER, CAN YOU SPARE A TANK?

"The general problem which confronts us and our statesmen," a business economist states,

---

[42]The "war on poverty" initiated under President Johnson reveals much concerning the weak impulses in that direction, as compared with military expenditures, e.g. For a thorough explanation and description of the whole matter, see Ben Seligman, *Permanent Poverty: An American Syndrome* (New York: Quadrangle, 1968), especially Chapters 9 and 10.

is that a large section of the labor force turned surplus in the mid-1930's, and since then, year in and year out, there has been this 10 to 12 million excess of manpower to deal with. Administrations came and went over the years, but always the hard nut remained about the same. The particular programs of this or that party seems to have had little effect on the size of the surplus, more likely it would affect only how the surplus was split.[43]

The "split" the author refers to is between rising military employment or rising unemployment and under-employment.

The editors of the *Monthly Review* have conducted an intensive analysis of this question. Using figures for December, 1970, they argue that the then official rate of 6.2 percent should be 9.1 percent, and would be were it not that male labor force participation rates have declined sharply in the age group twenty-five to sixty-five. Unless we assume that those in that group are "members of a new leisure class (a high improbability considering that they are poor), the explanation must be that such people have given up hope of earning a living in the normal way in the economy today."[44]

In 1970 about a quarter of manufacturing productive capacity was lying idle. Taking that as a starting point, the authors go on to calculate the role of military outlays in obscuring the stagnation of the American economy. In 1970 there were 2.9 million members of the armed forces, 1.2 million civilian employees of the Department of Defense, 3.0 million employees in defense industries, and 7.1 million employed because of the indirect effects of military spending. Adding in the unemployed— 7.9 million by their calculations—Magdoff and Sweezy come to a figure of 22.1 million dependent upon military activity, plus the unemployed, or 25.6 percent of the labor force, including armed forces. That figure is slightly above the official figure for unemployment in 1933, the worst year of the Depression. *Jeremiad's* calculations are much lower; still, he says, "Combining the military with the unemployed, when the total touches down at 10 million, as it did in 1965, that is prosperity. When it exceeds 12 million, as at the end of 1970, you have bad times."[45]

---

[43] *Jeremiad: Economic Intelligence,* no. 44 (July 24, 1972). This monthly newsletter, written by Jerome Schucter, is a witty and incisive commentary on the American economy. Address: P.O. Box 36496, Wilshire-La Brea, Los Angeles, 90036.

[44] This comment and the argument surrounding it is found in two articles, "Economic Stagnation and the Stagnation of Economics" (April, 1971), and "On the Theory of Monopoly Capitalism" (April, 1972), *Monthly Review.* The authors are Harry Magdoff and Paul M. Sweezy.

[45] Ibid. Speaking of the official estimates of unemployment, *Jeremiad* says: "For true unemployment there is no solution except to open a path from the worker to a livelihood. Such unemployment should be distinguished from the statistical unemployment rate. That rate is sculpted politically, according to a man-made definition of what to count as unemployment. As it diverges from the facts, it verges on the propagandistic." June 26,

The enormous military production of World War II lifted us out of the depression; the lesser expenditures of the Korean War lifted us out of a recession; the heating up of the American involvement in Indochina reduced unemployment to unusually low rates and raised inflation to unusually high rates. In the mid-1960's it appeared that hard-core poverty was declining; by 1969 it began to expand again. In the early 1970's, in the midst of substantial unemployment and inflation, corporate profit rates began to break all records—rising over 50 percent between 1969 and 1973. GM, making its highest after-tax profits ever in the first half of 1973 ($1.6 billion), sought price increases under Phase IV rules (as this went to print), and was expected to get them. All these matters were connected, and all can be looked at in terms of income and wealth distribution. To that we now turn.

READING SUGGESTIONS

The more or less technical matters discussed in this chapter can be better understood and appreciated if also approached through lighter works, fictional and non-fictional. They allow us to regain the flavors, bitter and sweet, of the so-called interwar period. Here is a short list of such works.

A very high percentage of people today are still responding to the trauma of the years between the two world wars. They were years of middle class euphoria in the 1920's and of despair in the 1930's; of desperate unemployment for workers; surprisingly to young people today, they were bitter years for the militarists, for they were years of pervasive anti-militarism (different in roots and manifestations from that of the Indochina War). For an overview beginning well before World War I and going into the 1930's, see John Dos Passos's exciting and informative trilogy USA* (The 42nd Parallel, 1919, and The Big Money). For the 1920's, anything of Sinclair Lewis, but especially Babbitt.* Anything of F. Scott Fitzgerald, but especially The Great Gatsby* and Tender is the Night.* The non-euphoric side is brought out in Upton Sinclair, Oil! (union struggles in the Los Angeles area) and Pietro di Donato, Christ in Concrete* (immigrant construction workers). The classic and most enjoyable social history of the decade of the twenties is F. L. Allen, Only Yesterday.* J. K. Galbraith's Great Crash* is a lively if bland analysis of the stock market debacle. Some idea of the period 1930–1960 can be gotten from Clancy Sigal's novel Going Away* (Boston: Houghton Mifflin, 1962).

1972. The long-standing politicization of government statistics was given a new twist in 1973 when President Nixon appointed two helpers from his re-election campaign (both non-statisticians) to head two key statistical agencies—the Commerce Department's Social and Economic Statistics Division and the Census Bureau—seen by statisticians as the equivalent of the Haynsworth and Carswell appointments to the Supreme Court.

Comparable to Allen, for the thirties (and more solid), is Dixon Wecter, *The Age of the Great Depression, 1929–1941.* Steinbeck's *Grapes of Wrath** tells more than just about migrant farm workers, and is must reading for any who wish to understand an important part of the American mind; his *In Dubious Battle** is a penetrating fictional inquiry into a farm workers' struggle in Salinas, California (and provides some insights into the contemporary struggles of the United Farm Workers). There is a very special and valuable work recently made available: Studs Terkel, a Chicago journalist and radio-TV commentator, has put together a broad range of human experience and responses from the 1930's, called *Hard Times,** in the recorded voices of people of all ages and from all walks of life who lived through the period—or, in some cases, the impressions they left with their children. It is a great way to learn about those years; it is also warm and enjoyable as moving reading. Representative fictional materials for the same period are collected in Harvey Swados, ed., *The American Writer and the Great Depression** (Indianapolis: Bobbs-Merrill, 1966).

Back to dryer stuff. To understand Keynesian theory, Dillard's book, cited earlier, is an apt summary. Useful controversies from right, middle, and left concerning Keynesian theory have been brought together in Robert Lekachman, ed., *Keynes and the Classics** (Boston: D. C. Heath, 1964). Lekachman's *National Income and the Public Welfare** (New York: Random House, 1972) is a clear and succinct statement of contemporary income and employment analysis. Lester V. Chandler, *America's Greatest Depression, 1929–1941** (New York: Harper & Row, 1972), is a readable and comprehensive survey of main processes and policies in the 1930's. A critical perspective on Roosevelt's New Deal may be found in articles by Ronald Radosh, "The Myth of the New Deal," in R. Radosh and Murray Rothbard, eds., *A New History of Leviathan** (New York: Dutton, 1972) and by Barton Bernstein, "The New Deal: The Conservative Achievements of Reform," in Barton J. Bernstein, ed., *Towards a New Past: Dissenting Essays in American History** (New York: Vintage, 1972) —a book of generally useful essays largely in accord with the interpretations of this work.

A critical Marxian analysis of the U.S. growth record since World War II is Victor Perlo, *The Unstable Economy: Booms and Recessions in the U.S. Since 1945** (New York: New World Paperbacks, 1973).

chapter five
Income, Wealth, and Power

Who can make a poem of the depths of weariness
bringing meaning to those never in the depths?
   Those who order what they please
   when they choose to have it—
   can they understand the many down under
who come home to their wives and children at night
and night after night as yet too brave and unbroken
   to say, "I ache all over"?
   How can a poem deal with production cost
   and leave out definite misery paying
a permanent price in shattered health and early old age?
   When will the efficiency engineers and the poets
   get together on a program?
Will that be a cold day? Will that be a special hour?
   Will somebody be coocoo then?
   And if so, who?

(Carl Sandburg, *The People, Yes*)

Capitalism is a system whose vitality is given to it by everyone trying
to make as much money as possible, and the devil take the hindmost.
From its beginnings to the present, capitalist development has taken
place within a pattern of income, wealth, and power characterized by
great inequality. That history has been marked by constant changes in
technology, in products, in markets, in institutions and in attitudes;
among all these patterns, those comprising income, wealth, and power
have been the most resistant to substantial change. Inequality is intrinsic to capitalism. It is another way of viewing the existence of exploitation; without inequality, economic expansion would be inexplicable.

   Variations in the patterns of inequality have of course occurred.
Given the complexity of capitalist development, and its dynamic
changes in economic structure, such alterations have been unavoidable.
In the 19th century, a simple division between property-owners and the

115

propertyless wage-earner was both cause and consequence of the unequal distribution of wealth and income. In our day, a more complex cause and effect relationship exists: (a) there is a sharp line to be drawn between *Big Business* and all other owners of (some) productive assets; (b) substantial income and wealth distinctions must be drawn between those who "own" *professional* labor power and those who do not; (c) in the non-professional ranks of labor, there are significant differences in the incomes of those whose labor power is protected and sustained by strong trade unions and those who are not. Within these *class* divisions, further distinctions occur because of racial and sexual barriers.

Arising out of the growing complexity of functions and incomes of modern capitalist society has been growing speculation concerning the emergence of a "new working class," or an "extended working class." The intention of these inquiries has been to establish the degree to which the members of the last two categories (b) and (c) might be expected to develop attitudes antagonistic to the continuation of a society whose prime beneficiaries are mostly those in category (a), those who control the productive assets of the economy. For despite the complexity, American society continues to move in ways resulting from a highly unequal distribution of power, wealth, and income, the key determinant of which is wealth. So long as capitalist society *remains* capitalist in its basic institutions—private property in the means of production, and production for profit—it will function "healthily" only insofar as the pattern of income and wealth distribution is highly unequal and can be expected to remain that way by those at the top.

Let us look briefly at the historical variations within the basic pattern. What is noteworthy about them is the small number of lasting changes, the directions in which they have moved, and the extent of overall *social* change required to accomplish them. The period of *least* inequality in the United States—if black slaves and Native Americans are excluded from the calculations—was in the several decades preceding 1850. After that came a long period up to the 1930's of *increased* inequality of income and wealth. Overlapping that period and extending to the present, and accompanied by greatly expanded State activity in both taxing and spending, has been a process where although it is possible to find some slight reduction of income inequality in the statistics, it is also necessary to show that both wealth and power have become more highly unequal.[1]

The lesser inequality of income and wealth for whites in the period 1800–1850, although it cannot be pinned down precisely, is suggested

---

[1] An informative analysis of the 19th century changes may be found in Alfred Conrad's essay "Income Growth and Structural Change," in Alfred Conrad and John R. Meyer, *The Economics of Slavery* (Chicago: Aldine, 1964). For points under discussion here, see esp. pp. 168–77.

not only by impressionistic data, but by the economic structure and processes of the period: widespread and growing access to land, a shortage of non-slave, non-indentured labor, and light industrial production. The years after 1850 constituted a major turning-point in American capitalist development, when heavy as well as light industrialization caught hold. From then on, income and wealth came to be held in a steadily more unequal pattern, as the small farmer disappeared, business became bigger, and the power of business in government became increasingly strong. The economic transformation was accompanied by a geographical shift in power, wrought by the convulsion of the Civil War.

It should be noted that as the distributive *shares* of income and wealth became more unequal, the *levels* of real per capita income rose. This pertained to ex-slaves as well, though as a group they, like their descendants today, remained at the bottom of the scale. An important by-product of rising real incomes was a mitigation of internal conflict.

Rapid and widespread industrialization made for more inequality; it also made for more instability of business activity and increased insecurity in employment, as noted in Chapters Three and Four. In turn, these changes marked the beginning of a new phase not only in private-State relationships, but, accompanying that, a new set of developments impinging upon the patterns of income, wealth, and power: a much enlarged role of federal, state, and local governments in taxation and expenditure. Setting aside careful analysis of this development for the moment, let it suffice here to say that although the distributional phenomena were of course much affected by the enormous increase of governmental fiscal activities, the resulting reduction of income inequality was at most marginal; nor have the changes benefitted those at the very bottom. On the contrary, through the role of the State in strengthening capitalism, "political capitalism" has been of considerable advantage to those at the top and in the middle ranges.

THEM THAT HAS, GITS

Income is a flow of money and purchasing power over time; *wealth* is a stock of things owned that have market value. Money income includes wages and salaries, social security benefits, dividends, interest and rents received, welfare payments, pensions, alimony received, net income from self-employment (for instance, from farming, or by doctors), and other periodic income. Wealth includes automobiles and homes as well as trucks and mines and corporate stock; but for analytical purposes the ownership of productive—that is, income producing—assets is the vital factor. Let us look first at the facts of *income* distribution.

The data on these matters come primarily from the federal census conducted every ten years, and from income tax forms (though individuals' data are not made public). There is of course reason to doubt the detailed accuracy of such information, but the general outlines provided by the data over time are reliable. One major reservation, however, concerns understatement of high *incomes* (due to the 50 percent exclusion of capital gains, the hiding of income in expense accounts, and the like) and the understatement of the real *wealth* of the wealthy. Nevertheless, the extreme disparity between the rich and the poor stands out:

> Since World War II, the poorest fifth of families has received less than 6% of money income; the richest fifth has received over 40%. Put another way, the average income of the 10.4 million families in the bottom fifth in 1970 was $3,054; the average income of the 10.4 million families in the top fifth was $23,100. If money income had been divided equally among families in 1970, the average income for each family would have been over $11,000.[2]

These figures are for "personal income distribution," and, as may be noted, they are generally couched in terms of "fifths" of the population,

TABLE 3

Percentage of Money Income Received by Each Fifth of Families and Individuals and by Top 5 Percent

Families and individuals ranked from lowest to highest income	1947	1957	1962	1967	1968
Total	100%	100%	100%	100%	100%
Lowest Fifth	4	4	3	4	4
Second Fifth	11	11	11	11	11
Middle Fifth	17	18	17	17	17
Fourth Fifth	24	25	25	24	25
Highest Fifth	46	43	44	44	44
Top 5 percent	19	17	17	16	15

SOURCE: Herman P. Miller, *Rich Man, Poor Man** (New York: Crowell, 1971), p. 50. This is the handiest compendium of facts and analysis on most of the matters discussed in this chapter—income, wealth, race, sex, education, and poverty—seen from a moderate viewpoint. Miller has been with the Bureau of the Census for about thirty years.

[2]Letitia Upton and Nancy Lyons, *Basic Facts: Distribution of Personal Income and Wealth in the United States** (Cambridge: Cambridge Institute, 1972), p. 1. This is an up-to-date and succinct statement, objectively bringing together available data from all major official and private sources. It is available inexpensively from the Cambridge Institute, 1878 Massachusetts Avenue, Cambridge, Mass. "Family" as used in income data means two or more people residing together, related by blood, marriage or adoption. The statistical size of the average American family today is about 3.6 persons.

from the lowest 20 percent to the highest. They are also available in terms of the highest 5 percent and the top 1 percent, as indicated in Tables 3 and 4. These are before taxes on incomes; but as will be shown later, taxes make no substantial difference in the shares. What is remarkable is the constancy of the distribution in the past twenty-five years.[3]

Using a broader conception of income, Joseph Pechman (one of the most authoritative tax economists) has compiled figures from 1966 that show a somewhat higher degree of inequality, especially for the top 5 percent "after adjustment for nonreporting and underreporting of income." (See Table 4.)

What about constancy of income shares if we go further back than 1947? Partially because the data are unreliable, and partially because the question of constancy is itself so controversial in the present period—when we are frequently told that inequality is lessening and that the poor are taking money from the rich—any arguments about comparisons over the past half-century are sharply contested. On close examination, however, the sharpness is more that of needles than of swords. The main warrior arguing for constancy is Kolko, who asserts:

A radically unequal distribution of income has been characteristic of the American social structure since at least 1910, and despite minor year-to-year fluctuations in the shares of the income-tenths, no significant trend toward income equality has appeared. . . . Throughout the 1950's the

TABLE 4

Families ranked from lowest to highest income	Income Range (dollars)	Percent of income received
Lowest fifth	0–3,070	3.2
Second fifth	3,070–5,890	10.5
Middle fifth	5,890–8,620	17.0
Fourth fifth	8,620–12,260	23.9
Highest fifth	12,260 and over	45.8
Top 5 percent	19,920 and over	19.1
Top 1 percent	44,560 and over	6.8

SOURCE: Joseph A. Pechman, "Distribution of Federal and State Income Taxes by Income Classes," Presidential Address, American Finance Association Annual Meetings, New Orleans, La., December 28, 1971, p. 6. Quoted in Upton and Lyons, op. cit., p. 16. Some in the lowest fifth have "negative incomes"; i.e., they fall into debt.

---

[3] *The Review of Radical Political Economics* (Summer, 1971), is devoted entirely to distributional questions, with seven essays examining "Capitalism, Inequality, and Poverty," from different vantage points. Most pertinent for our concerns here are pp. 20–43, "Income Distribution in the U.S.," by Ackerman, et al.

income of the top tenth was larger than the total for the bottom five income-tenths—about the same relationship as existed in 1910 and 1918. . . . While the income share of the richest tenth has remained large and virtually constant over the past half century, the two lowest income-tenths have experienced a sharp decline.[4]

An examination of Miller's data (Table 3) shows that whether or not he is correct in saying that Kolko's "statement is very questionable," (Miller, p. 51), the persistence of highly unequal income is unquestionable. There are occasional indications of something departing from long-run stability. *Year-to-year* fluctuations in distributional shares take place, but shifting percentage shares in a given year have less meaning than is apparent, if the year in question is unusually prosperous *or* depressed, for example, or if a new short-run trend has been at work. Thus, the mid-1960's were years of lessening poverty and lower unemployment, in association with the economic height of the Indochina War. After 1969, poverty, unemployment, and inequality in income and wealth distribution all increased.

Another important set of points requires emphasis. Those with the highest incomes and the greatest wealth benefit most from increases in the *national* income. They are in the best position to take advantage of the increased opportunities in expansion periods. In the early phases of an expansion out of a depressed period, although workers will find their incomes rising—not least because they are more fully employed—the *share* going to the lower income groups declines. In a sustained expansion that brings about full employment, the share of the lower income groups will later begin to rise, accompanied at the very peak of the expansion by falling profit rates (due both to rising wages and to softening markets for commodities). But a period of contraction means fewer jobs, and falling incomes for employed workers; although it also means falling incomes for those at the top, their *share* rises—and, of course, they are quite unlikely to suffer, as those in the lower income groups do. Over time, the gap between rich and poor widens obviously in absolute terms, if less so in relative terms. Thus (in *constant* 1970 dollars), between 1958 and 1968 the average income of the *poorest* fifth of families moved up from $1,956 to $3,085; of the *highest* fifth from $15,685 to $21,973. The difference in average incomes between the lowest and highest fifths increased from $13,720 to $18,888. The poor may or may not see their money incomes—and even, now and then, their income shares—rise; in general they do well to hold on to their

---

[4]Gabriel Kolko, *Wealth and Power in America** (New York: Praeger, 1962), pp. 13–15. Kolko's Table I, p. 14, shows the richest tenth receiving 33.9 percent in 1910 and 28.9 percent in 1959 (his latest year). This was something of a decline, but in relative terms not as much as the decline in the share of the poorest: the lowest tenth received 3.4 percent in 1910 and 1.1 percent in 1959. Note that Kolko is using *tenths,* not *fifths.*

relative share. But even when they manage to do that, poverty increases when the absolute gap widens. Poverty is a *social* condition. An American family receiving many times the money income of a family in India can be poorer than the Indian family. *Absolute* poverty exists when starvation enters the picture; poverty then is physical as well as social. But poverty is always first and foremost social. Marx puts it well:

> Rapid growth of productive capital calls forth just as rapid a growth of wealth, of luxury, of social needs and social pleasures. Therefore, although the pleasures of the labourer have increased [through higher wages], the social gratification which they afford has fallen in comparison with the increased pleasures of the capitalist, which are inaccessible to the worker, in comparison with the stage of development of the society in general. Our wants and pleasures have their origin in society; we therefore measure them in relation to society; we do not measure them in relation to the objects which serve for their gratification. Since they are of a social nature, they are of a relative nature.[5]

Marx's view helps to clarify why it is in periods of economic expansion that social protest tends to rise among those at the bottom of the heap. It is worth noting also that what is true of the distribution of income and wealth and the widening gap between rich and poor *within* this country is also true of the widening gap *between* rich and poor *nations.* When we look at the underdeveloped nations in a later chapter, we shall see it is a commonplace that the absolute and relative gap between the industrialized and non-industrialized nations has widened substantially in the postwar years of sustained expansion. And, of course, turbulence has increased in that same period. Let us now turn to the distribution and accumulation of *wealth.*

THE ACCUMULATION OF WEALTH

The old saw, "the rich get richer and the poor get poorer," has more to it than spite and envy. The rich own most of society's wealth, and wealth yields incomes that in turn are invested in more wealth, to produce even more income. More importantly, great *wealth* yields great *power.* The simple relationship between income and wealth emerges clearly from Figure 3, a *Business Week* chart which is an application of recent data to the so-called "Lorenz Curve":[6]

---

[5]Karl Marx, *Wage-Labour and Capital** (New York: International Publishers, 1933; originally published in 1849), p. 33. The data for the widening income gap in the preceding paragraph are from Upton and Lyons, op. cit., p. 4.

[6]The Lorenz Curve seeks to show degrees of inequality graphically: the straight line (45 degree angle) shows a relationship of exact equality between percent of persons and of income (or wealth); the greater the deviation from that straight line, the greater the degree of inequality.

FIGURE 3

Relation Between Income and Wealth

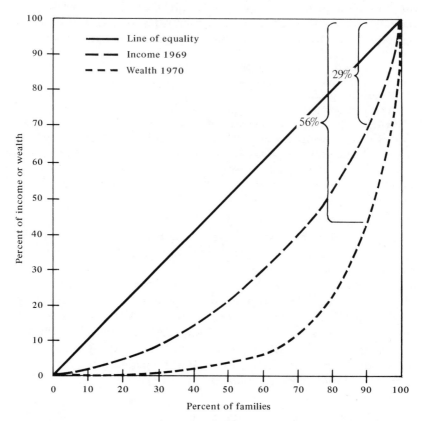

U.S. income is shared unevenly, but wealth distribution is more unequal.

With equal distribution:
  •each 10% of the people would get 10% of all income.
  •each 10% would own 10% of total wealth.

  But actually . . .

The top 10% of the people:
  •get 29% of income.
  •own 56% of wealth.

The bottom 10% of the people:
  •get 1% of income.
  •owe more than they own.

  SOURCE: *Business Week,* August 5, 1972.

Wealth measures the sale value of possessions and property. Almost everyone owns something of value; but only a small percentage of the population owns the society's income producing assets, the most vital part of which is its corporate stock. The considerably more unequal distribution of wealth than income is directly connected to economic power, and economic power is directly connected to political power. These connections mean that the wealthy are in a position to neutralize the apparent redistributive income and wealth effects of governmental income, estate, and inheritance taxes.[7]

In 1962, as was noted earlier, the highest fifth of *income* receivers had over 40 percent of personal income; in that same year, the highest fifth ranked by *wealth* size owned 77 percent of personal wealth. When we examine the corporate stock component of total wealth, the concentration is considerably higher. (See Table 5.)

If the figures in Table 5 are startling standing alone, behind them matters are even more startling, showing how wealth feeds wealth. The top 1 percent of personal wealth holders own 30 percent or more of all wealth, although the top 1 percent of personal income recipients receive "only" something under 10 percent of income. But all the wealth could be translated into income. Why is it not? First, because wealth produces income, and the law of the rich is "never live off capital." Second, the higher incomes involved would, if allowed to go higher through converting wealth to income, be taxed away, at least in part. Third, wealth

TABLE 5

Percentage Share of Wealth Held by Fifths, Top 5 Percent and Top 1 Percent, 1962

Consumer units ranked from lowest to highest wealth	Total Wealth	Corporate Stock
Poorest fifth	(−)[*]	(−)
Second through fourth fifth	23%	3%
Richest fifth	77	97
Top 5 percent	53	86
Top 1 percent	33	62

SOURCE: Upton and Lyons, p. 22.

[*](−) means less than 1/2 of 1 percent. These figures were derived by Upton/Lyons from Edward C. Budd, ed., *Inequality and Poverty*[*] (New York: Norton, 1967), p. xxii.

---

[7]Philip M. Stern has written two books showing the facts, procedures, winners and losers, and bases of our tax system, which works very much the opposite of its presumed intent: *The Great Treasury Raid*[*](New York: Signet, 1965), and *The Rape of the Taxpayer* (New York: Random House, 1973).

in the form of stock ownership (among other things) means increased wealth through undistributed corporate profits. Fourth, wealth means power. Last, in the case of the very rich, on what would they spend higher incomes? "Accumulate! Accumulate!" is what they have done.

It is a popular belief that stock ownership has become less unequal in recent decades, and in one sense that is so. The number of individual stock investors rose from nine million in 1956 to thirty-one million in 1970; but the wealthiest 1 percent of the population increased its percentage of stock ownership from 69.5 percent in 1953 to 71.6 percent in 1962.[8] *Business Week,* basing its analysis on the most recent scholarly studies of wealth concentration, concludes that "the degree of wealth concentration increased during the 1920's, decreased from 1929 to the late 1940's, and remained fairly stable in the 1960's." But they go on to cite the belief of Professor James D. Smith, a leading analyst of wealth distribution, that the figures since 1962 would certainly show no decrease in concentration of wealth; "if anything, it increased slightly." (Ibid.)

Whether or not there is great inequality in the distribution of income and wealth is not debatable; as such, it is not debated. But what to do about it, whether it is either desirable or possible to move toward more equality—such questions are very much debated. Setting aside radical voices, however, the arguments that range around this question uncritically take property rights for granted, and rarely question the desirability of the basic institutions that have created and that require great inequality. Thus, *Business Week,* although it had three major essays during 1972 on the distribution of income and wealth, all of which show the same data used by us above, comes out bemused and puzzled: "Neither side can come up with hard answers as to how it [income redistribution] can—or should—work." And, "some inequality may serve as an incentive for growth in a profit-oriented economy." "Some" inequality is not what their own essays show, nor are their conclusions more or less helpful than those of mainstream economists. The worst-kept family secret about the relationship between capitalist development and *great* inequality in the distribution of income and wealth is that they need each other.[9]

Nobody, and certainly not the rich, needs to be told that property-ownership is the key to high incomes. Nor could anyone seriously believe that being nonwhite, or a woman, is a matter of indifference to

---

[8]Ibid., p. 31. In addition to books already cited for data on income and wealth, see Ferdinand Lundberg, *The Rich and the Super-Rich** (New York: Lyle Stuart, 1968), a racy but thorough tome on the subject; and for basic work that is bone-dry, see Robert J. Lampman, *Changes in the Share of Wealth Held by Top Wealth-Holders, 1922–1956** (New York: National Bureau of Economic Research, 1960).

[9]The *Business Week* articles are those of April 1, June 17, and Aug. 5, 1972.

one's income. What is less accepted or understood is the systematic and long-standing *class* pressures to maintain the relationships that allow the gains from property, and that perpetuate the low incomes of all workers—men and women, whites and nonwhites. Discussion of such matters is normally in the nature of asides, or with the unexamined assumption that some good will, some intelligence, and some time are likely (if anything can or should be) to rid American society of such patterns.

A critical analysis of capitalist development teaches otherwise. The causes of existing patterns of income and wealth distribution are far from accidental and, so far as basic patterns are concerned, are unchangeable. Capitalism requires expansion; expansion requires savings and investment; the required savings and investment depend upon past and expected profits; persistent profitability in the economy is the telltale sign of both expansion and exploitation; it requires people who must work for what they can get even when that means they work part of the time "for nothing," that is, for the benefit of the employer and of capitalism's health. If the alternative to being exploited for those with little or no property is harsh, it is harsher still for the man who is nonwhite, and still more for women as compared with men.[10] Let us examine what *average* incomes are and mean.

THE ACCUMULATION OF MISERY

In 1971, the Bureau of Labor Statistics (BLS) calculated the annual money income a family of four needed to enjoy a "moderate but adequate" standard of living in "the average American city." About two-thirds of Americans live in urban areas, and most of those who do not get and spend in roughly comparable ways. The BLS figure for 1971 was $10,971. They also estimated the amount needed for a "minimum budget at a lower level of living" as $7,214 for an urban family.[10a]

The average annual *factory wage* in 1971 was $7,488 for fifty-two weeks of work. Thus the average urban and non-urban factory worker —those workers in the strongest unions—earned a bit over the urban *minimum* and far under the *moderate* level.

What do "moderate" and "minimum" mean? "Moderate," by which the BLS means a level of "accepted comfort and decency," provides one suit every two to four years for the father, a new winter coat every five years for the mother, and a new refrigerator and stove every seventeen years. A used car every four years. A movie once in six weeks. Nothing set aside for periods of joblessness, for illness, or for college education

---

[10]See the data in Table 6, below.
[10a]Raised to $11,800 and $7,600, respectively, in June, 1973.

for the family's children. "Minimum" pares everything down to food, clothing, and housing, and leaves nothing for other items.[11]

In 1971, *median* money incomes for American families rose above $10,000 for the first time, to $10,285. "Median" refers to the middle unit of an entire population; in this case, half of all families received less than and half more than $10,285. In purchasing power, the 1971 incomes were *less* than those for 1969 and 1970, however—which, calculated in 1971 dollars, were $10,423 and $10,289, respectively. The median income for *white* families in 1971 was $10,672; for black families it was $6,440, or 60 percent of the whites' income. In mid-1973, the Census Bureau reported that the 1972 percentage of all blacks' median incomes to all whites' median incomes was continuing the decline begun in 1970; the percentage is falling as the unemployment of blacks rises, and governmental programs are reduced. In short, we may say that roughly half of all American families in 1971 had money incomes below the "moderate but adequate" budget established by the BLS. About a third of families lived below the officially defined level of "deprivation" (about $7,000), and 25.6 million people received less than $4,137, the official "poverty line" in 1971—the highest number since 1967.[12] In this, the richest of all societies, the majority of the population is not, by its own government's standards, living well. But some few are living very well indeed.

In 1971, less than 1 percent received over $50,000. An idea of how very well the cream of that crop lives is given by data derived from *Business Week's* annual executive compensation survey. Executive compensation rose by 9.3 percent in 1971, in August of which President Nixon's wage-price (but not profits) freeze was imposed. Subsequently, during the wage-price freeze year of 1972, executive compensation rose an additional 13.5 percent (on average). *Business Week,* noting these increases, comments that "they appear to exceed the limits of 5.5 percent on salaries and 0.7 percent on fringes that were imposed by Phase II" (May 5, 1973). Increases in executive compensation were linked to increases in corporate profits. Some of the more spectacular examples may be cited.

Between 1970 and 1972, the two electrical industry giants, General Electric and Westinghouse, increased their profits (after taxes) by 61 and

---

[11]Donald Light, "Income Distribution: The First Stage in the Consideration of Poverty," *RRPE* (Summer, 1971), conducts a useful and critical examination of these concepts, only touched upon here. It is worth noting that although those who live in rural areas have generally lower expenses than urban residents, the figures for the "average city" understate by $1,000 or more the cost-of-living in the big cities such as Boston, Greater New York, Milwaukee, San Francisco, Chicago, Philadelphia, Los Angeles, and several others. All figures have to be adjusted upward to reflect the substantial inflation since 1971.

[12]*Characteristics of the Low-Income Population; Money Income, 1971** (Washington, D.C.: USGPO, 1972) is the source for all the data in this paragraph.

47 percent, respectively. Fred J. Borch, Board Chairman of General Electric received a pay increase of 34 percent in 1971, and an additional 21 percent increase in 1972—receiving $543,000 pay and deferred incentive compensation in the latter year. D. C. Burnham, Chairman of Westinghouse, did quite a bit better: in 1972 his salary was $236,000, his incentive compensation $180,000 and his profit on stock options was over one million dollars, for a total income that year of almost $1.5 million.[13]

These are not entirely exceptional figures. *Business Week* reported that GM Chairman Richard Gerstenberg was paid $889,963, Henry Ford II $887,795, Ford President Iacocca $873,852, and Chrysler Chairman Lynn Townsend $649,850 in 1972—incomes representing increases ranging from 27 to 205 percent over the preceding year. The increase in corporate profits and in executive compensation accelerated in 1973. While inflation worsened, unemployment remained stuck at 5 percent, and the nation was daily informed not just about Watergate, but about international monetary crisis, food shortages, depleted energy supplies, record new car sales, gas shortages, rising military expenditures, and presidentially impounded funds for expenditures on health, education, jobtraining, and other socially needed programs. It did not stretch the imagination to discern close connections between the various elements of the pattern of production, of income, wealth, and power distribution, and the coexistence of increased incomes for some and increased hardship for the rest.

OLIGARCHIC DEMOCRACY

How are such patterns maintained, in what is not only the richest but, by its own standards, the most democratic country in the world? The answer must begin with the role of power, the power to defend and to enhance the prerogatives of property. The holders of such power in capitalist society have been seen as "the ruling class" by Marx, "the vested interests" by Veblen, "the power elite" by C. Wright Mills, "the establishment" by Papandreou, and "the governing class" by G. William Domhoff. Their terminological differences arise from analytical differences in the way each of these men has viewed our society. Whatever those differences are, all agree on one matter: the holders of power are few in number, and at their center sit those who control—by virtue of concentrated ownership—the wealth of the society.

Americans are a strange lot when it comes to questions of power and class. Although workers "hate the bosses"; although it is universally assumed that "you can't beat City Hall" (which means also state and

---

[13]These data are taken from *UE News*, April 2 and 16, 1973; derived by them from annual reports of the corporations.

federal equivalents) and that "City Hall" is a nest of corruption; although the media are alleged to be in the service of powerful financial interests by figures as diverse as Abbie Hoffman and Spiro Agnew; although there is widespread recognition that schools and churches and social occasions divide clearly in terms of the wealth and income of those participating; although those at the top act and frequently speak in ways explicable only in class terms (FDR, for instance, was said to be "a traitor to his class"—quite mistakenly, as it happens); although all this and much more of the same sort is taken for granted, *class analysis* of American society is rejected and scorned, not only by the conventional social scientist but quite generally by all the people whose attitudes are noted above. This contrast between popular attitudes and systematic understanding is not at all apparent in other capitalist countries; it is very much an American trait. Why it should be so is of course a matter of our history, which thereby stands in contrast to the history of other capitalist societies.

Among all capitalist societies, the United States alone has no precapitalist history; for other societies, this was a history of clear-cut class relationships with power graded in terms of class. The United States was born in a *nationalist* struggle. Understandably, at the time that struggle could be seen as a social revolution as well. The distinction between a national and a social revolution requires clarification. Nationalist struggles unite people of different classes in pursuit of a common cause. They either succeed or fail. Social revolutions are struggles to alter the preexisting internal class structure of power. Their success or failure is thus a matter of degree, depending on the extent to which the class structure is changed. (The Vietnamese struggle is a combination of these two forms, which helps to explain its vitality.)

By this criterion, the American Revolution does not qualify as much of a social revolution, for its internal structural effects were peripheral and ephemeral. Despite this, however, Americans have historically seen themselves as living in a society characterized since the Declaration of Independence by widely diffused power and a fluid class structure, where movement from one level to another is a matter of pluck and luck and effort. Nor is it unimportant that a great measure of fluidity does exist. What is important about that fluidity, however, is not that it has existed, but that along with the social mobility has gone a *continuation* of the relative power of classes—indeed, as this book argues, an increase of power at the top. Why?

The upward mobility of American *individuals* has not altered the class structure because those who have moved up have been absorbed and co-opted by the stratum into which they have moved; only those who are willing to be thus co-opted get a chance to move up (except for a few "respectable" criminal and otherwise corrupt "deviant" exceptions, who get wealth by "out-system" means, and then buy in for themselves or their children). As will be noted again later, the educational process and most especially the higher levels of education are the prime socializing agents in this process of co-optation; once a "lower-class" person makes his or her way on to the upper reaches of the social ladder—whether in a corporation, in government, in the military, or in the professions—the absorption process is intensified. Or the person falls off the ladder. Social fluidity is one matter; class structure and the concentration of power is another. They can exist side by side, and they have and do in America. If one consequence has been analytical confusion in the social sciences, the other and connected result has been a virtually unchallenged role for the class that has gained and held power by virtue of its wealth and control of the upward mobility ladders.

But has there not been class *struggle* in the United States, between capital and labor? There has been, but it has taken particular forms that require careful analysis if their meaning is to be understood. Kolko, relying upon Veblen, has pointed to a key characteristic of the process in the United States:

> American society could also be understood as a class structure without *decisive* class conflict, a society that had conflict limited to smaller issues that were not crucial to the existing order, and on which the price of satisfying opposition was relatively modest from the viewpoint of the continuation of the social system. In brief, a static class structure serving class ends might be frozen into American society even if the interests and values served were those of a ruling class.[14]

The power of the ruling class in the United States has come principally from its ownership and control of the nation's productive wealth. That is a matter of class. But that power has also been enhanced by the depth and persistence of racial, ethnic, religious, and sexual discrimination, rivalry, and hatred. Whatever else in the United States may have held back the consciousness and strength of the working class, these divisions have surely been additional sources of weakness. Nor, of course, have such matters been confined to the United States. Discussing Ireland as a British colony, and the conditions of Irish workers in England (in a letter written in 1870), Marx said:

> And most important of all! Every industrial and commercial center in England now possesses a working class *divident* into two *hostile* camps, English proletarians and Irish proletarians. The ordinary English worker hates the Irish worker as a competitor who lowers his standard of life . . .

---

[14]Gabriel Kolko, "The Decline of American Radicalism in the Twentieth Century," in James Weinstein and David W. Eakins, eds., *For a New America** (New York: Vintage, 1970), p. 208. This book contains many exciting essays evaluating and re-evaluating American history. The point made by Kolko above suggests the analysis of ruling class "hegemony" made by the Italian Marxist Antonio Gramsci, which will be pursued more fully in our concluding chapter.

[,] feels himself a member of the *ruling* nation, and so turns himself into a tool of the aristocrats and capitalists of his country *against Ireland,* thus strengthening their domination *over himself.* He cherishes religious, social and national prejudices against the Irish worker. His attitude toward him is much the same as that of the "poor whites" to the "niggers" in the former slave states of the U.S.A. The Irishman pays him back with interest in his own money. . . . This antagonism is artificially kept alive and intensified by the press, the pulpit, the comic papers, in short, by all the means at the disposal of the ruling classes. This *antagonism is the secret of the impotence of the English working class,* despite its organization. It is the secret by which the capitalist class maintains its power. And that class is fully aware of it.[15]

Before examining further how such *non*-class relationships have operated, it is appropriate to explore very briefly the history of trade unionism in the United States, as trade unions were the main avenue taken by American workers to offset their weaknesses in the face of business power.

NOTHING TO LOSE, BUT. . .

American trade unions, by comparison with similar groups in other capitalist countries, are conservative. Neither in principle nor in practice are they class conscious; they do not seek basic institutional changes. They work within the framework of existing society, seeking to improve the economic conditions of their members *within* that framework. To succeed, some institutional change is of course required; broad changes are not. American unionism is generally characterized by the term "business unionism," or, sometimes, as "pork-chops unionism." There have been exceptions to these generalizations, but mainly in early or very bad times.

Right after the Civil War, groups such as the Knights of Labor formed which had as an important part of their aims a reconstitution of society, along lines which were then considered radical, although they might not seem so today. Even the very conservative American Federation of Labor (AFL) in the 1890's faced a moment when whether or not it would be explicitly socialist was debated (and rejected); before World War I about one-third of AFL members were also members of the Socialist Party. In the depression of the 1930's, the newly-formed Congress of Industrial Organizations (CIO) worked closely with New Dealers seeking broad social reform. And the most radical labor organization of all in America, the Industrial Workers of the World (IWW, called the "Wobblies"), was uncompromisingly anti-capitalist. The IWW was

---

[15]Quoted in Selsam et al., *Dynamics of Social Change,* p. 136. Emphasis in original.

ruthlessly and effectively crushed by the events surrounding World War I, the "Red Scare" of the 1920's, and the force of deeply hostile public opinion (including that expressed by the AFL), which more than once took the form of lynchings. Today a few so-called left-wing unions manage to hang on to life and members, but they survive because they are successful *business* unions.

How may the general conservatism of American trade unions be explained? It begins with the origins and the hopes of American workers, *and* with the socio-economic context within which they worked. From its beginnings until the 1920's, ours was a land of labor shortage, when the labor supply is set against the amount of land open to cultivation and the rapid rate of economic growth—with one important proviso: the "labor shortage" was not as intense as it appears in retrospect if the several millions of unemployed and severely under-employed blacks and whites in the South are taken into account and explained. From 1865 until the 1930's, migration from the underdeveloped South to the labor-hungry North was a mere trickle. Whites chose not to leave for an "enemy country," and blacks were generally restrained—by force of circumstance or by sheer force—from doing so. World War I and World War II, the agricultural depression of the 1930's and the mechanization and chemicalization of southern agriculture in the past generation gradually and then suddenly unlocked the substantial unused labor supply of the South substituting, in recent years, substantial urban for rural unemployment and under-employment.[16]

Given the foregoing institutional or artificially-created shortage of labor, the labor supply was persistently inadequate, despite a rapid rate of population growth. That rapid rate of increase was due in part to the high birth rate among residents, but the vital addition was due to heavy immigration, which was partly a result of the positive lure of the United States, partly due to the negative push of population pressure and political, social, and economic discontent in other countries. Acting as a link between the labor shortage and the influx of labor were American agents in Europe (and, later, in Asia)—sometimes of shipping companies seeking profits, sometimes of employers seeking workers, or of land companies seeking customers—who hawked the virtues of life in America much as soap is advertised today. The population rose from 31.5 million in 1860, to 63 million in 1890, to 106.4 million in 1920, about 29 million accounted for by immigration in that same period.[17]

---

[16]I have analyzed this question more fully in the essay "A Comparative Analysis of Economic Development in the American West and South," included in Harry Scheiber, ed., *U.S. Economic History: Selected Readings** (New York: Knopf, 1964), a generally useful collection of analytical studies.

[17]A useful analytical and factual study of the immigration process is Oscar Handlin, *The Uprooted* (Boston: Atlantic Monthly Press, 1951).

In the period between the Civil War and 1920, the proportion of male immigrants to the total immigration never fell below half, more often than not was above 60 percent, and in many years was above 70 percent. The men were overwhelmingly between fifteen and fifty years old, ready to become members of the labor force. Our total population more than tripled in this period. Still, in 1920 a congressional committee was told "there is a labor shortage in practically every industrial activity. It amounts to not less than that of 5 million men." From then on, excepting the peak years of World War II, labor moved into surplus.

But in those earlier years, the United States was one of the few countries where people were more likely to be needed than needy, poor though many were throughout. Wages and working conditions were terrible, but except for the most highly skilled trades, unions did not form. Why not?

The heavy percentage of foreign-born in the labor force provides one explanation. For immigrants America seemed a land of unparalleled opportunity and social mobility. Bad though conditions were, they were better than the harsh conditions of the home country, which usually meant the harsh conditions of the peasantry. Here there was hope, at least, hope for themselves and especially for their children; hopes not infrequently realized in the second generation. Why fight the bitter fight for unions if, perhaps, next year, or ten years from now, you would no longer *be* a worker?

Add to this the uncertainties and the hardships and the dangers of becoming involved in a union organizing drive and it may be understood why unions had difficulty in attracting converts. Employers' opposition to unions was unremitting and relentless, and they were greatly assisted by their friends in court and in the press—to say nothing of the pervasive view that *individual* hard work was the sure way to economic well-being. But the multiplicity of languages, religions, and national and cultural backgrounds of the labor force also rendered communication and solidarity among workers a most difficult thing. Employers did what they could to drive these wedges in deeper; "divide and rule" is as useful a stratagem for employers as it was for the British Empire.

Employers' determination to resist union organization took many forms: discrimination against union men on the job and in hiring, the use of labor spies within plants and unions, physical force or its threat, so-called "yellow-dog" contracts (where the condition of employment was to sign away the right to join a union), and the moving of plants to non-union areas in response to union activity. The press cooperated along the way in alerting the general public to anarchism, communism and other schemes to destroy all that is good, in the name of unionism. Local police, state militias, and federal troops could be relied upon to maintain "law and order," when and if the occasion arose, and private police (for example, "the Pinkertons") could do the job when it became especially nasty. And then there were the laws of the land and their interpretation by a friendly judiciary.

The law did not forbid unionism; it merely made the rights of labor quite explicitly inferior to those of property. In 1842 it was decided that a trade union was *not* a conspiracy (in *Commonwealth* v. *Hunt*); workers had a right to organize. Local, state, and federal courts up until 1930 interpreted that decision as meaning the right was effective only when it did not interfere with employers' rights—and strikes were seen as such interferences. Unions without the right to strike are like armies without weapons. Antitrust legislation was used more frequently against unions ("combinations in restraint of trade") than against business until 1914, when the Clayton Act exempted unions from such laws, but in 1921 that too was reversed (*Duplex Printing* v. *Deering*).

By 1915, about 8 percent of the labor force was in unions (2.5 million workers). World War I and its accompanying upswing in production and the need for cooperation between business, labor, and government allowed the figure to double. Although the labor force increased between 1920 and 1933, union membership declined from five million to fewer than three million. The 1920's were a period of friendship between business and government; they were the years of Harding, Coolidge, and Hoover, of the "American Plan," of the "Red Scare," of "welfare capitalism." The American Plan was an open shop—*non-union* shop—program. Its nature was epitomized by Mr. Dooley, the journalistic creation of Peter Finley Dunne, in a dialogue with his friend Hennessy: "But," says Hennessy, "these open shop min ye menshun say they are f'r unions if properly conducted." "Sure," says Mr. Dooley, "if properly conducted. An' there we are; an' how would they have thim conducted? No strikes, no rules, no contracts, no scales, hardly iny wages and damn few members."

In 1929 the Great Depression began. The prestige and power of the business community suffered. Businessmen had taken credit for all that was great in America; now business had somehow to explain how its genius had brought 25 percent unemployment, falling prices, bankruptcies, and the broad range of disasters of the Depression. Their explanation, which often placed the blame abroad, as did President Hoover, fell on deaf ears.

Enlightened corporate leaders had for decades seen the advantages of trade unionism, with effects both before and during World War I. But the largest number of businessmen were not so conscious of their own best interests over the long run, and in the euphoric 1920's even the "enlightened" leaders had changed their minds somewhat. In the Depression this view revived, and was given strength by the general unrest and by organizing drives of workers themselves. The government responded.

Inadequate legislation favoring unionism was made a part of the same law that created the National Recovery Administration in 1933. The inadequacy centered on the lack of provisions concerning business practices to fight against unionism, and of provisions that would enforce the legislation. These were substantially remedied by the Wagner (National Labor Relations) Act of 1935. After its passage the number of organized workers rose rapidly—from the low of 2.9 million in 1933, to 4 million in 1936, 7.3 million in 1938, 9.5 million in 1942, 13 million in 1946, and about 18 million by 1960, after which the rate of growth slowed down and stopped.

A casual reading of that numerical development might indicate that the labor legislation of the 1930's was the *cause* of this upsurge in trade union membership. It is perhaps more surprising that trade union growth was held back until the 1930's, than that it took place in and after that period. The development of mass production industries, the steady growth of the labor force, the virtual cessation of immigration in the 1920's, the loss of prestige by business after 1929, and the widespread social unrest of the Depression all must be given full weight in explaining the development of unions. So must the struggle of workers. The Wagner Act removed the legal obstacles to union organization and deprived employers of some of their traditional anti-union weapons. But the Act did not *establish* trade unions: the fight for union recognition was the major cause of industrial disputes between 1935 and World War II. Many of these disputes were extremely bitter and bloody; the waterfront strike in San Francisco of 1934 and the Republic Steel Strike of 1937 were the bloodiest of all.

If the increase in the ranks of organized labor after 1935 resembled a flood, the Wagner Act was not the cause of the flood so much as the opener of the flood gates. Be that as it may, the legislation was important, and since then there has been an increasing reliance upon government by both business and labor to develop "anti" or "pro" labor legislation. Since World War II, the balance has tipped in favor of business—with the Taft-Hartley Act of 1947 (which reduced the benefits of the Wagner Act), and the Landrum-Griffin Act of 1959 standing out prominently. Of no little importance for the future of industrial relations was the process by which this more recent legislation was supported and framed: it occurred in an atmosphere of klieg lights, spectacular and unrepresentative revelations and headlines, and the whole gamut of techniques increasingly associated with congressional investigations. As one authority has put it:

> The method by which the provisions of the [Landrum-Griffin Act] were enacted justifies the most extreme cynicism toward the legislative process.

Quite simply, the purposes of the various amendments were consistently and deliberately misrepresented to the general public, and for a good reason: Without the tremendous pressure exerted by public opinion, the Landrum-Griffin bill might never have passed the House. In a sense . . . it represents the failures of our democracy, for which all interested groups are in part to blame. Organized labor brought the new restrictions on its own head by insisting that amendments to the NLRA which it favored be included in any new legislation dealing with racketeering, corruption, and democratic union practices, and liberal legislators like Senator Kennedy yielded, presumably against their better judgment, to the union demands. Organized industry exploited the popular concern over dishonesty in labor-management relations and the lack of democracy in internal union affairs, and rallied support for NLRA amendments having little or no relevance to those issues. Finally, the average citizen continued to avoid acquainting himself with the basic problems involved, and fell back on the ingrained American habit of declaring, "There ought to be a law!"[18]

I'M ALL RIGHT, JACK

Up to this point in our discussion of organized labor we have been examining the development of a *trade union movement,* not a *labor movement.* The difference in terms is by no means a semantic one. Trade unions do and must fight for decent wages, working conditions, pensions, and, not least, their own continuity (which is called union security). Were they to cease to do so, general deterioration on all those matters would ensue. The union seeks to control the market in which labor power is sold; just as businesses seek to control the markets in which they sell their commodities. The goal in both cases is monopolistic control of the market; both cases are instances of what we have called "private mercantilism" earlier.

Without a trade union movement a labor movement could have no foundation of strength. But a labor movement goes beyond the terms of unionism; it is *political,* in the deepest sense of the term. A labor movement seeks State power, and seeks to gain it through being, or becoming affiliated with, a socialist movement.

As noted above, American trade unionism has had its political periods. One was from 1870 into the 1890's, before industrialism had taken a strong hold. The issues in that early period had to do with the money supply, with monopoly, with the manner of electing senators, and the like, issues affecting people in general, rather than workers in particular. Trade unions as such had little basis for national efforts, nor against

---

[18]Benjamin Aaron, "The Labor-Management Reporting and Disclosure Act of 1959," *Harvard Law Review,* vol. 73, no. 6 (April, 1960), pp. 1126–27. Both the Taft-Hartley and Landrum-Griffin Acts are amendments to the Wagner Act, or NLRA.

nationally powerful corporations. Urban workers did cooperate with the angry farmers of the period to bring about, finally, the Populist Movement, which had a radical wing. In the 1930's, the CIO worked closely with what they hoped would be a continuing and ever-more liberal New Deal, and a social context favorable to the needs of working people. Since the 1940's, trade unions have stayed political, but in a narrow sense; at the leadership level (at least) this has more often than not meant working *with,* not against, the interests of corporate power and the military, and this has been more than symbolized by the hawkish and conservative positions of the leader of the AFL-CIO, George Meany and Nixon's Secretary of Labor, Peter Brennan. Labor leadership functions within the context of a rigid bureaucratic structure, which it is to the leadership's interests to exploit and maintain; the best means of doing that is for them to concentrate the efforts of the union on "wage-only" types of issues—quite apart from their own political attitudes.

But the political attitudes of labor leaders, however they may have begun, are not fixed in concrete. They are apt illustrations of the co-optation process noted earlier. The clear tendency of Big Business is to make it evident that they will only "do business" with business-minded unions—except when conditions warrant an attempt to destroy them, too. They do this by coming down with overwhelming power—their own and power that they can muster in the media and the courts—on socialist-minded labor leaders and movements.[19] Only those leaders and unions that find ways of working *within* the system find survival and success a feasible matter. Samuel Gompers, the first leader of the AFL, spread the slogan "reward our friends and punish our enemies." Business has found that to be a useful strategy in its dealings with organized labor, also.

It is more than understandable that trade unions would concentrate as much as they have on job control; the alternative is utter helplessness in the face of business power. In confining themselves largely to that aim and in doing so little to organize the overwhelming majority of *unorganized* workers, however, the unions have also found themselves adopting much the same aims and means as their business opponents. Thus, not only do unions attempt to control the supply of labor and use the strike as their principal weapon—both essential means—but they

---

[19]A striking instance of this was in the attempt of the Waterfront Employers Association to have the leader of the longshore union, Harry Bridges, deported. Six trials occurred (beginning in the 1930's), in which the charge against Bridges (an Australian by birth) was that he was a member of the Communist Party and therefore deportable. The employers had the constant cooperation of the Immigration Service and what was proved to be their stable of paid informers. By the time of the sixth trial (after World War II), the *employers* moved to end the process, having found that the ILWU was a stabilizing influence on the waterfront.

have also resorted to gangsters, racketeers, and physical violence for both defensive and offensive purposes, against both business and rival union organizers. The record in all these cases shows not only that the tactics of labor find their counterparts in the tactics of business, but also that business used each of these tactics first (and simultaneously). In the absence of a prolonged and deep commitment to fundamental social change on the part of labor—a labor movement—little else could be expected.[20]

None of this should be construed, it must be repeated, to mean that labor's efforts to organize or their uses of strength have been either unnecessary or damaging from the viewpoint of *all* workers. Unorganized workers have gained from the successes of the organized; the organized themselves have gained more, and have also learned organizational discipline which has been and can still be of fundamental importance for larger struggles. Nor would it be wise to overlook the difference between the functioning of the top bureaucracy of labor and the quite different functioning of *local* leaders, to say nothing of the growing militancy and enlarged focus of rank and file union members. Still, much more is needed if the ordinary people of this country are to have a decent existence in an economic, political, and social sense. Without the participation of trade unions in that larger struggle, the prospects for working people in this country are seriously, perhaps fatally, diminished. It is not only the success of trade unions in making some headway on "pork-chops" issues for themselves that holds them back from a broader view; it is also the degree to which organized workers participate in the patterns of racial and sexual discrimination and fear that so much characterize our history.[21] This is the Achilles heel of labor's strength in America; it is quite likely to be the terminal cancer of any viable American body politic. Further examination of this point is in order.

ALL AGAINST ALL

We have to go back to the 1880's, at the very latest, to tie labor history in with the more general social history of America. Although immigra-

---

[20]An analysis and history of these matters (up to the early 1930's) is provided by Louis Adamic, *Dynamite** (New York: Viking, 1934). C. Wright Mills, *New Men of Power* (New York: Harcourt Brace Jovanovich, 1948) provided an early study of the nature and probabilities of labor bureaucracy.

[21]Which is not to overlook the many efforts made by unions throughout their history who fought for the breaking down of racial barriers—most notably in the Communist-led unions in the 1930's—and "equal pay for equal work" in the face of sex discrimination. Whether self-interested or not, such efforts are no less noteworthy, not least because unions were usually unique in pursuing them.

tion had been increasing since the 1850's, as we have seen, it was during the 1880's that the great waves of immigration from the poorer parts of Europe and from Asia began. By 1910 over one million immigrants a year were arriving, mostly from southern and southeastern Europe (over 200,000 southern Italians alone came in that year). These people came at a time when industrialization had taken strong hold and when the conditions of factory and city were becoming increasingly ugly. From the viewpoint of settled Americans (who were themselves immigrants from an earlier period, and from "better" areas of northern Europe such as England and Germany) these newcomers were also "increasingly ugly." Their language, their religion, their appearance—strange, "swarthy," Catholic, Jewish—set them against their predecessors, who, apart from the Irish, were mostly Protestant, and likely to be reasonably well-established.

America had been well-prepared for a translation of all this into divisions and hostility that were many-faceted. It had been prepared by our habituation to oppressing and even exterminating red, black, and brown peoples. The Populist Movement of the 1890's, which saw un-precedented political cooperation between poor whites and blacks, was the occasion for an intensification of racism. From the mid-1890's on, Jim Crow laws spread and deepened, and lynching became so common that it went unnoticed in the press (there were as many as a thousand a year officially recorded). The prior and continuing oppression of Native Americans joined with stepped-up oppression of black people and a rapid growth of American nationalism, religious bigotry and attitudes of cultural superiority. Savage developments in the eastern half of the country combined with savage developments in the western half, as Spanish-speaking and Asian immigrants were mistreated and killed (the lynching of Chinese was common in San Francisco at the turn of the century) while being exploited in the fields, mines, factories, and railroads.

Racial oppression and ethnic and religious hatreds did not begin in the United States, it should go without saying. But the competitive and combative atmosphere of the United States, taken together with the long-standing and well-entrenched acceptance of the Puritan work ethic and its corollary of economic individualism, made it easy for bigots and unscrupulous businessmen to exploit those pervasive inclinations. Given the enormous power and prestige of business in this country, workers would have had difficulty under the best of circumstances in forming unions or developing a labor movement. But workers accepted and developed internalized obstacles in their thinking and behavior, obstacles to thinking of themselves in terms of class solidarity.

The "Wobblies," never very influential in American labor or politics, lived by the slogan "an injury to one is an injury to all." The development of America has allowed most white men to see injuries to some as necessary to their own well-being—or even as desirable in and of themselves. Solidarity is a precious and delicate plant; it can scarcely grow or survive in a desert windstorm. It would be foolish to posit some inherent defect in the "American character" to explain the depth and pervasiveness of racism and sexism in our country, as foolish as it would be to ignore their existence in other countries. But it is not foolish to note how these characteristics have become accentuated and institutionalized in the United States to the point where it now appears that the very possibility of a decent future depends squarely on whether or not Americans can find ways to eliminate these practices and attitudes from our society.

Racism is one of the two leading social cancers that lead some human beings to view others as being less than human; the other is sexism. Historical and contemporary records point conclusively to one set of facts: nonwhite people and women of any color have been systematically deprived of basic human rights, have been systematically discriminated against in the kinds and levels of education normally available, have been systematically denied access to higher levels of work, and have been paid less for the same work when they could get it.[22]

TABLE 6
Median Incomes, 1964

FOR MEN	
Nonwhites' as a percentage of whites'	66%
FOR WOMEN	
Nonwhites' as a percentage of whites'	69%
FOR WHITES	
Women's as a percentage of men's	59%
FOR NONWHITES	
Women's as a percentage of men's	52%

SOURCE: Marilyn Power Goldberg, "The Economic Exploitation of Women," originally in *Liberation* (October, 1969). Reprinted in part in *RRPE* (Spring, 1970), in David M. Gordon, ed., *Problems in Political Economy: An Urban Perspective** (Boston: D. C. Heath, 1971), and in Edwards et al., *The Capitalist System*, cited earlier. These are U. S. Department of Labor data.

---

[22]There is at least one important difference between racism and sexism that gives the former a different *economic* meaning than the latter. It is that women share the status and class of their fathers and husbands, quite generally. That is of course part of the meaning of sexism. But it does mean that there are fewer women as a percentage of all women who are *poor*, say, than blacks as a percentage of all blacks. *Within* a given class or racial category, women are worse off than men—as measured by jobs available, pay for the same jobs, etc., as Table 6 suggests.

Summarizing the data, Goldberg points out that so far as money incomes are concerned, "this relative earning position, moreover, has not improved in the last twenty-five years, except for nonwhite women. White men have the highest median income, then nonwhite men, then white women, and finally nonwhite women." In December, 1972, the U.S. Department of Labor's Women's Bureau reported that the gap between men's and women's salaries and wages had widened substantially in the preceding years: full-time working women's wages as a percentage of men's had dropped from 64 percent in 1955 to 57 percent in 1970. (*New York Times,* December 28, 1972)

Incomes are of course an important measure of life in this society, but they are only a quantitative measure, and not an adequate measure even of that. It would of course be desirable if nobody's income were below the government's "poverty line" or, even better, if nobody lived below the level of "deprivation." That so many people live below those lines in this very rich society should tell us that the elimination of poverty is not an economic question, nor are its origins or its consequences to be measured in narrow economic ways. It has been calculated, for example, that something under $14 billion annually would eliminate all family money incomes below the poverty line. A society with a GNP well in excess of a trillion dollars whose governments spend in excess of three hundred billion dollars annually could not be economically strained by such a piddling amount. (Especially when we consider that other costs of government would thereby be reduced, and that other costs of government *should* be reduced.) That such a possibility is neither known about nor supported by most Americans is not a matter of economics or resources; it is a matter of attitudes and power.

The attitudes are those that look down upon the poor, and that despise and fear the nonwhite segment of the poor, which most white Americans would be surprised to learn constitute only one-third of the total officially described as poor. The power *not* to act along such lines is held at the top, but it is supported by the vast middle, who are mostly white, and mostly ordinary working people. Even were the money spent, to repeat, poverty would not be eliminated—not just because poverty is a relative matter, but because it is a social matter in the fullest sense. Its origins and its meanings are to be found in a complex pattern of inadequate education, health, and housing; in racial and sexual discrimination; in political powerlessness; in demoralization and a profound sense of hopelessness and disbelief. That such patterns are allowed and encouraged to exist in a society at once so rich and so proud of its watchwords of freedom and equality points to the profound dehumanization of the largest percentage of Americans.

How has American capitalism managed to so dehumanize Americans? We need only think through what has been said earlier in other connections. Americans from the beginning were told and were convinced that a capitalist economy would, when functioning successfully, achieve not only maximum incomes, but the freest (and best) of societies. The fact that this was believed while at the same time Native Americans were being killed and shoved aside, and Africans enslaved, means that racism, a virus carried over from Europe, had found a particularly receptive host in the United States. The success of American capitalism relied upon many things, of course, but, most relevant here, such success depended upon a single-minded concern with economic gain. This single-mindedness was made possible by a society that led its people to believe that other matters would somehow take care of themselves, or that they would be taken care of by others, in a government in which all would be represented by periodic voting.

For those at or near the top of society, the social context thus contained only one serious obstacle to their search for money and power —the competition of others also at the top. For those on the bottom, the simple struggle to eke out a tolerable level of life was all-consuming. Competition in markets came to mean competition of one segment of society against the other, as people became commodities, and both subjects and objects of gain. People as well as products have price tags. Life becomes commercial life; life becomes commercialized; it becomes dehumanized, quantified, trivialized—alienated.

Such talk has become common these days, as we now hear of the need to think of "the quality of life"—although it is difficult to conceive why what is obvious to most people must now be worked up as though it were a complicated new problem. Withal, the social scientists continue to think and work in quantitative terms, to seek to quantify the qualitative; and because quantification can never be the starting point of social analysis, the quantitative data and measures that are employed have themselves become part of the problem. The history of the "war on poverty" in the United States is a case in point.

POVERTY AMIDST PLENTY

The degree to which so many Americans have walled themselves off from the ugly side of our reality was captured well by Michael Harrington, when he spoke of "the invisible poor."[23] In 1962, when the United States was congratulating itself on having to face the problems of affluence, there were by a highly conservative estimate (see Wilcox's quote below) nine million families plus five million unrelated individuals living at annual incomes below the official poverty line—that is, about

---

[23]In his *The Other America** (Baltimore: Penguin, 1962).

one-fifth of the nation. Poverty cannot be understood, let alone eliminated, by thinking of it in purely quantitative terms; but it would be a step in the right direction to use accurate and meaningful quantitative definitions, at the very least. Because the government's definitions have become *the* definitions, it is important to show just how inadequate—some would say ludicrous, others obscene—those definitions are.

It was in 1964 that the government, responding to Harrington's book and the civil rights turmoil of the time, developed an estimate of the number of poor in America. This was done by the Council of Economic Advisers, at President Johnson's order. It is worth quoting a respected textbook on how that estimate was accomplished:

> The Council's estimate was based upon a study by the Social Security Administration of the income needed to support a nonfarm family of four. The SSA had established two standards for such a family, both based on estimates of dietary costs prepared by the Department of Agriculture: [1] a "low-cost" budget, permitting the minimum diet consistent with the food preferences of the lowest third of the population and adequate to avoid basic nutritional deficiencies. ... The resulting budget stood at *$3,955.* This called for a far higher level of expenditure than welfare agencies were allowing for families receiving public assistance. *To meet the administrative need of these bodies,* the SSA prepared ... [2] an "economy budget" based on a *deficiency diet designed for temporary or emergency use* ... set[ting] the total budget at *$3,165.* On the basis of this figure, the CEA adopted *$3,000* as its family poverty line ..., [and] $1,500 as the line for a single individual. It thus found ... some 35,000,000 people, a fifth of the nation, to be in poverty in 1962.[24]

Poverty must be "defined" by someone; as things go these days that someone means the government. Inadequate though the definitions have been, both qualitatively and quantitatively, they may seem less so in the future if recent plans materialize. The *New York Times* reported on April 4, 1973, under the headline "U.S. to Redefine What 'Poverty' Is," that the Office of Management and Budget (directed by Roy Ash, formerly head of Litton Industries, one of the fancier conglomerates) is "quietly examining the possibility of doing away with federal use of the word 'poverty' and of changing the income figures used to define the poor, 'because current usage exaggerates the [rising] number of poor.'" Presumably the new definition will be well-established by 1984; until the dispensation is provided, we will go on with the Johnsonian style.

The $3,000 estimate of 1964, which has increased since by the rate of inflation to $4,300 in 1973, still is the universally used criterion for

---

[24]Clair Wilcox, *Toward Social Welfare* (Homewood, Ill.: Irwin, 1969), pp. 26–7. Italics mine. The "emergency use" diet was first concocted by the Office of Civil Defense for a post-nuclear period! The article by Donald Light, cited earlier, is useful for this section.

estimating the extent of poverty in the United States. As we saw earlier, the Bureau of Labor Statistics—an agency with more of a civil service and less of a vulgarly political position than the Council of Economic Advisers, which is appointed by and serves the President—calculated $7,214 as necessary for a "minimum budget for food, clothing, and housing, with little left over," for 1971. If poverty is to be defined in quantitative income terms, that figure seems more compelling than one designed for "emergency" periods: poverty is not only an emergency but a persisting condition.

To understand its persistence requires going beyond figures and into relationships, which can be seen as a set of vicious circles. To be born poor is to live in inadequate housing in over-crowded neighborhoods with bad schools, and little or no recreational facilities; it is to be mired down in an atmosphere of hopelessness—to say nothing of poor health, of crime, of price-gouging in the stores, of job discrimination, and of political underrepresentation. The psychological impact of such living can only be imagined (or read about) by those who have not experienced it directly; but it takes little imagination to perceive that those who are born poor are likely to stay poor and to have children who will be poor —with here and there an exception that proves the rule. Why, in a rich society like the United States would poverty for tens of millions of people persist? Why would poverty be institutionalized?

One way to begin to answer such questions is to ask another question: Who benefits from the persistence of poverty? And who pays? The easy and the most widespread answer suggests that nobody—except the welfare recipient—benefits, and that the upper layers of the society pay. But analysis shows otherwise, which it will be worth pursuing here. Two recent essays will be cited, one from the liberal and the other from the radical quarter.

In an article entitled "The Uses of Poverty: The Poor Pay All," Professor Herbert Gans has listed and discussed thirteen "functions" of poverty. "Functions" refer to "those observed consequences of a phenomenon which make for the adaptation or adjustment of a given . . . set of interest groups, socio-economic classes, and other population aggregates with shared values that 'inhabit' a social system." In brief, the useful functions posited by Gans are: 1) The existence of poverty ensures that society's "dirty work" will be done; 2) The very low wages of the poor subsidize a variety of economic activities that benefit the affluent (as domestic servants, for instance), and the poor pay a disproportionate share of all taxes (see Chapter Eight); 3) Poverty creates jobs for middle-income people who "serve" the poor, such as social workers, prison guards, etc.; 4) The poor buy goods that others wouldn't, which is profitable to those who produce and sell them. These four functions are *economic* uses of the poor; the remaining nine are social and political.

They include the self-defined elevation in moral and social standing that middle-class attitudes toward the poor allow to the middle-class; the absorption by the poor of the costs of socio-economic change, being powerless to do otherwise (most vividly, these days, in being pushed out of their homes for freeways, urban renewal, etc.); their availability as cannon-fodder for wars; their utility as a basis for arguing against liberal or left social change.[25]

Howard Wachtel, writing as a radical economist, does not dispute the kind of points made by Gans, but he seeks to explore the *causes* of poverty. He points out, quite rightly, that everything said about the *uses* of poverty is consistent with an attitude that places the *causes* in the poor's shortcomings as individuals. Those shortcomings usually fall under the headings of laziness, shiftlessness, and the like. But most of the poor 1) work full-time but at wages that leave them (and their families) underneath the official poverty line, or half-time because they cannot gain full-time jobs; 2) are handicapped and unable to work; or 3) are retired, having worked at low incomes when younger.[26]

How people get into and get stuck in such a situation was suggested by the metaphor of the vicious circle, above. More concretely (and only in part), we may look at the relationship of education to jobs, and of the jobs of the poor to the existence of the "dual economy." And finally we may examine the role of the State in the perpetuation of poverty. By now everyone must be aware of the "tracking system" (which in the early years of schooling classifies children according to tests and performance that do not always accurately reflect cultural background, thus forcing them toward lower or upper income occupations by virtue of the curricula in which they are placed) in primary and secondary education, and the relationship between that and subsequent education, to say nothing of the wretched quality of the primary and secondary schools attended by most of the poor (whether white or nonwhite).[27]

---

[25]Herbert Gans is Professor of Sociology and Planning at M.I.T. This article will be found in *Social Policy* (July/August, 1971).

[26]Wachtel's analysis, "Capitalism and Poverty in America: Paradox or Contradiction?" is in *Monthly Review* (June, 1972), along with two other essays supplementing his views by David Gordon and Barry Bluestone. Bluestone's essay is a version of the Statement before the Joint Economic Committee of Congress referred to earlier, on the dual economy.

[27]For extended discussion of the general role of education in maintaining poverty and class distinctions, see Samuel Bowles, "Contradictions in U.S. Higher Education," in James Weaver, ed., *Modern Political Economy*, pp. 165–200, his "Unequal Education and the Social Division of Labor," *RRPE* (Fall/Winter, 1971), and Herb Gintis, "Education, Technology, and the Characteristics of Worker Productivity," *American Economic Review* (May, 1971). See also the fine book by Miriam Wasserman, *The School Fix, NYC, USA** (New York: Simon & Schuster, Clarion, 1970), for an intensive study of one school system in full display.

Education, beginning at the very first years, can and should be a process in which the young not only realize their creative and practical possibilities in terms of their life's work, but also a process whereby human beings learn to appreciate and to understand nature, society, human culture, and themselves. Instead, and especially for the poor, schools have taken on the quality of disciplinary barracks (and, for the better off, as Maynard Hutchins once put it, "play pens"), disillusioning and embittering both students and teachers, to say nothing of parents and taxpayers. Presumably, in a society as rich as ours something better is economically possible. Given the concentration of power that exists in the society, it may be assumed that if the powerful had the will to change the situation, they could find the way. That the educational system deteriorates, rather than improves, allows one to conclude that a system designed for human needs and possibilities is not high on the priority list of those with power, if it is on the list at all.

The young who are maleducated and miseducated quite naturally find themselves able to get only the meanest jobs once they drop out of school or graduate. They get jobs in what Bluestone and O'Connor call the competitive (or "peripheral and irregular") sector, where productivity, power, and incomes are low. What the State does to mitigate these conditions—through manpower training programs and the like—will be examined in our last chapter. There we will see that at the very best, State programs do no more than hold the line, and that more often they contribute to making a bad situation worse.

AFFLUENCE AND REALITY

It seems appropriate now to recall our criticism of the notion of "prosperity" in the 1920's (discussed in Chapter Four), and to relate that to the current notion of "affluence." Like so much else in the way of judgment in America, the *judgment* of affluence originates in the upper middle class and has a quantitative basis; it depends upon the height of real per capita income, absolutely and in comparison with other *nations*. If affluence is meant to suggest more than that, the notion dissolves— if, that is, we assume that affluence has some reference to the well-being of the *society* as distinct from a small fraction of its people; if we define that well-being in quantitative terms that do not include the military and the mountains of wasteful and trivial (to say nothing of offensive) production; if we examine what is available to the population in terms of convenient transportation, clean air and water, health, educational and recreational facilities, as well as insurance against natural and man-made disasters. If we combine qualitative with quantitative judgments,

in short, we may reckon our society as being closer to general impover-
ishment than to affluence.

Earlier, we pointed out that if (as is impossible in capitalist society)
money income had been divided equally among all families in 1970,
each would have about $11,000, and that in 1971 it took just about that
amount for the average family to sustain a moderate budget in the
average city. Only two-thirds of the population lives in cities, of course,
and it costs less to live outside the city, generally. But that figure is a
before-tax figure; and all taxes take about one-third of the GNP. If we
were to deduct a third from the $11,000 (or $12,000, taking account of
GNP increases since 1971), the national average would be down to just
about the amount needed for a *minimum* budget. Of course, some taxes
are used for expenditures that are life-serving, but it stretches the imagination to believe that is the case with most governmental expenditures,
if one takes account of the military, the excessive highway system,
interest payments on the national debt (which is accumulated mostly in
or for war and going almost entirely to upper income groups) subsidies
to upper income farmers and agricultural corporations, stockpiling corporations, and the like. Partisans of almost any viewpoint could quibble
until doomsday about the arithmetic of such conjectures, but what
would remain, after all was said and done, would not be a level or
quality of life that would suggest "affluence."

Like the notion of the prosperity of the twenties, the affluence of the
recent past is for most Americans a cruel joke. So was the "glory that
was Rome" for most Romans, something other than glorious. The decline and fall of the Roman empire has been cited innumerable times by
critics of western society, as though what happened there and then can
happen here and now. It cannot, because the societies have more differences than similarities. Some of the similarities are nonetheless telling.
One of the most respected of the historians of Rome, in a chapter
entitled "The Disorganization of Public Service," wrote (in 1898) an
analytical condemnation of Roman society that brought together the
interaction of poverty, inequality of income and wealth, overweening
power and rampant greed that with only minor adjustments might have
been written of our country today:

> It will be seen that in a society in which poverty is almost branded with
> infamy, poverty is steadily increasing and wealth becoming more insolent
> and aggressive; that the disinherited, in the face of an omnipotent govern-
> ment, are carrying brigandage even up to the gates of Rome; that parents
> are selling their children into slavery; that public buildings are falling into
> decay; that the service on the great post roads is becoming disorganised.
> ... [F]raud and greed are everywhere triumphant, ... the rich are growing
> richer and more powerful, while the poor are becoming poorer and more
> helpless. ...

The overwhelming tragedy of that age was the result not of violent and sudden calamities; it was prepared by the slow, merciless action of social and economic laws, and deepened by the perverse energy of government, and the cupidity and cruelty of the rich and highly-placed.[28]

READING SUGGESTIONS

The history of labor has been treated only superficially above; those wishing to gain an adequate basis for judgment will find no shortage of books. No one book on such a controversial area can stand as sufficient. A good place to begin is with Len De Caux, *Labor Radicals** (Boston: Beacon Press, 1970), which takes the story from the Wobblies up to the very recent past by one who was part of it and a fine writer to boot. The classic source book and compendium is John R. Commons, et al., *History of Labor in the United States,* 4 vols. (New York: Macmillan, 1918–1935). Of the several Marxist studies of labor history in America, the most comprehensive is the multivolume work of Philip Foner, *History of Labor in the United States** (New York: International Publishers, 1947 *et seq.*). Much has been written of the colorful "Wobblies." The definitive study is probably Melvyn Dubofsky, *We Shall Be All** (Chicago: Quadrangle, 1969). A convenient survey is Patrick Renshaw, *The Wobblies** (New York: Doubleday; Anchor Books, 1968). The drama and vitality of the Wobblies is caught best in the anthology by Joyce L. Kornbluh, *Rebel Voices** (Ann Arbor: University of Michigan Press, 1964).

Turning to inequality, poverty, racism, and sexism: the most penetrating analysis of American poverty is that of Ben Seligman, *Permanent Poverty,* cited earlier. A useful book of readings is Robert E. Will and Harold G. Vatter, eds., *Poverty in Affluence** (New York: Harcourt Brace Jovanovich, 1970). An excellent analytical treatment of urban blacks' economic situation is William K. Tabb, *The Political Economy of the Black Ghetto** (New York: Norton, 1970). Two excellent studies of broader scope are Robert L. Allen, *Black Awakening in Capitalist America** (New York: Doubleday; Anchor Books, 1970), and Raymond S. Franklin and Solomon Resnik, *The Political Economy of Racism** (New York: Harper & Row, 1973). Patricia Cayo Sexton, *Spanish Harlem** (New York: Harper & Row, 1965), studies the conditions of Spanish-speaking Americans. G. Osofsky, *Harlem: The Making of a Ghetto** (New York: Harper & Row, 1966) examines the history of black people in New York City through the 19th century and up to about 1930; in doing so he reveals how pressures and policies have worked to create and maintain patterns of discrimination from the very beginning.

---

[28]Samuel Dill, *Roman Society in the Last Century of the Western Empire** (New York: Meridian, 1958), pp. 228–9, 244.

A profound recent work on inequality and the context within which it is created and accepted is William Ryan, *Blaming the Victim** (New York: Vintage, 1971), wherein the author attempts the most difficult of tasks: trying to show people the ideological and mythological fog within which their attitudes move.

References to works on sexism could be multiplied as each day passes, for the literature is growing rapidly. A book of readings that makes a good starting-place is Robin Morgan, ed., *Sisterhood is Powerful** (New York: Random House, 1970). The economic aspects of sexism are explored in Margaret Benston, "The Political Economy of Women's Liberation," *Monthly Review* (September, 1969); M. and J. Roundtree, "More on the Political Economy . . .," *Monthly Review* (January, 1970); Peggy Morton, "A Woman's Work is Never Done," *Leviathan* (May, 1970); and URPE in its *RRPE,* vol. 4, no. 3 (July, 1972), has an entire issue, *The Political Economy of Women,* with about twenty essays ranging over a broad range of relevant questions. Eli Zaretsky, "Capitalism, the Family, and Personal Life: Part 1," *Socialist Revolution,* vol. 3, nos. 1 & 2 (January–April, 1973), after a cogent review of major analytical contributions of the Women's Movement, goes on to provide a penetrating and original historical analysis (a model of what Marxian analysis can be) of the development of sexism and the family under capitalist conditions.

The literature concerned with oppression of Native Americans is growing also. A powerful historical treatment (of the period 1860–1890) is Dee Brown, *Bury My Heart at Wounded Knee** (New York: Bantam, 1971). A study of contemporary conditions from a moderate standpoint, and perhaps therefore all the more shocking, is Edgar S. Cahn, ed., *Our Brother's Keeper: The Indian in White America** (New York: World, 1969). Also consult the bibliography of *To Serve the Devil* (cited earlier) for further readings on racism as it has affected all groups in the United States.

The term "class" (working class, ruling class) has been used frequently in the text. My own understanding of the origins and the meanings of class distinctions have been woven through the materials beginning with Chapter One. For other viewpoints, and for definitional treatments of this vital and complicated matter, see T. B. Bottomore, *Classes in Modern Society** (New York: Vintage, 1966); R. H. Tawney, *Equality** (New York: Capricorn, 1961; originally published in 1929); G. William Domhoff, *Who Rules America?** (Englewood Cliffs N.J.: Prentice-Hall, Spectrum, 1967) and his *The Higher Circles** (New York: Vintage, 1971). *Power, Politics and People: The Collected Essays of C. Wright Mills,** edited by Irving Louis Horowitz (New York: Oxford University Press, 1963) contains many essays on class, power, ideology, education and other issues most relevant to many of the chapters of this book. Marx and Veblen use class analysis throughout their writings, and I won't attempt to cite particular works. Mention of the "new working class" was made early in this chapter; on that, see Herb Gintis, "The New Working Class and Revolutionary Youth," *Socialist Revolution,* vol. 1, no. 3 (May–June, 1970). Finally, see the penetrating studies of Richard Sennett and Jonathan Cobb, *The Hidden Injuries of Class** (New York: Knopf, 1972) and of F. Piven and R. Cloward, *Regulating the Poor: The Functions of Public Welfare** (New York: Vintage, 1971).

chapter six

Nature and Nurture;
Country and City

Black spruce and Norway pine,
Douglas fir and Red cedar,
Scarlet oak and Shagbark hickory.
We built a hundred cities and a thousand towns—
But at what a cost!
We cut the top off the Alleghenies and sent it down the river.
We cut the top off Minnesota and sent it down the river.
We cut the top off Wisconsin and sent it down the river.
We left the mountains and the hills slashed and burned,
And moved on.

(Pare Lorentz, from the soundtrack of the film, *The River*)

They are herding our hearts down freeways.
The architects of America say
This is how it will be in another century:
We will join with armies of geese
In the cities of weeds,
Living on grass, in love with our own dung.

(Floyce Alexander, *Los Angeles*)

The problems we now face in our environment and in our cities are problems of whole systems in dynamic imbalance. These problems have existed in significant degree from our very first years; they are simultaneously physical and social, economic and political, psychological and historical and ideological, in their origins and in their continuation and worsening over time. Can conventional economics grapple successfully with such problems?

Conventional economics is abstract; it is concerned with purely quantitative *market* relationships; it takes both nature and historical time as "given," as it does also with technology; it has both a limited and an incorrect view of human psychology; and it totally ignores ideological and developmental matters. Such an economics can provide little understanding of either the nature or the origins of what now mounts to the crisis stage. Indeed, it is precisely what economists consider most necessary and most desirable—that is, maximization—that, in America's historical development, accounts for much of what has "gone wrong." Those who have exploited our natural resources, whether farmers, mineral or timber companies, or whatever, and those who have "developed" and ravaged our cities, have been businessmen or have moved in tandem with them. To provide a society dominated by such motivations with a market economics of maximization is like providing an alcoholic with directions to the nearest bar.

In the 19th century and the first part of the 20th there was already awareness of both environmental and urban problems, and around the turn of the century movements to urge reforms emerged in both areas: the "conservation movement" and the "progressive movement." Their views as to the nature and the resolution of these problems did not lead them to examine basic institutions or to question the processes fostered by those institutions. They were reformers who, though often idealistic, were concerned with the economic and social inefficiency of rapacious resource use and of teeming and unsightly cities. They were concerned with making the existing system work better, more efficiently, and less turbulently, over time.[1]

The conservationists and urban progressives, who were often the same people, sought to bring order out of the chaos induced by the rapid and pervasive industrialization and urbanization of the turn of the century. Their contemporary counterparts are the liberal ecologists and urban planners. Their viewpoint is partially, but only partially, valid. They seek to eliminate dangerous and destructive resource utilization and deep inadequacies in urban existence, an aim entirely praiseworthy. But they view these problems as *extrinsic* to the American system. Quite correctly, they assume that American capitalism does not *need* blighted cities, polluted air, cut-over land, and wasted resources. Yet they fail to see that for capitalist development to proceed satisfactorily in its own terms—as distinct from human terms—the economy cannot be constrained so as to *forestall* blighted cities, polluted air, and the rest. This analytical failing means that mainstream-liberal policy recommendations must be at best inadequate and at worst damaging. The problem of the inaccurate compass being worse than none at all, once more.

---

[1]See Faulkner, *The Decline of Laissez-Faire,* Chapter 15 ("The Era of Reform"), and also his *Quest for Social Justice* (New York: Macmillan, 1931), a social history of the progressive period. The best treatment of the conservation movement is Samuel P. Hays, *Conservation and the Gospel of Efficiency* (Cambridge: Harvard University Press, 1959). James Ridgeway, *The Politics of Ecology* (New York: Dutton, 1971), traces the development back to the English Industrial Revolution, through the pre-World War I period, and up to the present.

To repeat an important point: the prime reason for the *economic* dynamism of American capitalism has been precisely that it has been *socially* unconstrained. Now, when discussion is no longer about problems, as earlier in the century, but about crises, the universe of discourse must alter to meet our sense that time is running out.

Economists and other social scientists, once in the background of such discussions, have today moved more to the fore. Whether economists have anything to contribute depends upon whether or not economics moves toward the dynamic perspective of political economy (and similarly, in the appropriate ways, for the rest of social science). If it does so, and as it does so, it will have to be informed by some firm idea of the continuity of our development, of what brought us to where we are today, and of the manner in which business impulses have meshed with social and political developments to push us ever more rapidly to our critical present. The story begins with farmers, and their much idealized "way of life."

FARMING AS A WAY OF BUSINESS

The United States is the most industrialized of all societies. Yet, our social nature remains inexplicable if we ignore the dominating role played by farmers in the shaping of our history, our outlook, and our domestic and foreign policies. The first settlers came here for many reasons, but they all found themselves exploiting the land (and shoving aside or slaughtering its original inhabitants). Up to the end of the 19th century, and despite the great surge of industrialization that began around 1850, the numbers, the prestige, the economic importance, and the social outlook of farmers continued to take a leading role in setting the tone of American life. The tone was businesslike, and it was expansionist.

It began that way. Farming is, of course, "a way of life," as its proponents so often say. But American agriculture has been given its qualities and direction by those who are best at making money from the cultivation of and speculation in land. Less than a decade after the first settlers set foot at what became Jamestown, Virginia, their livelihood was dependent upon tobacco exports to England. So intense was their concentration on the marketing of tobacco that the Governor of Virginia (in 1616) had to *require* that each colonist plant at least two acres of corn for himself and each male servant, to avoid starvation.[2]

---

[2]These "indentured servants" were before long outnumbered by African slaves. A useful overall history of American agriculture is U.S. Department of Agriculture, *Farmers in a Changing World* (Washington: USGPO, 1940), especially the first three hundred pages or so. Like many governmental studies written in the Roosevelt years, this book is remarkably objective, which can not usually be said of those issued today.

There were of course great differences in the agriculture of the southern and northern regions of the American colonies. But the differences were in the meanness or generosity of climate and soil, not in intentions. For those who set the tone of farming, the intention was to make money, not subsistence, from the land. The South was by far the most productive region, with its rich soils and long growing seasons. Beginning with tobacco in the 17th century, the South went on to raise indigo (for dyeing), rice, cotton, and sugar. Slaves were used in tobacco cultivation; but large-scale slavery awaited large-scale cultivation: plantations. Plantations began with rice and indigo, but became most characteristic with sugar, and, of course, cotton. Cotton became king as three developments merged: the British industrial revolution (whose leading sector was cotton textiles), competition from Mexican long-staple cotton, and the invention of the cotton gin in 1793 (which made practicable the use of short-staple cotton, the variety best-suited to the southern lands). The entire range of southern agriculture was commercialized, and dependent upon foreign markets—entirely dependent before the Revolution, and critically so thereafter.

The economics of southern farming kept the plantation owner and the small farmer alike in debt, as they responded to market conditions and unfavorable bargaining terms set by powerful brokers, shippers, and financiers in (usually) London. Indebtedness combined with the rapid exhaustion of the soil (especially in tobacco and cotton cultivation) to make the southern agriculturist an expansionist in two ways. He had to keep moving westward in search of more fertile lands; his marketing focus was necessarily international.[3]

In the North, nature was less generous than in the South, but still very generous indeed by comparison with, say, typical European conditions. The colonies in New York, Pennsylvania, and New Jersey raised grains and livestock, for domestic but also for export sale mostly to the Caribbean and the Mediterranean. The harsh climate and rocky soils of New England made those settlers into part-time farmers, and into part-time loggers or handicraftsmen, whalers and fishermen, until commerce and manufacturers took hold enough to create urban markets for their diversified farms. But, like their counterparts in the so-called Middle Colonies and in the South, the New England farmers were always looking westward, and were always tied into foreign markets, directly or indirectly, for their economic well-being.

There was always a multiplicity of reasons for westward expansion from all the Colonies, and there continued to be long after independence. But tied to those other reasons—exhausted soils, excessive com-

---

[3]See Eugene Genevose, *The Political Economy of Slavery** (New York: Pantheon, 1965), especially Chapter 4.

petition, a simple restless itch to move on—was one constant: land speculation. We cannot know the degree to which the westward movement would have been slowed without land speculation, but we may be sure it would have been a significant reduction quantitatively, and that the whole quality of the process would have been much altered. On that score, there is no disagreement among historians. Veblen put it in his own way:

> Habitually and with singular uniformity the American farmers have aimed to acquire real estate at the same time that they have worked at their trade as husbandmen. . . . They have habitually "carried" valuable real estate at the same time that they have worked the soil of so much of their land as they could take care of, in as effectual a manner as they could under these circumstances. They have been cultivators of the main chance as well as of the fertile soil. . . .[4]

FARMERS, POLITICS, AND POWER

The passion for increasingly more land, in a country predominantly agricultural in its functions and outlook, meant that the political issues roiling American life in the century before the Civil War would revolve around the land, its value, and its uses. And so it was. *Land policy*—the accessibility, the size, and the price of western lands—persisted as a boiling issue. And, since the ownership of lands always required access to money and credit, monetary policy and control over banking were also destined to be a continuous source of political controversy. Because the market value of lands was, in important part, a function of their earning power, and because that in turn was vitally dependent upon the foreign trade of the United States, tariff policy was a key issue. Finally, to enhance and to realize the possibilities of real estate speculation and the marketing of commodities, an adequate transportation network (canals and railroads) was essential. It was around these issues that power struggles took place in the century before the Civil War. They contributed to the War for Independence and they were decisive for the outbreak of the Civil War. The farmers won on all of them; or, so it seemed.

In 1763, the British "drew a line" the length of the Appalachian range —the "Proclamation Line"—beyond which American colonists were forbidden to invest, trap, or farm. Probably no single act of the British was more unanimously opposed throughout the Colonies than this. It brought together northern and southern farmers, merchants, frontiersmen, and financiers, and revealed to the colonists that a century and a

---

[4] *Absentee Ownership*, p. 135.

half of westward movement, for them, would have to be halted. This in turn meant that their economic hopes and even their solvency were doomed, to the advantage of British capitalists. The resistance of agriculturalists to that order found its more positive counterpart immediately after the Revolution, in the Land Ordinances of 1785* and 1787 establishing the procedures for settling the West; in their steady pressure to reduce the minimum size of land purchase, and the cost per acre; in their pressure on local, state, and federal agencies to build canals and railroads; in the successful battle (in Jackson's regime) to destroy the credit-controlling Second Bank of the United States; in the movement toward free trade of the 1840's; and in the ability of northern industrialists and financiers to persuade western farmers to join in the battle against the southerners in the Civil War. This last was with the inducement of a more generous land and transportation policy, and the fear that unless southern power could be displaced, western lands would fall under an unfavorable political dispensation.[5]

If farmers were winning all these battles, they were doing so, increasingly after mid-century, as unwitting tools of what Veblen calls the "massive vested interests" of the rising industrial state. Farmers found themselves after the Civil War faced with sharply falling prices, with monopolistic railroads and commission merchants, and with monetary and tariff policies cut to the needs not of farmers but of industrialists and financiers. The farmers were becoming, in short, an internal colony of the United States—they who had been the ideal, the presumably incontrovertible source of American virtue.

Before the Civil War, farmers had been political but, because of their pervasive strength, loosely so. After the Civil War, they began to organize. The last quarter-century was dominated by the political struggle that ensued. The manner in which the farmers both won and lost had consequences reaching far beyond anything they sought or, except in an occasional nightmare, dreamed of. The farmers sought only to maintain and expand the value of their lands and an ever-expanding market for their livestock and their crops. To gain those limited ends, they wittingly and unwittingly greased the skids for a vicious speed-up in racism, for what has become an American empire, and for an agriculture less of farmers than of corporations.[6]

---

[5]The controversies affecting the evolution of the American State, and the meaning of, for example, the Second Bank, are examined on pp. 255–60, Chapter Eight.

[6]See, for part of the story, C. Vann Woodward, *The Strange Career of Jim Crow** (New York: Oxford University Press, 1966), and his *Tom Watson: Agrarian Rebel** (New York: Oxford University Press, 1963), which clarify the dual nature of populism, moving between reform and racism. The treatment of farmers and foreign policy that follows is derived largely from the conclusive study of William Appleman Williams, *The Roots of the Modern American Empire** (New York: Random House, 1969).

MORE CORN, MORE HELL

It will be recalled that the several decades after the Civil War were marked by worldwide industrialization, by marked improvements in technology, in transportation and in communications, by pervasive national and international trade and competition; and by a tidal wave of economic imperialism. One of the innumerable consequences of those processes was falling prices, whose obverse side was rising production. The bushel price of wheat in 1871 was $1.24; in 1894 it was 49 cents; the production of wheat rose from 173 million bushels in 1859 to 468 million bushels in 1884. But all production and all prices were moving along such lines: the wholesale price index for *all* commodities fell from 135 in 1872 to 69 in 1896.[7]

In that context, the classic rule of American economic life kept its hold: survival of the fittest. The "fittest" in farming were those whose lands could enlarge, whose technology could improve, and whose marketing and financial arrangements could be arranged most efficiently and least expensively. But whether large or small, the farmers joined in a campaign from the late 1860's until the end of the century to alter the setting in which that contest would be fought out. This era of agrarian discontent, or the "Agrarian Uprising," took shape first as a national movement, with the founding of The Patrons of Husbandry ("The Grange"), in 1867. Soon one woman coined the slogan by which the movement came to be identified: "Raise less corn and more Hell." The farmers raised more of both.

Along with falling prices (beginning in the early 1870's), which was the result of impersonal forces working in the national and world economies, there were developments that were by no means impersonal, and the farmers fought all of them. In 1873, silver had been "demonetized." That act, passed by the powerful Republican Party, meant that the United States went on a gold standard, and that its supply of circulating money was reduced; this exacerbated already severe deflationary trends. "Remonetization" emerged as a searing issue, uniting farmers with urban workers; it joined easily with anti-big business, anti-railroad, anti-tariff, and other comparable issues. Sitting at the center of all this was, however, an effort on the part of farmers to find "a new frontier," which could compensate for the slowing of westward expansion[8] and the

---

[7]See Shannon, *Farmer's Last Frontier,* for the history of this period.

[8]New lands were of course still being settled in the 1870's, and 1880's; but the slowing down of the process was quantitatively real, as suggested by the "closing of the frontier" which was announced by the Census Bureau in 1890. The qualitative deterioration of the frontier movement was bound up with the fact that the available lands were relatively arid and more suited to large grazing than to small cultivated tracts, and that the Homestead Act of 1862 (whose stated intention was to encourage small-scale settlement and ownership: in effect, 160 acres of land free with five years of settlement and cultivation) had come to benefit large timber, mineral, and railroad corporations almost exclusively.

deterioration of prices (always a problem, whether severe or moderate, for debtors, which farmers always are). In the decades before the mid-1890's, the farmers sought solutions in an expanding *foreign* trade, which they sought to facilitate by lowered tariffs, cheaper and better transportation, and a return to silver. Later, when these measures, too, proved inadequate they encouraged and supported the overseas imperialist ventures of the United States, to serve the same purposes.

In the first stage of those overseas developments, farmers received aid and comfort due to conditions entirely out of their range of influence: agricultural hardships in Europe, brought about by the spread of disease and a long period of unfavorable weather. In the midst of the unprecedented and severe depression that began in 1873, exports of crude foodstuffs began to increase spectacularly, strengthening the entire economy.[9] It was then also that the American trade balance shifted decisively from being "unfavorable" (that is, an excess of imports over exports) to "favorable."

If the meaning of those years, when the United States was lifted out of depression and into a new balance of trade position, was not lost on the farmers, neither was it lost on industrialists. The United States had from its very first years depended on foreign markets for its expansion; now it was dependent on them for resolving what became a recurring problem: excess productive capacity, both agricultural and industrial. The next chapter, which is concerned with the United States in the world economy, will examine this development more closely. Here it will suffice to say merely that the 1870's taught both Americans and Europeans for the first time what became a full understanding in the years to come: "The United States," as Williams puts it (Ibid., p. 22), "was rapidly becoming the most powerful nation on earth."

When the agricultural crisis of Europe subsided, the Europeans, for the first time but by no means for the last, saw that they would have to raise barriers and find alternatives to the American export invasion. Alternative sources of supply in Argentina, in Russia, and in India were encouraged, all under the direct or indirect control of the European imperial powers; and, especially in France and Germany, the path toward effective tariff barriers on both agricultural and industrial products was pursued with increasing haste. By 1892, the French had climbed the first steps along that path, with the famous Méline Tariff; the Germans had arrived a few years earlier. With slight variations since then, the course of European tariff policy has been consistently protectionist, and increasingly designed to protect against American imports. The Ameri-

---

[9]Exports of crude foodstuffs: 1875, $79 million; 1876, $94 million; 1877, $155 million; 1880, $266 million; 1881, $242 million. Exports of manufactured foodstuffs: 1875, $110 million; 1877, $150 million; 1880, $193 million; 1881, $226 million. Williams, op. cit., p. 20.

can Marshall Plan (1948–1952) had as an important component its design to find expanded markets for American exports, and not least among them agricultural exports. In addition to drawing American farmers once more into support of an expansionist foreign policy, this development has helped to make farm products the hot center of protectionism in the Common Market countries.

THE SYSTEM JOINED

It is customary to point out that after 1896 the farmers' revolt subsided, to be replaced in the 20th century by farmers' pressure groups, the key transforming development being the rise of farm prices after 1896 (and especially during World War I). But this leaves out an important point, a point given short shrift in most histories of the United States: the whys and wherefores of our turn toward overseas imperialism at the turn of the century. Farmers were very much part of that turn, and among its conscious beneficiaries.

The discontent of farmers beginning to be voiced in the late 1860's developed into the Populist Movement (and the People's Party) by 1892 —combining in the process urban worker with rural discontent and active cooperation between black and white farmers. It was the first vigorous coalition of that sort, and apart from some small labor and socialist groupings in earlier years, the first, and perhaps unwitting, attempt to find an *internal* rather than an *external* resolution of America's economic and social problems. The response of northern business and southern white leaders was to mount vigorous anti-liberal, anti-left, and contrived racist programs. Undercut by internal divisions and external pressures, Populism shifted to the right and dissolved, and both racism and overseas expansionism were propelled into new strength.

In the heyday of 19th century Populism, almost all farmers (and their allies) were ranged against big business; today, the dominating elements in agriculture *are* big business. The rural and urban contingents of Populism sought to bend State power to the needs of the common people; today, Big Agriculture and Big Labor work with Big Business and Big Government to defend themselves *against* the common people. In 1892, Populism stood for a broad range of social and economic issues; by the election of 1896 most of its leaders could be satisfied with the promise of rising prices and land values and expanding foreign markets even if that meant finding allies among previous business enemies and embarking upon a new form of colonialism. As Williams says:

The farmers who were quasi-colonials in the domestic economy thus became anti-colonial imperialists in foreign affairs, as a strategy of becoming equals at home.[10]

The farmers already in 1895 were agitating to have the United States support the Cuban struggle against Spain, and then to guarantee that Americans would have enlarged access to Cuban markets, investment possibilities, and the like. Although American farmers had no similar interest in Asia at that time, they found it possible to support the logic of those who did—the processors (of cotton, meat, and flour) and manufacturers who had visions of an endless Asian market.[11] Nor were they indifferent to the meaning of an isthmian canal—initially in Nicaragua, but ultimately in Panama (a "nation" created by the U.S. out of Colombia for that purpose).

Like the years that first produced the farmers' revolt, the mid-1890's were years of serious depression. The response laid down then has served as a template for American foreign policy ever since:

> The economic impact of the depression, and its effect in producing a real fear of extensive social unrest or even revolution, had completed the long and gradual acceptance by metropolitan leaders of the traditional farm emphasis on overseas market expansion as the strategic solution to the nation's economic and social problems.[12]

The farmers did not *want* war in 1898, nor did they expect it; they did not want war in the repetitive years of military intervention and gunboat diplomacy in the Caribbean, Central America and Asia that carried us up to World War I. But they did want expanding markets and agricultural prosperity. From the very beginning, when anything stood in the way of economic aims—whether it was the rights or the lives of Native Americans or blacks, or the possibilities of peace—it was relegated to a secondary consideration by most white farmers. After due habituation, people can find justifications for victimizing others in the

---

[10]Ibid. p. 25. "Anti-colonial imperialism" as a political stance for farmers meant 1) opposition to colonialism, which in turn meant 2) contesting for power in colonial areas against European powers (e.g., Spain), and seeking 3) to gain equal access to all markets in the world on a basis of free competition. In practice, given the already-established technological superiority of both American industry and agriculture, this meant a growing economic empire for the United States without the traditional political institutions of colonialism. Thus, "anti-colonial imperialism."

[11]That such "visions" were largely groundless, and given their force by a larger nationalist-expansionist drive, is well-argued by Marilyn Blatt Young, "American Expansion, 1870–1890: The Far East," in *Towards a New Past,* * op. cit.

[12]Williams, p. 41.

presumed characteristics of their victims, rather than in their own purposes.

American farmers did not invent American racism or American imperialism. But at a critical moment in our history, the last years of the 19th century, farmers lent their great prestige and their numbers to the forces that were moving along those lines. It was a turning point for American history, as much as it was for American farmers. The indifferent slaughter of buffaloes and of Native Americans became a habit easily applied to the slaughter of Filipinos (at least 500,000); the precedents for genocide in Indochina were established long ago.

The American agricultural sector lost what life it could call its own as the 20th century moved on; but the idealized picture and many of the ways of the farmer persist. It is these that are probably called to mind when "the silent majority" is invoked. Not all that is thereby suggested is good and not all of it bad. Much of what Americans value, and much of how they calculate, is derived from the fact or the myth of the farm and the country town that was the social, political, and economic center of the farmer's life when he wasn't tilling the soil. As Veblen (who grew up on farms in Wisconsin and Minnesota) pointed out,

> It has come to be recognized that the country town situation of the nineteenth century is now by way of being left behind; and so it is now recognized, or at least acted on, that the salvation of twentieth-century democracy is best to be worked out by making the world safe for Big Business and then let Big Business take care of the interests of the retail trade and the country town, together with much else. But it should not be overlooked that in and through all this it is the soul of the country town that goes marching on.[13]

The "country town" mentality Veblen refers to is that of Harry Truman, of Eisenhower, of Nixon—and of George Wallace, LBJ, and McGovern. Saying this suggests that there is and has been a division of thinking and attitudes among farmers, as well as other Americans, throughout our history. Those who won out have become part of the system of calculation and expansion that is the warp and woof of American history. There were and are others: farmers who love the land, and what it grows, and the pleasures of living on it; farmers who helped to swell the socialist and anti-imperialist movement led by Eugene Debs; farmers who are black and brown and yellow; and so on. Since the collapse of the People's Party in the mid-1890's, that other side of

---

[13] *Absentee Ownership*, pp. 152–53. And see Sinclair Lewis, *Main Street*, for a vivid example of Veblen's point.

farmers has been moved far from the levers of agricultural power and influence, and plays only a minor role in overall farm production.

AGRICULTURE AND AGRIBUSINESS

Throughout the 19th century, the farmer was socially, politically, and statistically a predominating force; by the end of the century he was losing out in all but the statistical category. The numbers of farms and farmers continued to increase up to 1935 in absolute terms, while falling in relative terms as the economy came to depend increasingly on industrial production and the growth of services (finance, distribution, etc.). After 1935, farming and farms went into an absolute decline. Long before the numbers began to turn downward, the role of farming had undergone a transformation in the American political economy.

The last great effort of farmers to affect broad American policies was embodied in their impact on foreign policy around the turn of the century. Afterwards, although farmers would intermittently and diversely join in national political movements, their principal political activities would be as a particular interest pressure group, lobbying for price supports, output controls, favorable tariff policies, and government-subsidized research. The decline in their numbers tells part of the story why; their success as a pressure group did much to facilitate that decline.

In 1870, over half of the American people were engaged in agriculture. By 1930, fewer than a quarter were. Today the number is under 5 percent. There were about one-and-a-half million farms in 1850. The number rose to four million by 1890, and reached a high point in 1935, with about seven million farms. By 1940, the number had dropped below six million; in 1973 there were fewer than three million, the lowest number in the past century. Fewer than a tenth of today's farms produce well over half of all agricultural output. One percent of all farms (mostly corporations) produced 25 percent of total farm output in 1972. As elsewhere in the American economy, there is a "dual economy" in agriculture, with over a million very small and poor farms at one end, and a few hundred thousand large or very large farms at the other. (When farm income rose at least 20 percent between 1972 and 1973, in connection with rapidly rising food prices, it was estimated that 90 percent of the increase went to 200,000 giant farms.)

The effectiveness of farmers as a pressure group began to take hold in the 1920's, and especially under President Hoover. Those first steps led directly to the present close cooperation between large farms, government, and agricultural colleges, and to the industrialization of agriculture. Since 1950, farm productivity has risen twice that of manufacturing industry, the gains going to the very largest farms while the small idealized farmer has been squeezed out of farming and into the cities.

In the long history of American farming, to have been a tenant farmer was a sign not of failure but of first steps toward ownership. But after World War I, as agriculture industrialized in the midst of widespread over-capacity, farm tenancy and share-cropping became virtually indistinguishable: it was the way *down,* or out. The mass exodus from farming was accelerated by the Depression and the Dust Bowl tragedies accompanying it; the exodus was pushed toward completion by the great step up in electrification, mechanization, and chemicalization in farming after World War II. Millions of farmers went bankrupt and were "tractored out" in the 1930's, and became part of a migratory labor force or of the unemployed. The military and production needs of World War II came just in time.[14]

Beginning in the Hoover Administration, a set of policies has evolved which seeks to prevent low prices and market instability for a broad range of farm products—keeping prices up through government loans and purchases, and supply down through production controls. The largest farms are the prime beneficiaries of these governmental programs. Thus, in 1967, the poorest 20 percent of farmers received 1.1 percent of government payments; the richest 5 percent of farmers (often corporations) received 42.4 percent of government payments. Total governmental payments in that year were over $3 billion. It could not be otherwise, for farm policies as presently constituted are tied to output: the larger the output, the more the gains from the program, and vice versa. Though carried out in the name of the small farmer, these programs have been pushed through and administered by representatives of the farm pressure groups representing the largest farmers. The result is a program that makes the rich richer and allows the poor to stay poor, or forces them to get out of farming.[15]

---

[14]The squeezing out process of the poorest farmers continues, even more tragically. The affected people become part of the "migrant" labor force in the East for a few years, and then settle in the northern slums—the last of the tenant farmers. The "Dust Bowl" was a product of the misuse of the arid lands west of the Mississippi, which should not have been used for grain or cotton cultivation. See the important article by Paul W. Gates, "The Homestead Law in an Incongruous Land System," reprinted in Scheiber, *United States Economic History,* Chapter 10, which shows the misuse of the land and the manner in which a law presumably designed to foster widespread ownership did much to deliver the public domain to large land, mineral, railroad, and timber companies. Steinbeck's *Grapes of Wrath* is an unforgettable portrait of the Depression/Dust Bowl exodus of the small farmer.

[15]The data are drawn from "The Effect of Taxes and Government Spending on Inequality," in Edwards et al., *The Capitalist System,* p. 243, put together by James T. Bonnen. For a long overview, see Murray Benedict, *Farm Policies of the United States, 1790–1950* (New York: Twentieth Century Fund, 1953). Edward Higbee, *Farms and Farmers in an Urban Age** (New York: Twentieth Century Fund, 1963) shows the inequities in current programs within agriculture and as between some farmers and all city-dwellers.

Agricultural controls and subsidies are of course paid for by the general public through taxation. If the public thinks about the matter at all, it finds some satisfaction in its belief that the programs are helping "the little guy." Meanwhile, the small farmer goes out of existence, as the policies work themselves out:

Thus, the total number of farms dropped from 5.9 million in 1947 to 2.9 million in 1970, while the average number of acres per farm doubled (rising from 196 to 387 acres). In 1959, large farms with sales amounting to $20,000 or more per year represented 13 percent of all commercial farms and accounted for 52 percent of total sales of farm products; by 1969 19 percent of all farms with 73 percent of total products sales were in this category. . . . The number of small farms with less than 100 acres has declined precipitately (from 3.0 to 1.4 million) between 1950 and 1964. . . . Among the farmers squeezed out were about 500,000 crop-share tenants in the South, largely from cotton plantations. . . . [which] means not only cutting off cash income but also loss of housing and of the minimal security derived from having a plot of land.[16]

Little known to the general public, but of great importance to the large farmers, have been governmental programs financed by federal and state funds that undertake research on the whole range of matters affecting agricultural productivity. These programs have done much over the years to stimulate and improve mechanization, seeds, soil management, and the like; they have also been prime movers in the general chemicalization of farming. Chemicalization, which undoubtedly has had an extraordinary impact in raising the productivity of farm land, has an equally extraordinary impact on the destruction of the environment —and not a few human beings. The case of DDT is only the best known example of a long list of chemicals which have poisoned the soil, the waters, and surrounding foliage in such fashion as to unhinge the balance of nature, a balance that depends upon insects, birds, and small animals who are poisoned by presently-used chemicals.

The contemporary ecological imbalance is tipped most drastically in dangerous directions by *industrial* production and the use of industrial products, and most especially the automobile and petroleum products. But there is, in the contemporary agricultural pattern, a specially disturbing quality to the problem, for agriculture provides our food. That our food should be provided in ways that poison as well as sustain us, and that it should be produced in ways that destroy as well as replenish natural forces is frightening; that all this is the direct result of governmental subsidies for research in the Department of Agriculture and in the land-grant universities is shocking. At a U.S. Senate hearing in the

---

[16]U.S. Dept. of Labor, *Manpower Report of the President** (USGPO, Washington, 1971), p. 119. This is a valuable source of data on a broad range of problems affecting the labor force, poverty, etc.

summer of 1972, the current status of these relationships was summarized as follows:

> a land-grant complex, a system composed of Federal research agencies and big universities in each state created in the last century with endowments of public lands or their monetary equivalent . . . , whose research was originally intended to serve consumers as well as rural communities, [but is] now focused largely on the development of big machines for vast farming enterprises, the breeding of crops for mechanized harvests and studies of chemicals for big corporations and big producers . . . with little regard for the quality or safety of products for the consumer or the small farmer. One result . . . has been to drive farmers and workers off the land and into the crowded cities.[17]

The land-grant universities referred to all have Schools of Agriculture, and they in turn have Departments of Agricultural Economics. The methodology of agricultural economics is, like its parent's, neoclassical, and its purposes are also to show how efficiency and profits can be enhanced. There are, however, some differences: 1) "ag econ" has more of an empirical component than "econ"; 2) it is designed explicitly to serve the agricultural community, whereas general economists believe they are serving either nobody or everybody; and 3) the understanding that agricultural economists have of their role is provided to them by an annual reminder from state legislatures (and/or the Department of Agriculture), which pays their salaries and provides their research grants.

There is also at least one matter other than neoclassicism that the two groups of economists have in common: they are addicted to what E. J. Mishan calls "growthmania." That is, they are responding wittingly or not to the omnipresent need of a capitalist economy to expand, and to continue to expand. As Mishan puts it, "They continue to give expression to the basic doctrines of their fathers and spin rhetoric out of the growth theme in blithe unconcern of the spreading jungle of problems stemming directly from the material prosperity of the last decade or so."[18]

For farmers, as for capitalist businessmen in general, expansion of markets was essential. Economic expansion was aided critically all along

---

[17]Reported in the *New York Times,* June 20, 1972.

[18]E. J. Mishan, *Technology and Growth: The Price We Pay** (New York: Praeger, 1969), p. xv. Mishan goes on to say that for such people, "any doubt that, say, a four percent growth rate, as revealed by the index, is better than a three percent growth rate is near-heresy; is tantamount to a doubt that four is greater than three." (Ibid.) Mishan was one of the very first of the mainstream economists to question the sacrosanct quality of growth, and his analysis is useful. It is also, however, limited, in that he sees "growthmania" *as* a mania; that is, as being irrational, rather than as intrinsic to the system.

the way by attendant geographic expansion—across the continent, first, and over the seas, later. It is unnecessary to recount here the laudable achievements that were part of that process in American history; our history books do little else. It is necessary, however, to underscore what is generally neglected. What were looked upon as aberrations or excesses, regarding the treatment of both human and nonhuman resources, were intrinsic to the process of American growth and development. And, if we wish to understand the pervasiveness and intractability of today's range of "problems," we must see them as the more severe contemporary manifestation of what has existed all along.

Since over two-thirds of all Americans now live in cities, most of the problems afflicting America today show themselves in the cities. Racism, poverty, pollution, violence, transportation mess, urban sprawl, health and housing and educational deprivation—all these and more swirl around in tight and deadly embrace in our cities; all are explicable in their current as in their historical conditions as "by-products" of a process of development in which profit and power—not natural balance, not human needs and possibilities, not social balance—were the guiding criteria. The deterioration of nature has been relatively silent, and hidden unless studied; it is quite the opposite with the deterioration of daily life in our cities. That the exploitation of *all* of nature would go hand in hand with exploitation of the *human* component of nature was foreseen by Marx, long ago:

> In modern agriculture, as in the urban industries, the increased productiveness and quantity of the labor set in motion are bought at the cost of laying waste and consuming by disease labor-power itself. Moreover, all progress in capitalistic agriculture is a progress in the art, not only of robbing the laborer, but of robbing the soil; all progress in increasing the fertility of the soil for a given time, is a progress towards ruining the lasting sources of that fertility. The more a country starts its development on the foundation of modern industry, like the United States, for example, the more rapid is this process of destruction. Capitalist production, therefore, develops technology, and the combining together of various processes into a social whole, only by sapping the original sources of all wealth—the soil and the laborer.[19]

The great and rich land space of continental United States was swept over and conquered in a process so swift and violent that it has been called "the rape of the land." Heedless of any natural balance or of human beings standing in the way, the exploiters of the land moved for greed more than need, for power more than for satisfaction. So it has been too with the way our cities have grown and changed and deterio-

---

[19] *Capital,* vol. I, pp. 506–7.

rated, in one wave after another. So too with the poisoning of our air and water. What land speculators were to farming, real estate and urban development interests were and are to our cities; as in farming, the entrance of government into the picture in this century has meant not a mitigation but an intensification of a long-existent process. The more rapid and more pervasive economic expansion of this century has brought with it more misuse of the land, more deadly cities, and an environmental condition so severe that to most it is terrifying.

The Jeffersonian dream of an agrarian democracy is not even remembered these days; the nightmare of urban decay and suffocation has taken its place. How did the city get that way, and how does it continue to move?

CIVILIZATION AND ITS DISCONTENTS

There was, not so long ago, a firmly-held notion that cities were the repository of all that is most precious in western social development. If that was a belief held too carelessly, there is even less to support the one that now spreads and grows: the cities embody all that is to be avoided. Furthermore, as this view spreads, it becomes a self-fulfilling prophecy.

American cities at their best were never, for a majority of their inhabitants, fit places to live, whether in the 19th or the 20th century. But apart from a small handful of people, mostly young, who can find ways to experiment with rural living, the alternative to *making* our cities fit places to live is quite probably the disintegration of what we mean by civilization. That we have done so little, and done it so badly, on that score testifies to how very slender the civilized base has been for our social development.

A careful analysis of how our cities came to be, how they have changed over time, and how they have sunk into their current desperate state, if combined with an analysis of how all that related to our overall socio-economic development, would quite probably tell us that a complete reorganization of our cities *and* of our society is necessary to make either livable or, in an acceptable sense of the term, civilized.

Recorded history begins with cities, at that stage of social development when production and productivity had advanced to the point where a significant number of the population could be sustained even though they did not produce their own food; when a relatively complicated division of labor had emerged, requiring government and writing. All this (and much else involved) appears to have come forth a millennium or two before Christ in the rich river valleys of the Indus, the Tigris and Euphrates, and the Nile. In the ancient period, cities were of course serving commercial purposes; but their religious, military, and administrative functions seem more frequently to have been dominant. During the medieval period, cities emerged and grew primarily because of their locations, which favored the development of commerce. In the capitalist epoch, cities have arisen, expanded, and decayed almost entirely in response to economic needs and possibilities.[20]

In the United States, the cities of the eastern seaboard—most notably Boston, New York, Philadelphia, Baltimore, Charleston, and Atlanta—waxed or waned as the changing patterns of agriculture, manufacture, foreign and domestic trade, finance, and transportation altered. They, and the cities that grew up in the trans-Appalachian West, fought strenuously and self-consciously to place roads, canals, and railroads in such manner as to become magnets for the trade, the industry, and the finance that could not otherwise flourish. In the early 19th century the competition along these lines between towns and cities was intense. If the emergence of Manhattan, for example, from a small village to becoming the nation's most populous city is to be understood, the story must begin with its advantages as a trading center: it was on the edge of the Atlantic, connected to the interior by the Erie Canal, and favorably located between New England and the South.

The same factors also affected other cities throughout the U.S.: Chicago, Omaha, Cincinnati (which was vulgarly known as "Porkopolis"), New Orleans, St. Louis, Detroit, Los Angeles, San Francisco, or Seattle. Transportation advantages, due to location near water routes, or emergence as a railroad center, made towns into commercial centers; then they emerged as centers of industry and finance, and in the process, as large population centers.

The reasons why the cities grew give important clues as to the criteria employed—and neglected—along the way regarding the quantity and quality of what we may call human services: housing, transportation, health, educational, and cultural-recreational facilities. These services came into being as responses to essentially market rather than human criteria, the sole exception being, in some cities, cultural facilities.[21]

The medieval European city often tended to develop in rings, moving outward from the initial walled city to "suburbs," one ring after an-

---

[20]In the United States, the principal exception to the last generalization would be Washington, D. C., which was, however, a quite minor city until the political economy of the U.S., around the turn of the century, required an explicitly strong central government. The best introduction to the historical and current development of cities is Lewis Mumford, *The City in History** (New York: Harcourt Brace Jovanovich, 1961). A narrower and controversial economic interpretation is Jane Jacobs, *The Economy of Cities** (New York: Random House, 1965).

[21]They responded to the "market," also; but museums, concert halls, libraries, parks, and the like, were more often created for non-market reasons: the tastes (vulgar or cultivated) of the rich; the complicated social convictions of an Andrew Carnegie (who financed innumerable public libraries in America); the strong European influences on Americans that diluted the pure American fluid of commercialism.

other; or, it was controlled in its design from the beginning, as were many Central European cities. By comparison, the spatial development of American cities was haphazard. As the structure of the economy, both locally and nationally, changed, new patterns of production and new inflows of people ensued. What began as commercial districts became industrial, or financial; initially residential districts became commercial or industrial; initially suburban areas became part of the "central city." Perhaps the most vivid example of the latter development is Harlem, once a village separated from the bustle of New York by miles of "country."[22]

CITIES AND SUBURBS; SPRAWL AND DECAY

American urban development can be viewed as having three reasonably clear-cut stages: 1) most of the 19th century, 2) the forty years or so ending just before World War II, and 3) from World War II to the present. The earliest period covers the growth of cities proper; the second sees the emergence of malignant growth including the significant expansion of suburbs; the latest brings us megalopolis, urban sprawl, and the dying city.

Throughout the 19th century, American cities muliplied and grew; but it was in some kind of rhythmic balance with the growing economy. Immigration became a river and then a torrent after 1850; agriculture was becoming relatively less important (although it was producing more and more, with its rising productivity); and industrialization became the prime creator of urbanization. It was not until the turn of the century, however, that the kinds of urban problems now familiar to us began to become obvious—widespread slums, rampant health problems, poverty, blatant corruption, and the like. What Lincoln Steffens had to say about St. Louis at the time of its World's Fair (1904) might have been written yesterday:

> The visitor is told of the wealth of the residents, of the financial strength of the banks, and of the growing importance of the industries, yet he sees poorly-paved, refuse-burdened streets and dusty or mud-covered alleys; he passes a ramshackle fire-trap, crowded with the sick, and learns that it is the City Hospital. . . . Finally, he turns a tap in the hotel, to see liquid mud flow into wash basin or bath tub.[23]

---

[22]Gilbert Osofsky, *Harlem: The Making of a Ghetto,* cited earlier, in tracing out the long-standing oppression of black people in New York (from the city's earliest years to 1930), incidentally provides a useful view of the process of urban development. See also Robert G. Albion, *The Rise of New York Port* (New York: Scribner's, 1939), and, for a more general history, Taylor, *Transportation Revolution,* op. cit.

[23] *The Shame of the Cities** (New York: McClure, 1904), p. 31. Even earlier conditions are described by Jacob Riis, *How the Other Half Lives** (New York: Hill and Wang, 1962), originally published in 1890.

Immigration and industrialization both speeded up substantially after 1900, and a net migration from rural to urban locations became a constant. In 1920, for the first time, there were more people in our cities than in the countryside.[24] The cities that grew fastest were those already largest. Into these rapidly expanding metropoli in every region of the country streamed people who would take up the lowest-paying and dirtiest jobs. They were from the poorer areas of Europe and Asia, and they were black and Spanish-speaking Americans moving from country to city. Their cheap labor was much desired, but they were in attitude despised and in fact neglected by the "WASP" power structures which ruled almost all American cities. They were despised as Catholics or Jews, as poor, as black, brown, yellow, or "swarthy"; for them, the cities, never well-planned, and only partially attractive and pleasant, were sink-holes.

Much sentimental claptrap has been written about how the poor and oppressed of the cities after the turn of the century were "taken care of" by the political bosses and machines then dominant; even today respectable opinion not infrequently lauds a Mayor Daley of Chicago as the last of an unfortunately vanishing breed. The machines did have a function, of course, a function much like that a bandage has for a running sore. There is reason for nostalgia among the respectable people today concerning our cities of half a century or more ago, but it is not because they were livable. Rather, it is because the cities then *seemed* tractable and manageable; they were still growing, still serving indispensable economic functions.

Since World War II, it is megalopoli, not cities, that grow; many of the functions performed in and by cities are now taken care of in once suburban *residential* areas that are now also "suburban" *industrial* areas; and the cities have been filled by a forced migration of rural people, who are heavily nonwhite. This process has been occurring even with fewer and fewer industrial jobs to be found; with fewer jobs of *any* kind to be found. In order to be manageable today, the cities would have to be managed in critical part *for* and *by* the despised poor and nonwhite residents who constitute their largest segments. Such a politics goes against the American grain.

A few American suburbs developed in conjunction with the steam railroad after 1850. But the first significant suburban development went along with the electric urban, interurban, suburban railway, as the 20th century began. What continental railroad developers were to westward expansion, electric railway (including subway) developers and their real-estate cohorts were to urban-suburban development.

In the years just before World War I, automobiles began to be mass-produced, and that brought about the next major suburban movement.

---

[24]See Faulkner, *Decline of Laissez-Faire: 1897–1917,* especially Chapter 5.

The possibilities associated with the electric railway and the automobile were fairly well exhausted before World War II, especially under the negative impact of the Depression. Since 1945, population has risen by more than fifty million; there has been a whole generation of high and sustained national income; the automobile (one for every two Americans) has become almost a universal possession; and the nation's industrialization, urbanization, and suburbanization have moved to levels of apparent saturation although doubtless there is more on the way. In the process, both the causes and the consequences of suburbanization have altered.

Suburban development prior to the 1930's was made possible by transportation developments that were taken advantage of by predominantly upper income families. The suburb, typically, was separated from the city by open stretches of country, and provided an opportunity to combine the advantages of city with country life. The suburban railway made its few stops, providing a leisurely and even a pleasant interlude; and some few drove to work and back. There were no "freeways."[25]

All that began to change as we moved into and out of World War II. The changes were first evident in and around Los Angeles, a "city" that drew people from all over the nation, but especially from the Midwest and South, as its oil wells, its aircraft production, its light and cheap labor manufactures, its warm climate and its glamor provided both jobs and dreams. The model it established for the rest of the country is well-captured by Mumford:

> Los Angeles has now become an undifferentiated mass of houses, walled off into sectors by many-laned expressways, with ramps and viaducts that create special bottlenecks of their own. These expressways move but a small fraction of the traffic per hour once carried by public transportation, at a much lower speed, in an environment befouled by smog, itself produced by the lethal exhaust of the technologically backward motor cars. More than a third of the Los Angeles area is consumed by these grotesque transportation facilities; *two-thirds* of central Los Angeles are occupied by streets, freeways, parking facilities, and garages. This is space-eating with a vengeance. The last stage of the process already beckons truly progressive minds—to evict the remaining inhabitants and turn the entire area over to automatically propelled vehicles, completely emancipated from any rational human purpose.[26]

---

[25]Except as rare phenomena, such as the Bronx River Parkway, connecting the then richest county in the nation (Westchester) with the most populous city, New York. See Sweezy, "Cars and Cities," cited earlier.

[26] *The City in History*, p. 510. In 1907, horsedrawn vehicles in New York City moved at an average speed of 11.5 miles per hour; cars move at six miles per hour today. It is generally recognized that the Los Angeles style of one day becomes the national style soon thereafter. Nathaniel West's novel, *Day of the Locust*, written in 1940, evoked that style exactly. The novel ends suddenly, with a race riot at a movie première.

There are still American cities that do not fit that model; but most that do not are racing madly to catch up with those that do. Greater Boston, Greater New York, Greater Cleveland, Greater Atlanta, Greater Houston, and of course Greater Los Angeles, all vie with each for growth, come what may. The San Francisco Bay Area, thought by many, as recently as a decade ago, to be exempt from such deterioration has instead come to stand as perhaps a pluperfect example of how very strong the drives are to "catch up" in the race. The Bay, enormous and convolute, ringed by hills in turn sloping into graceful valleys, is presently shrinking and dying as a body of water. Over 40 percent of the water area of the Bay has been filled in during this century. Steadily increasing amounts of effluent from the Navy, private industry, and residences have combined with intermittent oil spills to kill off much of the underwater life of the Bay, and to render its waters dangerous to humans. In addition, its valleys have seen orchards replaced by residential and industrial sprawl, now suffocating beneath smog. That all this is not yet enough is suggested by a two-page advertisement in the *New York Times* of April 25, 1972: "Metro San Jose" (south of San Francisco), whose population has risen more than ten times since 1940, boasts in the ad of its "runaway construction," its airline passengers, its new car sales—with the ad asking for more of the same.

The personal automobile has almost entirely replaced the dilapidated and expensive interurban railway; the suburbs have developed their own ghettoes,[27] their own smog, indeed their own suburbs. Industry has accompanied the automobile to the suburb, and the city has lost its ability both to provide a decent livelihood for a high and growing percentage of its residents, as well as to pay for its needed services.

All major American cities now lurch from one fiscal crisis to the next. The daily news announces school closings today, cessation of bus service the week after. Firemen, policemen, refuse collectors, teachers, and hospital workers organize and strike for better incomes and working conditions, attempting to stave off the city's slashes, rising taxes, and the rising cost of living. The Urban Coalition announced in 1971 that it expected that most major and many minor American cities would literally be bankrupt by 1976.[28]

---

[27]Westchester County, N. Y., still one of the richest in the nation, also has the highest percentage of welfare poor (per capita) in the nation.

[28]There is insufficient space here to treat meaningfully the range of urban crises now pervading the whole nation. But each of them—jobs, housing, education, poverty, crime, health, transportation, and the environment—is taken up systematically in terms of analysis and proposals, by "conservative, liberal, and radical" analysts, in the book of readings edited by David M. Gordon, *Problems in Political Economy: An Urban Perspective*, cited earlier. Each section concludes with a comprehensive bibliography and suggestions for further reading. The book constitutes an efficient starting-point for serious students of these questions. A succinct economic analysis may be found in Daniel Fusfeld, "The Basic Economics of the Urban and Racial Crisis," URPE Conference Papers (December, 1968), available also as URPE *Reprint No. 2*.

NOTHING FAILS LIKE SUCCESS

The listing of America's urban afflictions has become a persisting drone in the background of daily existence, like the whine of mosquitoes. We have already been bitten, and we know more bites will come. The items on the list are by now all too familiar: housing problems that regularly combine insane, ugly, and costly urban construction with a steady worsening of a lifelong housing shortage; maddeningly inadequate public transportation; schools bursting with tensions while the hope of learning drains away; spreading drug addiction and crime and intensifying police brutality; increasing costs for decreasing medical care; welfare needs that are met by "workfare" laws and falling welfare budgets, as the cost of living rises; a "serious" level of unemployment in over sixty cities in 1972; a slow but steady increase of those officially classified as "poor," despite—or because of?—a War on Poverty. And smog, and power blackouts, and. . . .

The crisis of the cities is another way of describing a serious deterioration in the way people live; for people live—work, reside, go to school, get addicted, busted and pushed around—mostly in the cities. Over two-thirds of the population live in the 224 "metropolitan areas" of the nation. The separate states also suffer from fiscal crisis; but theirs derives in large part from the cities'. Cities and states wait impatiently for Washington to bail them out; President Nixon proudly proclaims his "sharing" of five billion dollars of annual federal revenue with the regions, while simultaneously cutting back federally-funded urban programs in amounts equal or greater to the "sharing," and while raising arms expenditures. Whatever American mayors may think, seldom a voice is heard wondering if perhaps the trillion plus spent on arms over the past twenty-five years might not have a central responsibility for the cities' persisting fiscal crisis.

The rash of emergency announcements of recent years suggesting that the living conditions and fiscal mechanisms of urban life have come unstuck are of course accurate. But the inadequacy of living conditions in our cities is not new. It would be difficult to match the squalor and brutality found in 1900 Chicago as depicted by Sinclair in *The Jungle,* or their continuation as vividly described by O'Farrell in *Studs Lonigan.* The inadequacies have been there all along. But the new emigrants who mostly filled the cities tolerated what no longer is tolerated; what they found intolerable could be camouflaged or pacified by petty handouts, or hidden from view in ways no longer possible. The camouflage has peeled away under the hot blast of an unsuccessful war; belief in the basic beneficence of the system for tens of millions of Americans has shriveled in the same period. The system no longer delivers hope to the poor.

But it has not been the *failure* of the system that has caused these rude awakenings; it has been its *success*, as success is defined in this system. For the past generation (to look back no further) American capitalism has flourished as never before: real income per capita up more than 60 percent since 1946, an average rate of real growth of 3.5 percent, one or more automobiles and TV sets in almost every house, and many more houses than ever. That all this has been accompanied by militarization, imperialist expansion, war, large-scale corruption, waste and trivialization, is of course true. Withal, the economic system has been at its very best in the one way that is counted in our system as most important: it has done what it is designed to do, which is to produce goods—any old goods—and to yield profits and luxurious living to those within the top 10 percent of the population. When they can breathe, the 20 percent or so in the next layers down, moreover, have done better than that many people have ever done in other times or places. The system has succeeded; it can do no better. GNP, after all, is over one-and-a-quarter trillion dollars (1973).

The problems of the cities are now acute not only for those who live and work in them (and less directly, for those in the larger metropolitan areas surrounding the cities) but also for those who own city real estate, and whose plants, offices, and stores are still located in the cities. Industrial and commercial firms may move to the suburbs as fast as decorum and costs will allow, but there are certain limits to that process, as there are limits to the exodus of middle American homeowners. Apart from considerations of human misery, there are billions to be lost if the cities are not "saved."

This threat, which has placed the urban crisis on the front pages for the past few years, has been made more vivid by the turbulence also seen on the front pages. The Urban Coalition, a grouping of representatives from the very largest corporations, especially insurance, has sought to enlist the voluntary cooperation of businessmen in bringing new life to the cities. The federal government has joined with local governments to renew and redevelop the decayed central cities. These and other programs have done both a lot and a little. Slums have been wiped out and replaced by shiny new buildings; but they have been office buildings, stores, or middle and high income apartment houses. Urban renewal, as the saying goes, has been urban removal for the former residents of the slums—removal, that is, to still other slums—thus increasing rents while compressing the population. Black people call the process "Negro removal."

The intensity of the urban problem guarantees that its existence is known to all; its social, political, and economic dangers to those at the top of the society have guaranteed that all levels of business and government have initiated or become part of innumerable programs with the stated intentions of eliminating poverty, slums, mess, and sprawl. Many of the programs died on paper. Those that have been implemented have been accompanied by a worsening of the problems they have sought to cure, sometimes because of the programs, sometimes despite them. Why?

Certainly a key part of an answer to what has gone wrong must begin with a fundamental reality: remedial programs are run by those who have been responsible for the problems they seek to cure. The programs are run by those at the top—the top of federal, state, or local governments, or of the appropriate bureaus; the top of the economy, or their accepted representatives on the national, regional, and local levels. Whether the reference is to manpower training programs where resistant unions as well as businessmen have a say; to urban development and renewal where real estate developers, banks, and construction companies move into decision-making positions; or to transportation and environmental reform where *all* power groups move in; whether in these or other instances, "the vested interests" have the largest say.

Take urban renewal. In the shaping of federal urban housing and renewal programs, the process normally begins with the best of intentions, in or out of Congress. Immediately a variety of pressures comes to bear: to place administration and control of programs on the local level, which means under the control of those in power, not those with the need; *not* to allocate adequate funds; *not* to compete with existing housing. One study sums up the resulting situation as follows:

> Our survey has shown that the men and women who make basic public housing policy at the local level are in no sense representative of the client group the programs are intended to serve. A substantial proportion of the commissioners do not favor adding to the stock of publicly subsidized housing, nor use of newer forms of public housing, nor many of the "liberalization" trends, including increased tenant participation. . . . [The authority] inserts, at a critical level of internal decision-making, an intervening layer of part-time, lay commissioners who act as a brake on the program by failing to keep abreast of new trends and techniques and by representing a microcosm of middle-class white views about the poor, their housing, and the responsibilities of government.[29]

Urban renewal does not make cities a better place to live for their residents, whose housing continues to deteriorate, who find jobs increasingly difficult to find, and so on. But it does help the construction

---

[29] Chester Hartman and Gregg Carr, "Housing Authorities Reconsidered," *Journal of the American Institute of Planners* (Jan., 1969). Quoted in David Gordon, op. cit., p. 361. The entire section on housing in Gordon's book is worth reading for this matter. For an equally critical but conservative viewpoint see Martin Anderson, *The Federal Bulldozer** (Cambridge: The M.I.T. Press, 1964).

industry, the banking industry, the real estate industry. It does so by building high-rise office buildings, shopping centers, and freeways cutting through the residential areas of the very people who are supposed to be benefitting. The scandals associated with the development run the gamut—for example, disclosures of extensive corruption of the Chicago Federal Housing Authority in 1972, the same year a multi-million dollar housing development in St. Louis was *torn down,* after only a few years' existence—but they are not to be seen as scandalous. This is the way the "development of our cities" takes place. The essentially private power structure that built our cities in the past in response to speculative and market stimuli is now a complex private-public structure that "rebuilds" our cities, in response still to the lure of profits, still buttressed by "cooperative" politicians. The process is not new; what gives it the smell of scandal is that it is carried out in the name of those who are in fact harmed by it. But that is scarcely new, either.

Meanwhile, and with no improvement in sight, the mosquito drone intensifies, and not a few are carrying malaria. Intense concern with the urban crisis began in the Kennedy Administration. It continued in the Johnson Administration, but as the War in Indochina deepened, the War on Poverty and Urban Blight devolved into skirmishes. Under Nixon, the rhetoric of urban rescue found its principle in Daniel Moynihan's "benign neglect"—which has the virtue, at least, of bringing rhetoric and reality closer together.

THE EFFLUENT SOCIETY

So goes the American city, with millions of Americans living badly and many dying prematurely. And then we have the problems of the environment—our air and water especially, in the cities and the countryside. The scope and spread of industrialism in America are regularly hailed as totems of our success. The equally extensive existence of environmental damage is viewed much as a drunken hangover might be —the unfortunate by-product of a great spree. But hangovers go away, normally; ecological imbalance worsens dynamically, affecting even, indeed especially, those who gain the least from its causes. The causes are deep-seated in our society. "What is at stake in the ecological crisis we face today," says Murray Bookchin,

is the very capacity of the earth to sustain advanced forms of life. The crisis is being drawn together by massive increases in "typical" forms of air and water pollution; by a mounting accumulation of nondegradable wastes, lead residues, pesticide residues and toxic additives in food; by the expansion of cities into vast urban belts; by increasing stresses due to congestion, noise and mass living; by the wanton scarring of the earth as a result of mining operations, lumbering, and real estate speculation. The result of all this is that the earth within a few decades has been despoiled on a scale that is unprecedented in the entire history of human habitation on the planet.[30]

The ecological crisis, as Bookchin points out above, has many facets: the spoliation and waste of resources; the poisoning of our food and the sources of our food; what is coming to be called visual and aural pollution; and, of course, the pollution of air and water. The causes of each and all of these are found in the normal operations of our economy; here we will examine only pollution as it most directly affects urban life— air, water, and solid waste pollution.

Air, water, and solid waste pollution were familiar problems to the cities of England in the early 19th century. Sewage, garbage, foul drinking water, noxious air, and heedless expansion combined to produce intermittent cholera, sewer explosions and consequent fires, as well as significant reductions of productive efficiency.[31] It was to the self-interest of those with the most power in England then (and especially in London) to eliminate such problems. What is interesting is not that they made the attempt to do so, but that it took decades for substantial progress to be made, and that as the 20th century arrived the progress was still lagging behind the problem. The problems today are considerably more intense. They are by no means confined to the United States (if anything, they are more intense in Japan); but the United States, as the largest industrial power, the largest user of raw materials, of electric energy, of automobiles—of everything—sits at the center of the problem not only for itself, but for the world. (We are 6 percent of world population; we use 33 percent of the world's energy.)

Air pollution presses most noticeably and painfully on urban-suburban dwellers. Threatening though it quite clearly is, whether in oncoming years it will be more deadly than poisoned water and waste pollution only time will tell. All forms are connected, in any case. Let us begin with water and waste pollution.[32]

The means, or attempted means, of maintaining our production and our cleanliness are among the principal causes of water pollution: the disposal of industrial and bodily wastes, of our soaps, and the washing away of insecticides and pesticides. Yet in every case, alternative ways

---

[30]"Towards an Ecological Solution," *Ramparts* (May, 1970). Excerpts are reprinted in *The Capitalist System*, pp. 388–92.

[31]Ridgeway, *The Politics of Ecology*, discusses both causes and attempted reforms in that period, and relates them to our present.

[32]Gordon, op. cit., provides a concise summary of forms and causes of urban pollution, pp. 458–59.

can be and must be found. Additional factors are the increased runoff of water brought about by filled-in swamps and denuded hillsides, the closing off of local for distant water supplies as the major cities expand and reach out for "reliable" water, the increased use of water by industry and the resulting pollution of major rivers and lakes. Add it all together, and it may be understood why, as President Johnson pointed out in 1967, "every major river system in the country is polluted." So are most of the lakes and bays, and even parts of the oceans.

Quite simply, through organic and inorganic chemical residues, through sewage and heat and algae, clean water is rapidly becoming an increasingly scarce resource. In the economics textbooks over the past century, water, like air, has been classified as a "free" good. Free to business, perhaps; for American society it will cost billions of dollars for tens of years to get us back to the point where our water resources are safely usable, let alone free. Business made the profits from our reckless development; the entire population will have to finance the remedies— if there are remedies.

In a socio-economic system as highly interdependent as ours, no single activity can be isolated in terms of its meaning. But we can point to complexes of activities and the relationships and processes within which they spin. Let us look at *paper* (and containers), first, and then go on to examine the most central of all complexes in the American economy, *automobiles* and *petroleum*.

ROAD MAP TO DISASTER

Most of *solid waste* pollution does not emanate directly from the cities. But that which does is mostly composed of paper, plastic, and throwaway bottles and cans. The average trash disposal per person per day in the United States is seven pounds, which adds up to over three billion *tons* per year. Some of this helps to pollute the water; some of it takes up land space; some of it is dumped into the ocean. Ecology reformers urge us—regarding air and water and solid waste pollution—to use bio-degradable soap, white (instead of colored) tissues, and returnable bottles; they urge us not to use the car, not to use the air conditioner or the TV on hot days; and buy a bike.

Meanwhile, the economic system has its needs if it is to continue without basic change. Reformers urge self-restraint on us all; yet business must continue to sell its products. Whatever else that means, it involves the *increased* use of packaging, paper, automobiles and gasoline. The automobile-petroleum complex is of course the major air polluter; but it connects with the pollution associated with paper, packaging, and consumerism in general, as it does with the growth of bureaucracy.

The bureaucracy of business is and has for long been more pervasive and substantial than that of much- (and deservedly-) maligned government; it is necessary if accounts and records are to be kept and profits to be made. Consumerism is just as much a product of advanced industrial capitalism. Modern industry must have mass markets, even with high military production. Mass markets mean, increasingly, advertising, sales promotion, credit, and packaging. Paper and plastic production is, of course, one of the major polluters of our waters through poisonous chemical wastes, and one of the great destroyers of forests which are in turn the natural preservers of both air and water. No matter what individual consumers do about disposing of their own waste, they will continue to see an increase in packaging, advertising, and useless printed materials—and pollution. The situation is even less susceptible to mitigation regarding the automobile-petroleum complex.

Four-fifths of all American families own automobiles; about a third have two or more cars. About 60 percent of urban air pollution is due to the *use* of motor vehicles (varying widely from city to city, of course). If car users were to cut their driving by half, that would surely have a beneficial effect on the air, which would remain polluted, however. But more important, we may believe that the auto and oil companies would find ways to bring us back to normal. That is their business. In all the advertising of the auto and oil companies (GM alone spent over $300 million on advertising in 1971), there is nary a word about buying fewer cars, or driving less; nor are there suggestions as to ways of finding alternative modes of transport. "Earth Day," the nation-wide demonstration of concern over the environment, took place in 1970; in 1973 car sales broke all records, as did gasoline consumption.

Barry Weisberg has formulated the importance of the automobile-petroleum complex succinctly:

> No other factor has exercised such a predominant influence upon the direction and definition of the American industrial empire. In terms of capital formation, patterns of employment, the extent of marketing penetration, transportation, energy, urbanization, ecological imbalance and American foreign policy, they are unrivaled in influence. The impact of their economic priorities upon the public policy of the United States is unsurpassed by any other lobby or combination of lobbies. The network of subsidiaries, affiliates, and joint ventures runs into the tens of thousands and affects the political economy of virtually every nation. Automobiles and petroleum determine the political composition of governments and the chemical composition of the atmosphere.[33]

---

[33] *Beyond Repair: The Ecology of Capitalism,* cited earlier, Chapter Five. The foregoing quotation appears on p. 98; much of the data to follow are also drawn from this excellent study of these two industries.

As we saw in Chapter Four, the emergence of the automobile as a widely-owned commodity in the 1920's was the principal developmental/growth factor in the prosperity of that period. Setting aside its meaning for petroleum and construction (of buildings, suburbs, roads, etc.), consider the demands put on other industries by the automobile. It accounts for these percentages of the gross market consumption of the following products: steel, 21 percent; aluminum, 10.4 percent; lead, 54.7 percent; nickel, 14.3 percent; natural rubber, 68.8 percent; zinc, 36.5 percent. Automobiles represent about a quarter of *all* retail sales. The industry estimates that one out of every six jobs in America is dependent upon the automobile—it is responsible for 16 percent of the work force, 13 percent of GNP, involving more than eight hundred thousand businesses. There are more automobile mechanics per car than physicians per capita. General Motors alone accounts for over half of all passenger cars produced in the U.S. and directly employs almost eight hundred thousand people. As noted in Chapter Three, its sales in 1972 were over $30 billion; its profits (after taxes), over $2 billion. Moving alongside the automobile industry is the petroleum industry. GM is the largest industrial corporation measured by sales; EXXON is the largest measured by assets, and second in sales.

Dependence upon this pattern of production, jobs, consumption, and transportation has become an addiction in the American economy (and moves toward that extreme in other industrial capitalist societies). But the process did not create itself, nor does it go on without the aid of pushers. There are of course, as the foregoing data show, thousands upon thousands of street and road contractors, motel operators, repair shops, suburban shopping centers, fast-food shops, gas station operators, mechanics, salesmen, etc., etc., whose profits, incomes and lives would be substantially disrupted were this complex to be lessened in our lives by, say, the proliferation of mass urban transit systems. But if they are among the dependent beneficiaries of the status quo, it is the auto, oil, and major construction companies who are its most powerful supporters. Up to very recently, they have been almost unopposed in the use of their power and influence both to expand the use of the automobile and to hinder even the maintenance of public transport.

These groups have also been the moving force behind the Highway Trust Fund, which has spent $32 billion on highways since 1956. (Its supporters claim another $300 billion will be needed over the next fifteen years, ten times the rate since 1956. For every $50 spent on highways, the federal government has spent one dollar on mass transit.) This lobby is also among the principal combatants of effective pollution controls, as revealed in the initiative campaign for and against the so-called Clean Environment Act in California in 1972.[34] Nationally (in

---

[34]See Weisberg, ibid., pp. 128–32, and the San Francisco *Bay Guardian,* July-August, 1972.

1973), the lobby was successful in relaxing and postponing emission controls, and in preventing Highway Trust Funds to be used for mass transit projects.

Quite apart from the air pollution provided by motorists is that provided by the industries which are producing the stuff of pollution (not least of which are the auto and oil industries). In the San Francisco Bay Area, for example, official estimates state that industry is responsible for 54 percent of the visible air pollutants; and that ten corporations (four petroleum, four chemical) alone were responsible for 70 percent of all industrial pollution. The same ten corporations contributed about one-seventh of the $1.5 million used to defeat the Clean Environment Act.

The corporations that pollute the environment with their production, that induce us to use their products so that we do likewise, and that use their power to derail serious efforts to reverse these processes, are doing what is natural and necessary for them. They grow or decline as the system they now control grows or declines; and the law of growth to which all have become habituated knows only quantitative expression: *More!* As Mumford says, "the internal problems of the metropolis and its subsidiary areas are reflections of a whole civilization geared to expansion by strictly rational and scientific means for purposes that have become progressively more empty and trivial, more infantile and primitive, more barbarous and massively irrational."[35]

As if all this were not enough, in 1972 and 1973 public clamor arose, or was created, about an "energy crisis." That this crisis surfaced just as the Watergate exposures began to mount was perhaps a major reason why the general public, small oil refiners and independent retailers, and (among others) many attorneys-general of the separate states voiced the suspicion that the crisis was more contrived than real. Another major reason, of course, was that the prices of gasoline, heating oil, and natural gas rose rapidly and threatened to rise even more, at a time when the public was already plagued with accelerating general inflation.

On the grounds of rising gasoline prices alone there were ample reasons for suspicion: the major oil companies reported spectacular increases in profits after taxes for the first quarter of 1973 (the exact period in which the "crisis" hit the news): EXXON's profits were up 43 percent. Not only were independent discount-price retailers being denied supplies and shutting down, but the majors were building a rash of new stations at the same time—sometimes in the same places, only larger. But there was more to it than that, important though rising prices and profits in the short-run are to the oil companies.

Data made available in mid-1973 (in publications such as the *Wall Street Journal* and *Business Week*) indicated that the energy crisis of the

---

[35] *The City in History*, p. 554.

moment was a business creation. But there is little doubt that in a decade or so energy shortages of all kinds will be real and growing. The tumult and shouting of 1973 appear to be an attempt on the part of the major energy suppliers to shape the future so that the ultimate real shortages can be turned to their advantage, in the form of greater profits and greater power. As James Ridgeway points out:

> These companies know, as the average citizen does not, that the energy crisis could be the most important political and economic issue of the last quarter of the twentieth century. Not only does the production, distribution, and use of energy underlie the entire environmental movement, but also energy is the foundation of the modern industrial state.[36]

Over two-thirds of the world's oil is controlled by seven companies, five of them American. As known oil reserves in the United States run out, dependence grows daily on oil found either in political hotspots such as the Middle East and Southeast Asia (of which more in the next chapter), or in areas such as Alaska where environmental damage is a high probability. The major oil companies, knowing this better than anyone else, naturally choose to make their investment decisions without interference from environmentalists, antiwar types, or others. The "energy crisis" facilitates an increase in the *political* power of the oil companies, as the demand for their products becomes ever more desperate. This is all the more likely because the same companies have increasingly gained control over fuels other than oil: coal, uranium, and gas. EXXON, for example, is the single largest owner of coal deposits in the United States. As Ridgeway shows in meticulous detail, the oil companies have worked out an effective pattern of ownership and cooperation over competing fuels, and with those companies and facilities that transport (tankers and pipelines), accommodate (seaports), finance and own energy and other companies (banks, insurance companies, foundations and universities), are major users (nonferrous metal and power producers for example)—and, of course, with the agencies that regulate (the Federal Power Commission, and various state agencies).

Against such patterns of ownership, control, influence, and cooperation, the environmental movement seems a very small David with poor aim, pitted against an enormous and agile Goliath. Oil is the single most powerful industry in the United States and in the world; along with the automobile industry (and both are tied in closely with the most power-

---

[36]James Ridgeway, *The Last Play: The Struggle to Monopolize the World's Energy Resources* (New York: Dutton, 1973), p. 3. Analytically and factually this book is unquestionably the best guide to understanding the energy crisis; it also provides many insights into the sources and uses of corporate power.

ful financial institutions), its power is both unprecedented and unmatched, in the market and in politics.[37]

Environmental imbalance is systemic, the result of our system running at its necessary speed in ways that suit the system's criteria. It is not the result of self-indulgence, of people driving to work instead of biking, walking, or taking non-existent mass transit facilities, for example. The environmental costs have been very high up to now; they have only just begun to mount.

THE BELL TOLLS

What most people know about environmental imbalance is that if we don't take care, people will die. But even casual students of this question know that people died from poisoned air in Belgium in the 1930's, that over 4,000 deaths in London in the 1950's were authoritatively attributed to "smog," and that deaths related to pollution are now reported regularly in Europe, the United States and Japan. The people who die are those who have emphysema, or a heart condition, or who are otherwise weak—the poisoned air finishes them off. And there are the deaths due to poisoned water, or from fish poisoned by poisoned water, or . . . something. The cause of all this is well-known: the uncontrolled process of industrialization and consumerism. What is the cure?

The cure dwells in the halls of power. But the halls of power are presently filled with killers of the environment, even though they may soothe us with TV commercials showing either that there is *no* problem, or that if there is, it isn't *their* fault. Legislation, when passed over the substantial and well-financed opposition of the polluters, is soon diluted and controlled by their representatives. Cry the beloved country though we may, either singly or in massive crowds such as those on Earth Day, public action is the only means by which ecological imbalance can be replaced by ecological balance. But public action is presently dominated by local, regional, state, and federal bodies whose criteria center first around profit and power, and then, perhaps, on the preservation of life. That those with power are toying with their own lives as well as ours simply tells us that not only the powerless are dehumanized by this society.

It speaks volumes that it should be necessary through great effort to place an initiative for a "Clean Environment" on a state ballot, something any legislature could and should do without the powerless having

---

[37]The relationship between the oil industry and Presidents Kennedy and Johnson is discussed briefly in Chapter Seven; here we may refer to a bright survey of Nixon's connections with oil, and with other powerful supporters in what the author calls "the Southern-rim." See Kirkpatrick Sale, "The World Behind Watergate," *New York Review of Books,* May 3, 1973.

to spend time and money to push such legislation. When such ballot measures are defeated by massive scare advertising, paid for by the very companies whose TV ads seek to soothe us, that tells us something more —about the companies and about the deluded voters.

This kind of threatening situation led Veblen, on the eve of World War I and after suggesting what had to be done, to go on and say, "But history records more frequent and more spectacular instances of the triumph of imbecile institutions over life and culture than of peoples who have by force of instinctive insight saved themselves alive out of a desperately precarious institutional situation, such, for instance, as now faces the people of Christendom."[38]

Setting modern war aside, one cannot imagine a more effective system for destroying life than that within which we now function; except that war cannot be set aside. It grows from the same social matrix as the destruction of the environment and the death of our cities; the principal difference is that the destruction by war is deliberate whereas that coming from our economic system is a "by-product." The social outlook guiding both disasters is the same, as is the technology. Growth for its own sake, production for its own sake, consumption for its own sake, and power for the sake of continuing the rest—these are the drives that have shaped the modern world, whose leader (at this writing) is presently the United States.

Human beings can do better on this continent, and they have. The civilization of the Native Americans, before we crushed it, was a marvel of balance between human beings and nature, and among themselves. Listen to this Chief as he speaks to a French officer in the early days of settlement:

> As to us, we find all our riches and all our conveniences among ourselves, without troubles, without exposing our lives to the dangers in which you find yourselves constantly through your long voyages; and whilst feeling compassion for you in the sweetness of our repose, we wonder at the anxieties and cares which you give yourselves, night and day, in order to load your ships. . . . Now tell me this one little thing, if thou hast any sense, which of these two is the wisest and happiest? He who labours without ceasing and only obtains with great trouble enough to live on, or he who rests in comfort and finds all he needs in the pleasure of hunting and fishing?[39]

We cannot return to that condition of easy and natural balance, nor are there many Americans who would even if it were possible. But we

---

[38] *Instinct of Workmanship*, p. 25. By 1914, everyone expected war; however, its length, spread, and endless disastrous consequences were not expected by the "respectable people" who brought it about.

[39] Quoted in *To Serve the Devil*, vol. 1, pp. 43–4.

can seek to live at peace with our environment, our fellow human beings, and ourselves in an urban and industrial civilization. We can, but not so long as the bulk of Americans continue to strive for profit and power and an overflowing cornucopia of increasingly contrived and expensive consumer goods—strive as donkeys strive for carrots fixed beyond their noses. The bulk of Americans cannot achieve what they seek.

The time has come to take thought, to reflect on what the genuine needs and pleasures of life are, and to find some symmetry between our ends and our means. Those ends are not mysterious, or the province of a few: we wish ourselves and our loved ones to eat well, to be comfortably clothed and housed, to learn through education what we can become and do, to be healthy, to enjoy nature and the works of the species; to have control over our lives. Each of these ends moves away from us, not closer, with each passing year. We count as our treasures what we have been socialized to count as treasures, though they defile our lives and make robots of us all: the automobile, the TV, the encapsulated suburban existence, the gleaming high buildings, the ever-rising GNP, "fast" food. We are moving in the wrong direction for human beings.

Cities at their worst in the past had valuable qualities to them that our planners now rush to obliterate. They had neighborhoods, they were disorderly, they bustled with the diversities of our ethnic and religious backgrounds, they had some life of their own, and the people in them knew them as homes, not as way stations to the next job, or as places with airports, motels, freeways, and ghettoes. There is in our present processes a dynamic which guarantees its intensification—unless the people take hold. "We must," as Lincoln said in the midst of another crisis, "disenthrall ourselves."[40]

READING SUGGESTIONS

We have glimpsed only the surface of the issues raised in this chapter, although many of the references footnoted will take the reader below that surface. Here are a few more suggestions. Theodore Lowi, in his *End of Liberalism** (New York: Norton, 1969), shows the deep inadequacies of present ways and means of liberal policies and politics, and most

---

[40]What cities have been in America is discussed systematically and humanely by Jane Jacobs, in her *Death and Life of Great American Cities** (New York: Random House, 1961). See especially the first chapter. Richard Sennett, *The Uses of Disorder** (New York: Random House; Vintage, 1970) provides a penetrating analysis of the psychological dangers of the artifical order of urban/suburban existence, and offers some wise proposals for change.

effectively in his discussions of urban reforms—not least because he speaks as a liberal. Among Mumford's many fine books, his *The Highway and the City* (New York: Harcourt Brace Jovanovich, 1958) is a profound study of the relationships suggested by the title. Health and education are among the critical problems of our cities. Barbara and John Ehrenreich, *The American Health Empire** (New York: Random House; Vintage, 1971) help us to understand why that is so regarding medical care. Educational problems and possibilities have called forth many fine books in recent years; I have found two of the most illuminating to have been Jonathan Kozol, *Death at an Early Age** (Boston: Houghton Mifflin, 1967) and George Dennison, *The Lives of Children** (New York: Random House, 1969). Miriam Wasserman's *School Fix,** cited earlier, is valuable for understanding city politics as well as education. Studies of how cities "work" are badly needed. Two that commend themselves are Mike Royko, *Boss** (New York: New American Library, 1971), an easy-reading treatment of Chicago's Mayor Daley; a more penetrating study is by Edward C. Hayes, *Power Structure and Urban Policy: Who Rules in Oakland?** (New York: McGraw-Hill, 1972). A useful book of readings, ranging broadly in both focus and viewpoint, is Joe R. Feagin, ed., *The Urban Scene** (New York: Random House, 1973). The Steffens essay on St. Louis is included in an excellent anthology of the "Muckrakers' " writings—critical attacks on corruption, monopoly, poverty, etc., in the first years of this century—edited by Harvey Swados, *Years of Conscience: The Muckrakers* (New York: World, 1962).

chapter seven
Imperialism,
American-style

While this America settles in the mould of its vulgarity,
  heavily thickening to empire,
And protest, only a bubble in the molten mass, pops and
  sighs out, and the mass hardens,

I sadly remember that the flower fades to make fruit,
  the fruit rots to make earth.
Out of the mother; and through the spring exultances,
  ripeness and decadence; and home to the mother.

(Robinson Jeffers, *Shine, Perishing Republic*)

Peoples of all nations live in part by myths; the hardiest of these, and probably the most dangerous, have to do with their nation's foreign relationships. Two such myths stand out for Americans: we have been a self-sufficient national economy; and our external relationships have been benign.

By comparison with other capitalist nations we have been, of course, relatively self-sufficient: Great Britain, for instance, must import half of its food and four-fifths of its raw materials, whereas our total foreign trade seldom rises above 5 percent of our GNP. In this, as in other social relationships, however, quantitative measures taken alone are misleading. From the beginning, our economic development has been critically dependent upon our foreign economic dealings. In the last century that dependence has steadily increased, until today the American economy is dependent not just for its health, but for its very functioning, on its commodity exports, resource imports, and foreign investments. That dependence has grown along with the growth of an American empire, seldom seen as benign by those who live under its controls.

Nobody would dispute the generalization regarding dependence upon external economic relationships in our colonial period, of course. When we achieved our independence, it was the terms not the importance of those relationships that changed. America's foreign economic relationships and policies have been in a state of constant flux, from Independence to the present; both ends and means have changed—a necessity for a society whose economic structure is changing rapidly, in a rapidly changing world. The one constant in that history, however, is the conscious dependence of the United States on the rest of the world.

Those who have argued otherwise have been transfixed by the natural wealth and great size of the United States, which has of course set it apart from other nations. What has made us *like* other capitalist nations is that we have been a large and wealthy *capitalist* society. Capitalist societies have everywhere and always been vitally dependent upon their external relationships, have always functioned critically within an international setting. This has been much obscured, however, because almost all history is written and seen as *national* history, abetted by patriotic sentiments, education, and the sheer availability of such historical materials. And most history has been as superficial concerning capitalism as a system as it has been concerning the global setting within which national capitalist economies have functioned.

Capitalist economies must continually expand, as we have seen. The cutting edge of expansion often moves more easily and more profitably abroad than at home; yet it would be as unwise to attempt to isolate foreign from domestic functioning as to ignore one or the other, in what is a system of dynamic interdependence. At any one time one capitalist nation is dominant in the world economy. The very use of its dominance, however, leads to the emergence of a new leading power. Furthermore, the most powerful capitalist economy is not only the vital center of world capitalist expansion (or contraction); it is also the leading imperialist power. All these generalizations will now be examined in greater detail.

Americans quite generally see the United States as the leading capitalist, or "free world," power, and take great pride in our status as Number One. Most Americans do not see the United States as imperialist *at all,* let alone as the world's leading imperialist nation.[1] Yet the United States *is* that nation, not only in the minds of radicals but also in the view of many spokesmen in the other capitalist powers (themselves the second-level imperialist nations), to say nothing of the views of Third World countries. Most Americans would choke on terms like "the American Empire"; yet, the British Empire, the French Empire, and Imperial Ger-

---

[1]Typically, historians see the United States as having begun and swiftly ended its imperialist career in the years between the Spanish-American War and World War I, with a few pieces left to tidy up in the Caribbean in the 1920's. For a representative position, see Faulkner, *The Decline of Laissez-Faire,* Chapter 4. For a more realistic view, see Williams, *Contours of American History,* throughout, and the fundamental study of Walter La Feber, *New Empire: An Interpretation of American Expansionism, 1860–1898** (Ithaca: Cornell University Press, 1970).

many were terms bringing pride to most of the citizens of those countries. Anger and consternation ensued as their empires began to decline, and the United States, directly or indirectly, took over.

One reason Americans so quickly deny our imperial status is the pervasive lack of understanding of what imperialism is and does; another reason for the denial (for most Americans) is a systematic miseducation—what Veblen called "a trained incapacity"—regarding American history and American capitalism. Preceding chapters have sought to shed light on the latter; now we must explore the development and the nature of imperialism.

Imperialism is an historical process; to attempt a one-line definition of it (for instance, "the extension of political power by one state over another")[2] is to promote more confusion than enlightenment. As we now seek to show what imperialism has been and is, our discussion will move within a framework of several questions: *When* and *why* does a society expand its influence and control over other areas? *Where* is it likely to do so? *What* does the relationship mean to the imperialist and to the imperialized society? *How* are the relationships developed and maintained, and *how* and *why* do they change in nature and in meaning over time? *Who* benefits and *who* pays, at either end of the relationship? In seeking to answer these questions we shall first set forth a very general statement, and then explore the specific historical developments preceding and accompanying America's emergence as Number One.

IMPERIALISM: BECOMING AND BEING

The seeds of both capitalism and nationalism are to be found in the medieval trading cities: for example, Florence, Milan, Lübeck, and Bruges. So are the seeds of mercantilism and *modern* imperialism, which is sometimes called "the New Mercantilism."

"Buy cheap and sell dear" was the slogan emblazoned on the medieval merchant's escutcheon. The implementation of that policy abroad had two sides to it: *protection* and *privilege*. Internally for the towns it required a third policy, what the great historian of mercantilism Eli Heckscher called *"provisioning."*[3] "Mercantilism," Heckscher states, "is medieval town policy writ large." In an important sense, that is so; it is also useful to say that modern imperialism is "mercantilism writ large." But there are important differences between town economy, mercantilism, and imperialism—and of the meanings of protection,

---

[2]Quoted critically by James O'Connor, "The Meaning of Economic Imperialism," in Robert I. Rhodes, ed., *Imperialism and Underdevelopment: A Reader** (New York: Monthly Review Press, 1970), p. 101. This is an excellent article in an excellent collection.

[3]Eli Heckscher, *Mercantilism* (London: Allen & Unwin, 1935), 2 vols., is the basic work. See his brief discussion "Mercantilism," in the *Encyclopaedia of the Social Sciences.*

privilege and provisioning for each—differences given by the development of capitalism and of accompanying industrialism. The similarities and the differences both deserve comment.

The medieval trading town functioned very much as a unit in facing the external world. Surrounding it was the countryside, the source of its foodstuffs (and sometimes of its fibers and ores, used in medieval industry and trade). The provisioning policy of the towns had as its aim the guarantee of a steady and cheap supply of what the towns needed to consume and produce, an aim that placed the ruling merchant class in opposition to the surrounding feudal nobility and that ultimately brought the merchant into alliance with the rising monarchs who were also in conflict with the nobility. When those alliances were effective, the modern nation-state was the result. The merchants sought a united front in their dealings with other medieval traders in far-flung towns; Italians, Germans, and Flemings dealing with England, for example. The Italians and the Flemings in the 12th, 13th, and 14th centuries were most powerful, and could function effectively in a pattern resembling "free trade." In the 14th century, the individually weaker German towns banded together in the Hanseatic League, a grouping of about seventy towns acting as a powerful unit in their trading activities over the face of Northern Europe and England.

In their own towns, the merchants sought price and wage policies that provided stability and a supply of exportable products at costs that would allow profits. The famous "just wage and just price" policies of the medieval towns were "just" up to the point only where the ruling merchants could flourish in their inter-regional activities. Much of what was "bought cheap" was a result of exploitative relationships outside and within the towns; what was "sold dear" was a function of the strength of the merchants elsewhere and that strength was enhanced whenever and wherever possible by trading privileges and by both economic and military protection. By the 14th and 15th centuries, the degree to which the necessary protection and privileges were forthcoming was becoming a matter of national or quasi-national power at both ends of the relationship.

While nation-states replaced trading cities as the focus of commerce and industry, the aims of foreign policy remained much the same, although means could and had to change: the scope of affairs had enlarged, and so had the power of the contestants. Provisioning policy now meant the assurance of domestic and external sources of food and raw materials; in turn this led to a colonial policy whose aim was to control the trade and resources flowing from the colonies and to prevent rival states from having access to those same areas. There were great gains to be made from success, and great losses to be suffered from the success of others—losses measured in profits, and in national economic and military strength. The medieval town policy of "buy cheap and sell dear" became a national policy; it became "beggar thy neighbor." One nation's strength was seen as inversely related to the strength of the others.

This was all pre-industrial, in the early years of capitalism, from the 16th into the 18th centuries. As the 18th century melted into the 19th, means changed. Both needs and possibilities were stronger; the developing changes were reflected in a new meaning for provisioning, privilege, and protection. Summed up, the new meanings created modern imperialism. At this point it becomes necessary to draw the distinctions between mercantilism and imperialism.

Capitalism in the days of mercantilism was not industrial. Colonial policies tended to have seaports and coastlines as their geographic locus. The great gains in trade were typically made from high value–low bulk commodities: pepper and tea, sugar and slaves, gold and silver. This might be expected in an era of long, slow, and dangerous voyages. As modern industry developed, the patterns changed. Steamships and railroads tied continents together, allowing and requiring hinterlands to be penetrated. Bulkier, lower-value commodities were needed to supply growing industry and industrial populations with raw materials and foodstuffs. The relatively short-term commercial investments of the earlier period were added to by necessary long-term investments—in expanded harbor facilities, in railroads, in mines and in plantations. The political impact of *mercantilist* colonial policy was typically manifested in effective relationships with *local* rulers and the regulation of privileged and protected trade between colony and metropolis. The new *imperialism* required,

> as the colonial system of earlier centuries did not, a large measure of political control over the *internal* relations and structure of the colonial economy. This it requires, not merely to "protect property" and to ensure that the profit of the investment is not offset by political risks, but actually to create the essential conditions for the profitable investment of capital. Among these conditions is the existence of a proletariat sufficient to provide a plentiful and cheap labour-supply; and where this does not exist, suitable modifications of pre-existent social forms will need to be enforced (of which the reduction of tribal land-reserves and the introduction of differential taxation on natives living in the tribal reserve in East and South Africa are examples).

Thus the "political logic of imperialism" is

> to graduate from "economic penetration" to "spheres of influence," from "spheres of influence" to protectorates or indirect control, and from protectorates *via* military occupation to annexation.[4]

---

[4]Maurice Dobb, *Political Economy and Capitalism* (London: Routledge, 1937), pp. 239–40. This analysis is in Chapter VII, "Imperialism," one of the most astute analyses of the development, emphasizing the differences between the earlier and later stages of capitalist expansion.

There has been much discussion of which comes first, political/military or economic expansion: Does trade follow the flag, or does the flag follow trade? Both happen, and they also walked hand in hand from the beginning. The gains and the rivalries associated with mercantilism and imperialism were handmaidens of colonial and imperial *strategies*—for instance, control of seaports and coaling stations, the development of naval stations for refueling and battle readiness—if for no other reason than to keep them from rivals. There was a graceful interaction: strategic considerations facilitated economic advance; economic advance required strategic considerations. Chickens and eggs.

The late 19th century wave of imperialism swept the globe; the sun never set on the British flag; next door, in some contiguous colony European flags also waved in the sun. Imperialism became direct, and control became direct. Colonial governments were *colonial,* and their "legal" masters were in the metropoli. Thus did the 19th century end and the 20th century begin.

After World War I, the seams began to give; after World War II, the seams tore apart. Earlier, mercantilism had given way to imperialism; after World War II, imperialism gave way to *neo-colonialism,* sometimes called "welfare imperialism." The strain on traditional imperial ties—those of England and France, of Holland, Italy, Germany, and Japan—had first appeared after World War I, in conjunction with strains developing *within* these major capitalist powers. The depression of the 1930's greatly increased the strains; World War II gave the *coup de grâce* to traditional imperialism. The older imperialist powers lacked the financial and military resources necessary to hold on to their territories, whether they knew it or not. Britain knew it better than some others, loosing its hold on India and most of its other colonies. France was less prudent; it spent much of its treasure and let the blood of Frenchmen and the peoples of North Africa and Indochina flow for years before it let go, almost bringing itself down in the process.

The United States stood waiting. As the only major capitalist power strengthened by World War II, the United States was able and eager to move into the "vacua" created by European and Japanese collapse. Our movement was in the name of preserving freedom and of promoting economic development. With these slogans on our banner, we strode forth to create the largest, the most profitable, and the most costly imperialist network in world history, as befitted the most powerful nation in the world's history. Our style was not to control ports or nations, directly, as in days of yore; we controlled only the finances, the economies, and the military of our neocolonial empire—ways we had learned in our prep school days after the Spanish-American war.

America's expansion overseas after World War II was not confined to hitherto colonial areas. Our hegemony was global: inroads into Europe,

Canada, Central and South America, the Caribbean, the Middle East, South and Southeast Asia and Japan, and steel rings around the USSR and China. But our impact on the world was substantially diverse, depending upon whether the affected area was developed or underdeveloped when we took a strong hand: in Western Europe, Canada, and Japan, our influence helped to rescue and to speed up economic growth and development; in the rest of the capitalist world, our impact continued that of the earlier pattern—we deepened its *under*development.[5]

With the 1970's, a dramatic and uncertain new era opened up, both in the developed and in the underdeveloped sectors of the globe, as well as between them. The developed capitalist nations of Canada, Western Europe and Japan came increasingly into conflict and competition with the United States; the underdeveloped countries moved into one degree or another of resistance. They did so because of their own great needs, and encouraged by the Vietnamese, who had raised the costs and exposed the limits of American expansionism. Adding to the growing uncertainty has been the emergence of the multinational corporation— which, we shall see, lessens the power of national governments while increasing the power of international capitalism.

Up to now we have put forth a string of heady generalizations, which merely point to answers to our questions regarding imperialism—when and why, where, what and how, and who?—but which do not as such constitute adequate answers. The when and the why move in terms of needs and possibilities; the where in terms of what is useful and necessary and possible, regarding relative strength; what imperialism means is profit and power for the strong, exploitation and increased weakness for the already vulnerable, development for the advanced and underdevelopment for the undeveloped. In this chapter and earlier we have also seen that geographic expansion is critically encouraged and abetted by *economic* motivations, but that it is more complex than that. We shall also see that although the growth of advanced technology and monopolistic structures of industry speeds up imperialistic expansion, such expansion has clearly taken place before and without such structures. Great Britain and the United States were prime examples of that in the 19th century, before monopoly developed in either nation—Great Britain with its overseas empire and America with its continental expansion.

All these generalizations require much in the way of support and elaboration. Let us begin first with a central question: Does capitalism

---

[5]Following André Gunder Frank, we shall argue that capitalist control of what became colonial areas transformed *un*development into *under*development—i.e., a relatively stable into a retrogressive process—later in this chapter.

require imperialism? And, a somewhat different question: Where there has been imperialism, has there always been capitalism?

CAPITALISM AND IMPERIALISM

Empires litter the pages of history—Persian, Phoenician, Greek, Roman, Carthaginian, Holy Roman, to mention only a few. Although commercialism was an important part of the lives of some of these societies, only by misusing the term could we classify them as capitalist. And, on the other hand, the modern Swiss are surely capitalist, but, internationalist though they and their connections are, it would stretch the term to call them imperialistic. Still, as a world economic system capitalism has always *been* imperialist; or such, at least, is our argument. How and why is this so?[6]

The most persuasive argument stating that capitalism does *not* require imperialism—indeed, that capitalism and imperialism are *opposed* in their general features—was that put forth by Joseph A. Schumpeter. His definition of imperialism, one of those troublesome one-liners, helps to obscure the problem from the beginning. "Imperialism," Schumpeter says, "is the objectless disposition on the part of a state to unlimited forcible expansion."[7] By "objectless" Schumpeter means expansion for its own sake, and he observes that "objectless tendencies toward forcible expansion, without definite, utilitarian limits—that is, non-rational and irrational, purely instinctual inclinations toward war and conquest —play a very large role in the history of mankind."[8] Probably that was true in the past, and doubtless such inclinations persist in the present. What is at issue, however, is whether and when such inclinations become "objectful" and useful, indeed necessary for the maintenance of a social system such as capitalism, quite apart from whatever role expansionism might have played where *not* necessary. Here O'Connor is apt. "In connection with economic expansionism," he says,

> pre-capitalist and capitalist societies differ in five general ways: First, in pre-capitalist societies economic expansion was irregular, unsystematic, not integral to normal economic activity. In capitalist societies, foreign trade and investment are rightly considered to be the "engines of

---

[6]We shall find it convenient and appropriate here to follow closely the position taken by James O'Connor, in his article "The Meaning of Economic Imperialism," cited earlier. Our compressed summary should not be taken as an adequate substitute for the fuller position put forth by O'Connor.

[7]Joseph A. Schumpeter, *Imperialism and Social Classes* (New York: Kelley, 1951), p. 7. Edited and with an introduction by Paul M. Sweezy, a former student of Schumpeter's, and also his respectful critic. The original essay was written in 1919.

[8]Ibid., p. 83.

growth." . . . Second, in pre-capitalist societies the economic gains from expansion were windfall gains, frequently taking the form of sporadic plunder. In capitalist societies, profits from overseas trade and investment are an integral part of national income, and considered in a matter-of-fact manner. Third, in pre-capitalist societies plunder . . . was often consumed in the field by the conquering armies. . . . In capitalist societies, exploited territories are fragmented and integrated into the structure of the metropolitan economy. . . . Fourth, in pre-capitalist societies debates within the ruling class ordinarily revolved around the question whether or not to expand. In capitalist societies, ruling-class debates normally turn on the issue of what is the best way to expand. Last, in relation to colonialism . . ., land seizure, colonist settlement, or both was the only mode of control which the metropolitan power could effectively exercise over the satellite region . . .; capitalist societies have developed alternative, indirect, and more complex forms of control.[9]

A basic reason for the inability or refusal of Schumpeter and of other conventional social scientists to see the connection between capitalism and imperialism is their inability or refusal to see the role played by expansion and exploitation in capitalist development; or, to put it more accurately, their belief that the necessary expansion will take place under benign circumstances. For Schumpeter, expansion abroad is necessary, but it takes place through the "rational" mode of free trade; expansion at home takes place through the turbulent but effective impact of technological development on the growth and the institutions of capitalism. But capitalism's entire history has been characterized by obstacles placed in the way of free trade, apart from the exceptional decades of the late 19th century, which were decades also of raging imperialist expansion. Technological development, far from breaking down monopolies, as Schumpeter hoped, facilitated their entrenchment.

Growth and development are socially difficult to initiate and to sustain: they require expanding markets and resources and a docile labor force; they entail change throughout the society, not just in its economic institutions. In comparison, markets, resources, and cheap labor are readily obtainable abroad. What might take decades and much civil conflict to achieve at home can be achieved abroad more quickly, with less or no domestic conflict. Granted that it has been a relatively common matter for the populations of the powerful societies to become excited over foreign dangers and possibilities, real or imagined. But why do they become excited? What induces them to pay taxes, to make sacrifices, even of their blood? Whatever may be said of the pre-capitalist world, and whatever may be said of the "common man's" inclination to "go West," what may and must be said of the modern capitalist world is that the business community has seen the butter for its bread—and sometimes the bread itself—in what have become the colonial and

---

[9]Op. cit., p. 103.

neocolonial areas of the world. That the major share of profits and trade derive from relationships among and between the *developed* countries seems to contradict this assertion, but only if we fail to see the capitalist system as a *global* division of labor, and the crucial role played by the natural resources (especially oil) in the underdeveloped countries.

In Great Britain and the United States, the two leading imperialist powers of the last century, and also the two leading capitalist powers in their time, the principal voice shaping public policy both at home and abroad, directly and through the channels of public opinion, has been that of business. As Veblen said,

> Representative government means, chiefly, representation of business interests. The government commonly works in the interest of the business man with a fairly consistent singleness of purpose. And in its solicitude for the business men's interests it is borne out by current public senti- ment, for there is a naive, unquestioning persuasion abroad among the body of the people to the effect that, in some occult way, the material interests of the populace coincide with the pecuniary interests of those business men. . . . It seldom happens, if at all, that the government of a civilized nation will persist in a course of action detrimental or not osten- sibly subservient to the interests of the more conspicuous body of the community's business men.[10]

But even assuming that the imperializing process has been at the behest—or at the very least with the acquiescence of—business, has it been necessary, *required?* There is finally no way of finding an unequiv- ocal answer to that question; we can only point to constant associations and explain why the associations have occurred, still leaving open whether or not they *had* to occur. Perhaps, for example, capitalism could have existed without poverty; it has not, so we must explain why poverty exists in the midst of riches. Similarly (although I doubt it very much) capitalism *might* have grown and been sustained without over- seas expansion and control; but what would have taken the place of the stimuli and gains from that expansion and control has never been ex- plained. Professor Tom Kemp has put this point exactly:

> To claim that "imperialism" was not a necessary stage in capitalist devel- opment is to imagine that the colossal development of the productive forces which took place in the nineteenth century could have proceeded without the bringing into being of a world-wide economy dominated by the leading capitalist powers. It is to imagine that somehow the character- istics of early industrial capitalism could have become permanent, with- out the growth of combines and monopolies, as an atomized collection of owner-financed firms. It is to assert that there was no relation between

---

[10] *The Theory of Business Enterprise,* pp. 286–87. Veblen's attention to such matters is most intense in his *An Inquiry Into the Nature of Peace . . .* * (New York: Macmillan, 1917).

the politics of states and the dominant economic interests within them. It is to assume that the powerful economic forces released by capitalism were kept in tow by old-line statesmen, demagogues and ideologues. It is to argue, with Schumpeter, the most clear-sighted and consistent representative of this school, that the characteristics of "imperialism" were atavistic survivals foreign to the true nature of capitalism, adopted by the bourgeoisie only as the result of a betrayal.[11]

Some readers will have been persuaded of the hand-in-glove relationship between capitalism and imperialism by now; some others never could be. Let us conclude this general part of the discussion with an observation of Harry Magdoff's on the same question:

> Imperialism . . . is so intertwined with the history and the resulting structure of modern capitalist society—with its economics, politics, and ruling ideas—that this kind of question is in the same category as, for example, "Is it necessary for the United States to keep Texas and New Mexico?" We could, after all, return these territories to the Mexican people and still maintain a high-production and high-standard-of-living economy. . . . Or one might ask, "Is Manhattan necessary for the United States?" It would surely be equitable to return land obtained from the Indians in a sharp deal. . . . Such a move to wipe out a terrible blot on the conscience of white America could be socially useful. Moreover, a new financial headquarters of the United States (and the capitalist world) could be designed to avoid slums, smog, pollution, and traffic crises. . . . The relevant question is not whether imperialism is necessary for the United States, but to discover the "rationality" of the historic process itself: why the United States and other leading capitalist nations persistently and recurringly acted in the imperialist fashion for at least three-quarters of a century.[12]

The foregoing has been an attempt to provide a skeletal framework for understanding what led to imperialism and what it is and means. Now let us flesh out that framework with historical matter.

THE BATON OF ECONOMIC POWER

Capitalism and nationalism emerged together in world history, and induced comparable attitudes and behavior. Economic individualism

---

[11] Tom Kemp, *Theories of Imperialism* (London: Dobson, 1967), pp. 165–66. As the book's title suggests, this is a survey of various theories. It is by far the very best study of its kind.

[12] *Social Policy* (September/October, 1970) in an exchange between Magdoff and S. M. Miller, Roy Bennett, and Cyril Alapatt, "Does the U.S. Economy Require Imperialism?" Magdoff's portion of the exchange, "The Logic of Imperialism," is reproduced in *Monthly Review* (October and November, 1970).

and competition have their counterpart in nationalism and national rivalries. It would be foolish to believe that any one merchant, industrialist, or financier could attribute his economic successes entirely, or even mostly, to his own doings, independent of the larger economic context within which he makes his gains; similarly, it would be foolish to attribute the economic "successes" of a particular nation to *its* own doings, independent of the world economy. In the past several hundred years, there has always been one country in the lead. It has been economically strongest, and supreme in the technology, and dominated the patterns of trade, finance, and production of the time. And it has had its way in shaping and using the political and military forms of the time.[13]

In the early dawn of capitalism and nationalism, before either existed as such, Venice and Florence—both territorial states, not nations—carried the baton of leadership. In the late medieval and early renaissance periods, Venice ruled the Mediterranean; Florence, not a naval power, drew its strength from its trans-alpine relationships. Florentine capital and trade stimulated what became the more dynamic northern rim of Europe—principally Antwerp, Holland, and later England—at the cost, finally, of Florentine collapse in the 14th century, as a result of growth elsewhere.

Economic advance in the medieval period was principally a result of growing inter-regional trade, which in turn stimulated and required urban industry and finance. The dynamic process that has characterized world economic history ever since worked slowly but inexorably even then: the leading area benefitted from its dominant relationships with lesser trading partners; the latter, transformed in the process, ultimately took over the lead. The nature of that process persists in the present; the scope and content have changed: national/international in scope, industrial in content.

The 16th century brought rapid overseas expansion, newly-found resources, and the need for expensive military forces on both land and sea. Traditional political and social patterns broke down, giving way chaotically to the emergence of new nations, new religious institutions, and the beginnings of capitalism. The Italians had brought Western Europe to that point; for centuries the Italians did not go beyond it, but the earlier "backward areas" did.

Beginning as cities, the Venetians, Milanese, Florentines and Genoese grew into territorial states, and spent much of their time and resources

---

[13]France in the 18th century (and Spain in the 16th) constitute partial exceptions to the generalization. Compared to either the Dutch or British economies, the French was institutionally and technologically retarded; yet France (like Spain, earlier) was seemingly "the leader," by virtue of military effort—but at the cost of distorting the more (in the long-run) rewarding economic relationships.

fighting each other while extending their economic relationships to the east, west, and north. The scope of these relationships required an alteration in the traditional medieval pattern of inter-regional politics, a pattern given its nature and its sweep by the pervasive Church. In the 15th century, the Italian states invented diplomacy, as a means of undertaking and securing their negotiations abroad. In doing so, they hastened the birth of the nation-states that came to exist in strength in the 16th century, and whose rivalries would provide the massive and enduring conflicts that brought us to the present. It was a new world. As Mattingly has said,

> Our modern notion of an international society composed of a heterogeneous collection of fictitious entities called states, all supposed to be equal, sovereign and completely independent, would have shocked both the idealism and the common sense of the fifteenth century. Such a society would have seemed to philosophers a repulsive anarchy . . .; and the concept would have been equally uncomfortable to practical statesmen.[14]

The transformation from medieval to modern economies took centuries; it took longest of all for the Italians. Benefitting for centuries from their location in the Mediterranean, central both for trade with the rich Near East and the emerging trans-alpine North, the Italians had little inclination to seek greener pastures. Columbus was hired by Spain; Cabot, also an Italian, was hired by England. The hinge on which the door opened for modern economies—that is, larger in scope, industrial in production—was the exploration and exploitation of overseas territories. Marx put it vividly:

> The discovery of gold and silver in America, the extirpation, enslavement and entombment in mines of the aboriginal population, the beginning of the conquest and looting of the East Indies, the turning of Africa into a warren for the commercial hunting of black-skins, signalised the rosy dawn of the era of capitalist production. These idyllic proceedings are the chief momenta of primitive accumulation. On their heels treads the commercial war of the European nations, with the globe for a theatre. It begins with the revolt of the Netherlands from Spain, assumes giant dimensions in England's anti-jacobin war, and is still going on in the opium wars against China, etc.[15]

---

[14]Garrett Mattingly, *Renaissance Diplomacy** (London: Cape, 1955; Penguin, 1965), p. 24. Up until about 1400, he points out, the West "still thought of itself as one society. Christendom was torn by the gravest internal conflicts, by religious schism, doctrinal dispute, and the endemic warfare of class against class. . . . But Latin Christendom still knew itself to be one." (p. 16)

[15]*Capital*, vol. I., p. 751.

In the 15th and 16th centuries, Portugal and Spain swept over the Far East and the New World. Their social and economic institutions were anachronistic; their gains drained away into Northern Europe, and especially into the hands of those who busied themselves in Antwerp—"a center of unbridled capitalism." Antwerp's location was central to the sea and overland trade of the North; it was granted a monopoly over the Portuguese spice trade first, and of the Spanish trade later (under Charles V). It was a glorious period, and a short one; it ended when Spanish largesse became Spanish destruction. Antwerp's typical figure, Tawney remarks, "was the international financier," serving the hustling merchants and princes who fattened on this enlarged world.[16]

TRADE WAR, WAR OF TRADE

The fall of Antwerp after the mid-16th century, due to religious and civil strife and the depredations of the Hapsburgs, was followed by the rise, not of a city—which for centuries had been the centers of economic strength—but of a region: the United Provinces, with Holland at their lead, and Amsterdam at the center of Holland. It was the first approximation to an economically viable *national* unit. Though tiny in population (perhaps two million), and bereft of the normal run of soils, minerals, timber, and the like (and with much of her "soil," the so-called polders, built up out of the sea, and protected by dikes), the Dutch rose to heights never before reached economically. Industry, trade, and finance combined with an enormous fleet to allow the Dutch to rule the world in the 17th century, and to remain financially strong throughout the 18th century. France and England struggled in that century to wrest the baton from the Dutch, and from each other.[17]

---

[16]Tawney, *Religion and the Rise of Capitalism*, p. 67. His discussion of the rise of Antwerp, pp. 67–9, ends with a characterization which with only a few alterations, fits today's world all too closely: "Nourished by the growth of peaceful commerce, the financial capitalism of the age fared not less sumptuously, if more dangerously, at the courts of princes. Mankind, it seems, hates nothing so much as its own prosperity. Menaced with an accession of riches which would lighten its toil, it makes haste to redouble its labors, and to pour away the perilous stuff, which might deprive of plausibility the complaint that it is poor. Applied to the arts of peace, the new resources commanded by Europe during the first half of the sixteenth century might have done something to exorcise the specters of pestilence and famine, and to raise the material fabric of civilization to undreamed-of heights. Its rulers, secular and ecclesiastical alike, thought otherwise. When pestilence and famine were ceasing to be necessities imposed by nature, they reestablished them by political art" (pp. 69–70).

[17]Excellent histories of the period of Iberian and Dutch dominance are J. H. Parry, *The Spanish Seaborne Empire* (New York: Knopf, 1966) and C. R. Boxer, *The Dutch Seaborne Empire* (New York: Knopf, 1965).

Until the 17th century, the colonization of the world was in the hands of the Portuguese and the Spanish, while the Italians continued their hold on the Mediterranean although increasingly with competition from English and French merchants. In the 17th century, the Dutch gained control over whole areas (e.g., the Netherlands East Indies) or unique trading privileges (as in Japan). Their trade branched out from Holland to Scandinavia, to Africa, to all of the Americas, and to Asia. The Dutch East India Company was quite probably the most powerful single economic organization the world had seen up to that time, the General Motors of its day. Its intra-Asian trade was more profitable than its Asian-European trade, which was very profitable indeed. Some idea of the relative economic strength of the Dutch (and, as well, of the nature of "mercantilist" thinking) is given by a famous argument of Colbert (first minister of King Louis XIV of France) in 1669:

> Commerce is carried on by 20,000 vessels and that number cannot be increased. Each nation strives to have its fair share and to get ahead of the others. The Dutch now fight this war [of trade] with 15,000 to 16,000 vessels, the English with 3,000 to 4,000 and the French with 500 to 600. The last two countries can improve their commerce only by increasing the number of their vessels and can increase the number only by paring away from the 15,000 to 16,000 Dutch ships. . . . It must be added that trade causes perpetual strife both in time of war and in time of peace between all the nations of Europe to decide which of them shall have the greatest share.[18]

The Dutch, lacking natural resources of their own, imported them from all over the world, processed them, and sold the higher-value product, once more, all over the world. They had begun to do that in the medieval period, with fish from the North Sea and the Baltic. That led to shipbuilding; to enhanced trade; to industries processing the grain (into gin, as well as flour), the cocoa, the coffee, the tobacco, the diamonds, the fibers, etc. From it all, the Dutch became the leading trading, industrial, financial, and shipping nation. In finding its way to that eminence, the Dutch—like the Italians before them—opened up and stimulated other areas.

The other areas included France and England, both larger in population and richer in natural resources than the Dutch; both were able also to copy, or to reproduce, the economic sources of Dutch strength. The English became much better at it than the French, although, at the opening of the 18th century if there seemed to be any serious rival for Dutch power, it was the French. As the 18th century wore on, it increasingly became the scene of an Anglo-French struggle on land and sea, in Asia (especially India), in the Carribbean and North America, and on the

---

[18]Quoted in Heckscher, op. cit., vol. 2, pp. 26–7.

Continent. When the French were finally defeated at Waterloo, the underlying economic strength of the British had been decisive.

British economic strength was given its critical edge over the French by the trading proclivities and abilities of the British, derided by the French as "a nation of shopkeepers." In the 18th century, France was by far the richer (for the benefit of a small fraction of its people) of the two nations, as it was twice England in population, and blessed with the best and broadest agricultural resources of any European nation. But in the emerging capitalist world where trade was vital, the natural riches of France, requiring little foreign trade, turned out to be dynamic disadvantages. Recall Colbert's calculation of the relative number of English and French vessels: England, although it had a much smaller population, had at least five times as many ships. Ships, shipbuilding, and sailors strengthened fighting as well as trading capacities.

France, rich and the dominant military power of Europe, was continually involved in continental warfare. The splendor of its Court had another side to it: its power, its corruption, and its taxes bled France dry, and influenced the pattern of French production toward the elegant. The economic power of the future lay with those who moved toward the mass production of the mundane. While France was achieving cultural and military supremacy in the 17th and 18th centuries, England was improving its technology and spreading its trade. In England, there was a bourgeois revolution in the 17th century, and an industrial revolution in the 18th century; in France, the consolidation of absolute monarchy in the 17th century, and a weak bourgeois revolution in the 18th century. In England, Adam Smith; in France, Napoleon.

WORLD ECONOMY AND IMPERIALISM

The 19th century belonged to Great Britain. The Dutch although economically supreme in the 17th century, presided over a string quartet by comparison with the symphony orchestrated by Great Britain in the 19th century. The Dutch scrambled continuously, in and between wars; the strength of Britain achieved the *Pax Britannica*. Industrialism and modern technology made the difference: it was a difference in scale and penetration, entailing differences in all aspects of social existence. The 16th through the 18th centuries were given their dynamism by trade, and overseas relationships were mercantilist; the 19th century was industrial in its dynamic, and imperialist overseas. These contrasts require further emphasis.

Industrialism means many things; England, as the first industrial nation, was characterized by: increasing specialization within the economy, and the sharp decline of agricultural sufficiency; increasing use of coal and iron in production, and for transportation; increasingly capital-intensive production (that is, the use of machinery, with high fixed costs) and the consequent need for mass markets; the need to guarantee that no part of this increasingly interdependent system would break loose and bring it all down. For England especially, the new industrialism meant the need to import the major portion of its foodstuffs and raw materials. These were not produced, generally, at ports or coastal strips, but in the hinterland. The iron steamship made it possible to carry bulky and low-priced commodities more cheaply and more reliably than sailing ships; the railroad made it possible to penetrate whole continents. The process of realizing these needs and possibilities led to the annexation of whole territories. In addition to privileged trade, there was privileged investment; instead of colonial outposts, an empire; instead of forts, occupying armies; instead of dots on a map, whole areas colored pink.

The British were not alone, either in need or in possibility. But they were strongest in both. The last part of the 19th century saw them in rising competition with the other "Great Powers"—being part of that competition is what *made* a nation a "Great Power"—and, by its very end, with Japan and the United States. In turn, control over overseas areas was necessary to keep others out, as well as to make what gains there were from getting in, oneself. Control of the high seas was sufficient to this end in the 19th century (sea power playing the role that air power and nuclear missiles do in this century). To say that the 19th century was the century of the *Pax Britannica* is to say that Britain's navy was without serious competition; there was not even a close second. Apart from a few abortive maneuvers toward overseas expansion by the French and the Americans in the 1860's, Britain's role as world ruler was unchallenged until the 1890's. The umbrella of control was based on a virtual monopoly of naval and mercantile sea power; under that umbrella, British business thrived overseas, and a period of the freest international trade and most unified international monetary system in capitalist history was created. Nor is it unimportant that the peace established by Britain allowed American development to proceed unhampered by foreign violence or the necessity to sustain a significant army and navy. As will be seen later, American hegemony after World War II created a similar worldwide condition for the capitalist system —but now with something Britain did not have: competitors of great strength with a different and, now, also of the same ideology.[19]

---

[19]A most illuminating analytical approach to this question has been provided by Frederic C. Lane, the great economic historian of (especially) the Mediterranean world, in the four essays that comprise Part Three of his *Venice and History: The Collected Papers of Frederic C. Lane* (Baltimore: Johns Hopkins Press, 1966). The leading concept in Lane's analysis is "protection rents and costs," where rent (as used by economists) is a return to monopoly—in this case the monopoly of organized violence—and the costs are those of military supremacy.

The period 1815–1915 is usually described as "a century of peace." It was, if by peace is meant no war between "the great powers." But it was a century of desperately sought alliances, of scrambling for coaling stations and, toward the very last years of the century, of an arms race.

Britain's economic well-being in the 19th century depended squarely on buying, selling, and investing all over the world. The relationships developed with the United States and with Germany are most informative in showing how the very process of British success in these economic activities meant the creation of even mightier rivals, as had been the case with those who had carried the baton of power in earlier times.

Britain's two principal customers for consumer and capital goods, and loans were Germany and the United States. In return, Britain took in foodstuffs and raw materials, gold, commissions, profits, and interest. But the importation of goods and capital for the United States and Germany meant an enhanced ability to develop their own economies, and a movement toward industrialization. Doubtless the British relationship was more necessary for Germany than for the richer United States; in both cases, however, Britain was creating rivals in trade, industry, finance, and for imperial space. In the 1890's, voices were already being raised in England to curb its free trading policies in favor of protection and to anticipate an open conflict with Germany, which was expanding its navy, competing with increasing effectiveness in world markets, and seeking to catch up in the race for empire.[18]

LIKE FATHER, LIKE SON

While America was a colony of the British, American foreign trade moved within a complicated and extensive system of restrictions, prohibitions, requirements, and subsidies, all designed to enhance British profits and power. Initially this model of mercantilist policy worked to the mutual benefit of Britain and the colonists; by the mid-18th century, the same system harmed the Americans and benefitted the British.

The first policies toward America taken by the British (in the 17th century) had two main designs in mind: to strengthen British trade and shipping at the expense of the Dutch, and to strengthen the colonies (through subsidies and guaranteed markets) as potentially strong economic and strategic assets. It was classic mercantilism, and the Ameri-

---

[18]See Ross J. S. Hoffman, *Great Britain and the German Trade Rivalry, 1875–1914* (Philadelphia: University of Pennsylvania, 1933), Alfred E. Kahn, *Great Britain in the World Economy* (New York: N.Y.U. Press, 1946), and Albert Imlah, *Economic Elements in the Pax Britannica** (Cambridge: Harvard University Press, 1958). The classic work describing and analyzing the overall financial network is Herbert Feis, *Europe: The World's Banker** (New Haven: Yale University Press, 1930).

cans had almost two centuries of habituation to such policies, before breaking loose from Great Britain.[19]

Among our very first steps after Independence was the creation of our own mercantilist system. Alexander Hamilton was the most productive economic thinker in those first years, issuing one *Report* after another. His *Report on Manufactures* (1791), revolving around the need to develop industry and to protect it in its "infant" stages, set the stage for a coherent and tight protectionist trading policy, with subsidies mixed in. Like the European experience on which it was modeled, American protectionism recognized the importance of foreign trade: protectionism was designed not to reduce its volume but, through selectivity, to minimize its costs and enhance its gains. The mercantilism of Hamilton has appeared and reappeared in our history, interspersed with movements seemingly going in the opposite direction; it continues today.

Daniel Webster's career, involving a complete turnaround on foreign economic policy, reflects the changing position of the New England economy. As a Congressman from New Hampshire (1813–1817), and Massachusetts (1823–1827), Webster represented the trading center of the United States and was an ardent free trader, an anti-protectionist. Later, as a Senator from Massachusetts and U.S. Secretary of State (both in the 1840's), Webster utilized his orator's talents on behalf of protectionism. New England was becoming the home of American "infant" industries. In the 1820's, he was an opponent of protectionist Henry Clay, whose "American system" was designed to give American farmers a "home market" composed of buyers earning incomes from manufactures in America; a decade or so later, he and Clay were protectionist allies, leaders of the "Whigs," a party whose explicit business concerns foreshadowed the Republican Party that emerged just before the Civil War.

After the death of Clay and Webster (both in 1852), the Whig Party disappeared; it had been split earlier over the question of tariffs (as well as over the extension of slavery), with the Northern Whigs supporting tariffs, and the Southern Whigs pushing for freer trade. The latter won out, in 1846, with the Walker Tariff, which reduced protective tariffs while seeking to increase revenues through high tariffs on domestically non-competing goods (such tariffs are called "revenue tariffs"—for example, on coffee). Those who opposed the Walker Tariff favored increasing trade also, so long as the trade that took place did not injure American industry.

Nobody then doubted the critical quality of American foreign economic relationships which, in that early period, involved borrowing

---

[19]The nature and intensity of the rivalry between the Dutch and the English is definitively treated by Charles Wilson, *Profit and Power* (New York: Macmillan, 1957).

steadily from Britain, and paying back through the rising exports of (almost entirely) agricultural products, and especially cotton. When the conflict between southern and northern interests brought the nation to the edge of civil war, the South assumed that the importance of the relationship between cotton exports and British textiles was such that Britain would actively and effectively intervene on the South's side. That Britain did not testifies to the less evident but nonetheless more powerful relationships already existing for trade and investments in the North; however, the South's assumption testifies to the acknowledged importance of trade in the United States at that time. It grew more important in succeeding decades.

FROM YOUTH TO MATURITY

The United States, as the first colony to be exploited in a modern way and the first to rebel, had very early on begun to view the Western Hemisphere as its backyard. We could not expel the British from Canada; but from the rest of North America, the Spanish, the French, the Russians, the Dutch and the English were bought out or pushed out. The Monroe Doctrine set the tone as early as 1823: there would be no further European colonization or attempts to implant monarchy in this hemisphere; the United States would not meddle with existing colonies nor in internal European affairs. By the end of the century, we had begun to meddle in others' colonies; after World War I we began to take a hand in European affairs.

The Republican victory that brought Lincoln to the presidency also set the stage for a set of foreign economic policies suited to emerging industrialism. Strong protective tariffs were passed in 1862, and immigration was stepped up through the revival of indentured labor. In 1873, with the "Crime of '73," silver was demonetized so as to integrate the American economy with the emerging international gold standard. And, as we saw in Chapter Six, American exports of unfinished and processed agricultural commodities expanded substantially in the late 1870's, deepening a dependence on exports for that production which continues to this day.[20] In that respect, as also with our international financial, trading, and industrial relationships abroad after the Civil War, the American economy transformed itself from one that was relatively passive and dependent upon foreign economic relationships for its health, to an increasingly aggressive economy upon whose health

---

[20]Apart from war years, and those of the Depression of the 1930's, agricultural exports normally have provided at least one-sixth of farm income. For example: 1910, 16 percent; 1963, 17 percent.

most of the world became dependent. That transformation was all but accomplished in the 1920's; it was obvious to all by the 1950's. The data which follow suggest some of the quantitative signs of the process.

Up until the 1870's, the United States was in the category of an "immature debtor" nation: it owed other countries (mostly England) on net balance, and it imported more than it exported. That stage was changed into "mature debtor" (that is, it was still in debt, but was now exporting more than importing) in the 1870's, due in large part to the upsurge in agricultural exports. But when Europe's agricultural crisis ended, our exports continued to exceed our imports for an entire century, except for three years, 1888, 1889, and 1893. In 1971–72, the balance reversed.

In the midst of World War I, we became an "immature creditor" nation, as our rising export of capital brought us to a position of being owed by the world on net balance, and as we continued to export more than we imported. A "mature creditor" country presumably imports more than it exports, and pays for it with earnings in addition to those from merchandise exports (from investments, shipping and insurance services, etc.). When our balance of trade went negative (that is, our imports exceeded exports) in 1971, we became a mature creditor nation, but we did so with a widespread feeling of uneasiness that in some quarters verged on panic. Let us now examine some of the tendencies underlying these changes.

Our transition from immature to mature debtor was accompanied by our growing productive—and therefore exporting—power; this in turn meant a changing economic structure. From being an exporter chiefly of crude raw materials and foodstuffs (e.g., cotton and wheat), we became an exporter *also* of semi-finished and finished manufactures (e.g., steel and machinery). Table 7 shows how the absolute amounts grew over time, and how their relative positions changed.

Note that between 1890 and 1910 the United States had changed from a net importer to a net exporter of finished manufacturers; and in the same period it changed from being a net exporter to a net importer of crude materials. Table 8 shows the rising importance of the United States in total world exports and in the export of manufactures. As in Table 7 the absolute amounts traded rose substantially over these years. The figures for 1950 are misleadingly high, because all industrial countries other than the United States had yet to recover from the impact of World War II. Since 1957, U.S. percentages have declined (in 1969 our percentage of world exports was down to 16 percent) but absolute amounts have more than doubled.

The notion that the United States has only a slight dependency on its foreign economic relationships stems directly from the percentage that exports and imports bear to our GNP. Except for the war-affected years

TABLE 7

U.S. Exports and Imports, Selected Years 1820–1957 (Million $)

| | Finished Manufactures | | Crude Materials | |
	Exports	Imports	Exports	Imports
1850	$ 17	$ 95	$ 84	$ 13
1870	56	174	214	57
1880	93	197	243	142
1890	133	231	309	180
1910	499	368	574	578
1930	1,898	757	829	1,002
1940	2,330	409	464	1,011
1950	5,741	1,504	1,886	2,465
1957	11,786	3,527	3,109	3,186

SOURCE: Adapted from *Historical Statistics of the U. S.*, p. 544. Between 1930 and 1950, figures are much distorted by the impact of depression, trade restrictions, and war and postwar phenomena.

TABLE 8

	U.S. Exports as % of World Exports	U.S. Exports of Mfrs. as % of World Exports of Mfrs.
1899	20.5%	11.6%
1913	22.1	13.0
1929	27.0	20.4
1950	32.0	26.6
1957	30.0	25.3

SOURCE: Data calculated from A. Maizels, *Industrial Growth and World Trade* (Cambridge: Cambridge University Press, 1965), pp. 426–27 and p. 434. An abridged paperback edition appeared in 1970: *Growth and Trade*[*] (same publisher).

between 1915 and 1920, exports have been at or below 5 percent of our GNP in this century; imports have been at or below 4 percent. Table 9 indicates how this compares for other industrial countries.

This handful of countries is responsible for 90 percent or more of all industrial production in capitalist countries; and the U.S. produces at least half of that. The U.S. exports and imports about one-sixth of all exports and imports in the world, with one-sixteenth of world population. The ten countries listed in Table 9 export and import about two-thirds of all exports and imports (in the non-socialist world). Finally, the best customers for the leading trading and industrial nations are each other, as they have been throughout the industrialization period of the past century or so. Since the late 1940's, for example, the countries to which we export and from which we import most are Canada, Great Britain, West Germany, and Japan. As in the internal relationships of each capitalist society, those at the top buy and sell most to each other; those at the bottom, whether depressed income groups or depressed nations, see the gap between themselves and the rich steadily widening over time. The dual economy phenomenon is pervasive, nationally and internationally.[21]

ADOLESCENT GIANT, SICKLY DOTARDS

When World War I broke out, the United States was $3 billion in debt to the rest of the world; when the war ended, the rest of the world was $6 billion in debt to us (exclusive of war debts). The United States had taken over Britain's place as the industrial, commercial, and financial center of the world. For better and for worse, the reality of our new position was not matched by a suitable or a coherent foreign policy for several decades. When, after World War II, that policy fell into shape, its very success would be our undoing; this process had been true of Britain and of the Netherlands, earlier.

The "immature creditor" status of the United States after 1918 was more than an economist's dry classification; it describes well our state

TABLE 9
Exports as a Percentage of GNP, 1968

U.S.	4
West Germany	23
United Kingdom	18
France	14
Japan	10
Canada	24
Italy	18
Netherlands	43
Belgium-Luxembourg	38–76

SOURCE: see *Fortune* (August, 1971), pp. 144–49.

---

[21]The bases for the generalizations regarding world trade were first developed by Folke Hilgerdt, in two studies for the League of Nations, *The Network of World Trade* (1942) and *Industrialization and Foreign Trade* (1946). His studies were extended in the massive book by Maizels, cited above. Ingvar Svennilson, *Growth and Stagnation in Europe* (Geneva: United Nations, 1954) contains much additional data. It also offers an at least partially effective analysis of the stagnation of European economies between the two world wars —the main focus of his book.

of mind, and the immature policies with which we related to the rest of the world.

A creditor nation is a net exporter of capital, a net lender to private parties and governments abroad. Debtor nations can only maintain a healthy balance in *their* external relationships if they can sell in the markets of the lending countries (and earn foreign exchange)—as, for example, the United States could when, in the 19th century, it was able to export increasing amounts of its production to Europe (and as the underdeveloped countries today cannot). The United States, from the Civil War on, was a high protective tariff nation with only an occasional deviation. That was perhaps understandable up to World War I; from then on it stood in conflict with our creditor position. Nonetheless, our tariffs rose again in the 1920's, and were jacked up to their highest levels ever in 1930. If the free trade policies of Great Britain in the 19th century were taken as the proper standard for the world leader, the United States was breaking the rules of the game. In the fragile world economy after World War I, for the economic leader to break the rules meant that the game would be lost by everyone.[22]

But Great Britain could *not* be taken as the standard for foreign economic policy after World War I, nor would it be by the United States, despite the entreaties of liberal economists from 1920 on. Why not?

First, when Britain began to rule the world economy, there were no other significantly industrialized economies. A free trade policy maximized both exports and imports, and the imports did not constitute a threat to British industry. Ricardo had advocated such a position decades before Britain adopted it; it made sense for that economy. Subsequently, economists transformed Ricardian notions into eternal verities, good for all times and places; Ricardo had been concerned with one time and one place, and he had assumed away foreign competition. When the United States moved into dominance it faced Great Britain, Germany, Japan, and a handful of lesser industrial countries as competitors. All were hungry for markets, all were bristling with protective devices.

Second, when Britain forged its international policies, the major powers had been and would remain at peace with each other. Britain ruled the sea lanes, as both merchant and naval power. The United States came into supremacy in the midst of world war, itself a result of great instability and conflict. The years after World War I were merely a resting period until World War II. In that resting period, the world was

---

[22]American policies and the relevant economic data for the 1920's and 1930's are thoroughly examined in Hal Lary, et al., *The United States in the World Economy** (Washington: Department of Commerce, 1943). The study is in effect a call for the United States to grow up, essentially along earlier British lines. As such, it has a quaint ring to it.

rocked by revolution in Russia, and outbreaks of revolutionary and counterrevolutionary developments in the fragments of the broken Hapsburg empire; by a frenzied inflation in Germany; by fascism in Germany and Italy; by worldwide depression, and the collapse of colonial economies. Had the United States pursued a set of "mature" foreign economic policies from 1920 on, some of these developments *might* have been averted; however, most of them would have been untouched by anything the U.S. might do. It was no longer the 19th century. Different trading policies were needed; different policies to run an empire were needed, also. The United States after World War II—for better and for worse, once more—developed those policies. They will be analyzed shortly.

Something else made our possibilities quite different from those of Great Britain in the 19th century: the internal balance of power and the social outlook of Americans concerning power and influence. The United States could not reproduce the experience or adopt the principles of 19th century Great Britain, merely because the U.S. was dominant in the world economy. Our behavior as world economic leader is not explicable solely in terms of the differences between the 19th and the 20th centuries; much of the explanation lies in the nature of American politics. In part because our independence was won through war, the United States—despite its perennial dependence on the world economy —is nationalist in its mood and in its policies; always, and now as a nationalistic empire.

From the Embargo Act of 1807, through the "Buy American" campaigns of the 1830's, the 1890's and the 1930's; from the geographic expansion that has characterized our history from its first moments up to the present; from Secretary of the Treasury Alexander Hamilton to Secretary of the Treasury John Connally, the United States—in moods varying from buoyant to desperate to arrogant—has shaped its internal and external policies on the steady assumption that this country has special qualities that give it special rights. Other countries use their power to advance their national interests, of course. The United States has assumed that *its* national interests, after all is said and done, are to the interest of other countries; and if that is less clear to others than to Americans, so much the worse for them.

Thus, protective tariffs for "infant industries" can easily be justified, but their continuation to "protect" monopolistic industries whose size and efficiency is unrivalled in the world (as was the case, for example, with steel since the late 19th century, and up to recently) has no justification except the power that continues them and the profits that ensue. Thus, it is understandable that older industries (such as cotton textiles and shoes) have resisted being phased out by cheaper imports, but it is quite another matter for protection to work the miracle of allowing such industries to *expand* over time, which has curtailed the possibilities of repayment of debt by developing countries where the cheaper product is made. Thus, it is not strange that financial investment follows the highest returns; but it is more than irresponsible, it is dangerous when lenders turn away from renewing and extending loans to pursue the will-o'-the-wisp of a ballooning stock market, as happened with Latin American loans when Wall Street boomed away in 1927 and 1928 (facilitating the collapse of those already weak economies). Finally, protectionism was by no means the exclusive possession of the United States, but for the leading national economy to break all world records in the critical year of 1930 was sheer recklessness.

During the Depression, the world broke out with a rash of economic nationalism, marked by import quotas, export subsidies, increased tariffs, competitive devaluation, exchange controls, and the like, to the accompaniment of a steadily falling volume of world trade and rising international hostility.

In 1933, a "World Economic Conference" was convened, in the hope that the mutual throat-cutting accompanying the Depression could be halted, or even reversed. The key nation in strength and influence was the United States, but President Roosevelt, "after a brief interval in which it seemed that he would throw his force into the World Economic Conference, abandoned international responsibility, even disparaged it by fostering nationalist devices, though not without the face-saving afterthought that a prosperous America would do most to produce a prosperous world."[23]

NEW FRONTIERS: THE MUSCLES FLEX

When Great Britain moved to full free trade in the mid-19th century, it did so knowing it had nothing to fear from foreign competitors. The United States has never made such a fulsome move toward free trade in its period of pre-eminence. But in 1934 we took a small step in that direction, with the Reciprocal Trade Agreements Act (RTAA) and the Export-Import Bank (Eximbank); other steps of the same limited sort have been taken in subsequent years. Our conscious needs for expanded foreign markets, taken together with confidence in the ability of our production to compete effectively in an open market (the basis for our "Open Door" policy for China, decades before) made for the institutionalization of a new world trade position.

It is often said that the United States had thus finally abandoned its long "isolationist" stance for a new "internationalism." It is more ap-

---

[23]Broadus Mitchell, *Depression Decade*, p. 57.

propriate to see the earlier position as nationalism with an inferiority complex, and our developing position since the 1930's, our rising interventionism, as nationalism with a superiority complex. Be that as it may, the RTAA was designed to increase trade through negotiated, bilateral, mutual tariff reductions, between the United States and one nation at a time; the Eximbank was aimed at increasing exports to Latin America (primarily), through loans to governments to finance purchases from American companies. In the context of the Depression, neither of these measures had much effect; the effects have been more substantial since World War II.

When World War II began, it abruptly shoved aside the Depression and transformed the context within which foreign economic policies would and could be made. But the war did not prevent plans from being made, some of them aired in the 1930's, all of them aimed at market expansion. The nature of the problem was seen clearly by Dean Acheson in 1944, when as Assistant Secretary of State he told a Congressional hearing:

> We cannot go through another ten years like the ten years at the end of the twenties and the beginning of the thirties, without having the most far-reaching consequences upon our economic and social system. When we look at that problem, we may say it is a problem of markets. . . . We have got to see that what the country produces is used and sold under financial arrangements which make its production possible. . . . You must look to foreign markets.

But couldn't the United States consume everything it produces?

> That would completely change our Constitution, our relations to property, human liberty, our very conceptions of law. And nobody contemplates that. Therefore, you find you must look to other markets and those markets are abroad.[24]

Soon an impressive collection of men from the world of corporate industry and finance began to construct programs that mixed economic expansion with the politics of Cold War. Their names, in addition to Acheson's, are very familiar by now: John Foster Dulles, Averill Harriman, James Forrestal, John J. McCloy, A. A. Berle, Jr., Robert Lovett, Douglas Dillon, Dean Rusk, Christian Herter, George Ball. . . . Most of these men were associated with both the Council on Foreign Relations

---

[24]Quoted by William A. Williams, "The Large Corporation and American Foreign Policy," in David Horowitz, ed., *The Corporations and the Cold War** (New York: Monthly Review Press, 1969), pp. 95–6. Lloyd C. Gardner's essay in that same collection, "The New Deal, New Frontiers, and the Cold War," is very useful, as is his book *Economic Aspects of New Deal Diplomacy* (Madison: University of Wisconsin, 1964).

and the State Department, the Department of Defense, and the CIA, moving back and forth between corporate offices, the Council, and governmental position with ease. The journal of the Council, *Foreign Affairs,* is generally conceded to be the most influential journal of its kind.[25]

Beginning in 1941 with the Atlantic Charter (constructed by Churchill and Roosevelt) and coming to fruition in the Dumbarton Oaks and Bretton Woods conferences of 1944 (both with widespread international representation), the United States used its power to shape the new international organizations that were institutionalized in 1945 and 1946: the United Nations, the International Monetary Fund (IMF), and the International Bank for Reconstruction and Development (IBRD, or World Bank). All these organizations would be dominated by the lop-sided power—military, political, and economic—of the United States in the postwar world. The IMF was designed to stabilize the international monetary situation over time (and to function as a substitute for the "automatic gold standard" which had served the same function before 1914.) The World Bank was designed to lend for capital projects. The assets of both institutions were dominantly American from the beginning; and the United States has been the prime decision-making power in both organizations—as it has been in the Inter-American Development Bank, a later development.

In the decade following 1945, the United States created a whole new framework within which its entire foreign policy would move. Unlike the UN, the IMF, and the IBRD, which were all international in their construction (no matter how dependent on the U.S. they may have been), the next steps were devised by and for the United States. The drama began with Winston Churchill's famous "Iron Curtain" speech at Fulton, Missouri, in 1946. In the next year a whirlwind of institutional innovations began to form:

1947 *The Truman (Greece-Turkey) Doctrine.* Truman asked for and received $400 million from Congress "to help free peoples to maintain . . . their national integrity against aggressive movements that seek to impose upon them totalitarian regimes." Control of the Balkan area before World War II had been in British hands, now too weak to continue.

The National Security Act. Created the "National Military Establishment," incorporating the pre-existing Department of the Navy with the new Department of the Air Force and Department of the Army under the Department of De-

---

[25]For an extended discussion of this matter, see G. William Domhoff, "Who Made American Foreign Policy, 1945–1963," in Horowitz's volume.

fense. (The latter had more candidly been called the War Department since 1789.) This Act also created the Central Intelligence Agency and, of course, the National Security Council, the pivotal center of policy-making.

1948 *The Marshall Plan.* At a commencement address at Harvard in June, 1947, General George Marshall (then Secretary of State) proposed what became in 1948 the European Recovery Program. In its four years of operation, the program gave $14 billion to eighteen Western European nations (including Greece and Turkey) for a broad variety of investment projects. Over 70 percent of the amount was spent for American goods. The program was sold to Congress on those grounds and as a means of "rolling back the tide of Communism."

Organization of American States (OAS). All nations but Canada in this hemisphere were charter members. Its purpose, according to our State Department, is to protect the hemisphere from "the interventionist and aggressive designs of international communism."

Selective Service Act. The United States had had a military draft only during the Civil War, World War I, and, beginning in 1940, for World War II. The Selective Service Act of 1948 built the draft into our postwar history.

1949 *North Atlantic Treaty Organization* (NATO). The military counterpart of the Marshall Plan.

Point Four Program. Announced in Truman's inaugural address, it was a program of technical assistance to "underdeveloped areas." It has continued to the present in one form or another.

1950 *Subversive Activities Control Board.* Created by the McCarran Internal Security Act, aimed at controlling and restricting "domestic communism." In the same year Senator Joe McCarthy and the Korean War joined in, creating some kind of symmetry between domestic and foreign affairs.

American Military Assistance Advisory Group (MAAG). Created to assist and advise the French in Indochina. In 1951 we began to assist France in financing the war; by 1952 we were paying three-quarters of the bill.

1951 *Japanese-American Treaty.* A mutual security pact, one of whose provisions allowed the U.S. to "administer"

Okinawa, one of our principal military bases in Asia. The treaty was renewed in 1960 and 1970. The U.S. has now agreed to phase out of Okinawa, but the military bases remain.

1954 *Southeast Asia Treaty Organization* (SEATO). The counterpart in Asia of NATO.

1955 *Middle East Treaty Organization.* Another NATO counterpart, made up originally of Iraq, Iran, Turkey, Pakistan and Great Britain, with a participating American military mission. Iraq withdrew in 1959, and METO became CENTO *(Central Treaty Organization).*

The United States, in a very few years, had jumped headlong into the international arena, armed with both economic and military supremacy. There was some vocal opposition in the first few years; for example, from the conservative and influential Senator Robert A. Taft, and from the liberal-left, whose numbers peaked in the period surrounding the 1948 election.

The trade union movement, existing as the separate AFL and CIO (until 1955, when they merged), provided both opposition to and support for growing American intervention around the world: opposition from left-wing unions in the CIO (all of which were expelled between 1949 and 1950), and substantial and growing support from the non-left CIO unions and the entire AFL.[26] In 1947, organized labor was skeptical of the Marshall Plan; at its convention in 1948, the CIO endorsed it. In 1949 both the AFL and the CIO cooperated in the creation of the explicitly anti-Communist International Confederation of Free Trade Unions; in the 1950's, labor officials were accepting funds from the CIA (secretly) for anti-Communist activities abroad. And so the web of cooperation between organized labor, the cold warriors of Washington, and corporate leaders became tighter and tighter until, in 1966, George Meany (then President of the AFL-CIO) could proclaim that criticism of the war in Vietnam "can only pollute and poison the bloodstream of our democracy."[27]

---

[26]The unions expelled were the United Electrical Workers, the Mine, Mill, and Smelter Workers, the Fur and Leather Workers, the Food, Tobacco and Allied Workers, the Marine Cooks and Stewards, the Fishermen, the International Longshoremen's and Warehousemen's Union, and the American Communications Association. See Ronald Radosh, *American Labor and United States Foreign Policy** (New York: Random House; Vintage, 1969), pp. 435–36.

[27]Ibid., p. 4. Pp. 3–29 and 435–52 provide a summary and an evaluation of organized labor's contribution to the Cold War, including secret cooperation with the CIA.

DOLLAR SHORTAGE TO DOLLAR GLUT

The election of 1952 brought General Eisenhower and Richard Nixon to the White House. The old-fashioned "isolationist" wing of the Republican Party had been suppressed and a working consensus on anti-Communism abroad and at home had been created between the GOP and the Democrats. Organized labor and agriculture worked in harmony with organized business on the highest levels; the gains made from rising exports and arms production assured that almost any conflict could be ironed out with minimal trouble—at least, for those at the top of business, farming, labor, and government.

Foreign economic affairs approached the euphoric for the United States. The American economy had to find expanding markets abroad for its extraordinary productive capacity, and additional outlets for capital. After World War II, the rest of the world was desperately short of productive capacity. The condition after 1945 came to be known as a "dollar shortage"; that is, the world wanted more from us than it could sell to the dollar area (principally the U.S., but including Canada and much of Latin America). Our economic strength in that period was the basis for our ability to create the American-dominated political framework suggested by the list above. Within that framework, our strength increased; and so, by the mid-sixties, did others'. To many in the world, that Germany and Japan lead the parade of our competitors provides wry amusement.

Already in the Truman Administration, one matter in addition to markets and investment outlets was seen as vital: America's increasing and (in the popular view) surprising dependency on raw materials imports—of small quantities of strategic materials such as tungsten, chromium, columbium, and the like, and, looming in near future, of large quantities of petroleum, iron ore, and similar materials.

In 1951, the International Development Advisory Board's *Partners in Progress* ("The Rockefeller Report") made the connection between raw materials dependency and foreign policy explicit. In 1952, the President's Materials Policy Commission issued a five-volume report ("the Paley Commission Report") entitled *Resources for Freedom.* In the report, past, present, and future supplies of raw materials were studied, evaluated, and measured against new demands and technology. The conclusion was twofold: by the 1970's, the United States would be vitally dependent upon imported raw materials, qualitatively and quantitatively; and its foreign policies must reflect and fulfill that need. Our policies had begun to do so in the years immediately preceding the Paley Report; they did do considerably more in the years to follow. The means adopted turned on American investments in the countries possessing the needed resources, and on political/military arrangements suited to assuring secure flows of both profits and the raw materials themselves. The geographic framework entailed was imperial in its scope; the policies were imperialist in their nature. The Cold War provided the rationale for those policies, in the name of defending the entire "Free World" against Communist aggression.[28]

The fifteen or so years following 1945 were of course marked by upsets large and small, at home and abroad: the Chinese Revolution, the Cold War, and the semi-defeat in Korea; and there were four recessions between 1948 and 1961 (despite the enormous amounts of production going into arms and abroad). But in general, that period was one of optimism and confidence; indeed it was one of complacency regarding American economic and military strength. Problems arose, and would continue to do so; but with the whole world seeking American consumer and capital goods and accepting our leadership, what's to worry?

THE TROUBLES OF THE PAX AMERICANA

When the 1960's began, the United States seemed unchallengeable in the world, and few indeed were challenging the American system at home. By the end of the sixties, doubts and turbulence at home had become widespread, due to racial unrest, to intractable and inexcusable poverty, to the Indochina War, to a growing malaise and alienation. In the same years, power grew elsewhere: the other industrial capitalist countries had gone beyond recovery to bursting strength. Third World countries were finding ways to resist and to show independence—Tanzania, Cuba and Vietnam in their ways, Peru and Chile in theirs, the oil exporting countries (through the Organization of Petroleum Exporting Countries [OPEC]) in theirs. And the Soviet Union and China were now major and stable powers. If, as emperor, the United States was by no means yet naked, neither were its clothes dazzling.

From the 1940's on, American governmental and private activities abroad provided a high and rising demand for American production and

---

[28]See Harry Magdoff, *The Age of Imperialism: The Economics of U.S. Foreign Policy** (New York: Monthly Review Press, 1969). His data on the importance of foreign trade and raw materials imports, in Chapter 2, are an excellent example of how what seem to be insignificant quantities are in fact qualitatively critical. In the past few years, many fine books have exploded the Cold War rationale, and shown the conscious duplicity involved in its propagation. Some of those will appear in the Reading Suggestions at the end of this chapter; here the most readable will be noted: Carl Oglesby and Richard Shaull, *Containment and Change** (New York: Macmillan, 1967), Part One. Written by Oglesby, this traces the Cold War up from its beginnings in the years surrounding the Soviet Revolution into its full savage consequences in Indochina. Without perhaps wishing to do so, Halberstam's *Best and the Brightest* goes far to underpin Oglesby's and others' critiques of the Cold War.

thus stability and growth for the economy, while simultaneously enhancing and protecting the empire and the gains from it. Both deliberately and unwittingly, however, these activities sped up the transformation of pre-existing industrial economies in Europe, Canada, and Japan, as well as the processes of social change in the dependent non-industrial economies in Asia, the Middle East, Africa, and Latin America. By the mid-sixties, the consequences of all these changes were appearing: economically in the worsening of America's balance of trade and payments position, and politically/militarily in the softening of our alliances and, most notably, in the Indochinese military disaster. The first postwar administration to sense the possibility of these difficulties was that of John F. Kennedy.

Kennedy's advisors knew the American empire was already well along by 1960; they also knew it could not function in the same terms as its predecessor, the British Empire—economically, politically, or militarily. For us to adopt the status of "mature creditor," different means were necessary, as they were also if we were to hold down challenges to existing and vital patterns of dependency. The contrasts between Britain in its heyday and the threats and possibilities facing the United States were noted generally above; some elaboration is now appropriate.

In Britain's day, "internationalism" could and did mean free trade. Britain's competitors did not appear until the end of the 19th century, and then as *newly*-industrialized nations. The United States came to eminence in the midst of already existent industrialized and highly nationalistic nations. By 1960, as a result of American policies of investment and encouragement, these other nations—and especially Germany and Japan—were becoming technologically competitive or even superior to us, in ways not so in 1934, the year of the RTAA. American loans and investments facilitated the modernization of foreign industries, and as a condition of Marshall Plan aid we pushed the Europeans into patterns of cooperation—most noticeably the European Common Market—which strengthened the separate economies and enabled them ultimately to stand against us in a united front relating to, say, tariffs. Comparable steps stimulated the Japanese economy.

Our export surplus rose to over $7 billion in 1964; it has dropped steadily ever since, and became negative in 1971 for the first time in this century. The Trade Expansion Act of 1962, usually seen as the legislation topping Kennedy's priority list, aimed to prevent that. The Act was designed to encourage the necessary expansion of European and Japanese exports, but *only* insofar as our own exports could expand at least as fast, thereby maintaining and increasing our export surplus. Britain could accommodate an import surplus without internal damage, in its day; policy-makers for the United States believe we cannot. Why not?

Britain's import surplus was "paid for" by the returns from its over-seas investments; that is, on balance, inflow from overseas investments exceeded capital outflow, as is also true for the United States now: for example, in 1971, the net excess of interest and dividends from foreign investments over new capital outflow was $4.8 billion. On balance, therefore, it is not American investment abroad that exacerbates our balance of payments problem; quite the contrary. Until 1971, our trade balance was also positive. Setting aside net tourist expenditures by Americans (the excess of Americans' expenditures abroad over foreign tourists' expenditures here, which is now under reversal by the devalua-tions beginning in 1971), and also setting aside the exacerbating effect on our payments deficit of short-term and speculative capital outflows (caused by the troubles of the American economy at home and asso-ciated instability in the world monetary system), there has been one major source of trouble for our balance of payments: what Lane would call the "protection costs" of empire. U.S. governmental expenditures abroad (gifts, loans, and military)—which were $6.2 billion in 1971, for example—create and maintain the world hegemony allowing the world capitalist system to function, and provide the foundation for the net inflow of "protection rents." However, as Sweezy and Magdoff point out, this entails a "vicious spiral: direct investment income is essential to pay the costs of empire, but the costs of empire are basically deter-mined by the need to protect the investment income and this is certain to grow as time goes by."[29]

Given our enormous governmental expenditures abroad and our do-mestic habituation to and dependence on an export surplus, the United States can only function as a secure Number One power if *we* find ways to initiate a substantial and persistent expansion of *world* trade. Only thus can our exports keep ahead of our imports *and* can other countries find adequate export markets for themselves, and all rest easy with a persistent American payments deficit. Failing the requisite rate of worldwide economic expansion, the United States faces an insoluble contradiction (within the framework of maintaining its empire): domes-tic considerations require a trade surplus while global considerations require us to run a trade deficit. In the words of an economist for the First National City Bank, "it is politically difficult for the U.S. to main-tain a liberal [that is, relatively free trade] import policy unless we also run a trade surplus."[30]

---

[29]"Balance of Payments and Empire," *Monthly Review* (December, 1972).

[30]Quoted in *Fortune* (August, 1971) in the article "U.S. Foreign Trade: There's No Need to Panic," p. 186. *Fortune's* optimism seems misplaced, for the analysis in that article did not anticipate the trade reversal of 1971, let alone its worsening in 1972: "In the *late* 1970's the trade balance may well turn negative—and stay negative for many years thereafter." (My emphasis.)

But why did Britain's empire not entail the kinds of problems that ours does? Britain's empire was global, as ours is. But the costs of empire in the 19th century (after all adjustments for prices, size, etc.) were much lower than today, and they occurred within a simpler domestic and international context. The technology of 19th century imperial order was minimal for Britain, which relied on naval power almost exclusively, and seldom had to use it. By contrast, the United States had three and a half million men and women under arms in the late 1960's, and over two thousand bases spread-eagling the globe.[31]

Britain presided over a balance of power in the heyday of advancing imperialism and easy subjugation of weak countries; the United States seeks to preside over a world with accomplished and threatening revolutions in Asia, the Middle East, Latin America, and Africa, and has to do so with something less than enthusiastic support at home. The costs of empire today are staggering, in dollars and in political strains. The increasing competitiveness of Europe and Japan began to nibble away at our trade surplus in the early 1960's; the Indochina War fed a domestic inflation that finally tore great chunks of our surplus away; more recently a new force—the multinational corporation—has acted to reduce our *national* economic competitiveness, to destabilize the international currency system, and to place further pressure on our trade and payments position. But that is by no means the end of what this giant new force means. It requires separate examination.[32]

---

[31]Writing in 1970, Colonel James A. Donovan stated, "In addition to the 600,000 military men in Southeast Asia, there are 300,000 U.S. Ground and Air Forces stationed in Europe and South Korea. Tens of thousands of Americans serve in warships on the high seas. There are over 1,200,000 U.S. fighting men stationed overseas at 2,270 locations in 119 countries. Additional divisions, air forces, and fleets stand by in the continental United States prepared to execute numerous contingency plans for every area in the world deemed to be of interest to the defense and welfare of the United States and its allies." *Militarism, U.S.A.** (New York: Scribner's, 1970), p. 2. Donovan is now retired from the Marine Corps. The most penetrating factual and analytical study of contemporary American militarism as a counter-revolutionary force is Michael T. Klare, *War Without End: American Planning for the Next Vietnams** (New York: Knopf, 1972).

[32]The trade deficit was over $2 billion in 1971, and three times that in 1972. The payments deficit rose from $4 billion in 1970, to about $30 billion in 1971; it fell to about $12 billion in 1972. Our gold stock, which was over $24 billion in 1949, had declined to $10 billion by 1972. Further than that it will not drop, because President Nixon "closed the gold window"—i.e., ceased to allow dollars to exchange for gold—in 1971. For a useful analysis and much data on this process, see Frank Ackerman and Arthur MacEwan, "Inflation, Recession and Crisis . . . ," in *RRPE* (August, 1972). Those wishing to explore the mysteries of devaluation, gold, and the like will be helped by Richard Du Boff, "Dollar Devaluation and Foreign Trade," and Jacob Morris, "Monetary Crisis of World Capitalism," in *Monthly Review* (March and January, 1972, respectively). See also Ernest Mandel, *Decline of the Dollar: A Marxist View of the Monetary Crisis** (New York: Pathfinder Press, 1972) for a series of illuminating essays written over the period 1964 to 1972.

BIGGER THAN A BREADBOX

The 20th century is earthquake country: war, revolution, vast changes in social behavior, wildly contrasting periods of economic expansion and contraction, a widening gap between rich and poor, and a constant reshuffling of political forms and relationships all over the globe recall the extraordinary turbulence of the 17th century, except that both the pace and the spread of change in this era have been considerably more substantial. Into this already highly unstable world a new and exceptionally powerful business institution has entered: the multinational corporation (MNC).

Whether the MNC will function so as to strengthen world capitalism —or the power of any particular nation within the world structure—or tend to make things come unstuck is presently impossible to know; the fate and the meaning of the MNC will be determined by the major currents of world economic and political life over the next decade or two. What is certain, however, is that the MNC will be one of the major currents in that process; it is the most dynamic force now at work in the world economy, and it has done much to add to the power of private corporations in the leading capitalist nations.

As we saw in Chapter Three, a few hundred MNC's already control over 15 percent of world *production*, and they are growing at a rate of 10 percent a year. What is an MNC? Why are they? What do they do, why do they grow, with what means and consequences?

All MNC's are international corporations, but the reverse is not so. By definition, an international corporation has operations, with sales outlets (or mineral production, for example) in more than one country; such international operations provide the long background for the emergence of the true MNC. But the MNC is more complicated than that, both in its bases and its meaning. As suggested by Hymer (in Chapter Three), the MNC can be understood by comparing it with the *national* corporation as it evolved in the United States at the end of the 19th century, and subsequently. Indeed, one way to find the most apt comparison is to note the behavior of those corporations that moved their operations from the New England area to the South, especially during and after the 1920's—in response to cheaper labor, resource availability (for example, cotton or timber), tax advantages, and favorable marketing conditions. The MNC operates in all its facets—manufacturing, marketing, finance—over the face of the world as though the world were one nation. The 1960's technology of communications and transportation was one basis for this development; as we shall see, economic and political questions (rapid growth rates, lower labor costs, the need to avoid protective tariffs, etc.) were the propelling causes. The

American giant corporations took the lead in the process, as they sought new outlets for their great capital, and rising profits from extended operations; the giant corporations of Europe and Japan soon joined the parade. The latest phase of the process is the rapid upsurge of European and Japanese investment and production in the United States (as well as in other areas).

When the truly *national* corporation developed in the United States in the late 19th century, it broke through local and regional political controls and its rising power transformed the private-public political structure to the advantage of the corporations, which at first sought a laissez-faire setting and subsequently (just before World War I) began to move toward centralized controls suitable to their needs. Up to now, the MNC has had something of the same effects: freed from politically-imposed limitations in their headquarters country, able to bring effective pressures to bear on their host countries, and increasingly seeking to create a *world* structure of relationships suited to their needs, while simultaneously acting as both an expansive *and* a destabilizing force in the world economy.

American corporations began to control manufacturing production facilities in Europe as early as the 1920's—for instance, General Motors' take-over of Opel in Germany and Vauxhall in England. Today's process is different. In the earlier period, the relationship meant that the American firm controlled and profited from the production of German or British autos. "But by 1970 General Motors were turning Vauxhall and Opel into two integrated components of an international production machine."[33]

The first major wave of American direct investment in postwar Europe was as a means of moving along with the rapid growth of their economies, *inside* European tariff and other obstacles. "Between 1958 and 1963, over 3,000 American companies either set up subsidiaries in the European Common Market countries, or gained control over already existing firms within it."[34] This says nothing of American investment in Britain, or in other non-Common Market countries in the same years. As the new technology of transportation, communications, and control improved—and it improved at increasing rates—the original motivations were added to. What had first been seen as a necessity for political reasons was transformed into a new possibility for economic reasons. The European giants joined in. Some of them, especially the oil compa-

---

[33]Hugh Stephenson, *The Coming Clash: The Impact of Multinational Corporations on National States* (New York: Saturday Review Press, 1972), p. 22. Stephenson is editor of the (London) *Times Business News*. His book is an excellent source of information on this development.

[34]Ernest Mandel, *Europe vs. America** (New York: Monthly Review Press, 1970), pp. 22–3. The Common Market began in 1957.

nies, were also long-experienced in multinationalism. Now, as Hymer points out, "the multinational corporate system is no longer an American system, but is, at the very least, a North Atlantic system both in the sense that Europeans have joined the ranks and in the sense that American firms have become less tied to the United States."[35] Let us look at some representative and important facts concerning the MNC's:[36]

— Among these giants, the very largest are the Americans: EXXON, ITT, GM, GE, IBM, Ford, Chrysler, et al. The largest American corporations are also the largest MNC's. In almost all the established industries, the largest European MNC is smaller than any of the top *three* companies in that industry based in the United States. Petroleum is an exception: of the seven largest oil companies, the second largest is Royal-Dutch Shell.

— Many of the largest American companies have around half or more of their fixed assets outside the United States: EXXON, ITT, Singer, Colgate-Palmolive, Mobil Oil, National Cash, Corn Products, Goodyear, Sperry Rand. The same is true for many smaller companies, such as International Packers, Burroughs, Heinz, Pfizer, Gillette, et al.

— Profits for many giant American corporations depend for as much as a third, a half, or more on foreign operations—e.g., Eastman Kodak, International Harvester, Minnesota Mining and Manufacturing.

— Seventy percent of ITT's employment is in mid-Europe.

— Forty percent of all American direct investment in France, West Germany and the United Kingdom is owned by EXXON, Ford and General Motors.

— American companies control 95 percent of European production of integrated circuits; 80 percent of electronic computers (IBM alone has 65 percent); 30 percent of European car and vehicle production.

— About half of the largest 500 American corporations now have substantial manufacturing interests outside the United States. Forty of these have more than one-third of their total physical assets abroad. One consequence is a steady decline of American exports of finished manufactures (by 29 percent between 1955 and 1964) and an increase in the exports of semifinished goods, that is, of components and materials (an increase of 326 percent between 1955 and 1964).

---

[35]Op. cit.
[36]Derived from Stephenson, op. cit., *passim.*

- The largest private employer in Formosa (Taiwan) is the General Instrument Corporation (of the U.S.).
- In 1970, half of the largest three hundred American corporations had subsidiaries in Spain.
- Japan, though much affected by American military and trading relationships, was almost totally without American investment. In 1970 Japan began to undo its restrictions on foreign capital. In 1971, Chrysler, Ford, and GM all set up joint-venture companies in Japan. The process is expected to continue, because Japanese companies have begun to join the multinational parade and must give a *quid pro quo* in order to do so. In 1973, Sumitomo gave $2 million to Yale University; Mitsubishi gave $1 million to Harvard Law School. (How multinational can you get?)
- Not only American companies are involved, of course. Between 1962 and 1968 British investment in the U.S. doubled, to almost $2 billion, and to something over that in the Common Market countries. In turn, over 15 percent of all British manufacturing industry was owned by foreigners, and over two-thirds of that by Americans. Over two-thirds of Canadian industry is foreign-owned, mostly by Americans.

These, and similar facts, are impressive indications of a major change in the structure and functioning of the capitalist world economy. This is all the more so when we recognize that the corporations are among the most powerful within their own societies *and* in the other societies where they operate; that what they produce—whether consumer goods, like TV's or autos, or capital goods, like computers—are among the most valued today, and that their financial strength and flexibility guarantee that there will be increasing difficulties for those not already giants to join the race or to keep from being beaten down by those who win it.

It may be seen that what is now taking place through the MNC is a global replaying of what happened in the American economy with the rise of the giant national corporation. In the United States in this century, the main dynamics of both economic and political life have been provided by the giant corporation. Much of what has happened has been a result of their direct needs and desires; very little has happened that they saw as incompatible with their own interests. Labor policy, monetary and trade policy, tax policies, resource policies, and the like, have changed in complicated ways throughout this century; they have never veered very far, for very long, from the ways found acceptable by Big Business. Is it likely that the consequences of monopoly/oligopoly in a national economy will be reproduced on a global scale by the MNC? Of necessity, because the scale *is* global, there are important differences; because the power is great and concentrated and capitalist, there are important similarities. The best we can do at this point is to ask what seem to be the most important questions, and in doing so underscore the differences and similarities.

1. What does this "interpenetration and international concentration of capital," as Mandel calls it, mean for jobs and wages in the advanced capitalist nations? The MNC is the ultimate in capitalist strength and flexibility. It moves in and out of areas, products, and techniques with an ease hitherto unknown. Its flexibility is labor's weakness. Labor's greatest weapon has always been the striking union. MNC's can redistribute production in the face of a strike; they do so even without the threat of a strike. One aim of the MNC is to find the geographic area of maximum labor advantage in terms of some optimum combination of wages, skills, and labor strength. Sometimes this means East Asia (wages in Taiwan in electronics are 1/20th of those in the U.S.), sometimes Northern Scotland; sometimes, even, the United States. The MNC rapidly moves out of reach of the *national* trade union. A telling example: in 1971, Ford (U.K.) decided to resist wage-demands of the well-organized British auto workers. Henry Ford II met with the British Prime Minister (Heath), who agreed that even at the cost of major labor unrest, such resistance was desirable. Ford switched some of its production to its Cologne factory, whose work force consisted mostly of newly-recruited, non-union, *Turkish* migrant workers. They had recently replaced *Italian* migrant workers, who had slowly become unionized, and whose work contracts were allowed to lapse. Such workers have few rights in the host country. Ford won out in the British dispute, unsurprisingly.[37]

If organized labor has any possibilities of fighting against that kind of power, it is at the moment dependent upon its ability to organize *international* trade union cooperation; i.e., between American, British, and German (and perhaps other nations') autoworkers, in the foregoing case. Steps along those lines in a few industries have been attempted, and others may be expected to follow. The prospects for American unions being able to take such steps effectively are significantly reduced by their membership in the International Congress of Free Trade Unions (ICFTU), a Cold War creation which places barriers even to *discussions* with many of the most relevant (Communist, or presumed to be Communist) unions abroad. The principal trade union federations in both Italy and France, for example, are Communist-dominated. Quite apart from that self-inflicted weakness, however, American organized labor is likely to find its strength effectively and steadily reduced as that of the MNC grows.

2. What will the MNC mean to tariff policy? Or, a variation on that question, is it likely that either smaller business *or* labor can hope for

---

[37]The full story is given in Stephenson, pp. 157–58, along with other similar incidents.

tariff protection to protect sales and jobs at home? Tariffs lose their meaning when production takes place *within* the national boundaries, a fact that was one of the principal stimuli to the initial growth of the MNC. What becomes necessary, therefore, are barriers to the flow of *capital* across national boundaries or, given the already substantial existence of MNC's in the world, even the forcible expulsion or expropriation of MNC capital. Anything can happen, of course; as matters now stand, it seems most unlikely that the most powerful corporations in the world, corporations whose sense of business identity appears to be stronger than their sense of national identity, but whose power within their own and other nations' governments is high and rising, would allow such developments to get very far. The kind of political pressure required to make such an eventuality probable would have to be substantial and broad-based, and nationalistic in its orientation; the future may see such a movement, but at present none is in sight. Organized labor is the most likely spearhead of such pressure, but that would seem to conflict with its need to organize internationally.

3. What are the effects of the MNC on the international monetary system, and on the balance of payments and trade conditions for individual nations? The MNC's include almost all of the very largest corporations in the world. They are giant producers, with sales amounting to about half a trillion dollars annually. They have and must have large financial reserves. They are constantly shuttling investment and working capital from nation to nation, and taking in flows of profits and interest. To quote Stephenson on part of this picture:

> International corporations may at any given moment have an overall balance sheet in a dozen or more currencies. This gives them both the commercial *need* and the commercial *means* to protect their interests by "speculating," or (more politely) "taking positions" in the foreign-exchange markets.[38]

Among the most active and largest of the involved MNC's are the international oil companies. Stephenson quotes an oil-company treasurer as saying "when I write a cheque, it is the bank that bounces."[39] Giant national corporations *in* the United States have the same kind of importance in the financial situation; but there are of course no balance of trade and payments or foreign-exchange rate problems directly entailed by domestic operations. It is Stephenson's considered opinion that the international monetary crisis of 1971, which led to the U.S. going off the gold standard, to dollar devaluation, and to the Nixon wage-price freeze, was due to "the increasing monetary freedom of the international company" (p. 138). In 1973, the U.S. Tariff Commission came to the same conclusion. "In August of 1973, influential British opinion

[38]Ibid., p. 123.
[39]Ibid., p. 126.

had it that 'America is at the centre of what is potentially the most dangerous monetary and trading crisis since 1931.' "[39a] Now a new international monetary system is in the making. One major reason for its necessity is the MNC; its shaping will be largely determined by the MNC.

4. Other questions concerning the MNC are being raised as the world becomes conscious of its existence and its importance. Here we shall end with our final question: What does the great and growing strength of the MNC mean to the relationships between the leading capitalist countries and the dependent economies of the Third World? Our answer will stress that the historical relationships between these two sets of countries—comprehended in the terms mercantilism, colonialism, imperialism, and neocolonialism—have meant retrogressive development for the Third World, and that the MNC will intensify that process.[40]

BACKWARD INTO UNDERDEVELOPMENT

There are more than three and a half billion people in the world. The distribution of income within the capitalist portion of the world (which contains over two-thirds of world population) is very much like that within each capitalist country, except more so. If we divide the countries of the world into "rich" and "poor," 69 percent of the people live in poor countries. In 1965 they received 15.5 percent of capitalist world income. The *average* annual per capita income in the poor countries was $167; in the rich countries it was $2,040. Two additional facts: 1) most of the people received much less than the average in both rich and poor countries (i.e., the median is lower than the average) for the distribution of income is highly unequal in both; 2) the gap between rich and poor countries has widened since 1965.[41]

The gap that widens today has been widening since the first penetration of Europeans into these areas; nor are the West's lamentations and worries about the gap new. Both the sorry facts and the attitudes of *noblesse oblige* are constants of this history from the beginning. Not until this century did the attempt grow to explain the whys and wherefores of the relationship: why the capitalist powers systematically penetrate the rest of the world and what the consequences are for both ends of the relationship.

[39a]Editorial Comment, *Manchester Guardian Weekly*, August 25, 1973.

[40]For further general discussion of the MNC, see the two-part essay in the *Monthly Review*, "Notes on the Multinational Corporation" (October and November, 1969).

[41]Between 1960 and 1970, per capita output in the rich countries increased 43 percent; in the poor countries 27 percent. See *New York Times*, July 10, 1972, in its summary of data in the latest *Statistical Yearbook* (for 1971) of the United Nations. The income figures above are taken from "Capitalism and Underdevelopment in the Modern World," by Thomas E. Weisskopf, in *The Capitalist System* (cited earlier), p. 444.

The first attempt was made by J. A. Hobson in 1902. Hobson was a radical (but not a socialist); he sought to show that Great Britain benefitted little from its empire, and argued that the impulse to empire (at least in his day) was due to the inability of Britain's own population to consume what it produced: "The taproot of imperialism," Hobson said, "is the unequal distribution of income."[42]

Hobson's analysis was picked up and transformed by Lenin. Writing in the midst of World War I, and using Germany as the basis of his analysis, Lenin saw imperialism—"the highest stage of capitalism"—as having its "economic quintessence" in monopoly capitalism. The growth of giant industry, its organization along monopolistic lines, its intermingling of industry and high finance, its needs for investment outlets, markets, and raw materials, its competition with other capitalist states, and its control over State power all combine to push advanced capitalist states inexorably over the globe—and into conflict with each other.[43]

Lenin's analysis of imperialism has been central to the development of anti-imperialist analysis, despite the general recognition that the spread of imperialism was substantial (e.g., by Great Britain) *before* the stage of "monopoly capitalism," and that the specific conditions of German capitalism formed too narrow a base for an understanding of imperialism in the 20th century. The development of this analysis has been swift since World War II.

The key contributions have been those of Paul Baran, Harry Magdoff, and André Gunder Frank. Baran, in his *Political Economy of Growth** (New York: Monthly Review Press, 1957), modernized and broadened Lenin's analysis and went on to analyze not only the imperialist *impulse* but its *consequences* on the "backward areas," including his assessment of the possibilities of their freeing themselves from capitalist domination. Harry Magdoff's *Age of Imperialism* focuses especially on the American empire in its contemporary phase. Frank, in a series of essays shortly to be commented on, centers his attention on the meaning of "dependency" for the underdeveloped areas.[44]

For understanding the gap between rich and poor nations, the widening of that gap, and the systematic worsening of conditions for the peoples of the underdeveloped countries, Frank's analysis is compelling.

---

[42]See J. A. Hobson, *Imperialism* (London: Allen & Unwin, 1902), p. 81.

[43]V. I. Lenin, *Imperialism** (New York: International Publishers, 1939). Written in 1916, and published first in 1917. Lenin's contemporary and associate Nikolai Bukharin probably contributed to Lenin's views; he also took a view less restricted to German conditions. See his *Imperialism and the Accumulation of Capital** (New York: Monthly Review Press, 1972, written in 1914).

[44]Here it is worth recalling the excellent survey and analysis by Tom Kemp, *Theories of Imperialism,* cited above, a study of which will show that our own presentation of the development is cursory—and deliberately so.

It moves within several "hypotheses": *First,* "in contrast to the development of the world metropolis, which is no one's satellite, the development of the national and other subordinate metropoles is limited by their satellite status." The "satellites" are the underdeveloped countries. *Second,* "the satellites experience their greatest economic development and their most classically capitalist industrial development if and when their ties to their metropolis are weakest." (As, for example, during the Depression of the 1930's, or during World War II.) When the ties grow strong again, Frank argues, *under*development, that is, retrogressive development, once more ensues. *Third,* "the regions which are the most underdeveloped and feudal-seeming today are the ones that had the closest ties to the metropolis in the past." Related to these hypotheses are two more: *Fourth,* what are thought of as latifundia or haciendas today (the "feudal-seeming" plantations) were born as *commercial* enterprises in the dim past; and, *fifth,* that the decline of these plantations as viable institutions is due to a decline in the demand for their products. Putting all these arguments together, Frank concludes that the economies and the societies of the Third World (and his focus is primarily Latin America) have undergone a process of deterioration and distortion due to their coerced relationships with the developed countries. They have gone backward into underdevelopment.[45]

It has been customary among American historians to believe that the United States, because of its great domestic market and abundant resources, did not *need* the overseas empire it began to develop in the years just before and after 1900; from that observation, conventional observers have gone on to see us as having gradually abandoned what we picked up. The great resurgence of American interventionism after World War II is seen as an attempt by the United States to defend freedom and to help the weak to become strong. The facts can be seen otherwise.

American overseas experience began to take on its current shape with the Spanish-American (more accurately, the Spanish-Cuban-American) War. From then on, we developed strong relationships with a growing number of countries spreading out from Cuba to the Caribbean and Central America, from the Philippines into the Pacific. All this was before World War I.

The period after 1914 was hectic and without a persisting pattern. World War I, the Depression, and World War II had massive disruptive

---

[45]Frank is a prolific writer. The argument above may be found in his essay "The Development of Underdevelopment," in Rhodes, *Imperialism and Underdevelopment,* Chapter 1; as Chapter 1 in James D. Cockcroft, André Gunder Frank and Dale L. Johnson, *Dependence and Underdevelopment** (New York: Doubleday; Anchor, 1972); and as Chapter 1 in his own *Latin America: Under-Development or Revolution** (New York: Monthly Review Press, 1969). His other works support his hypotheses.

effects. The hold of the traditional imperial countries (Great Britain, France, Belgium, Holland, Germany and Italy) was shaken by World War I and the Depression; World War II almost totally transformed their colonial relationships. Into that shambles strode the United States —because it could, and because, to maintain order in the world capitalist system, it had to.

Academic economists, encouraged and prodded by corporate and governmental needs and funds, made the study of "the development of the underdeveloped" into a recognized area of economics.

Unsurprisingly, American mainstream economists transported both their economics and their attitudes into the new field; so did business and government leaders. All these uncritically assumed: 1) the aims of the United States regarding the Third World countries are benign, and generously so; 2) if our activities' consequences have been in any respects negative, let alone unsuccessful, in producing development, that is accidental or due to the shortcomings of the poor countries; 3) "pragmatism and moderation" (in the phrase of W. W. Rostow) are the appropriate means to development and independence and that revolutionary movements act as destructive obstacles; 4) the methodology of conventional economics is sufficient to the end of understanding and specifying developmental processes.

What de Tocqueville said of political institutions applies with full force to the whole range of imperialistic relationships—and, as well, to the comic-tragic qualities of development economics:

> The physiognomy of a government may best be judged in its colonies, for there its features are magnified and rendered more conspicuous. When I wish to study the merits of the administration of Louis XIV, I must go to Canada; its deformity is there seen as through a microscope.[46]

When American postwar intervention in the underdeveloped areas became institutionalized, beginning with Truman's Point Four program in 1949, the economic and political characteristics of the affected countries were already desperate: deep poverty, dangerously high rates of population growth, oppressive governments, illiteracy, malnutrition and disease, and a long list of social traits that added up to human misery. A generation later all these characteristics have continued and intensified. Our intervention, like that of the Europeans before us, far from "developing the underdeveloped," has produced and speeded up a process of underdevelopment.

---

[46]Quoted by Baran, op. cit., p. 249. This compares with the famous utterance of Lyndon Johnson: "Foreign policy is merely the extension of domestic policy."

CHARITY BEGINS AT HOME

We have seen that the expansionist drives of the United States are, so to speak, congenital traits; that this country has always been sensitive to the gains to be made from expansion, and, over time, has quite consciously seen expansion as a means of resolving domestic problems —economic, political, and social. After World War II, our inclinations along these lines were given more force, and provided more opportunities. Business and government leaders knew that we would require expanding markets and investment outlets abroad, and that our raw materials requirements would depend increasingly on external sources for their satisfaction. Add to that the collapse of European power in the colonial areas due to war-wrought weakness, an upsurge of independence movements in the colonial areas, and the existence of established revolutions in the Soviet Union and (by 1949) in China. The stage was set for a swift and pervasive expansion of American hegemony. It took somewhat different forms than European colonialism and imperialism, and was all the more effective for having done so. Because of the relatively greater power of the U.S., both the gains and the damage were greater.

In 1950, U.S. direct foreign private investment was $11.8 billion; by 1971 the figure had risen by almost eight times that amount (cumulatively) to $86 billion. It doubled between 1950 and 1956, doubled again by 1964, and doubled again by 1971. By far the largest share (about 68 percent) of this investment was in the developed countries, and over half of that in manufacturing facilities. Of the $26 billion invested in underdeveloped countries, almost all was in raw materials extraction, and the greatest part of that was in petroleum: about 70 percent. The investments in the developed countries are vital for enhancing competitive strength and profits, the investments in the underdeveloped countries are vital as guarantees of precious raw materials, for global strategy and, of course, for profits.[47]

The direct investments of American corporations in the poor countries are less than a third of total direct investment abroad, but they bring in about half of all profits from foreign direct investments. They bring them in to the very largest corporations; mostly, the big oil companies. The largest, EXXON, in 1965 had stated foreign assets of $4.5

---

[47]The figures above and immediately following are taken from *International Economic Report of the President** (Washington: USGPO, 1973) and from the comprehensive article by Thomas E. Weisskopf, "U.S. Foreign Private Investment: An Empirical Survey," in *The Capitalist System*, pp. 427 ff. Weisskopf points out that the investment in *non*-raw materials facilities in the underdeveloped countries has recently begun to rise rapidly.

billion, or 52 percent of all its assets. Its foreign sales were 68 percent of all its sales, and yielded 60 percent of its total earnings.

A useful sense of the comparative magnitudes of the giant corporations in the world is given by a 1973 compilation of the Library of Congress (reported in the general press), ranking the 100 largest entities in the world—countries and companies—for the years 1960, 1965 and 1970, ranking countries by GNP and companies by annual sales volume. (The comparison of production with sales is technically inexact, but valid nonetheless.) In 1960 there were 59 countries and 41 companies on the list; in 1965, 57 countries and 43 companies; in 1970, 49 countries and 51 companies. The companies are almost all MNC's. In 1970, GM was the 24th largest entity in the world, its sales higher than the GNP of Yugoslavia, Pakistan, and South Africa (25, 26, and 27, respectively). Then came AT&T. Then EXXON. Then Denmark. Then Ford. The largest non-American company, Royal Dutch Shell, was 36th, a bit smaller than Norway, a bit larger than Venezuela (much of whose economy Shell controls). In 1960 there were neither Japanese nor German companies in the top 100; in 1970, there were two Japanese (Hitachi and Nippon Steel), and six German companies (VW, Siemens, Farbwerke Hoechst, Daimler-Benz, August Theyssen-Hutte, and BASF).

The "Seven Sisters," the oil companies that control the world's petroleum (and much of its other energy supplies)—EXXON, Mobil Oil, Texaco, Gulf Oil, Standard of California, Royal Dutch Shell, and British Petroleum—were all in the top 100 "entities," and they are of course among the top MNC's in the world. EXXON, the largest of these, functions in ways similar to the others. Its operations are mostly outside the U.S., and (apart from its crude oil production) mostly in the developed countries. In 1972, EXXON had "36,420 retail outlets in 14 European countries, pumping more gasoline than EXXON sells in the U.S." (*Business Week,* July 29, 1972). But its oil reserves (and some of its refineries) are in the underdeveloped countries, and two-thirds are in the Middle East. It would be very surprising indeed if EXXON and its "Sisters" did not take a strong interest in the "political stability" of these source countries. Given the power of the oil corporations in their own nations' politics and the vital importance of oil not just for profits but for day-to-day private and industrial life in modern economies and the military, it would be even more surprising if national policies deviated from the policies desired by the oil giants. The oil companies have complex interests and a long-term vision, in keeping with their power. They negotiate with nations, and their decisions must be ratified by their own nations—as in the case of the Tehran and Tripoli Agreements of 1971, between the oil companies and OPEC (representing eleven oil *countries* in North Africa, the Middle East, Southeast Asia, Africa, and South America), which raised the take per barrel of the petroleum exporting countries. The companies can and do pass on such increases in the form of higher prices to buyers, and acquiesce for a variety of reasons (including the delicate military and political conditions in some of these areas, and the potential profits to be gained through higher prices not only for oil but for coal, gas, and nuclear energy supplies which they own). Today, and despite appearances to the contrary, there is no shortage of oil reserves; a decade from now there almost surely will be. The oil companies are likely to make policy in the future, as they have in the past. What the companies want and decide they need in the future is no more likely to coincide with what the peoples of either the consuming or the producing countries need than it has in the past.[48]

The United States, once overflowing with oil, abused and misused its resources (abused with irrational pumping practices by engineering standards, and misused by selling petroleum products for uneconomic purposes—such as heating oil). By 1966 we were already importing (net) an amount of oil equal to 31 percent of our domestic production. What is true of oil is generally true of other raw materials that are used in bulk (as compared with, say, molybdenum, used as an alloy). Table 10 indicates this trend.

Magdoff also shows (p. 47), that in the relationship between net mineral imports and consumption up to 1919, we were net exporters; after 1940 our position as a net importer of all minerals (except gold) rose steadily, from about 5 percent of consumption in 1940–1944 to 14 percent in 1961.

TABLE 10

Selected Minerals: Net U.S. Imports as a
Percent of Domestic Mine or Well Production

	1937–1939 Average Percentages	1966 Average Percentages
Iron Ore	3	43
Copper	−13	18
Lead	0	131
Zinc	7	140
Bauxite	113	638
Petroleum	−4	31

SOURCE: Magdoff, *Age of Imperialism*, p. 48.

[48]Two books that go far toward providing understanding of how the oil companies work abroad and at home are Michael Tanzer, *The Political Economy of International Oil and the Underdeveloped Countries** (Boston: Beacon Press, 1969) and Robert Engler, *The Politics of Oil** (Chicago: University of Chicago Press, 1961). A conservative economist's view of the current market conditions for oil, which sees claims of shortage as nonsense, is M. A. Adelman, *The World Petroleum Market* (Baltimore: Johns Hopkins Press, 1973).

The United States had to expand its power in the underdeveloped areas if they were to be kept in the capitalist orbit as sources of raw materials and of high profits; that it was able to do so is dramatically revealed by comparing its position in the Middle East just before World War II with the present. (See Table 11.)

The importance of oil to the functioning of the economy, and the power of the oil corporations in domestic politics, achieves a consensus in our domestic politics at the highest levels, even where differences exist on other matters, just as the consensus is broader on foreign than on domestic affairs. The trade magazine *World Petroleum* illustrated this in its comments on Presidents Kennedy and Johnson:

> The USA oil industry finds little to complain about in the Kennedy Administration. . . . The president even went out of his way to write a nice letter to the National Petroleum Council, an industry advisory group of 95 top oil and gas executives, a letter almost without precedent in the 18-year-old history of the council. . . . (Sept., 1963) Lyndon Baines Johnson . . . has the interests of the industry at heart, as shown many times during his career of 31 years in political life in Washington. . . . (Jan., 1964)[49]

What is true of international oil in the Middle East finds its counterpart wherever oil reserves are located—for example, in Venezuela and in Southeast Asia, where at least some of the doggedness of the American war is to be understood in terms of estimated oil reserves which, according to one petroleum expert, make the Louisiana oil resources "look like a postage stamp on an elephant's ass."[50]

TABLE 11
Oil Reserves in the Middle East

| | Estimates of Reserves Controlled (billions of barrels) | | | |
| | 1940 | | 1967 | |
	Amount	% of total	Amount	% of total
Great Britain	4.3	72.0	73.0	29.3
United States	0.6	9.8	146.0	58.6
Other	1.1	18.2	30.0	12.1

SOURCE: Magdoff, p. 43.

[49]Quoted in Michael Tanzer, *The Political Economy of International Oil and the Underdeveloped Countries,* pp. 57–8.

[50]This is discussed in my article "The Political Economy of War," *The Nation,* June 28, 1971, with an accompanying article by Michael Tanzer, "Offshore Oil Sweepstakes." The "offshore" area curves around Indochina.

What is true of oil is true of other vital raw materials; for example, a shortage of chromium in 1972 was critical enough to cause our foreign policy to defy the UN ban on imports of chromium from Rhodesia as a means of bringing pressure to bear on Rhodesia's blatant racist policies. So it goes, with tungsten (from South Korea), columbium (from Brazil and Mozambique), cobalt (from the Congo), and so on.

All this strengthens American corporations and supplies important needs for the American economy, as it presently operates. What does it mean for the underdeveloped countries?

BAD TO WORSE

There was, until recently, a broad consensus that the internationalization and militarization of the American economy—whether or not those were the terms used—was good for Americans. The results were jobs, profits, and national security. As domestic tensions and social and economic troubles have multiplied in recent years, however, what were formerly seen as blessings are increasingly seen as disasters in disguise, and not only by radicals. This change in attitudes has made it easier to understand the calamity that the United States and other powerful nations have imposed on the underdeveloped countries. If their conditions before our policies took hold were bad, their present conditions are worse. The choice facing most of these countries is to allow this tragic path to continue to unfold, or to find ways to break the hold of the powerful countries; in Frank's words, "underdevelopment or revolution." Both the powerful nations and the underdeveloped ones realize the truth of this ultimate choice.

Most observers of the changes taking place in the underdeveloped areas find it difficult to understand why their economies steadily deteriorate, and why their governments—presiding over increasing hardships for the majority—move toward increasing coercion. It is the same kind of puzzlement that middle class people express about the continuation of poverty among the poor, despite all the help given them by the middle class. For such observers, the cause is sooner or later found as shortcomings of the victims. And victim is the appropriate term.

The continuing poverty of poor countries compares on many counts with the continuing poverty here at home. Both take place in a world whose already great riches increase by the day. Both occur within the context of the dual economy: the rich get richer; the poor get poorer, and are accused of an innate capacity for bringing misfortune on themselves. Finally, in attitudes mixing exasperation with pity, the better-off conclude that, after all, some people *are* better than others.

Economists normally cite a list of "factors" which, in combination, enhance the possibilities of growth and development: resources, entrepreneurship, the quantities and skills of the labor force, the availability of capital, markets, and a State that contributes to (or at least does not detract from) the developmental process; and some economists argue that the process will move more rapidly if the development is "balanced" (all industries moving together) and others if it is "unbalanced" (a few strategic industries taking the lead). Thus, as the underdeveloped economies find themselves in increasing difficulties, the quite natural response is to pinpoint the manner in which any factor is not satisfied: their resources are poor (but so were Japan's and Germany's, among others); they lack a lively entrepreneurial group (although Asians and Middle Easterners, e.g., are also known as crafty and aggressive businessmen); their labor force is inadequate in its skill composition, and disposed to be inadequately responsive to market stimuli (as was also said to be true of the British workers during the Industrial Revolution); they are short of investment capital (as were all capitalist countries in their industrializing stages); their domestic markets are too skimpy to absorb industrial production and they cannot compete on world markets, except with their raw materials (as was true of all but the leading nations over time); their governments are corrupt, or ill-advised; their development is too balanced, or too unbalanced. And, on top of everything else, their populations grow too fast. Why can't they be more like, say, us?

The conventional explanation of why development fails in the poor countries has many inadequacies: the most commanding concern the profoundly unhistorical quality of those explanations, and with their studious avoidance of acknowledging the degree to which the plight of the underdeveloped economies is to the benefit of the rich countries. Every industrial capitalist nation depended critically upon its own geographic expansion, or upon the buoyant world markets created by others' expansion. The expansion, of course, was into the lands of the presently underdeveloped countries. Setting morality, politics, and warfare aside, there is simply no space left into which the poor countries can expand—except, perhaps, space already controlled by the rich countries. Apart from any other consideration, therefore, the underdeveloped countries today must develop without the ease provided by the external possibilities of expansion. Indeed, quite the opposite is the case: the external relationships of the underdeveloped countries press down on them, and are negative. They are negative regarding their worsening terms of trade. Their productive facilities are owned by outsiders or, when owned by their own nationals, owned by those who function at a level and in a way subservient to the outsiders, as a kept and servile business class. When they do produce manufactures, they find themselves walled out of the rich markets by protective tariffs, import quotas, and the like. As for their domestic markets, the duality of their economies means that, even more so than in the rich countries, the overwhelming proportion of the people are abysmally poor, and the small high-income group finds its satisfactions in luxury goods or bank accounts abroad.[51]

But what about all the aid given to the poor countries by the rich, and especially by the United States? And of the private investment by outsiders? Shouldn't those flows of capital have made a difference? They did: they made a bad situation worse. In the frequent international meetings attended by representatives of both rich and poor countries— e.g., UNCTAD (the UN Commission for Trade and Development)— representatives of the poor countries regularly complain of the tariff barriers erected against their manufactures, and about the deterioration in their terms of trade, that is, the purchasing power of their exports. The deterioration, serious in the 1920's and 1930's, set in again about 1958, and has gone on since.

The terms of trade are more easily controllable by the rich countries than by the poor; just as an oligopolist or monopolist can set prices, but a competitive producer cannot. The rich countries give aid: but normally there is a high proportion of military grants buried in dollar aid. The usual custom is to tie aid to purchases in the granting country, and aid has always been considerably less than private investment from abroad (and has been decreasing since 1966). What results is a stark fact relating aid and the terms of trade (the meanings of both of which are dominated by the rich countries): the poor countries lose a considerable amount of what they receive because of the deterioration in the terms of trade. UNCTAD calculated that losses due to worsening terms of trade were 36.5 percent of official aid in 1961, and rose to 42.8 percent by 1966. They have risen since.[52]

The rich countries invest in the poor countries in their own self-interest, of course. Corporations do so for profits; they receive the support of their governments (in subsidies, investment guarantees, and policies designed to maintain a "friendly climate for investment") because that's what governments are for, and because the governments have interests that coincide with those of the corporations, on both

---

[51]See Arghiri Emmanuel, *Unequal Exchange: A Study of the Imperialism of Trade** (New York: Monthly Review Press, 1972), for a penetrating and original analysis of these relationships.

[52]See Magdoff, p. 158. His chapter on "aid and trade" is informative on this and other relationships. What we have just stated about the terms of trade does not take into account (as Magdoff does), the increasing indebtedness forced upon the underdeveloped countries by their worsening position, which in turn reduces their net earnings from exports, and leads to further indebtedness. The question of aid is treated in a fascinating manner by Teresa Hayter, *Aid as Imperialism** (London and New York: Penguin, 1971). Working as a professional in a major aid agency, she discovered the differences between the rhetoric and the reality of aid.

economic and strategic grounds. The impact of private foreign investment is harmful to the poor nations; its net effect is to yield an income inflow to the rich, not to the poor. The U.S. Department of Commerce found that for the period 1956–1961, the ratio of inflow of profits and interest to the United States to outflow of investment from the United States with the underdeveloped countries was 164 percent; that is, in those years more came back to the U.S. than went out. For the years 1950–1961, the Department found (for Argentina, Chile, Peru, Venezuela, Colombia and Mexico) that remittances of profit and interest to U.S. investors exceeded new private U.S. investment by $3.9 billion.[53]

Expansion into the underdeveloped countries, and exploitation of their people and of their resources have provided the critical *margin* of dynamic capitalist development for the developed countries. They act as if they knew it, all along. In the mercantilist period, no bones were made about it; in the past century or so, exploitation is done in the name of the "white man's burden," *"la mission civilisatrice,"* or, for the United States, "the preservation of the free world, and the development of the underdeveloped."

The free world seems to be free only for private investment. It is difficult to know what other kind of freedom is meant in places like Greece, South Korea, Thieu's South Vietnam, the Union of South Africa, Brazil, Chiang's Taiwan, the Dominican Republic, Guatemala, and Iran, among other cherished diadems of the free world. Except for a few small societies that have fought their way out of it, that "free world" has been preserved. Saved for freedom, it continues to underdevelop backward into a perverse and ever more repressive form of capitalism, displaying all of its evils but none of its virtues.

---

[53]This pattern is characteristic, and the figures have, if anything, increased in recent years. In 1966, Chase Manhattan Bank, seeking a relaxation of the restrictions on overseas investment demanded by Johnson's 1965 "Voluntary Balance of Payments Program" (itself brought about by the payments crisis associated with the Indochina War), issued a brochure stating the facts about petroleum investments and urging that oil companies give "complete reporting" in order that the government would see that such investments reduced rather than increased the payments deficit, because of the "quick payback" period. Some of their facts are worth quoting at length: ". . . these investments have yielded dollar inflows that are considerably larger, year by year, than the new investment outflows. In balance of payments terms the petroleum industry is more profitable than the average U.S. foreign investment: in 1964 it accounted for about a third of net U.S. overseas investment, yet produced over 50% of total U.S. direct investment income." *Balance of Payments of the Petroleum Industry,* Chase Manhattan Bank, 1966, p. 4. They add that the "payback period" is three years; i.e., the rate of profit is 33-1/3% per annum. Every year since 1957 has shown a rising excess of inflow over outflow. The Bank addressed this brochure to the petroleum companies to enhance their truthfulness, and to the government to enhance its understanding. The data from the Department of Commerce are cited in Frank, *Latin America* . . ., pp. 151 and 162–63.

The developments of the past half-century would have passed comprehension for Schumpeter and Hobson, the only two mainstream economists who set about to analyze imperialism with any seriousness. Both thought capitalism to be rational in its essence, and both thought imperialism to be irrational—as well as immoral. Seeing it in its best light, Schumpeter prized capitalism; Hobson was not opposed to the system as such, only to its excrescences. Imperialism was one such, and it was due to the other main excrescence, a highly unequal distribution of income. Rid the society of the latter and there would be no need for the former: "The only safety of nations lies in removing the unearned increments of income from the possessing classes, and adding to the wage-income of the working classes or to the public income, in order that they may be spent in raising the standard of consumption."[54]

Schumpeter counted on free trade, the rational way, to be the hallmark of capitalist development. There has been less of it since he wrote (1919) than before. Hobson's hope for a redistribution of income "from the possessing classes" has not been met, but the "public income" has risen from what was little in his day to hundreds of billions annually now. But it has accompanied the spread not the decline of imperialism.

Schumpeter's and Hobson's ideas have an attractive quality to them; subsequent history shows that their attractiveness is not matched by sufficient analytical cogency. Lacking in both cases is an understanding of the role of exploitation in capitalist development, and of how and why a small group of powerful individuals and enterprises formulate national policies seen as rational for themselves and for the system they wish to defend, but which in comparison with an alternative *system* are certainly irrational for the people in their own and other societies.

These two men have not been alone in framing attractive ideas, nor alone in having their ideas buffeted by cruel winds. They and other well-intentioned analysts have failed to develop a theory of power, a theory of the State, that would support their leading ideas. The validity of these ideas depends upon their compatibility with how power is developed and by whom, how it is used and by whom, and for what purposes. Such questions take us now to an examination of the State.

READING SUGGESTIONS

This chapter, despite its length, has only scratched the surface of what needs to be known. In addition to looking further at many of the works cited in this and other chapters—e.g., *Monopoly Capital* and *Contours of*

---

[54]Hobson, op. cit., p. 89.

American History—serious readers will find some of the following books especially helpful.

Immanuel Wallerstein, *The Modern World-System: Capitalist Agriculture and the Origins of the European World-Economy in the Sixteenth Century* (New York and London: Seminar Press, 1973) is a work of original and comprehensive scholarship which, in clarifying the emergence of capitalism, develops an analytical framework (core, semi-peripheral, and peripheral societies) of great use for understanding current patterns. William Ashworth, *A Short History of the International Economy Since 1850* (London: Longmans, 1964) is an unexciting but useful summary and analysis of major institutional, technological, and economic developments. The literature on imperialism is expanding rapidly. URPE has put together a very useful bibliographical collection on all geographic areas and many analytical topics in its *Case Studies in Imperialism and Underdevelopment, RRPE* (Spring, 1971). See also its *Dependency and Foreign Domination in the Third World, RRPE* (Winter, 1972), and *Capitalism and World Economic Integration: Perspectives on Modern Imperialism, RRPE* (Spring, 1973).

A neglected but important aspect of the current situation is treated succinctly and critically by Herbert I. Schiller, *Mass Communications and American Empire** (Boston: Beacon Press, 1971). The book of readings by Rhodes has been cited; another such collection (which overlaps a bit) is K. T. Fann and Donald Hodges, eds., *Readings in U.S. Imperialism** (Boston: Porter Sargent, 1971). William A. Williams, *Tragedy of American Diplomacy** (New York: Dell, 1962) provides a strong analytical summary of the major directions of American foreign policy, especially since the 1890's. Joyce and Gabriel Kolko, *The Limits of Power** (New York: Harper & Row, 1972) is an intense examination of the crucial period 1945–1954. David Horowitz, *Empire and Revolution** (New York: Random House; Vintage, 1969), emphasizes U.S.-USSR relationships, real and concocted. An interesting collection of Marx's many mostly journalistic pieces on these matters is Shlomo Avineri, ed., *Karl Marx on Colonialism and Modernization** (New York: Doubleday Anchor, 1969).

There is an enormous amount of literature on underdeveloped areas. One of the useful books is David E. Novack and Robert Lekachman, eds., *Development and Society: The Dynamics of Economic Change** (New York: St. Martins, 1964). Pierre Jalée, *The Third World in World Economy* * (New York: Monthly Review Press, 1969), has put together facts and figures otherwise difficult to find, within a sound analysis. Chandler Morse et al., *Modernization by Design* (Ithaca: Cornell University Press, 1969), is an attempt from several social disciplines to achieve a realistic appraisal of problems of development; Morse's chapter relates "economic" and "non-economic" matters scientifically, in the best sense of that much-abused term.

Finally, some books of a different sort. Felix Greene, *The Enemy**
(New York: Random House; Vintage, 1970) is a powerful and most
readable attempt to explain to us that we *are* an imperialist power and
what that means to those whom we oppress *and* to ourselves, as a nation
and as individuals. One of the bloodiest meanings is detailed in the
so-called Cornell Study, *The Air War in Indochina** (Boston: Beacon
Press, 1971), edited by Raphael Littauer and Norman Uphoff. Its low-
keyed and heavily statistical analysis is overwhelming and horrifying.
Without saying the words, it shows that the final result of imperialism,
unless overthrown, is genocide. *The Pentagon Papers** (New York: Bantam, 1971) show clearly (if not fully) how and why the government
deceived us as the process took shape. Noam Chomsky in his *American
Power and the New Mandarins** (New York: Vintage, 1969) and *At War
with Asia** (New York: Vintage, 1970) provides a penetrating and horrifying historical analysis of the process. His *For Reasons of State** (New
York: Vintage, 1973) contains essays mostly sparked by the Indochina
war, but with an importance going beyond the war and into the nature
of contemporary American social tensions and power. His analysis of
the Pentagon Papers (Chapters 1 and 2) shows how very limited those
Papers' contents are, by comparison with the full story of aggression
and deception.

chapter eight
The State

Was it for this our fathers kept the law?
This crown shall crown their struggle and their ruth?
Are we the eagle nation Milton saw
Mewing its mighty youth,
Soon to possess the mountain winds of truth,
And be a swift familiar of the sun
Where aye before God's face his trumpets run?
Or have we but the talons and the maw,
And for the abject likeness of our heart
Shall some less lordly bird be set apart?
Some gross-billed wader where the swamps are fat?
Some gorger in the sun? Some prowler with the bat?

(William Vaughn Moody, *An Ode in Time of Hesitation*)

All agree that what the State has or has not done has been of great importance in the social and economic development of modern societies. Beyond that simple statement, disagreement sets in and soon becomes sharp. When has the State's role been beneficial and when harmful? When vital and when of small consequence? How does one measure the State's importance, and within what temporal and functional framework? How does the State relate to private groups, at any time and over time?

Asking these questions, or others as yet unasked, places an examination of the role of the State in a context of ideological and theoretical dispute and it raises still another question: to what degree and in what ways does the relationship of the State to economic development manifest and in what ways does it conceal the changing structure and functions of *power* in modern capitalist societies?[1]

---

[1] A good part of these introductory pages follows closely my position in "The State, Power and the Industrial Revolution, 1750–1914," *URPE Occasional Paper No. 4* (Spring, 1971), concerned with Great Britain, France, and Germany.

The activities of governments have been much studied by historians, but very much as though "government" and "State" are the same entities. The larger and more decisive meaning of the State and, therefore, the role of *power,* remains a vast *terra incognita.* It is power that informs and is informed by the complex relationships between public and private institutions; at the center of that complex will be found the State system, supported by and maintaining the political and social system over which it rules. To explore and map out the ground that comprehends power, socio-economic stability and change, and the State is slippery work; if we are to understand our past and have any say whatsoever in our future, that effort is essential.

THE EASY WAY

Historians and social scientists who have dealt with the government, the State, and power in capitalist society customarily have been motivated by a particular tension and have operated with a particular assumption. Typically, neither the tension nor the assumption has been explicit. The tension has been between those who thought it desirable to minimize the role of the government and those who wished to see a broadening of its powers. The assumption has been the pluralist notion that government in capitalist societies, like the functioning of the economy, is a response to the forces of competition. Some elaboration of both these points is necessary.

For example, Great Britain is seen to have had a "weak State" in the 19th century; Germany a strong one. The terms of the historical discussion are confined to easily discernible, hotly debated, and explicit policies: statutes, regulations, fiscal, monetary and commercial policies, subsidies, and the like. Seldom is there an analysis of what governments did *not* do, or what *ceased* to be done (for example, in the way of social and human protection), let alone what the State was responsible for that did not appear in specific actions or that did not "appear" at all.

This last-mentioned role of the State, what we may call its nonactions, is by its nature the most obscure. When understood it is among the most revealing of the relationships between private power, governmental activities, and social conditions. Put together with the more obvious manifestations of power, this aspect of social existence allows a long step to be taken toward an understanding of the State. An absence of such understanding encourages the following kind of misleading observation concerning social conditions in industrializing Britain; the statement is made, it should be noted, by a respected economic historian who has done more than others to study "the State":

... in the age of laissez-faire the role of government in economic affairs was largely a passive one. ... The social evils in town and countryside that followed in the wake of the Industrial Revolution might have been alleviated at an earlier date if the governing classes had been better informed about the great changes that were taking place in the mines and factories. ... The government was inactive because it saw no good reason why it should do anything.[2]

"The governing classes," it may be assumed, contained men who were the creators and beneficiaries of the very conditions of which the author thinks they were ignorant, ready in a trice to employ the coercive power of the State to subdue those who sought to change those conditions, power that had been used to abolish social protections at "an earlier date" (as discussed in Chapter Two).

The "social evils" mentioned by Henderson were due to the absence of social controls at the time, as the "self-regulating market economy" held full sway. Given their earlier abolition, their continuing absence can be explained in good part by "non-decision making," a phenomenon analyzed explicitly in a recent study:

... non-decision making is a means by which demands for change in the existing allocation of benefits and privileges in the community can be suffocated before they are even voiced; or kept covert; or killed before they gain access to the relevant decision-making arena; or, failing all these things, maimed or destroyed in the decision-implementing stage of the policy process.[3]

Those involved in protest activities in recent years have experienced all these deflecting techniques in full measure; indeed, it is the success of such techniques in maintaining the status quo that has led many to an enhanced interest in the way power works.

Non-decision making is a principal means of maintaining the status quo, or of slowing and guiding the changes away from it. It is the monopoly of those who have great power in society; those who are deflected, ignored, suffocated, and whose proposals are "maimed or destroyed" are those with less or no power. In capitalist democracies the guiding assumption of conventional social theorists, the assumption on which their "theory of the State" is founded, is *pluralism*. The pervasiveness of this assumption, and the confusions surrounding it, require

---

[2] W. O. Henderson, *The State and the Industrial Revolution in Prussia, 1740–1870* (Liverpool: University Press, 1958), pp. xiii–xiv. The reference in the quote is to Britain.

[3] Peter Bachrach and Morton S. Baratz, *Power and Poverty: Theory and Practice** (New York: Oxford University Press, 1970), p. 44. Both the theory and the practice discussed in this excellent work are significant additions to what we have known. The empirical focus is Baltimore.

that it be looked at critically. After doing so, we shall attempt an analysis of power, and of the nature and role of the State in the United States.

Few economists have a "theory of the State," or are even conscious of the need for one. In the fragmentation characteristic of the social sciences, economists who might feel that need can, so it is believed, turn to the political scientists. The latter would be much offended at the suggestions above that the State has been neglected. They do have a theory of the State: pluralism. The only thing wrong with it is that it takes for granted the very matter most requiring examination: power. In this neglect, the political scientists have matched their economist counterparts who take private property and basic capitalist institutions for granted. But, as Ralph Miliband points out,

> A theory of the state is also a theory of society and of the distribution of power in that society. But most Western "students of politics" tend to start, judging from their work, with the assumption that power, in Western societies, is competitive, fragmented and diffused: everybody, directly or through organised groups, has some power and nobody has or can have too much of it. In these societies, citizens enjoy universal suffrage, free and regular elections, representative institutions, effective citizen rights, including the right of free speech, association and opposition; and both individuals and groups take ample advantage of these rights, under the protection of the law, an independent judiciary and a free political culture. As a result, the argument goes, no government, acting on behalf of the state, can fail, in the not very long run, to respond to the wishes and demands of competing interests. In the end, everybody, including those at the end of the queue, gets served.[4]

Pluralism as the basis for thinking about the State assumes that sovereignty resides in the voter and that political outcomes depend upon competition among those vying for those votes. Neoclassical economics, the body of theory that guides economists' thinking, has its parallel assumptions. Not the voter, but the consumer is sovereign; business firms vie with each other for the consumer's vote—that is, the consumer's dollar. Economic demand determines economic supply; political demand determines political supply. It is a comforting set of beliefs for those who accept it; all that is ignored is the underlying reality in society that makes some considerably more equal than others. All that is ignored is power, who has it, how it is obtained, how used, how distributed, how lost. A theory of the State without a theory of power is, in the old saying, like Hamlet without the Dane.

---

[4]Ralph Miliband, *The State in Capitalist Society* (New York: Basic Books, 1969), p. 2. Harold J. Laski, *The State in Theory and Practice* (New York: Viking, 1935) is an earlier, modern, and still relevant attempt by a Marxian political philosopher to understand the modern State.

POWER, POWER, WHO HAS THE POWER?

What *is* power? It is the ability to act effectively, to make things go one's way, or to keep them so. The Latin root for the noun "power" and the verb "to be able" is the same. Power is the ability, for present purposes, to make or to influence decisions and non-decisions. Where does it come from? Most simply, power is held by those who control what is valued in their society; what has been valued; what is coming to be valued. What is valued may be tangible (like productive assets or weaponry) or intangible (like the ability to formulate or represent cherished beliefs or aspirations).

Control over the means of material survival places its possessors at the center of power in any society, although the forms and functions associated with such control have differed quite substantially in history —a priesthood in Ancient Egypt, the Church and warriors in medieval Europe, for example. Control over productive wealth in a capitalist society as *a* source of power comes closest to being *the* source of power. This characteristic is one way of defining capitalism; it also helps to explain the great dynamism of capitalist economic development.

Still, complexity in the structures of power exists in a capitalist as in any other kind of society; this complexity is substantial and, upon reflection, obvious. Power derives from different areas of society—economic, political, military, religious, cultural, social—and functions at different levels—local, national, international. Still, from this patterned and dynamic complexity, order may be derived; we may think of *structures* of power. Visually, we may think of a many-sided pyramid, its sides representing the diverse sources of power and its shape, narrowing to a peak, representing the concentration of power. Power changes hands over time, which requires that this visual representation be thought of as a moving film, rather than as a diagram. Nor should it be forgotten that those who have power at lower levels of the pyramid (e.g., those who control education, or police, or medical facilities on the local level) have power that for some purposes is just as vital as those who wield power at the top. Some examples are in order.

In medieval Europe, power was in the hands of those who ruled over religious and military affairs; they also controlled the productive land. Which came first, the chicken (religious and military power) or the egg (control of the land), need not detain us here; there were tangibles and intangibles involved. For the medieval serf, the locally-held power was most vital in determining the conditions of life.

Something concerning the chicken and egg argument seems worth saying. The simple Marxian view would argue that the "egg," i.e., control over the land came first; a more complicated view would see the long and militarized anarchy of the so-called Dark Ages as having its unifying factor in the Roman Catholic Church and its stabilizing factor in unremitting military activities. Church functionaries were often fighters; together they comprised the aristocracy of medieval Europe; the serfs supported them from the land. The "middle class" was virtually non-existent in the early Middle Ages; as it became more prominent through its expanding trading activities, it was leaned on increasingly by the feudal military and clerical nobility; the structure of power was altering in the process.[5]

The consequences of the successful discharge of the feudal military function included an increase both in political stability and in trade and industry; the unifying role of the Church began to break down, and to seem a hindrance. The Reformation of the 16th century had many sides to it, in as many countries; central to that struggle was a challenge that denied the fiscal and political prerogatives the Church had long possessed. In what had been an epoch whose deep attachment to religious belief is unintelligible to moderns, any major struggle for power had to revolve around the control of religious institutions and translate itself into religious categories: the confessional, the role of the priest, faith and works, and the like.

When the Church lost its hegemony in Europe, its place was taken by the descendants of those militarists who once walked hand in glove with the Church; as secular dynasties they now ruled over nations in a time of substantially larger and more expensive conflict. Merchants and financiers were quite frequently the handmaidens of this transition; they were required to finance the now mercenary (once feudal) fighting forces, and their trade and industry gave strength to the new nations.[6]

The stage was set for yet another struggle for power. From the viewpoint of capitalist development, its most decisive manifestation was in 17th century England: a struggle between what has been called "the divine right of kings" and "the divine right of capital." It was not a clear-cut struggle to its participants, nor would its eventual outcome—laissez-faire capitalism—be entirely clear for over a century after the dust settled. The age was still religious: thus, "the Puritan Revolution." It was the age of mercantilism, and of a class of merchants and financiers whose strength had increased along with England's: thus, "the bourgeois revolution."

---

[5]For the origins of feudalism, see F. L. Ganshof, *Feudalism* (London: Longmans, 1952). For the definitive view of the complexities of the period see Marc Bloch, *Feudal Society** (Chicago: University of Chicago Press, 1964) 2 vols. A simpler Marxian view is well-put in Marion Gibbs, *Feudal Order* (London: Cobbett Press, 1949). This treats only English society, which explains what I take to be the undue simplicity of the treatment.

[6]The classic process had merchants and incipient monarchs working together against a feudal nobility. Where that did not occur, or where it faltered, the nation-state did not arise until centuries later. See, e.g., G. Barraclough, *The Origins of Modern Germany* (New York: Putnam, 1963; originally published in 1949), esp. Part Four.

The English Civil War began in 1640 and ended in 1688. The motives of those involved were mixed, and any one of a particular religious, business, or military status might well be found on either side. But the bourgeois mentality was the most viable; by the close of the 17th century, the bourgeoisie had begun to move toward parity with the aristocracy (monarchy and hereditary peerage), even with the Established Church playing a subsidiary and supporting role to the latter. Thus the dynamic new economic forces and the more traditional political and social values came into an uneasy but workable balance, a balance that has yet to disappear totally in Great Britain. The structure of power had been decisively altered; the nation of shopkeepers had been born; capitalist control over production came to be valued *most* in the nexus of power.[7]

THE STATE AS A SYSTEM OF POWER

Who most valued this control over production? Not, surely, the simple folk who found themselves swept off the land and into the brutal conditions of the towns, the mines, mills, and factories, with increasing tempo and ruthlessness; nor the women and children who pulled coal carts deep in the mines or tended spindles for twelve or more hours a day. What is valued and why does not tell us much about the acquisition of power; the *who* is always important, the who and their location in the structure of power as society moves through time.

Except for revolutionary periods, alterations in the structure of power are brought about by those already sitting fairly high in the structure; the alteration allows them to move up even more. The Tudor and Stuart dynasties that led England toward the civil war that in turn reduced the power of the Crown did *not* value economic matters above all else; that honor was reserved for their own noble attributes. But of necessity the monarchs did value rising economic strength in England, without which England would be subdued by the feisty rivalries of the 16th and 17th

---

[7]The evolution of power structures was quite different elsewhere. In the United States the capitalist class, though its composition and base changed continually, started out on top, with no competitors from the past and the ability to sweep any potential competitors into its net or into the dustbin of history. The American businessman was able both to create and to control the political and social ("normative") sources of power—i.e., the system of government, the political system, and religious and educational institutions all accepted the directions and values established by business. The historically evolved patterns in Germany, Italy, Japan, and France were different from each other and from the United Kingdom and the U.S. See Barrington Moore, Jr., op. cit., for some of the appropriate analysis. For the English Civil War as a process, see Christopher Hill, *Reformation to Revolution,* op. cit., and Michael Walzer, *The Revolution of the Saints* (New York: Atheneum, 1968).

centuries. So men of trade, industry, and finance rose to positions of influence and importance, each step making the next easier. Politics and opinion, education and literature, paid increasing homage—if also more criticism—to the new men of affairs; religious standards subtly but surely altered in their favor. The Civil War was an announcement that the complex of new structures had reached an impasse, where existing political institutions, the formal structure within which power works, had to be revised. A new State system was needed; one suited to surging capitalism.

The modern capitalist *State system* has many components to it: government; administration and bureaucracy; military, para-military, and security forces; the judiciary; lesser (local and state) governments; legislative assemblies (federal and other).[8] To most contemporary minds all these classifications fall into one category: government. For some Marxists they add up to "the executive committee of the ruling class," that is, the owners and controllers of the means of production. The merits of the latter view come close to reality in ways that the pluralist notion does not; still, much is left unexplained that must be understood.

Marx made no attempt to develop a theory of the State, although that was one of his intentions. His observations on power and the State are trenchant and illuminating; like Veblen, however, Marx went no farther than illuminating observations. In both past and present, power is held and used in complex ways; those who would deny its present sources and uses and who seek to put something more humane in its place will have to work with all the necessary distinctions in mind.

The State system sketched above is the system through which power flows; within it power grows, for use within and outside the State system itself. The State system, like the larger social system which it represents, is oligarchic and pyramidal in structure: there is an élite at the top and people of some but not much power in the middle; the mass of participants in the State system (like those in the economy) are mere hirelings. Within each of the six categories noted above the pyramidal structure is reproduced. As between the categories there is a difference between higher and lower; e.g., top federal government positions are usually in the State élite; top local positions usually are not.

The *sources* of power are diverse, with control over the means of production the most vital. The framework through which power is *used* to affect the State system is the framework of politics: the political system. The forms or institutions of politics, like the sources of power, are diverse: power is applied through *pressure*—in and through political

---

[8]This structure, and much of what follows, derives from Miliband, op. cit., especially Chapter 3. See Chapters 4-8 for an elaboration of the component parts of the system. What I call "lesser governments" Miliband classifies as "sub-central."

parties, and directly on (or in) the agencies of the State through lobbies —whether industrial, agricultural, financial, labor, church, or professional lobbies (e.g., doctors and lawyers). In addition, the more powerful the interested party, the more able it will be to work directly on the top layers of the State élite, and have its representatives as members of that élite (for example, in the President's Cabinet).

These component parts of the political system are constantly seeking to bend the State system to their wills; they are also among the legitimators of that system and the larger society over which it presides. Let us examine in more detail these elements of State power.

COMPETITION AMONG THE FEW

In the American State system, the *government* is the executive branch: the president, his cabinet, and his top aides. The government is not the State, but the government speaks for the State. As Miliband puts it,

> ... the state ... is a nebulous entity; and while men may choose to give their allegiance to it, it is to the government that they are required to give their obedience. A defiance of its orders is a defiance of the state, in whose name the government alone may speak and for whose actions it must assume ultimate responsibility.[9]

Electoral contests for control of the government are contests for who shall interpret and represent the interests of the State. Except in revolutionary or counterrevolutionary periods, however, these contests take place within narrow limits—narrow enough, *usually*, that the expression "Tweedledee and Tweedledum" has come to characterize them more often than not. However, in times of rapid social change, contests for power *within* the system, reflecting divisions of opinion between the most substantial groups, lead to more important electoral choices. Ours are such times.

The next sector of the State system, *administration* and *bureaucracy*, includes the numerous public and semi-public agencies (such as the Federal Trade Commission, which is a public agency, and the Federal Reserve System, which is semi-public). These agencies are presumed to work in harmony with government, and usually do. Whether they do or not is not a matter of statute; they are not necessarily responsible to the executive. Their heads are frequently appointed for periods that extend beyond the government of one term. (The seven directors of the Federal Reserve Board, for instance, are appointed for fourteen years, staggered over time.) The largest number of the working members of such agencies are civil servants, subject to neither appointment nor election. Although presumably devoid of "political" inclinations, in fact

---

[9] *The State in Capitalist Society,* p. 50.

(and especially at the top) their political leanings are strong, and tend to be well-known when they come into conflict with the executive (e.g., Arthur Burns, as Chairman of the Board of Governors of the Federal Reserve System, at one time or another under Nixon). The persistent tendency for these administrators, as for virtually everyone at the top levels of the State system, is to be conservative—which tends to mean "liberal" in today's usage—and to be drawn from the top business or professional levels of society.

The *military, para-military,* and *security forces* of the State will receive a separate treatment when, later, we seek to evaluate the strength of the Pentagon in the current power structure; here they will merely be characterized. As the coercive elements of the State, they serve the government of the day and its foreign and domestic policies, although they are independent of executive control with regard to appointment for all but the very top positions. In the past thirty years or so, this coercive force has grown most. Again, Miliband:

> Nowhere has the inflation of the military establishment been more marked since the second world war than in the United States, a country which had previously been highly civilian-oriented. And much the same kind of inflation has also occurred in the forces of "internal security," not only in the United States; it is probably the case that never before in any capitalist country, save in Fascist Italy and Nazi Germany, has such a large proportion of people been employed on police and repressive duties of one kind or another[10]

The *judicial* sector of the State system is presumed to be independent of the interests of the government; it is concerned with continuity and adherence to established law. The top federal judges are appointed for life by the president; such appointments are among the juiciest plums in the orchard of patronage that enhances the power of the presidency. Presidents are often in conflict with one or another of Supreme Court and other federal judges; and this is an additional reason why presidents cherish their right to appoint. Viewed over the long-run, however, the range of conflict is narrow. The memory of man knoweth not the appointment of a federal judge who questioned the fundaments of the American capitalist system, least of all the sanctity of private property. Veblen puts it wryly: "In the nature of the case the [property] owner alone has any standing in court. All of which argues that there are probably very few courts that are in any degree corrupt or biased. . . . Efforts to corrupt them would be a work of supererogation, besides being immoral.[11]

What Miliband calls "sub-central government"—that is, local, county, and state governments—in the United States is a bewildering

---

[10]Ibid., p. 52.
[11] *Theory of Business Enterprise,* p. 282n.

array that reproduces in form and function most of the State system, but at a lower level of power and importance. For day-to-day questions of life, however, this sub-central system may be and usually is critical, in the areas of education, health, welfare, police, housing, and transportation, for example. This welter of governments is the prime channel through which much of the power of the State runs; it also is the channel through which the voice of local and regional interests and attitudes is conveyed to the State élite. They are, as Miliband remarks, "power structures in their own right" (p. 53).

The final segment of the State system is the *legislative assembly:* the two branches of Congress (with their counterparts in state and local assemblies). Historically, Congress has provided both conflict and cooperation for the executive branch, although always within the narrowly-defined limits that characterize the behavior of the other elements of the State system. In this century, there has been a marked tendency toward concentration and centralization in the economy, as we have seen; that tendency has had its counterpart in the concentration and centralization of power in the State system. The power of the federal government vis-à-vis the separate states has grown to a disproportion that would have seemed incredible to Americans at the turn of the century; this is also true of the power of the executive branch vis-à-vis Congress.

These developments toward concentration and centralization in the economy and in the State system are both cause and result of the internationalization and militarization of the United States. Already in the 1930's respected voices were expressing alarm at how "dangerously slow and inefficient" the processes of representative government are when considerations of foreign policy are at stake. By 1952, when Eisenhower took office, "consensus" on foreign policy had been achieved between the two major parties; consensus on foreign and military policy would thenceforth mean that the executive branch would decide first and induce Congress to go through the formalities of granting what became automatic appropriations afterward. The path that led us to our present condition began to be cut out in the first years of this century; it was smoothed by the key processes of *legitimation,* now to be examined.

IT'S ALL RIGHT. . .

Modern societies all use coercive devices of one sort or another to one degree or another; by far more important than coercion are the practices that bring about voluntary acquiescence. These practices fall under the heading of legitimation. Taken together with the public and private institutions that they legitimate, the ways in which acquiescence is achieved make a grim joke of pluralistic notions of political competition, as oligopolistic economic power and modern advertising make a mockery of notions of economic competition. Whether or not the processes to be described constitute conscious *deception* to achieve their consequences is not important; indeed, the high probability that what the legitimators do they do out of principled conviction rather than guile makes their impact all the more powerful.

Politically, we grow up within a universe of discourse in which certain matters are taken for granted and others lie beyond the pale. We are socialized to be deaf and blind and dumb on a range of matters, the more so the more basic they are to the society's functioning. The process is not much different in its results from that which affects our tastes in food. Certain foods, enjoyed in other lands, are seen as repulsive or as non-foods; so it is with political questions.

Of course *anything* can be discussed. Whether or not an audience will assemble or listen, or, if it does, will move in suggested ways, is a matter of who is saying what to whom. At any time there is an undesigned apparatus that sustains the largest elements of the status quo. The constituent elements of that apparatus vary from time to time and place to place, of course. They include: the major political parties; the media; the educational system; religious institutions; popular cultural life (including TV and organized athletics); public relations and advertising; the family. From cradle to grave, we are enclosed within certain options and views presented as reasonable; contrary options and views are easily dismissed as "idealistic," "foolish," "alien," "juvenile," or "dangerous" with regard to job, to security, to virtue, to almost anything. Legitimation is one side of a conservative process whose other side is socialization.

Those who are heard most clearly and most frequently in and from the apparatus noted above are those at the top of its parts: political leaders; the major commentators in the media; the establishment in the universities and schools; religious leaders; the most popular figures in entertainment and sports; the largest corporations; our parents. Parents become so through the processes of nature (and become less so in modern society); social leaders rise to the top because they function effectively within the existing system. Few people ever come to doubt a system that allows them to rise to high levels of income and status; most, indeed, find totally praiseworthy a system that is able to recognize their special talents. They are believers when they begin; true believers as they rise. By comparison, dissenters are usually seen as scruffy; usually of low income and status; often angry, distraught, complaining; or worse. All this should be obvious; let us look at the news media for illustration.

The Pentagon Papers informed Americans of the conscious deception practiced by Administrations on both the media and the public with regard to the war in Indochina. The Papers tell us nothing of the systematic bias of the news media in presenting what they know regarding controversies over foreign policy, labor struggles, protest groups, and the like.[12] In the media, too, there has been a process of concentration and centralization, with most Americans now getting most of their ideas —insofar as they are gotten through the media—through one "local" newspaper (usually owned elsewhere), and three national TV networks and their star commentators.

Those who own and control the media are of course businessmen, who are in it for money, and naturally inclined to keep from rocking the boat. If that is not always true of the reporters who work for the distinctly conservative publishers and network executives, the pressure is great for it to become so. News that smells of criticism is modified, truncated, or, more frequently, not presented. The reporter who would make his/her way does not make it by filing unprinted stories. Advertisers complain; readers and viewers complain; presidents and vice-presidents complain. Reporters ship out or shape up. The news takes on all the qualities of a rooting-section at a football game, with the newspeople rooting for our side—i.e., the status quo. Our generals are brave, resourceful, even humane; theirs are sneaky, treacherous, cruel. Businessmen are responsible; strike leaders are reckless of the interests of the economy and of their rank and file. Police are also brave, beleaguered, patient; protestors are violent, amoral, wild-eyed. Doubtless this systematic dichotomy in adjectives is for some commentators a matter of playing the game; for most it is a matter of developed conviction. The road to the top is a finishing school.[13]

---

[12]Thus, the hundreds of pages detailing thousands of incidents involving deception (mostly about Vietnam), found in Halberstam's *Best and the Brightest,* necessarily depend upon information accumulated over many years—but not brought to light systematically by those who knew until years, too many years, later. Everyone at the top—of the government, the media, of business—is on the "team."

[13]Despite the craven quality of most of the media, the few honorable exceptions have existed and have drawn the wrath of (especially) Presidents Johnson and Nixon, with the latter using the Federal Communications Commission and Spiro Agnew as weapons to achieve purification—unsuccessfully, Watergate allows one to believe. An excellent survey of "How the news media use bias, distortion and censorship to manipulate public opinion" is Robert Cirino, *Don't Blame the People** (New York: Random House; Vintage, 1971). Cirino documents the charges contained in the foregoing subtitle, for a long list of issues: hunger, auto safety, smoking, pollution, the Indochinese war, and much else. An older, marvelously written and deeply-revealing book is the series of essays by A. J. Liebling, *The Press** (New York: Ballantine Books, 1961). See also James Aronson, *The Press and the Cold War** (Indianapolis: Bobbs-Merrill, 1970). The collection of essays by I. F. Stone, *In a Time of Torment* (New York: Random House, 1967) adds up to news that only Stone saw fit to print, which required his own *I. F. Stone's Weekly.* His *Hidden History*

Turning to the more general process of legitimation, there can be little doubt that the most insistent and respected voice in the United States is the voice of business. That is only partly because most "professionals"—doctors, lawyers, publishers, entertainers, and athletes—have a high regard for making money, whatever else they may take seriously. Rather, it is because, as was noted in Chapter Three, a capitalist society depends for its health on a healthily functioning business sector. Policies that might militate against that would cause a "loss of confidence" among businessmen. For most people in the United States there is no lively awareness of or interest in an alternative to the capitalist economy; the possibility of such a loss of confidence is tantamount to the possibility of unspeakable economic disaster. In short, business has the open respect of the entire society, except for the few who criticize business, and who thus forfeit respect in the process.

The pressures brought to bear on the State system are therefore the pressures of business people or business-minded people; the people who occupy the top and middle posts of the State system are almost entirely people from the middle or upper class. Prior education, aspiration, and function prepare those who are called to be deserving of their responsibilities. The United States Senate, once known as a "rich man's club," still deserves that description for all but a very few; but so does the rest of the élite of the State system.[14]

FROM STATE TO STATES TO SUPERSTATE

The foregoing discussion applies as a sketch outline of the State system in the United States today. The 19th century conditions were different both in form and content. An examination of three of the conflicts that marked that century will serve the twofold function of highlighting the differences while at the same time revealing the central role of power in the process of social change: 1) the so-called Bank War; 2) the Civil War; 3) the Populist uprising. These conflicts represent,

---

*of the Korean War** (New York: Monthly Review Press, 1952) also pertinent in this connection, is now coming to be seen as the authentic and damning explanation of that war. The book was assiduously ignored by journalists and scholars until recently; its lessons have yet to be absorbed.

[14]C. Wright Mills, in his *Power Elite,* cited earlier, in his *White Collar** (New York: Oxford University Press, 1951), and in his *New Men of Power: America's Labor Leaders* (New York: Harcourt Brace Jovanovich, 1948) analyzes all this generally and with specific application to businessmen, the professions, and labor. G. William Domhoff, following in Mills's tradition, relates these matters to the social and political setting in a definitive manner. See *Who Rules America?* (cited earlier) and *The Higher Circles** (New York: Random House; Vintage, 1971).

respectively, the successful struggle for laissez-faire capitalism; the triumph of industry and finance over agriculture and commerce as the center of capitalist dynamism; and, finally, the last gasp of Jeffersonian democracy. Each sought to alter the State system or, as in the case of Populism, to restore an idealized past.

Bank War

One of the first achievements of the triumphant English bourgeoisie after their Glorious Revolution was the creation of the Bank of England; the First Bank of the United States, chartered for twenty years in 1791, was designed to serve much the same purposes for the United States. Both were "central banks"; that is, bankers' banks, endowed with the responsibility of influencing the supply of money and the rate of interest in the direction of the public interest. Mercantilist in their origins, central banks have become a key feature of all modern capitalist economies. The United States is unique in having created, allowed to lapse, re-created, and then destroyed its central bank. From the 1830's until the creation of the Federal Reserve System (our present central banking system) in 1914, the United States was the only major capitalist economy without a central bank, which was destroyed in the middle of Andrew Jackson's two terms as president.

The charter of the First Bank of the U.S. lapsed, amidst controversy, in 1811. The monetary chaos that followed encouraged the chartering of the Second Bank of the U.S. (1816–1836). One-fifth of the Bank's stock was owned by the federal government; the rest was in private hands. The Bank served as a repository for federal funds, most important of which were payments for public lands and customs collections. In that period, the latter amounted to about 90 percent of all governmental revenues. Currency at the time was in the form of banknotes; that is, promises to pay in specie to the bearer the face value of the banknote. The issuing banks were predominantly private banks chartered by state governments, and the Second Bank issued its own banknotes, the soundest of the time. When a Kentucky bank paid, say, $1000 to the federal government for a land purchase, or when a New York bank paid $1000 in customs collections for an importer, those banks were placing their notes in the hands of the Second Bank. The Second Bank became their creditor; it could demand specie in return for the note. The notes of the various banks came into existence in response to loans to the banks' customers. The banks, creditors to their customers, were debtors of the Second Bank. The latter's ability to demand specie was the power to curtail the lending capacities of the banking community. In turn, that meant that the Bank had critical control over the uses of the economic surplus. Power over the extension of credit then as now also meant power to influence the nature and direction of economic activity.[15] Then as now, such power is among the most important political powers; then as now, the power rests in mostly private hands, or in the hands of those congenial to the banking community.

The Second Bank itself made loans; that was its principal business. It was a profit-making institution, as well as one having public purposes. Quite naturally, other banks saw the Second Bank as a competitor, and one with extraordinary power. The Second Bank's directors and owners tended to represent the older and more powerful mercantile and financial interests of the new nation, and especially those in Philadelphia. By the 1820's, New York City was rising in strength, Baltimore was seeking to do so, and the West was opening up rapidly. The bankers, land speculators, and merchants in those and comparable areas saw the Bank as "the monster of Chestnut Street." Andrew Jackson, vowing to destroy the Bank, made it the central issue of his re-election campaign of 1832.[16]

Jackson, who had risen to the presidency because of his military exploits as the "Hero of New Orleans" (1815) and his campaigns against Indian tribes, was a planter and friend of the larger propertied interests in Tennessee. He was thought to speak for the common man. In his fight against Biddle and the Second Bank his most numerous supporters were the western farmers and the urban workers of the East. Standing less noisily behind them, however, were the bankers, merchants, manufacturers, and land speculators who saw the credit-restraining powers of the Second Bank as the last remaining obstacle to rapid increases in their fortunes. Jackson won re-election in 1832; the Second Bank, although its charter had four years left to run, was rendered ineffectual. The relatively concentrated financial and mercantile structure of power was

---

[15]Today, loans result in checking deposits for the borrower. Private banks no longer (since the 1930's) issue banknotes. The First and Second Banks of the United States were *creditors* of the banking community; the Federal Reserve System is a *debtor*. Member banks (about half of all banks, controlling about 85 percent of all deposits) must keep about one-fifth of their deposits on reserve in the Federal Reserve System. The latter exercises its influence on the supply of money and credit and the interest rate through means that alter the amount of reserves or the amount required. See any economics textbook for explanation.

[16]The Bank was located on Chestnut Street, in Philadelphia. The head of the Bank by the late 1820's was Anthony Biddle, an astute and strong-minded banker in his own right. The best and most comprehensive discussion of the relevant issues is Bray Hammond, *Banks and Politics in America From the Revolution to the Civil War* (Princeton: Princeton University Press, 1957). The most popular book, which received the Pulitzer Prize, is Arthur Schlesinger, Jr., *The Age of Jackson* * (Boston: Little, Brown, 1946). It is a model of intensive scholarship combined with unsupportable interpretation, as Hammond shows, dominated by Schlesinger's attempt to find historical justification for elements of the New Deal. Hammond's own book is very much dominated by *his* contemporary concerns; namely, to support a strong Federal Reserve System. History is seldom written by people without serious interests in their own present, which is a virtue, not a vice. But it is well for both the historians and their readers to be explicitly conscious of those interests.

displaced, pushed aside by a rapacious, rugged and uncontrolled laissez-faire capitalism. Politically, this meant that the jealousies of the individual states as against the federal government were institutionalized: the era of effective "states' rights" shifted into high gear. In practice this meant that raw economic power was the almost pure representation of State power for the rest of the century. The "great barbecue" would shortly begin.

Civil War

The forces unleashed by the destruction of the Bank led to a great step-up in all forms of economic expansion: banks multiplied (there were over 10,000 separate banknotes by the 1850's); trade and industry spread from the Atlantic seaboard out to the Mississippi; canals and railroads tied the broad land together; soils, minerals, and forests were exploited with abandon. A new economic structure took shape; the political structure lagged behind.

We need only summarize briefly what was discussed earlier concerning the South: the South by the 1820's was the leading sector of the American economy, with its King Cotton. The South's economic needs and its social system gave it a viewpoint on matters of the State profoundly different from that coming to be held by the manufacturers, merchants, and financiers of the North. But up to the Civil War, the South held the largest part of the strategic posts in the State system.

The South used its rivers and its coasts for the bulk of its transportation needs; the North needed canals and railroads. The South exported its cotton and imported manufactures; the North wanted protection for its growing industries. The South had a labor supply over which it was both economically and politically unchallenged; the North was faced with labor short in supply and politically free. The South's needs for westward expansion were modest as compared with the temptations and needs facing the North and West. In short, the South wanted a State system that was suited to planter capitalism; the North needed a system that would enhance industrial capitalism and rapid westward expansion.

Slavery was of course the major public issue of the Civil War. Whether or not it was the most important issue is another matter. We can do little to reconstruct the inner motivation of those in the past. But one can gain useful insights into what those involved in a struggle wanted most by seeing what those who won did with their enhanced power. The slaves were freed, of course. But within a few years the promises of "forty acres and a mule" were shelved; more important, arrangements were made between the triumphant North and the defeated South to allow the latter to regain full sway over its internal politics in exchange for northern control of the federal government and easy access to the investment possibilities of the South—in railroads, timber, land speculation, and the like.[17] The new State system removed all obstacles to the full possibilities of industrial capitalism in the United States. All obstacles but one, that is; that one, the lingering belief in America's promises as a democracy, underlay the Populist struggle toward the end of the century.

Vox Populi

The Populist struggle, perhaps because it contained so much of the hopes and fears of Americans, has been misrepresented in histories from its own day (the 1890's) until now. It is seen generally as having its center in the Middle West; actually, the South, and especially the Deep South, was its stronghold. It is viewed as centering on money fanaticism, which may represent its midwestern spokesmen, but did not represent Populism. It is viewed as being inextricably mixed with racism; in fact, the Populist movement in the South brought the only years—and they were few—in which racial egalitarianism was practiced, and in which poor whites and blacks fought shoulder to shoulder, politically and physically.[18]

The distinction must be made between populist tendencies and Populism. The former is a collection of conflicting notions which more often reflects the biases of those who recount them, rather than the nature of Populism. Populism was a movement based on the dire needs of its main participants and a nostalgic and hopeful view of what could be and was "supposed to be." It sought to reassert the hegemony of ordinary people, while not doubting the desirability of basic capitalist institutions. Small farmers, small businessmen, and workers were seen as the true heart and muscle of America; the State should be their instrument and their protector—against Big business, Big banks, Big railroads, and the misuse of government. Those were the Populists' wishes; their needs were the father of those wishes. They found themselves faced with ruinously falling prices and a shortage of credit; with extortionate rail rates and commission charges; with manipulated com-

---

[17]C. Vann Woodward, *Reunion and Reaction** (New York: Doubleday; Anchor, 1956) provides a definitive interpretation of the sordid "Compromise of 1877 and the End of Reconstruction," the consequences of which included the conservative-racist coalition still central to our social existence.

[18]C. Vann Woodward is probably the most astute and humane of leading historians on the South. His essay "The Populist Heritage and the Intellectual," in his collection *The Burden of Southern History** (New York: Random House; Vintage, 1961) is a balanced appraisal of Populism. See also Chapters 8 and 9 of his *Origins of the New South,* cited earlier. For black/white cooperation, see Jack Abramowitz, "The Negro in the Populist Movement," *Journal of Negro History,* vol. 38, no. 3 (July, 1953).

modity exchanges; with state and even more federal legislatures, and especially the Senate, that responded to the direct pressures of the most powerful. By 1896 they also found that the leadership of their movement had come under the domination of a distorted view of their aims —"free silver"—and a Nebraskan, William Jennings Bryan, who represented not only what was slightest in Populism but worst in America. Whether Bryan revealed his ultimate essence when he became Secretary of State under Wilson or prosecutor of Scopes in the famous "monkey trial" is a matter of dispute; but his essence lay somewhere other than in the central position of the Populists.

Populism was dying well before the election of 1896 gave it the *coup de grâce.* Taking no chances, the massive GOP campaign of 1896 was the first truly modern political campaign. Master-minded by Marcus Hanna, a Cleveland shipping, banking, transportation, and newspaper magnate, the campaign made regular assessments on businesses, engaged in widely-publicized scare tactics, and effectively scattered the opponents of big business rule, the "communists" of the day. In the South the period saw a new and more intensified set of segregation ("Jim Crow") laws, accompanied by waves of lynchings. By then the popular heart of Populism was muffled, its racial egalitarianism had been replaced by confusion and hatred, its social and political goals had given way to narrow economic criteria, measured by the level of farm prices. The removal of Populism sped up even more the consolidation of economic power that Populism had resisted. The State system moved toward "political capitalism," as the economy moved toward monopoly capitalism. Institutionalized racism came to be as much a part of the urban North as slavery had been in the South; white Americans went about their business and looked the other way. And, already in 1897, the drums of overseas imperialism had begun to sound for Americans who very soon would march to them, again and again. The present act of the American drama had begun; the mass of Americans became a background chorus to it, mixing laughs with screams, cheers with anger. Most stood silently, hoping for the best.

LOST DEMOCRACY

The opening years of this century for many Americans seemed very much like our own times; it was an age of dislocation.

The decline of political democracy and the rise of monopolies were not the only dark aspects of American civilization. Among those which called for remedy were the gross inequality of wealth, wide existence of poverty, racial inequality, the domination by big business of politics, religion, education, and the courts, the selfish and stupid waste of natural resources, carelessness of human life, exploitation of women and children. ... America's new rulers were the "robber barons" and her new God, Financial Success.[19]

The accompanying hue and cry of social criticism was begun by writers and reformers, conscious that things were getting out of joint; the policies that ultimately ensued were shaped and controlled by businessmen and the politicians who suited them. Reformers awakened business to the chaos of the time, threatening not least to business.

Able to organize their own kind, and powerful enough to move things, big business brought order out of that chaos. It was order cut to their needs and aims, cut to the needs of industrial capitalism. Thus the Progressive Movement, frequently seen as an anti-business reformist movement, resulted in a set of far-reaching changes which strengthened the hold of business on America. And the Progressives' "respectable reforms" also did much to take the steam out of popular discontent. For that to happen, the hold of business criteria had to extend itself deeply and consciously into the State system, which in turn had to be expanded and strengthened to assure domestic and international order.[20]

In the days just before the Nazi seizure of power, a respected German economist noted:

> The animosity of German capitalism against the state does not rest upon fundamental theoretical foundations, but upon purely opportunistic considerations. It is opposed to the state when control is in the hands of a political majority whose permanent good will it doubts. German capitalism, which would like to be freed of the power of the state, and which seeks to push back state intervention as far as possible, is constructed exclusively upon the most thorough intervention of the state.[21]

German capitalists had worked steadily to devise a State system suited to their needs throughout most of the 19th century. American business,

---

[19]Faulkner, *The Decline of Laissez Faire,* pp. 368–69.

[20]These generalizations, and many to follow, depend upon the important historical revisions about the period developed by Gabriel Kolko in *The Triumph of Conservatism,* and James Weinstein in *The Corporate Ideal in the Liberal State, 1900–1918,* both cited earlier. Probably without intending to do so, Robert H. Wiebe, *Businessmen and Reform** (Chicago: Quadrangle, 1968) presents data that allow the same conclusions. Kolko centers on the ability of the largest corporations to use the State to curb uncontrolled competition and to reduce instability; Weinstein emphasizes the role of the large corporations and their National Civic Federation in conscious displacement of laissez-faire, over the opposition of the smaller companies and the National Association of Manufacturers.

[21]Quoted in Robert A. Brady, *Business as a System of Power,* p. 294, from M. J. Bonn, *Das Schicksal des deutschen Kapitalismus* (1931).

operating in a much less stringent social and natural context, needed only to be left alone: laissez-faire (plus tariffs and gifts) was just right. The rapid and pervasive industrial development that swept America at the end of the 19th century, however, created a set of problems that individual businesses, no matter how large, could not resolve by themselves. Public institutions were needed to provide the requisite scope. Advanced industrial capitalism, even in the United States, requires social institutions that will prevent its precarious and fruitful interdependencies from becoming a source of breakdown, whether economic, social, or political. In short, *rationalization* becomes a necessity.

The term rationalization is many-sided in its meaning, for it is designed to cope with diverse problems. Brady, in his massive study of the German rationalization movement of the 1920's, comments that:

> rationalization was begun, and largely carried through, at a time when forces were converging to undermine the institutional framework of German capitalism. As the rationalization movement developed, it became increasingly clear that its progress was to be conditioned by the solution of numerous issues directly related to the radical and far-reaching changes that were taking place in the political, economic, and social institutions of the country. The drift to the two extreme wings, and the politicization of nearly the whole range of economic problems, meant that these issues were to be resolved, if at all, in an atmosphere of bitterness, struggle, and drawn compromise.[22]

Although both the timing and the content of the German movement were different from comparable developments in the United States, the impulses were fundamentally alike. In the U.S. their beginnings were in the Progressive Movement, in the decade or so preceding World War I. As Kolko notes:

> Progressivism was initially a movement for the political rationalization of business and industrial conditions, a movement that operated on the assumption that the general welfare of the community could be best served by satisfying the concrete needs of business. But the regulation itself was invariably controlled by leaders of the regulated industry, and directed toward ends they deemed acceptable or desirable. In part this came about because the regulatory movements were usually initiated by the dominant businesses to be regulated, but it also resulted from the nearly universal belief among political leaders in the basic justice of

---

[22]Robert A. Brady, *The Rationalization Movement in German Industry* (Berkeley: University of California Press, 1933), p. xiv. The "two extreme wings" were socialism and fascism.

private property relations as they essentially existed, a belief that set the ultimate limits on the leaders possible actions.[23]

THE BURDENS OF SUCCESS

The problems that led to these new political needs ranged through the whole society. The absence of a central bank and other control institutions in the economy allowed normal fluctuations to translate into severe panics and depressions. The depression of the 1890's was unprecedentedly deep; the "Panic of 1907" was a panic in more than name. The giant corporations that emerged from the immense combination movement of 1897–1904 behaved with no more recklessness than businesses always had; now, however, they were bulls in a china shop. National markets for interdependent industries meant pervasive and deeper crises. Business competition had always been alarming to the businesses competed with; the heavy industrialization of the new century made alarm an inadequate reaction. Financial manipulation was a popular business sport throughout the 19th century; in the 20th century it brought Wall Street and a host of other financial enclaves crashing down. Business could no longer afford to cavort heedlessly; it had to settle down.

Much the same was true of the exploitation of our natural resources, as was noted earlier. Mining the soil, cutting over timber lands, and the spoliation of mineral resources had brought great profits: if continued in the same way and in greater amounts, such exploitation would dry up its sources. Resource management was necessary: resource management by business. Nor were human resources in a different category. Housing, labor conditions, and welfare had never been a matter of keen concern for those who built the cities and hired the workers, but the scope of such activities had never been as great as they suddenly appeared to be in the new century. Urban housing and welfare reform and some mitigation of harsh labor exploitation were put forth as necessities; they would not stop the running sores, but they might at least cover them. Mostly, not even that happened.

---

[23]Kolko, op. cit., pp. 2–3. In another study, Kolko documents these generalizations about regulation for an industry interpreted quite differently by previous students. See his *Railroads and Regulation, 1877–1916** (Princeton: Princeton University Press, 1965). His main point is that though the impulses for regulation may arise outside the industry to be regulated (farmers, in the case of railroads), the industry comes to see regulation in its own interests, and shapes the legislation to assure that outcome. The conclusion, in the light of the history of regulated industries, seems inescapable; however, most conventional observers, seeing each reaffirming instance as an aberration, have let the conclusion slip through their flimsy analytical nets.

From the Spanish-Cuban-American War up through World War I, the presidency passed from McKinley to Roosevelt to Taft to Wilson. They were different types of men, and their reputations in history books emphasize those differences. But they had one characteristic in common: they provided unbroken continuity in the creation of the new "political capitalism." The solidifying developments within the State system took place in the first administration of Woodrow Wilson. The "New Nationalism" of Teddy Roosevelt translated easily into the "New Freedom" of Wilson. All four presidents found themselves occupied with foreign affairs more than any president since Jefferson: McKinley agonized into the Spanish-Cuban-American War; Roosevelt charged up San Juan Hill and created Panama and its canal; Taft served as the first American governor of the Philippine Islands; Wilson, promising to keep us out of war, sent troops to Mexico and got us into World War I. From then on public relations and manipulation would develop into a high art.

The continuity manifested itself in domestic as well as in imperial policies: all busied themselves with conservation, with urban reform, with "trust-busting," and with financial and industrial reforms. They were the midwives of "political capitalism," which took hold after 1900, and which has been altered and strengthened from then up to the present.

Those who have come to consciousness since World War II are likely to take the ways and means of political capitalism as the "natural" state of affairs; those whose consciousness was formed in earlier decades will remember that the "normal" state of affairs for capitalist society was assumed to be one in which the State was unobtrusive in economic and other affairs. The State in the United States has always operated so as to provide an acceptable or favorable context for capitalist development; in the 19th century it did so largely through "non-decisions," that is, unobtrusively—except for railroad subsidies, protective tariffs, and a few other explicit policies noted above. But in the 20th century the State's role became obtrusive, and explicit. The political outlets and institutions of the State had to be and came to be used to attain the desired conditions of stability, predictability, and security. Characterizing this development, Kolko says:

> *Stability* is the elimination of internecine competition and erratic fluctuations in the economy. *Predictability* is the ability, on the basis of politically stabilized and secured means, to plan future economic action on the basis of fairly calculable expectations. By *security* I mean protection from the political attacks latent in any formally democratic structure.[24]

---

[24]Kolko, *The Triumph of Conservatism*, p. 3. Italics in original.

There were many conflicts along the way, of course: between various aspects of the business community; between labor and business; between local and national politicians; between socialists, anti-business reformers, and those who represented business interests; between anti-imperialists and imperialists. There are always conflicts; more to the point is who wins out, and how; and one must remember that alongside those who seek what they get are those who, seeking something else, unwittingly assist those who win out.

Business criteria won out in these conflicts, but the criteria of *giant* business, not of business in general. As the century began, the giant corporations represented the most intense gathering of power in the society; because it was economic power, it translated into State power. These were the new monopolists; their breeding ground was the old competition. One of the consequences of the State system created in those years was that the movement from small to large to giant firm would be more under control than in the 19th century: the new laws and regulatory agencies put a curb on rapacious behavior within industries, much as Great Powers do with Lesser Powers in the world of Statesmanship, so that the large might be more secure against the possibilities of interlopers. It also meant a loss of whatever benefits the public may have derived from the uncontrolled warfare of business. The invisible hand that presumably transformed naked self-interest into society's well-being would have to find a different strength than price competition. The antitrust laws of the 1890's began by forbidding collusion and the "intent to monopolize." By the 1930's amendments made it illegal to engage in price competition. By the 1960's, except for curious exceptions, competition became "non-price competition," institutionalized to the point where laws against price competition were not needed.[25] In an economic world where advertising, product variation (e.g., automobile model changes), sales promotion, research and development, and lobbying became the chief means of enhancing corporate strength, the battle went to the already strong, even more than it had earlier.

One of the closest students of the "era of reform," in intending to characterize the beneficent qualities of the period, says,

---

[25]Laws forbidding price competition, such as the "Resale Price Maintenance Act" (1937), most generally called "fair trade" laws, emerged after the National Industrial Recovery Act was declared unconstitutional in 1935. The National Recovery Administration (NRA), a form of self-government in business, gave the power to fix prices *(inter alia)* to industry trade associations (in the form of "code authorities"); violators of these private agreements were punishable by law. The similarities between the provisions of the NRA and those for "self-management in industry" under the Nazis are, to say the very least, striking. See Robert A. Brady, *Spirit and Structure of German Fascism** (New York: Viking, 1937), Chapter X. A major difference is that the German laws were not declared unconstitutional.

By 1917 a change appeared evident in the entrepreneurial spirit and conduct of private business. The flush days of the "robber barons" had passed; leaders of business and of the larger institutions had begun to show some of the characteristics which distinguish them today [1951]. Risk and profit had become less important than security and power. . . .[26]

When the robber barons of feudal times passed from the scene, it was because their territories had come under the control of a count, a duke, a prince, or a king, with the financial assistance of the merchants upon whom the robber barons had preyed. The analogy therefore breaks down; in America the robber barons *became* the counts, dukes, and princes, and the king bent largely to their will. And, although the search for security and power is certainly what the "larger institutions" sought, they reduced risk and increased profits as a result.

The areas encompassed by these efforts cut through the entire economy, producing new laws and a new bureaucracy. Some examples:

Labor. The Clayton Antitrust Act (1914) exempted unions from the antitrust laws (although the exemption has been narrowed by judicial interpretation and subsequent legislation). The relevant parts of the Act are called "Labor's Magna Carta"; time has shown this label to be overly-effusive. In 1916, the Adamson Act provided for an eight-hour day for railway workers, the first such federal legislation. Their organization had made them among the most powerful unions (in a generally weak array) from the 1870's on; in 1926, the Railway Labor Act provided labor protections that were subsequently generalized in the Wagner Act (1935). The contest over the labor legislation of the Progressive Period well reveals the differences between "corporate liberalism" and the continuing raw laissez-faire attitudes of small business.[27]

Banking. The Glass-Owen Currency (Federal Reserve) Act of 1913 re-created the central bank for the United States. From the destruction of the Second Bank in 1832 until then, the country had been periodically rocked by banking collapse and financial panic. The National Bank Act of 1863, which passed for our national banking system until 1913, assured that when problems arose they would become more intense than without any "system" at all; this was not surprising, for the Act's original purpose was to help finance the Civil War. The Federal Reserve System was itself weak and ill-organized, as revealed by its contribution to the financial disasters of the 1920's. It was strengthened during the New Deal.

---

[26]Faulkner, op. cit., p. 379.
[27]See Weinstein, op. cit., Chapter Two, but also *passim.*

Taxation. The 16th Amendment was ratified in 1913, providing for an income tax. Although never very progressive, it was more so in 1913 than it is now (incomes below $4000 were exempt, and that was a large amount in 1913). Of taxation, more later.

Conservation. The Newlands Act of 1902 provided for the "reclamation" of arid lands through irrigation. What this meant was a bonanza for irrigation companies in gaining cheap access to the public domain, most of which was then arid. Teddy Roosevelt was an ardent conservationist.

Consumer Protection. Roosevelt was also an ardent supporter of good eating. Much impressed by Upton Sinclair's *The Jungle,* he joined reformers by creating the Pure Food and Drug Administration, and by passing the Meat Inspection Act (both 1906).

Business Regulation. The Federal Trade Act of 1914 added the Federal Trade Commission to the enforcing agency of the Justice Department. Under Roosevelt the courts first used the Sherman Antitrust Act (1890) prohibiting collusion and the intent to monopolize against business (Northern Securities Case, 1904). In 1911, it was used to break Standard Oil into seven separate companies although the Rockefeller family was not ordered to divest itself of its ownership in the new structure. Most authorities agree that the step-up in antitrust enforcement led not to more competition, but to oligopoly—today's form of monopoly. The Hepburn Act of 1906 and the Mann-Elkins Act of 1910 gave new powers to the Interstate Commerce Commission (created in 1886) in railroad regulation. The long-run effect seems to have been that the railroads, though presumably competing with other transportation industries (truck, air, autobus), have been able to raise rates and maintain profitability despite declining and deteriorating service.

Foreign Trade. The Webb-Pomerene Export Trade Act (1918) allowed companies involved in foreign trade to form selling cartels (a means of achieving a uniform sales policy for different firms); that is, they were exempted from the antitrust laws, as a means of sharpening the already sharp edge of American competition in the world economy. As competition in the world economy revived and became severe in the early 1970's, pressures mounted to revive this policy.

IN THE CATBIRD SEAT

Efforts by corporate liberals and their supporters to create a new State system after 1900 were halting, contradictory, and controversial; the onset of World War I speeded up the development, gave it coherence, and stilled controversy. The impact of the war on the economy was so beneficial, however, that in contributing to the upper echelon prosperity of the 1920's it also allowed a re-emergence of laissez-faire as the dominant business mood. The mood was one thing, the reality another.

The economic gains of the United States from the war need no further discussion; the institutional changes accompanying the sustained upsurge in production were equally significant. Businessmen, and especially those from the industries most closely connected with war production—metals, fuels, vehicles—were drawn into the councils of government as never before. They were predominantly from the large corporations. As would occur with even greater strength in World War II, the government sought to maximize production and minimize conflict in the economy. This entailed active and close cooperation between representatives of industry, agriculture, and labor, with industry as the dominant member. The Council of National Defense and the War Industries Board were the key agencies; their leading personnel were those who had also led in the creation of the new State system in the years leading up to the war.[28]

Subtly, but firmly, the easy use of State power by business became unchallenged and unchallengeable. The political habits of those who used that power and those who acquiesced in it were transformed. Those who might think differently were largely those who opposed the war and the system that presided over it: the Socialists (led by Eugene Debs). As has happened more than once, a general opposition to American involvement in a war was transformed into enthusiastic support when we became directly involved. The opposition was crushed, its leaders jailed, its ideas reviled.[29] The larger outcome was that it made possible the repression of the entire Left in the years after the war through the "Palmer raids" of 1919–1920 and the "Red Scare" that ensued (whose most famous instance was the Sacco-Vanzetti case[30]). In that period, as in the years after World War II, a major consequence

---

[28]See Soule, *Prosperity Decade,* Chapters I, II, and III.

[29]Even when, as in the case of the IWW, it took no stand against the war. For the cooperation of trade unions, the opposition by the Socialist Party, and the curious position of the IWW, see James Weinstein, *Decline of Socialism** (New York: Random House; Vintage, 1969), pp. 47–53, and his essay "The IWW and American Socialism," *Socialist Revolution,* vol. 1, no. 5 (Sept.–Oct., 1970), esp. p. 27.

[30]Wilson's Attorney General, A. Mitchell Palmer, organized raids on homes and offices of "suspected Communists." Thousands were arrested, hundreds jailed and deported. The socialist movement was still strong, the Russian Revolution was publicized as a direct threat to the U.S., immigration had been at its peak (almost a million in 1920), and strikes were numerous. Foreign-born people were most noticed among the radicals (and aliens could be deported by the Secretary of Labor if found to be "radical"). Sacco and Vanzetti were anarchist labor organizers accused and convicted in 1921 of a payroll murder in what is (and was) widely considered to be a frame-up. They were electrocuted in 1927.

of anti-Left campaigns was to remove whatever influence Left ideas had from the trade union movement, leaving the latter weak and docile. The "consensus" on foreign policy in the Cold War had its earlier counterpart in a "consensus" on domestic policy in the 1920's.

The mood of business could be laissez-faire in the 1920's because the reality was so firmly under their control as to require little in the way of explicit government intervention. The decade opened with Harding as president, followed by Coolidge and Hoover. If Harding had any distinction at all in the office, it was that he was a close competitor of Buchanan as the most mediocre of presidents, although as far as we know Buchanan lived at a somewhat higher moral level. Calvin Coolidge signified the temper of the times exactly. He gained the prominence he needed for presidential stature by helping to break a strike while he was Governor of Massachusetts. He was famous for saying little: "Silent Cal" was his affectionate nickname. What little he said was telling: "The business of America," as noted earlier, "is business." "The man who builds a factory builds a temple, the man who works there worships there, and to each is due not scorn and blame, but reverence and praise."[31]

As F. L. Allen notes in his entertaining evocation of the spirit of the twenties, *Only Yesterday,* "The great god business was supreme in the land and Calvin Coolidge was fortunate enough to become almost a demi-god by doing discreet obeisance before the altar" (p. 211). By some, the relationship between divinity and business was pushed explicitly. Bruce Barton, founder of one of the largest advertising agencies (BBD&O) wrote in 1924 what became perhaps the best-seller of the time, *The Man Nobody Knows: A Discovery of the Real Jesus.* Jesus, it appears, was "the founder of modern business."

> He picked up twelve men from the bottom ranks of business and forged them into an organization that conquered the world. . . . Nowhere is there such a startling example of executive success as the way in which that organization was brought together.[32]

THE GOD THAT FAILED

Hoover was a different breed of man. His critical view of the evolving State system has been misunderstood or neglected, largely because his

---

[31]Quoted in James W. Prothro, *Dollar Decade: Business Ideas in the 1920's* (Baton Rouge: Louisiana State University Press, 1954), p. 224. This is a revealing study of what businessmen thought at a time when they had the confidence to be candid about their social philosophy. When what is revealed is not frightening it is very funny.

[32]Quoted in Prothro, ibid., pp. 229–30. Judas Iscariot is viewed in that connection as being a bit overzealous, but of good spirit.

reputation became bound up so tightly with the Depression that began in his term. Hoover was a committed adherent of capitalism; but he opposed the direct use of the State to advance the interests of capitalists. He knew, as president, that what he opposed was already a prominent feature of capitalist development. He believed in self-reliance, but self-reliance in voluntary cooperation with others with the same needs. W. A. Williams states Hoover's position as follows:

> . . . Hoover feared that the corporation leaders would produce an American form of fascism. If labor became predominant, on the other hand, the result would be socialism or some willy-nilly variation thereof. . . . If each broad interest group in the economy continued its evolving attitude of viewing the government as a marketplace in which to compete for its share of the gross wealth, then the system would ultimately be dominated by a state bureaucracy which would lack even the distinguishing characteristic of a positive ideology. And wars engendered by struggles for predominance in the world marketplace threatened to produce a tyranny of even graver proportions because of the increased role and influence of the military.[33]

What Hoover feared from business was in place before he took office in 1928. Whatever cogency his ideas might have had was buried, as he was, by the avalanche of the Depression. The collapse of the economy was blamed on those who had taken credit for its achievements; everyone looked to the State for succor. As noted before, the effects of New Deal policies during the Depression were insubstantial; the major meaning of the New Deal was the manner in which it sought to flesh out the State system that has carried us into the present.

Sophisticated though corporate liberals were by comparison with small businessmen before World War I, they were not sophisticated enough to create a State system that would give any significant access to that system by those not in business. Their inclinations to do so were lessened by the roaring confidence of the 1920's. Business' fall from grace in the thirties allowed some kind of balance, however minimal, to be achieved—over the howls of rage and accusations of betrayal of some but by no means all business spokesmen. The State became explicitly interventionist in matters of the business cycle, monetary and fiscal controls, protection for labor and the aged, agriculture, and foreign trade. There were precedents for all these developments; the New Deal put them together in a new balance. The New Deal re-educated corporate leaders to what they had first begun to learn thirty years earlier; World War II and the Cold War showed them how valuable that education could be in profits, in social stability, in domestic and world power. The growth and developmental aspects of the years since the Depres-

---

[33]Williams, *Great Evasion,* p. 155.

sion were examined in Chapter Four. The stabilizing and tension-pro-
moting aspects of the new State system will occupy the remainder of
this chapter.

THE BEST LAID PLANS ...

The decade of the fifties comprised the years of the "great celebra-
tion," of the "silent generation," of the avuncular Eisenhower. The
upsurge of left-wing attitudes and organizations from the thirties and
forties had been squashed by spy scares, McCarthyism and the repression that gave it teeth, and by the often enthusiastic cooperation in these
endeavors by intellectual and labor leaders. Marx had become a four-
letter word, Veblen a barely-known freak, the influence and power of
the United States expanded all over the globe, and capitalism flourished
at home.

In the midst of this quiet and complacency, C. Wright Mills wrote his
Power Élite (1956), a biting appraisal of the State system at that time.
Leading American liberals, meanwhile, were getting the materials together that allowed them to pronounce "the end of ideology," and that
"the fundamental political problems of the industrial revolution have
been solved. . . ."[34]

Mills was the first academic social scientist after World War II to
recognize and explore the extraordinary role then being played by foreign policy and the military in the entire life of Americans and their
foreign satellites. The original quality of his argument, to say nothing
of its controversial nature, led to an immediate reaction from "liberal,
radical, and highbrow critics." Almost all of the reaction was scornful.[35]

As Mills saw it, the "power élite" has three components: "the corporate rich," the "political directorate," and the "warlords." For Mills, as
in our earlier discussion of the State system, the first two components
overlap: the "political directorate" holds the top posts of the State
system; those who occupy those posts are from the highest levels of
business—in fact, in spirit, or in association (for instance, corporate
lawyers). That is, the power élite reduces to two segments: corporate

---

[34]Daniel Bell, *The End of Ideology** (New York: Free Press, 1960), S. M. Lipset, *Political
Man** (Garden City, N.Y.: Doubleday, 1960), p. 406. The ideas leading to these conclusions were developed earlier in the British journal of elegant liberal opinion *Encounter*,
which was financed in part, it was subsequently shown and admitted, by CIA funds. Bell
and Lipset are among the most noted pluralists.

[35]The classifications are those of G. William Domhoff and Hoyt B. Ballard, eds., *C.
Wright Mills and The Power Elite** (Boston: Beacon Press, 1961), a very useful collection
of the criticisms and of Mills' response to some of them. Miliband's book, cited earlier,
is dedicated to Mills. Although among the most prolific and creative of American sociologists, Mills never rose above the rank of associate professor; nor, it might be added, did
Veblen.

rulers and the warlords of the Pentagon. How much power the Pentagon has, and the degree of autonomy with which it can or could use that power is now a matter of substantial controversy; when Mills first made his argument about the military, it was dismissed out of hand in all quarters.

The final test of greatness for an analytical or theoretical contribution does not depend upon its being indubitably "correct," but whether or not it leads to further questioning and research, and improved understanding. *The Power Élite* qualifies as such a work. The way in which Mills made his case stimulated others to their own hypotheses and studies, which were also stimulated by the increasingly *obvious* growth of the State system and its military component then and later. Much of the discussion has moved along lines that over-simplify and distort the real problems suggested by Mills; it has taken place largely within the *liberal* universe of discourse and analysis. At the same time, other analyses are developing that seem more to the point, analytically more promising and also more frightening in their import, and *radical* in both discourse and analysis. Seymour Melman's work is representative of the former at its best; James O'Connor's of the latter. Let us examine each in turn.

WARFARE STATE?

A professor of industrial management at Columbia University, Seymour Melman has emerged as a foremost liberal academic critic of the destructive tendencies of the U.S. Beginning (in 1965) as a critic of the military-related waste and the misuse of our entire range of resources he became a severe critic of the war in Indochina. Now he ranks as one of the most intensive students of the military-industrial complex in America. The opening words of his *Pentagon Capitalism* define his position clearly:

> An industrial management has been installed in the federal government, under the Secretary of Defense, to control the nation's largest network of industrial enterprises. With the characteristic managerial propensity for extending its power, limited only by its allocated share of the national product, the new state-management combines peak economic, political, and military decision-making.[36]

---

[36]Seymour Melman, *Pentagon Capitalism* * (New York: McGraw-Hill, 1970), p. 1. See also the book of readings edited by him, *The War Economy of the United States** (New York: St. Martin's Press, 1971). The earlier book is *Our Depleted Society** (New York: Holt, Rinehart, and Winston, 1965), in which his present stance begins to appear. Although it will be argued that Melman misses the main point of what he has studied, he stands out as one of a small handful of honorable and humane academics in a university establishment that generally works hand-in-glove with the military-industrial complex.

The data confronting Melman and all other students of the role of military production in the American economy make such characterizations plausible. A recent student of the matter, writing in 1970, has pointed out that:

> In the United States, 10 percent of our personal income and 20 percent of our manufacturing output are derived from this war industry. Indirectly, the livelihood of twelve to fourteen million Americans, including two-thirds to three-fourths of our scientists, now depends on this industry. The defense sector has had the fastest rate of growth of any area in the economy, and it accounts for more than half the research done in this country since the Cold War began.[37]

It is a truism that the key to understanding is in knowing which questions to ask; it is a characteristic feature of liberal criticism that it starts with wrong-headed questions. In our discussion of imperialism, it was asserted earlier that such a wrong-headed question was "Does the U.S. Economy Require Imperialism?" The authors who asked that question concluded that imperialism was unnecessary; there are other ways the American economy *could* flourish. The better question is, given that the United States is imperialist, why and how did it get that way, and what are its domestic and international consequences? Melman, concerned with the military-industrial complex, asks a similarly wrong-headed question: "Do capitalist nations require military production as a priority economic activity—because they are capitalist? The available evidence says 'no' " (p. 210). Melman shows, for example, that although Japan and West Germany had higher growth rates than the U.S. in the period from 1950 to 1965, they had substantially lower spending on the military as a percent of GNP; in 1966, Japan with about one-eighth our percentage expenditures had a growth rate that had averaged more than twice ours.[38]

Undoubtedly there are conceptual alternatives to the internationalization and militarization of American capitalism. Conceptually, there are alternatives to everything that happens. But there is the persisting reality: the United States has spent over a trillion dollars on arms since 1946, and has military bases all over the globe. It is not only conceivable that other ways can be found to keep the economy going; additional

---

[37]James L. Clayton, ed., *The Economic Impact of the Cold War** (New York: Harcourt Brace Jovanovich, 1970), p. 281. This quotation is from Clayton. The many essays in the collection are most informative in terms of background data.

[38]By 1967 the picture had changed. "By the end of 1971," *Der Spiegel* (the *Time* of West Germany) reports, "the German armaments industry had completed deliveries worth more than $24 billion to the West German armed forces alone and had expanded its market to include much of the rest of the world." (July, 1972) Similar trends are now at work in Japan, but such facts are not necessary to show that Melman is asking the wrong questions.

ways *have* been used and *are* being used. What is fundamental is that despite the extraordinary rise of *non*-military expenditures since World War II, military expenditures have risen even more, and the economy nevertheless finds itself with chronic excess capacity in both plant and labor. (These matters and supporting data will be brought forth subsequently.) Furthermore, despite the connected and extraordinary expansion of foreign markets and investment, the economy finds itself with persistent slack.

In recent years, military expenditures have been $70 billion or more per annum. The conceptual argument can be made that the replacement of military by peaceful governmental expenditures to that amount *could* sustain the economy as much as or more than the present pattern; or, that cutting both expenditures and taxes would release private purchasing power that *could* take up the slack in consumer and investment expenditures. Essentially this is the form Melman's hopes take. In addition to being irrational and immoral in our military spree, he argues, we are living dangerously: we may bring on the war we seek to prevent, and we are undoing, not preserving, capitalism. "The New State" is growing, like a cancer in our midst. He sees the Pentagon as the "single social force . . . [with] a controlling influence in changing, swiftly, the character of life in a large and complex society. . . ." Thus,

> Failing decisive action to reverse the economic and other growth of these institutions, then the parent state, if it is saved from nuclear war, will surely become the guardian of a garrison-like society dominated by the Pentagon and its state-management.[39]

Melman no longer accepts the notion, if he ever did, that the growth of the Pentagon was necessary to counter an *external* threat. He sees it now as a self-fueling, self-directed "para-state," which "both breeds and needs foreign and domestic crises" (p. 226). His view of *why* all this happens is his Achilles heel: profit-seeking is incidental to it. He sees the personnel who run the Pentagon, both civilian and military, as growing directly out of the managerial outlook of the modern corporation. And what motivates the modern corporation?

> I have emphasized here the idea of enlarging decision-power as the occupational imperative, the operative end-in-view of modern corporate management—as against the more traditional idea that profit-making is the avowed central purpose of management. Profit-making, as a step in the recoupment of invested money, has diminished in importance as an independent measure of managerial performance.[40]

---

[39] *Pentagon Capitalism*, p. 227.

[40] Ibid., p. 22. Viewing profit-making as a step in the "recoupment of invested money" makes investment sound like slipping on a banana peel.

Despite this persumed insouciance toward profit-making, corporate profits since World War II have broken all records, *after* taxes. The highest rates ever were recorded in the first quarter of 1972, and then broken in the second quarter once more: ". . . second quarter profits [were] at better than a $52-billion annual rate—more money than U.S. business has earned in any quarter in history." (*Business Week,* August 12, 1972) At this writing, the report on 1973 first and second quarter profits have been published: all previous records are broken. What would happen if they really tried?

Melman is not taken in by Cold War propaganda, but he gives no indication that he sees the creative connection between "the corporations and the Cold War." There was and is a high consciousness among the corporate leaders who served in or as advisors to the State of just what the alternatives were as between an American Empire or, failing that, "radical readjustments in our entire economic structure . . . , changes which could hardly be made under our democratic free enterprise system."[41]

Melman and other conscientious liberals may or may not have begun to see the role of the corporations in creating the current strength of the Pentagon; his fear, in any event, is that whoever and whatever created it, it has taken on a life of its own. It is, in his view, a Frankenstein monster. To date, the evidence is at best inconclusive for that view. The future is no doubt a precarious one; up to now, as the conduct of the Indochina War attests, the sober corporate heads are still capable of curbing the power of the military when it threatens to go too far. Thus, after essentially military advice was taken on that war in the Johnson Administration (the earlier penetration under Truman and Kennedy having been essentially non-military in its guidance) and the military failed, serious steps were taken to cut back on American personnel and expenditures. That the number of casualties to the people of Indochina rose markedly under the impact of the enormously expanded air war is quite irrelevant to the argument about the decision-making process. Businessmen have never been noticeably tender about human life. Under Nixon the war became manageable and was attenuated, *and* military expenditures rose; limits were set to the further expansion of the Empire; the future would entail digging deeper within its existing limits.

Perhaps because the Pentagon itself finally saw the Indochina War as a disaster to themselves; perhaps, in addition, because the expanding

---

[41]The argument is that of Will Clayton, out of Wall Street to vice-president of the Export-Import Bank, to Assistant Secretary of Commerce, to Undersecretary for Economic Affairs in the State Department, in the Roosevelt and Truman administrations. He was a key figure in the Committee for Economic Development, the organization which plays the same role now as that played by the National Civic Federation before World War I. The quotation is from an important article by David W. Eakins, "Business Planners and America's Postwar Expansion," in *Corporations and the Cold War,* cited earlier, p. 168.

military budgets (for fancy hardware) constituted a satisfactory meal for their appetites; or perhaps for other reasons, the Pentagon at this writing (1973) is functioning in ways satisfactory to the corporate world. The possibility always exists that corporate and military criteria will clash seriously; many Americans envisage that, and envisage the corollary of an attempted, even a successful, *coup d'état.* Whether this possibility moves to the realm of probability depends not upon the kinds of fears expressed by Melman, but whether the present social crisis in the United States deepens. In short, and in anticipation of what will now be discussed, the present and probable future role of the military in the State system is a function not of their ambitions but of the nature and depth of the problems facing American capitalism. A movement toward a military *coup d'état* is as unlikely as it is unnecessary in the foreseeable future. Should it become likely it will be as part of something larger: a business-supported movement toward American-style fascism. The strategic feature of the present State system is not a struggle between the military and the business world; it is a division within the business world itself.

WARFARE-WELFARE STATE

The major political tendencies in a society like ours cannot be evaluated without an analysis that centers on the power, the needs, and the modes of conduct of giant national and multinational corporations. Baran and Sweezy's *Monopoly Capital* sought to provide an analytical framework within which the key processes and relationships could be investigated and understood. The theoretical center of their analysis is "the tendency for the surplus to rise." What is the "surplus" and why does it tend to rise?

> The economic surplus ... is the difference between what a society produces and the costs of producing it. The size of the surplus is an index of productivity and wealth, of how much freedom a society has to accomplish whatever goals it may set for itself. The composition of the surplus shows how it uses that freedom: how much it invests in expanding its productive capacity, how much it consumes in various forms, how much it wastes and in what ways.[42]

---

[42] *Monopoly Capital,* pp. 9–10. In a valuable appendix to this book, Professor Joseph D. Phillips has made analytical and statistical estimates of the components and behavior of the surplus, pp. 369ff. The major components of the surplus are property income, the wastes of distribution, advertising, and selling, the incomes of those in the financial/legal sector, and, largest of all, government expenditures. These are defined as elements of the "surplus" in the sense that the incomes and expenditures involved are not necessary to maintain current levels of production and life. O'Connor, as we shall see momentarily, modifies this conception, showing the government to be a generator as well as an absorber of surplus.

Baran and Sweezy posit that the surplus as a percentage of GNP has risen from just under 50 percent in 1929 to a figure closer to 60 percent in the 1960's; the State (on all levels) absorbs over half of that surplus. Clearly an analysis of the State becomes critical for understanding the behavior of the society, whether or not one accepts fully the foregoing conception and estimates.

The characteristic feature of *all* modern industrial capitalist nations is not only that they are monopolistic in their economic structures but that the State system has become central to their life processes. James O'Connor's ongoing work is foremost among that which seeks to explicate this modern political economy. What follows depends basically on his efforts.[43]

O'Connor posits three sectors in the economy: 1) the monopolistic sector, 2) the competitive sector, and 3) the State sector. He assumes that the economy is marked by surplus capital and surplus labor. It is the interaction of all these characteristics that gives the economy and the State their quality and direction. The quality is that of a monopoly capital warfare-welfare State; the direction has combined imperialism, militarization, racism and sexism to bring us to our present condition; the future direction is problematic. Now, some elaboration.

The monopolistic sector is the pride of the American economy. It is where productivity, high profits and the highest wages are found. It is the world of the big corporation—such as GE, GM, IBM, ITT, EXXON —and of the most powerful unions (the teamsters and construction unions being notable exceptions). It is where the greatest concentration of business and labor power exists, and where productive capacity is in surplus.

The competitive sector is where most businesses, and as many workers as in the monopolistic sector, function. Unlike the monopolistic sector, productivity is low and technology non-dynamic; profits are low; wages do not allow livelihood; and labor is in surplus. This sector comprises small retailers, small manufacturers, real estate operators, and the like. Competitive business firms often have substantial power on *local* issues; their power on the national level is confined to their influence on the two major political parties.

The State sector (federal, state, and local) is responsible for State expenditures and activities. The nature and importance of that responsibility is well-clarified by O'Connor and warrants lengthy quotation:

---

[43]Brady's *Business as a System of Power* (1943) was the first study to show the similarity of tendencies among all leading capitalist economies toward both monopoly and "political capitalism." Andrew Schonfield, *Modern Capitalism,* cited earlier, covers some of the same ground for the years since World War II, from a conventional standpoint. O'Connor's analyses have appeared as essays in *Socialist Revolution,* vol. 1, nos. 1 and 2, and vol. 2, no. 2, as "The Fiscal Crisis of the State," I and II, and "Inflation, Fiscal Crisis, and the Working Class," respectively. *The Fiscal Crisis of the State* is an expanded and revised version of these early essays.

> State expenditures have a twofold character corresponding to the capital-
> ist state's two basic functions [accumulation and legitimization]: social
> capital and social expenses. *Social capital* is expenditures required for
> profitable accumulation; it is indirectly productive. ... There are two
> kinds of social capital: social investment and social consumption. ... *Social
> investment* consists of projects and services that increase the productivity
> of a given amount of labor-power and, other factors being equal, increase
> the rate of profit. A good example is state-financed industrial-develop-
> ment parks. *Social consumption* consists of projects and services that lower
> the reproduction costs of labor and, other factors being equal, increase the
> rate of profit. An example of this is social insurance, which expands the
> reproductive powers of the work force while simultaneously lowering
> labor costs. The second category, *social expenses,* consists of projects and
> services which are required to maintain social harmony—to fulfill the
> state's "legitimization" function. They are not even indirectly productive.
> ... The best example is the welfare system, which is designed chiefly to
> keep social peace among unemployed workers.[44]

In the process the State indirectly generates as well as absorbs and
redirects a growing part of the economic surplus. It is the most rapidly
growing sector. Although its function is to provide economic stimulus
and social stability it has been both source and mitigator of the tensions
accompanying the American social crisis. Its ways of doing both now
deepen the crisis.

Surplus capital is a way of characterizing the excess productive capacity and the corollary supply of investment funds which, in the absence
of the State sector, would have brought down American capitalism long
ago. The key role of the State has been to use up and to create outlets
for capital, in the military, in non-military goods and services, and
abroad. Given that fundamental development, American business has
been able through advertising and sales promotion to develop the "consumerism" that propels Americans to spend more than they earn whenever possible, on almost anything.

Surplus labor in a capitalist economy is the other side of the coin of
surplus productive capacity. In a rational society there would be neither;
in a society where marketability and profitability are the criteria of
production and of employment there must be both. Surplus labor was
seen as a "problem" in vivid terms in the 1930's. One of the most
widely-read authors at that time was Walter B. Pitkin, best-known for
his *Life Begins at Forty,* where he was speaking to the middle class. In
another book, *Let's Get What We Want* (1935), Pitkin, then extremely
popular in business circles, proclaimed:

---

[44]O'Connor, *Fiscal Crisis of the State,* pp. 6–7. His italics.

... most well-mannered debaters carry on with the White Lie of Democracy; and thus reach worthless conclusions. A land swarming with tens of millions of morons, perverts, culls, outcasts, criminals, and lesser breeds of low-grade humans cannot escape the evils all such cause. . . . So long as we have an underworld of 4,000,000 or more scoundrels willing to do anything for a price, and a twilight world of fully 40,000,000 people of profound stupidity or ignorance, or indifference, and a population of nearly 70,000,000 who cannot support themselves entirely and hence must think first of cost, whenever they buy things, we shall have a nasty mess on our hands.[45]

Liberal and radical critics of contemporary America usually join in one important error: they assume that military spending has risen to astronomical levels, which is true, but that non-military government spending has increased only slightly, which is *not* true. The basis for that error is a failure to appreciate the degree to which social sophistication is possessed by the corporate élite; put differently, it is failure to understand that the strongest impulse toward "liberalism" today is found in the largest corporations, the counterpart of what was true in the Progressive Period. Before providing some of the relevant data on this score, the view of David Rockefeller of Chase Manhattan Bank can serve as a *leitmotiv:*

In view of the emerging demands for revision of the social contract, a passive response on the part of the business community could be dangerous. Any adaptation of our system to the changing environment is far more likely to be workable if those who understand the system's problems share in designing the solutions. So it is up to businessmen to make common cause with other reformers . . . to prevent the unwise adoption of extreme and emotional remedies, but on the contrary to initiate necessary reforms that will make it possible for businessmen to continue to function in a new climate. . . . By acting promptly, business can assure itself a voice in deciding the form and content of the new social contract.[46]

The "new social contract" referred to by Rockefeller is a step beyond the present warfare-welfare State, an attempt to transform social expenses into social capital. To the so-called "military-industrial complex" it would add a "social-industrial complex." Some steps toward that "contract" have already been taken; as we shall see, the very factors

---

[45]Quoted in Brady, *Business as a System of Power* p. 268 n. Brady cites Pitkin also in *Spirit and Structure of German Fascism,* pp. 395–96, to show that the Nazis were not alone in their views in the capitalist world. The U.S. population when Pitkin wrote was about 126 million. Adding his figures gives us 114 million more or less worthless types. Many are called but few are chosen.

[46]*Wall Street Journal,* December 21, 1971. Quoted in O'Connor's *Fiscal Crisis of the State,* p. 227.

making for that "progress" are now serving to obstruct its further movement. To build a warfare state has not been difficult; the attitudes necessary to that construction, however, tend to militate against the construction of the welfare state. Especially is that so when America's long adherence to a naive individualism is taken into account. Violence and raw patriotism run deep in the American grain; concern for social balance has at best been a veneer. Building the American empire has been like rolling off a log; the other task set by the corporate élite has been like trying to roll that log up a steep mountain. Today the mountain has become cliff-like in its angle. The energy that lies behind the effort accumulates in the surplus population of the State and the competitive sectors and the power of corporation leaders; the resistance to it comes from small business and organized labor in the competitive sector and some of the powerful in the State sector. If only, a Rockefeller must think, those who resist would try to understand what O'Connor makes clear:

> ... both welfare spending and warfare spending have a two-fold nature: the welfare system not only politically contains the surplus population but also expands demand and domestic markets. And the warfare system not only keeps foreign rivals at bay and inhibits the development of world revolution (thus keeping laborpower, raw materials, and markets in the capitalist orbit) but also helps to stave off economic stagnation at home.[47]

What are the data supporting this development? Total government spending at all levels in the United States was 8 percent of GNP in 1890; in 1960 it was over 30 percent. Non-military governmental expenditures rose from 5 percent to 18 percent of GNP in the same period. Military spending is almost exclusively done by the federal government. State and local government spending, almost entirely non-military, increased seventy-fold in this century. Local and state spending is in the area of social capital (transportation, education, health), income maintenance (e.g., welfare), and fire and police forces. But the federal government also spends on non-military social capital (e.g., highways, education, housing and community development), on income maintenance, and various other forms of social consumption (food stamps, etc.). All categories of State spending rose in the 1960's. Although *federal* spending on the military rose by 75 percent, its income maintenance outlays rose by 100 percent. Local and state expenditures that fall under the heading of the welfare state rose even more. These data are taken from O'Connor, Chapter 4, as are Tables 12 and 13, which illustrate these tendencies for the Federal government.

---

[47]O'Connor, *Fiscal Crisis of the State,* pp. 150–51.

TABLE 12
Trends in Budget Outlays by Major Category, Fiscal Years 1960-71
(billions of dollars)

Category	Outlays				Average Annual Change in Outlays		
	1960	1965	1967	1969	1960–1965	1965–1967	1967–1969
National defense	46.0	49.9	70.6	81.4	0.8	10.3	5.4
Space	0.4	5.1	5.4	4.2	0.9	0.1	−0.6
Income maintenance	24.5	34.2	43.9	56.8	1.9	4.9	6.5
Education, health, manpower	2.5	4.1	8.6	10.3	0.3	2.3	0.8
Housing and community development	0.7	1.5	2.6	3.3	0.2	0.6	0.4
Physical resources	6.4	10.2	10.3	10.8	0.8	0.0	0.2
Interest	6.9	8.6	10.3	12.7	0.3	0.8	1.2
Other outlays (net)	4.9	5.9	7.8	6.2	0.2	1.0	−0.8
Sale of assets	−0.1	−1.1	−1.2	−1.1	−0.2	0	0
Total	92.2	118.4	158.3	184.6	5.2	20.0	13.2
Total, nondefense adjusted for asset sales	46.3	69.6	88.9	104.3	4.7	9.6	7.7
Annual % increase	....	....	....	....	8.5	13.0	8.3

SOURCE: Charles L. Schultze (with Edward K. Hamilton and Allen Schick), *Setting National Priorities: The 1971 Budget* (Brookings, 1970), pp. 11-12.

The State thus accomplishes many badly-needed functions for the maintenance of American capitalism: 1) the social capital provides facilities and skills (for example, highways and trained workers at all levels) that reduce the costs and increase the profits of business; 2) the social capital that takes the form of income maintenance enhances purchasing power; 3) military and para-military forces abroad and at home create and maintain a framework within which orderly business can be transacted; 4) the research and development associated with military production, an important part of social capital, enhances productivity and subsidizes investment in the monopoly sector; 5) jobs are provided: over 25 percent of the entire work force in the 1960's was estimated as owing its jobs directly or indirectly to State payrolls and contracts.[48]

---

[48]Ibid. Nor can one overlook the inestimable difference that would be made for *all* jobs if those estimated were to be reduced or cease to exist.

TABLE 13

Program Composition of the 1965 Federal Budget

(New Obligational Authority)

	Amount ($ millions)	Percent
National Security Programs	$ 59,820	44%
U.S. military forces	48,806	81.6
Scientific competition (NASA)	5,304	8.8
Foreign nonmilitary aid	2,826	4.7
Foreign military forces	2,325	3.9
U.S. passive defense	372	0.6
Political and psychological competition (USIA)	176	0.3
Arms control and disarmament	11	0.1
Public Welfare Programs	45,783	34
Life insurance and retirement	23,402	51.1
Public assistance and welfare	5,976	13.0
Aid to farmers and rural areas	5,398	11.8
Unemployment insurance	4,059	8.9
Health	3,303	7.2
Veterans compensation	2,121	4.6
Urban housing and facilities	1,533	3.4
Economic Development Programs	14,386	11
Transportation facilities*	5,154	35.8
Natural resources	4,278	29.7
Education, training and research	3,677	25.6
Aids and subsidies to business	1,277	8.9
Government Operations	15,616	11
Interest payments	11,102	71.1
Housekeeping functions	3,299	21.1
Judicial and law enforcement	451	2.9
Conducting foreign relations	395	2.5
Regulatory programs	237	1.5
Legislative functions	132	0.9
Total	135,605	100

*Transportation facilities consist of three major programs: land transportation ($3,980 millions), air transportation ($751 millions), and water transportation ($423 millions).

SOURCE: Murray L. Weidenbaum, "The Allocation of Government Funds," mimeographed paper based in part on a paper presented to the annual meeting of the Western Economic Association, Eugene, Oregon, August 27, 1964. Data computed from details in The Budget of the United States Government for the Fiscal Year Ending June 30, 1965 (Washington, D. C.: U.S. Government Printing Office, 1964).

It sounds like a fool-proof system; if it were criminal, it might be almost the perfect crime. The reasons why it is not fool-proof, why it is, indeed, in great trouble, are why O'Connor writes of the "fiscal crisis of the State." It all has to be paid for, through taxation of all kinds on all levels. And there is a tax revolt in the making, which arises not from careless construction or administration of the system, but from the very features that make the system necessary and that have made it possible. Veblen would say the system has the defects of its virtues; Marx would see it as the culminating set of inherent contradictions of capitalism.

The State system has exfoliated in all its parts; but some parts have grown more than others. They are the parts most satisfying and least controversial among those at the top and middle levels of power; the parts that hue most closely to America's long-standing love affair with money-making and with expansion (employing violence when necessary). The fuel of American dynamism has been the pattern of investment directed by profit and the work ethic accepted by the population. The resulting dualism in the economy has its corollary in the dualism of the State system. The non-military grows, but it cannot keep up with the natural, normal, and powerful tendencies to create and maintain inequality in the distribution of income and wealth.[49] Without the expansion of the "welfare" side of the warfare-welfare State, the United States would have moved closer to a revolutionary *or* counterrevolutionary condition. Even with that expansion, however, the essentially half-hearted efforts made have produced a situation of slowly-increasing tension and polarization, exemplified by the success of super-patriots like Nixon, Reagan, and Wallace with implicitly anti-black, explicitly anti-welfare slogans. The clearest manifestations of this process are in the fiscal crisis of the State, the head-on collision of rising tax resistance with rising needs for State expenditures. When to this is added the necessity of keeping inflation down at home in order not to exacerbate an already serious international trade and payments problem, the directly conflicting needs of the warfare-welfare state become apparent.

ARISE, YE WRETCHED TAXPAYERS

Everywhere and always, the State is supported by taxes—hidden or open, regressive or progressive. That is the same as saying that the status quo is supported by taxes; the burden of them is almost without exception *not* on those most able to pay. In the medieval world, the labor provided by serfs on the lord's domain was the principal tax of the time;

---

[49]Bluestone's analysis along these lines is recommended again in this connection. *Monthly Review* (June, 1972), pp. 65–71.

the principal tax in 19th century America took the form of tariffs, a tax on consumers. Local property taxes, sales and excise taxes, and payroll taxes now comprise the principal tax burden on Americans, and all such taxes are regressive. Income taxes, progressive in surface structure, are so widely-evaded by the well-off within the framework of the law that their effective progressiveness is minimal.

Tax grumbling does not occur simply because taxes are being paid, but when one or more developments occur: the percentage of income paid (in *all* taxes) rises to substantial levels; the uses to which taxes are put are objectionable; the distribution of the tax burden is seen as inequitable. All these developments come together in the United States today. Total taxes amount to about 30 percent of GNP; objections to non-military State expenditures are mounting rapidly; the tax burden is (as will be shown momentarily) highly inequitable. The upshot takes on the proportions of an incipient tax revolt.

Taken by itself, rising tax resistance would not constitute a fiscal crisis. The inexorable need for rising expenditures by the State, taken *together* with tax resistance, has produced the crisis. If expenditures continue to rise, resistance even to warfare spending (already beginning to surface) might become substantial.

Until very recently, the signs of today's fierce mood were hidden from sight. By the election of 1972, taxes had become a pervasive and heated issue. The objections to rising taxes grew as the taxes rose; and grew even more as knowledge spread and deepened about who was paying how much for what. The average taxpayer still has much to learn, but what is already becoming well-known is substantial.

The richer you are, the less likely you are to pay your full share of taxes. If you are rich enough, you may have to pay *no* direct taxes, and indirect (sales and excise, e.g.) taxes are regressive—that is, the higher your income, the lower the percentage. Among the pleasanter and more time-consuming duties of Congress is to devise tax breaks for the top levels of corporate and individual taxpayers. The salaries of Congressmen place them in the top 5 percent of income recipients, which is why their duties in this respect are taken seriously. Corporate and personal income taxes have been steadily reduced in the past decade in nominal rates; loopholes through the lowered rates have widened.[50]

When the federal income tax was initiated in 1913, a single person had an exemption of $3,000; today it is $650, and of course a dollar bought considerably more in 1913. In 1913, the initial rate of tax was 1 percent on the first $20,000 of taxable income; now it is 20 percent. In 1916 only 400,000 tax returns were taxable; today it is over 55,000,000. The big jump was from 4,000,000 net taxable returns in 1939

---

[50]Unless otherwise indicated, the data on these matters are taken from O'Connor, *Fiscal Crisis,* Ch. 8.

to 32,000,000 in 1950, the period encompassing the later New Deal and World War II, in which the new State system came to flower.

The progressiveness of personal and corporate income taxes is mitigated by loopholes; the progressiveness of the tax system as a whole is eliminated by *non*-income taxes at all levels of government. Property taxes are passed on to tenants. Payroll taxes are paid for in part by workers and in part by employers; they are regressive for the worker (because the tax is only on the first $7–8000) and even more so because the employer's contribution is passed on in the form of higher prices or lower wages. (See *Business Week,* July 15, 1972.) In the years since 1964, nominal personal income tax rates have been cut four times, from a maximum rate of 91 percent down to 50 percent; after 1966, payroll tax receipts began sharply to exceed corporate income tax receipts. Property taxes are the principal source of local receipts; state governments raise about two-thirds of their tax revenues from sales and gross receipts taxes. Income taxes on the state level account for only about 16 percent of revenues. Tax withholding, begun after World War II on the federal level and now spreading throughout the separate states, has overcome the lower-income population's ability to evade taxes, while legal loopholes have increased the ability of the well-to-do. The resulting pattern is not surprising.[51]

Average tax rates for federal, state and local taxes for 1965 reveal a pattern defying the notion that government power is used to redistribute income. Table 14 indicates the tax pattern for 1965. John Gurley estimates that the 200,000 families with average incomes (including capital gains) in excess of $150,000 a year pay *income* taxes of about 20 percent of their true incomes.[52]

The best that can be said of the tax system—a system which, since the framing of our constitution has presumably been shaped in terms of ability to pay—is that it is proportional to income and not, as most believe, progressive (that is, a system where taxes rise both absolutely and relatively as income rises). It is proportional between $2,000 and $15,000 per annum; for the poorest and all others, it is regressive.

---

[51]If the latest proposals for "value-added" taxes are legislated, the pattern will be even more regressive; the value-added tax is a fancy name for a complicated federal sales tax.

[52]In "The Real Impact of Federal Tax Policy," in Gordon, *Problems in Political Economy,* op. cit. There are at least two hundred millionaires who in 1970 paid *no* income taxes. For this and similar data, see Philip Stern, *The Great Treasury Raid,* cited earlier. The number of known millionaires increased from 27,000 in 1953 to 200,000 in 1969, according to *U.S. News and World Report,* December 15, 1969. *Fortune* (May, 1968) estimated that there were 166 individuals with over $100,000,000, many of them having accumulated their income and wealth since World War II, the period in which popular fancy has it that such accumulation was made impossible by the tax laws; in September, 1973, *Fortune* reported that at least "39 men had amassed wealth of $50 million or more [6 from $200 to $700 million]" between 1968 and 1973, exclusive of inheritance.

TABLE 14

Taxes as a Percent of Income

Income Class	Federal Taxes	State and Local Taxes	Total Taxes
Under $2,000	19%	25%	44%
$2–4,000	16	11	27
$4–6,000	17	10	27
$6–8,000	17	9	26
$8–10,000	18	9	27
$10–15,000	19	9	27
$15,000 and over	32	7	38
Total	22	9	31

SOURCE: Joseph Pechman, "The Rich, the Poor and the Taxes They Pay," *The Public Interest* (Fall, 1969), quoted in Richard Parker, *The Myth of the Middle Class* (New York: Liveright, 1972), p. 216. This is a generally useful book on income and wealth.

The highest effective tax rates are on the poorest segment of the population—44 percent for those with incomes under $2,000 per year. Income taxes are at about 5 percent for those in that group; most of what they pay is in the form of sales, excise, and payroll taxes, and hidden taxes passed on by landlords and corporations. About 40 percent of Americans receive annual incomes in the $6–15,000 range (see Tables 2 and 3, Chapter Five). They include workers from the monopolistic sector, small businessmen, and lesser professionals. The taxes they hate most are *not* hidden. This segment has been the largest purchasers of houses in the postwar years. Property taxes are now at a $40 billion rate per annum; 60 percent of that is paid by homeowners, the rest by businesses. The rates have been rising: in California, for instance, "the property tax take has climbed by 147% in the past decade." (*Business Week,* February 12, 1972) Over half of federal income taxes are to finance the warfare state; most of local property taxes, taken together with sales and excise taxes, are to finance the welfare state.

The incipient tax revolt is aimed most heatedly and most effectively at the financing of the welfare state; it combines, of course, with hostile attitudes toward nonwhites and the young and, as well, with the traditional schizophrenic view of Americans toward education. It combines with something deeper: the naive individualism and Puritanism so much a part of the American tradition has made us a people deeply distrustful of all public agencies but the military, and especially distrustful of income maintenance programs. "You get what you deserve."

The middle-income income receivers and taxpayers (i.e., those in the $6–15,000 range) have entered the outer rings of the charmed circle of American opulence in the very years that the warfare state has grown;

they see themselves and their tenuously-held possessions as being under dire threat, in order to assist a largely despised surplus population and an educational apparatus they see as being both costly and feckless. Their targets *should* be the military and the inequities of the tax system. Why aren't they?

Our history, our traditions and our non-social philosophy constitute the largest part of the explanation; much of that has been discussed in earlier chapters. It is also necessary to understand the culminating role played by the rise of the warfare state itself in shaping current attitudes, attitudes which militate against the acceptance by the "middle Americans" of the "welfare" side of the warfare-welfare State.

SHINE, PERISHING REPUBLIC

Overseas imperialism as a way of life for the United States is now at least three-quarters of a century along. For the past thirty years, militarism has joined with imperialism.

In my view and that of many others (those cited above, such as Oglesby, Kolko, Mills, I. F. Stone, Williams, Klare, Sweezy, Magdoff), American militarization has not been the result of external threats to our national safety but of a conscious and deliberate attempt to underpin economically and geographically expansionist policies, as outlined in Chapter Seven. To achieve that, given the anti-militarist attitudes common in the United States between the two world wars, a massive and sustained propaganda effort was necessary. Doubtless some of the propagandists, both high and low in power, *believed* there was a threat; doubtless some still do. There was, of course, a problem; the spread of socialism in Europe and Asia could not be taken lightly by a capitalist world always needing exploitation and expansion. But that was a political/ideological problem; if, in the past thirty years, it has ever had a military tinge to it that was a happily self-fulfilling prophecy.

Moving into the geographic and economic soft spots allowed by the weakening of all the other capitalist powers after World War II, the United States gained two additional bonuses: the stimuli from military production and a virtual end to domestic dissent, at least until recently. Capitalism, the free enterprise system, and freedom became synonymous; dissenters at home were dupes or worse, opposition abroad was part of an international atheistic Communist conspiracy to overrun the world. Humane attitudes toward public policies that would promote opportunities, jobs, and the amenities of life to the lower one-third of the population—that is, that would provide for social stability and higher overall productivity, the function of the welfare state—became suspect as "Communist" attitudes, adding to the long-standing resistance to social policies. Both the universe of acceptable discourse and the kind of person who could rise to high political levels shifted to the right. Why?

Education and popular discourse in the United States have done little to allow appropriate answers to that "why?", for they have tended to discourage widespread interest in social and historical analysis. The general inclination is to personalize historical processes, and to become attentive only in periods of great drama: we read and speak much of political figures, but study political relationships and what they represent very little. Thus, one can read through Halberstam's *Best and the Brightest* and learn an extraordinary amount about the individuals (Acheson, Rusk, Johnson, the Kennedys, Rostow, McNamara, the Bundys, Maxwell Taylor, Nixon, et al.) who conspired to take the United States to war against the peoples of Indochina, and about how they lied to the people, the press, and to each other in the process. The discussions are generally astute, and the information we gain is valuable, but the reader is left with an interpretation of the period based upon the strengths and weaknesses of *personalities*—in the absence of any other analysis. Similarly, in commenting on the revelations of Watergate a portrait of substantial accuracy is made concerning President Nixon:

> In the end, his long reliance on playing upon the baser part of people's nature, his professed conviction that they are children who must be disciplined before they can be trusted with responsibility, his readiness to resort to the most undemocratic means to retain and expand his control over them, and finally, his apparent belief that his personal interest is identical with the public interest together make up the character of the tyrant—the man who would assert himself by making his will the will of a nation.[53]

But Nixon's inclinations along each and every one of these lines were familiar to those who financed his campaigns and who voted for him from 1946 through 1972. Both his financial and his voter support increased steadily over that period of 26 years (notwithstanding electoral setbacks in 1960 and 1962).

In those same years, almost insensibly, Americans were led to accept as plausible what in earlier years they had thought dangerous or laugh-

---

[53]"Talk of the Town," *The New Yorker* (June 23, 1973). It is worth adding that for several years preceding 1973, this magazine had come to be the most persistent voice opposing the war and criticizing the diminution of civil liberties, outside of radical publications, a tradition begun with its devotion of a full issue to the horrors of Hiroshima, in 1946 (written by John Hersey). Intentionally, consciously, or not, the magazine has come to stand for the urbane values of a confident bourgeois—but not an imperialist or totalitarian—society.

able. Nixon was by no means the only such person who rose to high office or great power in that period. As military budgets and bases abroad rose to numbing levels, political contests were won increasingly (if never entirely) in terms of the patriotic strenuousness and vicarious bravery of the victors—making General Eisenhower first into a university president, and then a beloved but often befuddled president; making Joe McCarthy, a man of no evident scruples, into the most feared (and therefore one of the most powerful) of men; making Lyndon Johnson into a president, and potentially no worse than most and better than some from the past, but a president who was both able and inclined to continue our plunge into Indochina by presidential and governmental deceit both supported and prodded by the politics of the Cold War—and to do so while classifying his enemy as "a raggedy-ass little fourth-rate country," peopled by "little yellow dwarfs"; giving us, finally, Richard M. Nixon. Twice.

As a person, Nixon has earned the criticisms he receives; but something has to be explained about the society that elects and re-elects such a person. When Nixon began his political career in 1946, he did so on the basis of innuendo and a sneering anti-Communism. At first, he was viewed as a political aberration, at best. But he was a man moving with the times. As his power grew, he did not change, except that each step up the ladder, from Congressman to Senator to Vice-President to President, allowed him to delegate his gutter skills to others, while also bringing him that presumably un-American deference that Americans usually give to those in high office. Nixon stood in 1972 where he had always stood, off on the far Right; but the United States had moved over, making him a Centrist.

In changing so, Americans came to value what earlier they found valueless, or worse. It was not all a matter of ideas and fear-filled rhetoric. A very high percentage of Americans came to be dependent upon the militarized empire for their jobs and profits; or so they came to believe. As things have been, of course, the belief was correct, even though as things have stood more recently the real income and the jobs of Americans are in trouble *because* of our addiction to empire and militarism. From being the cutting edge of prosperity, America's imperial/military basis of production has become a two-edged sword: our external (and militarized) relationships in becoming so important to the United States, now that they have run into a period of troubles, have become the cutting edge of worsening economic and political problems.

The winding down of the Cold War, signified by more congenial relationships with China and the Soviet Union, is now assumed to be under way; for the system within which Americans *now* live, however, that consummation so devoutly to be awaited poses a social challenge of enormous proportions: the centralized, intertwined, and powerful corporate and State bureaucracy that fed and was fed by the Cold War seems presently out of control.

The dogged manner in which the United States pursued its horrifying and finally self-destructive war against the Indochinese peoples continued long after it was perceived as irrational by important elements of the business community (as early as 1967), leading as it did to inflation at home, to a deterioration of our international economic strength, and to corrosion of the structure of American institutions; our involvement in Indochina, which began under Truman, was both consequence and partial cause of the centralized patterns of power that had their most recent effusion in the processes leading to Watergate. It was not coherent actions by the business community or government leaders that led to our withdrawal from Indochina; it was the military and political strength and determination of the Indochinese peoples (not least the critical Tet offensive of 1968) and an antiwar movement headed by the powerless that finally led the "respectable" people of power in this country seriously to seek ways out; similarly, the breaking of the Watergate conspiracies depended upon a handful of reporters, one judge, and the breaking of discipline among the conspirators themselves.

Whatever else this tells us, it shows that a simple theory of the State, whether that State policy represents a pluralist consensus or the decisions of "the executive committee of the ruling class," does not hold now, if it ever did. Some Marxists to the contrary notwithstanding, it is clear that Marx, at least, never held such a simple theory. He saw that under certain developmental conditions, and especially those obtaining under imperialism, a State bureaucracy could grow that would pervert and distort the power relations more normally arising from capitalist rule. Writing of the bureaucracy of France's Second Empire (1852–1860) under Napoleon III, his formulation might have been made to characterize recent American history:

> Apparently the final victory of this governmental power over society, it was in fact the orgy of all the corrupt elements of that society. To the eye of the uninitiated it appeared only as the victory of the Executive over the Legislative, of the final defeat of the form of class rule pretending to be the autocracy of society by its form pretending to be a superior power to the society. But in fact it was only the last degraded and the only possible form of that class ruling, as humiliating to those classes as to the working classes which they kept fettered by it.[54]

The Indochina War was and remains a savage and destructive experience for the peoples of Indochina, many millions of whom have been

---

[54]Quoted by Shlomo Avineri, *The Social and Political Thought of Karl Marx*, pp. 50–51. This appeared in the original draft (but not today's published versions) of Marx's *The Civil War in France*.

killed, maimed, and displaced by it. Setting our own Civil War aside, it has probably been the most dislocating and unsettling experience in American history, to which Watergate is a loud coda. The War served as lightning flashes do, providing intermittent heat and light on the American scene, and it burned away much of the mythology of the Cold War. It helped many Americans to identify the United States as imperialist; it added new emphasis to what racism means; and it along with the spate of social analyses directly and indirectly stimulated by the war, along with Watergate, have forced Americans to be somewhat less casual about the corruption they have always taken for granted.

One cannot judge now what the ultimate consequences of the growing re-appraisal of American reality will be. As of now, the facts of life for the State system in America must be part of that re-appraisal: 1) Militarism has come into existence with civilian support under the leadership of a corporate élite (with the greedy prodding of the military); 2) although the quality of life in America has deteriorated in many if not all areas—demonstrably in the areas of health, education, the environment, drugs and crime, transportation, the viability of our cities, and the morale especially of the young—the largest proportion of Americans still appears to place the blame for all this not on rampant capitalist imperialism and racism but, as is so often true, on its principal victims at home and abroad.

So it appears, at the moment. For the longer run, appearances may be deceptive.

READING SUGGESTIONS

That the appearance of pluralist political competition, expressed customarily in electoral contests between the Democratic and Republican parties, is belied by a more carefully studied reality is the well-documented argument of Walter Karp, *Indispensable Enemies: The Politics of Misrule in America* (New York: Saturday Review Press, 1973). He shows the conscious and cynical cooperation between the two parties that has persisted and grown in this century, with the consequence of maintaining the power structure within those parties, and the rule of monopoly capital (to the gain also of their allies in the military and organized labor). Some of the details of these alliances are brought together in Morton Mintz and Jerry S. Cohen, *America, Inc.** (New York: Dell, 1971). Two books of readings also illuminating in these respects are Herbert I. Schiller and Joseph D. Phillips, eds., *Super * State: Readings in the Military-Industrial Complex** (Urbana: University of Illinois Press, 1972), and Robert B. Carson, Jerry Ingles and Douglas McLaud, eds., *Government in the American Economy: Conventional and Radical Studies on the Growth of State Economic Power** (Boston: D. C. Heath, 1973). Michael

T. Klare, *War Without End,* cited earlier, shows how this works out regarding the political economy of American counter-insurgency, past, present, and future.

URPE has several publications relevant to this chapter: *RRPE* Special Issue (August, 1970), *The War and its Impact on the Economy;* In *Conference Papers* (December, 1968) the essay by Daniel Fusfeld, "Fascist Democracy in the United States," a view somewhat gloomier than that presented in this chapter; *RRPE* Special Issue (August, 1972), *On the New Economic Policy: The New Economics and the Contradictions of Keynesianism,* cited earlier, contains essays that range from domestic to international to methodological emphases, all concerned with the State in one way or another. "The New Economics: Handmaiden of Inspired Truth," by R. Du Boff and E. S. Herman is especially useful in showing how the mainstream ("brandname") economists have cooperated in selling the ugly policies of recent administrations. Brady's *Spirit and Structure of German Fascism,* cited earlier, and Franz Neumann's *Behemoth: The Structure and Practice of National Socialism, 1933–1944** (New York: Harper & Row, 1966; originally Oxford University Press, 1942) make good corollary reading in this connection.

A useful collection of essays from the spectrum of opinion on power in the United States is Richard Gillam, ed., *Power in Postwar America: Interdisciplinary Perspectives on a Historical Problem** (Boston: Little, Brown, 1971). Dahl, the pluralist spokesman, can be compared with Sweezy, Mills, Eisenhower, and Kolko. The concluding essay by Robert Paul Wolff is especially useful. Many of Mills' essays have been collected in Irving Louis Horowitz, ed., *Power, Politics, and People** (New York: Oxford University Press, 1963) who has also put together a group of essays in honor of Mills, *The New Sociology* (New York: Oxford University Press, 1964) which is worth studying.

A careful and thoroughgoing presentation of Marxian views is Stanley W. Moore, *The Critique of Capitalist Democracy: An Introduction to the Theory of the State in Marx, Engels, and Lenin* (New York: Paine-Whitman, 1957). Confusion over the role of the State, and the states, in early American life is rife; Carter Goodrich, ed., *The Government and the Economy: 1783–1861** (Indianopolis: Bobbs-Merrill, 1967) contains a group of essays that clarify the early period.

Finally, Marxists from many countries in 1973 began a new journal to develop understanding of the State: *KAPITALISTATE.* Communications in the U.S. should be addressed to Professor James O'Connor, Department of Economics, California State University, San Jose, California 95114.

chapter nine

Epilogue: The Future Lies Ahead

These are transitional years and the dues will be heavy.
Change is quick but revolution will take a while.
America has not even begun as yet.
This continent is seed.

(Diane di Prima, *Revolutionary Letter #10*)

Neither knowledge of history nor of social analysis can tell us what the future holds; taken together, they can tell us where we are, how we got there, what to look for in the unfolding present, and what questions to ask. Marx and Veblen, who most and best combined historical analysis with social theory, differed greatly on what the developments they studied augured for the future; yet they shared a healthy respect for the shaping importance of the past.

Both saw change as continuous, and marked always by conflict. Veblen saw social evolution as a race between the life-giving and life-destroying, cooperative and predatory, elements in human nature and society, but he feared that "force and fraud" were more likely than love and reason to take the lead in that race. His final hope was his ironic reservation that to foresee the future was itself hopeless; it was a matter of "opaque cause and effect," of "blind drift."

Marx was more hopeful, about both our ability to foresee the future, and what the future held. His theory of social change saw capitalism creating both a final crisis for itself *and* creating its own gravediggers—the organized working class—who would replace capitalism with socialism.

Like Veblen, Marx had a fundamental respect for how much the present and future are products of history, which both men saw as the great submerged bulk of an iceberg. In a famous passage, Marx said:

> Men make their own history, but they do not make it just as they please; they do not make it under circumstances chosen by themselves, but under circumstances directly encountered, given and transmitted from the past.

The tradition of all the dead generations weighs like a nightmare on the brain of the living.[1]

The history of the United States is the history of a capitalist society. From its beginnings our political and social history took place in the stated terms of political democracy, human equality, and social mobility. But our economic history was shaped by capitalism's integral needs for economic and geographic expansion and only barely constrained human and resource exploitation.

Glorious though our political and social ideals may have been, our reality has been shaped predominantly by our economic development, which allowed white Americans to treat nonwhites as sub-humans or (along with women) as second-class citizens, to treat our natural environment as something to conquer, and, in this century, to view the rest of the world as our oyster.

Our long history of technological advance and economic expansion made us the primary world power in a world where economic power has been decisive. At home, quantitative economic achievement has encouraged and allowed the bulk of our population to be deflected from concern over the quality of their own and others' existence.

Will the future allow the continuation of these long-standing and deep-seated processes and relationships? It does not seem so. Although it is impossible to foresee what shape the American future will take, and whether we will shape it actively or passively, we may be reasonably sure that it will be substantially different from our distant and recent past. We are in a period of transition; for better or for worse, it is likely that the near future will see changes in basic political, economic, and social institutions. Why is this so? Can anything be said of likely directions?

TROUBLES, HERE AND THERE

The past decade or so has been one of unprecedented searching and turbulence for the United States. Even though the 1970's began with a calming of the surface turbulence, uneasiness and searching continue; we may remember that the raucous sixties were preceded by the "silent fifties." In the perspective we have advanced, the explanation for this development should be looked for in the changing conditions of expansion and exploitation.

The developmental changes for the United States that have shaped the past generation were begun during World War II and took their

---

[1]This is part of the opening statement of *The Eighteenth Brumaire of Louis Bonaparte,** available in many editions. It is contained in *Selected Works,* cited earlier, pp. 97ff.

current forms shortly thereafter: internationalization, militarization, and related and dependent patterns of domestic investment and "consumerism." The sustained economic growth since 1941 was made possible by these developments, guided by a growing State in close cooperation with the business community. But each of these developments has created conditions making it increasingly difficult for them to serve as continuing sources of sustained economic growth. Economic and geographic expansion and human and resource exploitation, which have for so long been sources of vitality for American capitalism, have now combined in their effects also to create a new time of troubles.

The nature of those troubles may be spelled out as a quick summary of what has been traced in preceding chapters: 1) the expansion of American influence and investment in the rest of the industrial capitalist world has produced a growing source of effective competition for American products—in markets both at home and abroad—as well as increased demands and uncertainty in financial and resource terms; 2) the expansion of American power into the Third World has become excessive in its costs and has quite probably reached its limits, from which we are now drawing back, and which is a new and potentially unsettling experience for the United States; 3) the militarization of American production has created economic stability, jobs, and profits, but also corruption, an enlarged bureaucracy, and resistance; in addition, the slowed rate of *increase* in military expenditures (sharply declining as a *rate* of GNP) reduces their effectiveness in supporting the economy; 4) "consumerism" finds its limits in the distribution and levels of purchasing power and the ability of business to manipulate tastes and encourage indebtedness, a combination that does not hold out endless promise unless a new boom in economic growth ensues, a process difficult to anticipate; 5) domestic private investment depends upon actual and expected increases in demand and profits, here and abroad, which takes us back to expansive tendencies coming from points (1) through (4) and which closes the circle.

But more is involved: the economic buoyancy and the policies and processes making for buoyancy since World War II have produced other developments that have been and are likely to remain sources of trouble within the system. The stimulating role of the State for expansion has required a rise of all taxes to a level (over 30 percent) which constitutes an already substantial and increasing drag on purchasing power; it has also meant the proliferation of bureaucracy in both the public and the private sectors; it has meant a growing dependence of the principal beneficiaries of State policies and also a growing attention to the activities and *non*-activities of the State. In short, rightly or wrongly, the State is increasingly seen as the cause of what is both wanted and disliked in current society. The State becomes a target in ways new to our history, and it is likely that people at all levels and in all quarters of society will become increasingly political as a result. The turbulence of the sixties is likely to have been only the first round in that process of heightened politicization.

Much more could be said of the destabilizing consequences of American economic growth since World War II. Let us note only two developments of as yet unascertainable but clearly momentous implications: 1) all the talk of affluence for the past years has underscored the relative deprivation endured by tens of millions of Americans, while the great wealth and productivity of our economy makes the continuation of such deprivation difficult to smooth over; 2) continued reliance upon rapid industrial growth as a solvent for social problems must be set against the widespread conviction that such growth must somehow be controlled if we are not to poison ourselves out of existence.

The upshot is a developing crisis. Economic and political in its roots, the crisis is not only social, but moral in its tensions; its ultimate resolution will have to comprehend all these dimensions, for better or for worse. If the United States is approaching a crisis, that means some basic alteration in American institutions is in the offing. Just when, just what, just how, is presently unknowable; but the tensions characterizing the totality of American existence seem unlikely to persist for long without some means being found of subduing or eliminating them.

In general, this must mean a substantial move either to the Right or to the Left—toward an American version of fascism or toward an American version of socialism. For most Americans, either possibility sounds outlandish; still, one or the other is likely before this century ends. We can only look briefly at the conditions that might lead to either. First, American-style fascism.

WAITING FOR RIGHTIE

A movement to the Right has been underway for some years now in the United States, assuming such a movement is defined by increasing power in the hands of a few and increasing powerlessness for the many; by the resort to physical and judicial coercion to solve domestic and international problems; by a growing resort to secrecy and manipulation in both private and public affairs; by a steady erosion of civil liberties; by a decline in policies seeking, however weakly, to set a floor to deprivation and oppression; by a growth of venality and corruption; by the emergence of authoritarian leaders.

All these developments have become part of our daily news in recent years. Do they add up to fascism? Some would say they do; but by fascism it seems more appropriate to mean not merely the emergence of such tendencies but their coming together in a new combination requiring a decisive closure on the traditional forms of political existence. To put it this way is not to encourage a relaxed view of obvious and ominous tendencies; it is to say that fascism is considerably more terrible in its reality than are the tendencies toward it.

When fascism emerged in other nations, such as Italy and Germany, it came in on the heels of a deep socio-economic crisis, and in conjunction with a substantial threat from the Left. Other countries' histories are not likely to be repeated by the United States, nor to suggest the same pre-conditions for social change in the United States; our capitalist history has been significantly different from others' and our evolution toward either fascism or socialism is also likely to have its own qualities.[2]

If and when the movement toward social crisis in America becomes more pronounced, and if it were to be joined by an actual or threatened economic collapse, it seems highly likely that American-style fascism would be attempted. It could be attempted in America even without economic collapse. Deepening racial fears and hostilities could threaten so much in the way of social chaos that only a strong authoritarian rule might promise any sort of stability; that, combined with increasing socio-cultural disintegration, with declining moral sensitivity, with yearning for simpler, more "virtuous" and less challenging days, could be used as an excuse to seize power and lead the nation back to a past imbued with fantasy. There are right-wing leaders who will do what they can to encourage such a development, as Watergate makes "perfectly clear."

Whether or not such leaders can move far in such directions depends not only upon the existence of crisis, but upon the existence of alternatives. That means the Left. Is the Left now or will it be in the foreseeable future able to muster an effective opposition to such tendencies, which are already very real? Or, even more, will it be able eventually to win out and create an American socialism?

TOWARD AN AMERICAN REVOLUTION?

The emergence of fascism in the United States would require "only" a *political coup d'état;* there would be no need to alter basic economic institutions substantially, except to move *more* toward coordinated planning, *more* toward economic nationalism, *more* toward a regressive

---

[2] Arno J. Mayer, *Dynamics of Counterrevolution in Europe, 1870–1956: An Analytic Framework** (New York: Harper Torchbooks, 1971) is an incisive and original analysis of great value for approaching these matters.

use of the State's taxing powers. But socialism would require a basic revolution of the whole range of institutions—economic, political, social, cultural—social ownership and control of the means of production, in turn enabling a structure of production and consumption suited to human needs and possibilities, a structure of power allowing and requiring democratic control of the society, and a social system (not least an educational system) that would contribute to equality and cooperation rather than to privilege and competition. To gain fascism is easy, by comparison: less is involved, and there is more power at hand to do the job. Harold Laski called fascism "capitalism with the gloves off," by which he meant capitalism without the political democracy that historically has accompanied it. Fascism is *counter*-revolutionary. Revolutionary change demands much, much more, especially if it is to be worthwhile.

For there to be a socialist society, there must be a socialist movement with the strength to cause and carry through a revolution. In turn, that requires an analysis that shows why socialism is necessary, and that convinces the largest percentage of the population of this need; a program that makes socialism attractive; a strategy that makes a socialist revolution possible. If that is what is meant by a revolutionary movement, the United States has none. The United States does have large numbers of people of all ages, colors, sexes, and conditions whose lives seem to them increasingly intolerable and alienating; it will seem so until the country undergoes a social reconstruction of revolutionary proportions.

At present, although there is a good deal of revolutionary rhetoric and a recent past of semi-revolutionary tactics, the United States lacks a revolutionary political base both because and despite the ways in which the existing system horrifies, frightens, disaffects and oppresses growing numbers of people, while demeaning and crippling the potentialities of the large majority. In one degree or another, some or all of this has been so throughout American history. Why then has America polarized in attitudes now, but, except for a branch of the Populists, not before?

The key elements appear to have come together in the past decade or so. In that period, the interactions of domestic and international developments flowing from the victory against the fascist armies but not against our own or others' fascist tendencies, combined 1) with a rhetoric revolving around peace, democracy, and equality; 2) with an economy whose technology was widely hailed as making all things possible; and 3) with a determined drive against "communism" abroad and at home that had the unexpected consequence of illuminating the inadequacies of American society. It was of course the young, both black and white, who most quickly noted the gap between the rhetoric and the reality, and whose customary impatience with temporizing first led them to seek ways to close the gap by bringing reality closer to rhetoric.

None of that was entirely new, although the coming together of disparate developments in a white glare of attention perhaps was. The aims of the young were voiced pervasively by almost everyone else—politicians high and low, educators, businessmen, clerics, et al.—while at the same time the society became more bent on war, active racism intensified, poverty programs were abandoned and, among other things, the leadership of the nation became steadily more mediocre, to say the least. That was true at all levels; at the highest level, what seemed barely possible under Kennedy came to seem implausible under Johnson and impossible under Nixon. This tragic evolution was necessarily matched by an enhanced process of repression and further corruption of the judiciary, victimizing those who sought to realize the expressed ideals of America. And all the while America deteriorated even further: in the seventies, more poverty, more corruption, more economic troubles, more hypocrisy on racism—but somewhat less war.

It is vital to note and to understand that only a very small number of the young ever engaged in the political struggles of the sixties; it is equally vital to note how very great the attention and furor was that attended their efforts. In the United States that has always happened, whenever Left or radical movements seemed to be more than mere exercises in free speech. That this has been more true in the United States than elsewhere is a consequence of our uncompromising and uncontested capitalism. It is a matter of what Antonio Gramsci calls "hegemony," which is a concept worth exploring. Hegemony is:

> an order in which a certain way of life and thought is dominant, in which one concept of reality is diffused throughout society in all its institutional and private manifestations, informing with its spirit all taste, morality, customs, religious and political principles, and all social relations, particularly in their intellectual and moral connotations.[3]

Gramsci developed the idea of hegemony as a means of understanding both the power of capitalism and the needs of the working

---

[3]Gwynn Williams, quoted in John M. Cammett, *Antonio Gramsci and the Origins of Italian Communism** (Stanford: Stanford University Press, 1967), p. 204. This book is fundamental to an understanding of Gramsci, leader of the Italian Communist Party in the 1920's, until imprisoned by Mussolini for 11 years (until just before his death in 1937). See also the excellent essays by Carl Boggs on Gramsci in *Socialist Revolution,* vol. 2, nos. 5 and 6, and by Eugene Genovese, in his *In Red and Black,* cited earlier. Gramsci's writings are now easily available. See his *The Modern Prince and Other Writings** (New York: New World Paperbacks, 1967) and the larger selection in Quintin Hoare and G. N. Smith, eds., *Selections from the Prison Notebooks of Antonio Gramsci** (London: Lawrence and Wishart, 1971). Although Gramsci's analyses are treated briefly here, it is my view that they are of substantial relevance for American conditions.

class if it were ever to gain power: "the working class, before it seizes State power, must establish its claim to be a ruling class in the political, cultural, and 'ethical' fields."[4]

It would be difficult to find an industrial capitalist nation in which the "hegemony" of the ruling class is as thoroughgoing in its spread as in the United States; as we approach crisis, it is that hegemony which is breaking down. But we shall move through that crisis into fascism unless an alternative vision of society is created, and unless those who would bring socialism educate and organize around that vision. The hegemony of the ruling class is not simply economic, nor simply anything; it is the consenting acceptance of the main elements of social existence by the mass of the population. That hegemony will not be displaced by an economic crisis; quite the contrary, in the absence of a strong socialist movement working with a socialist program of coherence and comprehensiveness, an economic crisis would hasten fascism.

It is widely accepted that revolutionary periods are preceded by developments in which those who subsequently make the revolution see their hopes become raised within the system, but then without chance of realization within that same system. But revolutionaries alone do not make a revolution. The revolutions that have occurred in the past have occurred only during or after a *crisis,* which itself results from the system's own normal, interacting ("dialectical") processes and relationships. Revolutionaries have been able to seize the opportunities presented by the social crisis. An "historical" crisis of the system is thus a necessary condition for revolution. But it is not sufficient unto itself, as the American Depression of the thirties shows.

When a capitalist system's "natural" evolution leads through crisis to institutional discontinuity, the stage is set for revolution *or* counterrevolution, that is, fascism. It is not enough to believe, as I do, that fascism is deeply contrary to basic human needs, that reason and decency and well-being in our well-informed and productive world *should* vitiate the possibilities of fascism and enhance the possibilities of democratic socialism; that, in short, fascism "can't work," and would therefore mean the later emergence of a still larger crisis. Fascism has happened frequently in this century; it can still happen here. Should it, in an age of nuclear weapons, faith in the "ultimate" triumph of socialism becomes a cruel figure of speech, a dangerous delusion. Fascism must and can be prevented only by simultaneous efforts on two fronts: struggles *against* its lurking potential and *toward* democratic socialism.

Many who participated in the protest movements of the sixties will quarrel with what now will be said, but it must be said: despite the rhetoric, the furor, and the great heights of emotion and activity of that

---

[4]Ibid., p. 205.

period, it was a period of revelation, not of revolution. The leading edge of that process was provided by young blacks, at least partially stimulated by minor institutional changes and a pleasing language of racial equality that began to be publicized—for the first time in our history, it is important to note—in the late fifties. The young blacks were joined by young whites who, unburdened by considerations of material striving, and later horrified or threatened by the Indochinese War, began to request and later to demand that this society live up to its fundamental promises. There was no excuse for not doing so, if their elders could be taken at their word. Both young blacks and young whites believed and acted, for a while, as though reason and the setting of virtuous examples would move society to fundamental change, almost as though they were priming a pump. Within a decade they had learned and others had been taught that the well is dry—or poisoned.

The process of revelation in the United States has been remarkable, not only in its swiftness—though its belated appearance is understandable—but also in the way in which the uncovering of one layer of oppression helped to reveal one after another layer of oppression, injustice, violence, material and spiritual deprivation, and repression. Now the United States can be compared to an onion, whose layers when peeled away finally reveal little worth preserving.

Still another remarkable feature of the last decade was that the impetus for change did not come from its expected sources, economic interest groups, but instead from those who, seeking to make America realize its promises, fought principally on grounds of morality rather than economic interest. The "Movement" thus lacked an adequate theoretical base, initially a perverse source of its strength. It is worth noting that the simultaneous existence of formal political democracy and economic autocracy, on the one hand, and widespread naïveté as to the manner in which the latter vitiates the former, on the other, raises interesting possibilities for the future, as it did in the sixties. A people that does not know it is *de facto* powerless can, by acting on mistaken assumptions, both improve its understanding and push further and more vigorously than it might otherwise do. At some point, in other words, the myth of American democracy could turn out to be a building block for a struggle to make the myth into a reality.

To become a Movement that is also a revolutionary movement, the moral and the analytical bases must be strengthened and combined, and these views will have to comprehend the numerous interests that are now and that remain to be articulated into both an analysis and a program. But morality and understanding only facilitate social change; they do not bring it about. That requires power.

Earlier it was noted that power arises from control over both intangibles and tangibles. The intangibles—morality, ideals, and understanding—are necessary if the nature of our developing crisis is to be grasped and in any sense dealt with. We may think of these as the normative sources of power. But unless the American crisis ushers in a complete breakdown of the existing power structure (as happened in Russia in 1917, but which is not yet to be expected in the United States), a socialist movement must have a non-normative source of power: it must have control over tangibles. In our society that means some control over the means of production.

Clearly, that in turn cannot refer to ownership, so it must mean control gained by the organization of the working class, defined in its contemporary and broadened sense. The working class has its sheer numbers to shut down production as its *potential* source of power; at the present time and in the foreseeable future, the potential has no counterpart in reality. Nor can it have until and unless the Left begins to operate in terms substantially different from its past.

This is another way of saying that the American Left must be both more and less American. Both the Old Left and New Left have adopted all too much of capitalist America's ways—individualist power drives, imagistic appeals, the search for simple or quick solutions, over-emphasis on narrow economic programs—and neither Old nor New have acted as though they understood the strength of American capitalism, or the degree to which the social system it has created has been accepted as natural and desirable by most Americans. Such shortcomings have been entirely understandable; but to continue with them is entirely too dangerous.

There are important, heart- and mind-warming signs that the defects of both Old and New Left *are* being overcome. There is much talk these days that "The Movement" has died out; that talk is based mostly on the dearth of media visibility for left-wing political activities—in part because the media have been intimidated and bored, in more important part because such activities are much less aimed at media coverage now than in the sixties, an entirely healthy sign. Hundreds and thousands of small community-oriented groups now function, centering on health care, new forms of education, improved housing and rent control efforts, "people's" presses and garages, and on personal liberation. In addition, virtually every profession now has its counterpart to URPE: there are radical caucuses and journals for (among other areas) sociology, political science, literature, the natural sciences and engineering, history, law, and medicine. And there are critical revolts in some trade unions. A recent and serious inquiry into the state of such matters yielded the following conclusions:

> There are tens of thousands and perhaps millions of people who have come out of the Sixties with new ideas, new ways of looking at America,

new perceptions of themselves, their families, and their communities, shorn of old loyalties and assumptions, no longer taking for granted the values and authority of things-as-they-are. These are the people, mostly but not exclusively young, who were truly "radicalized" in the last decade and haven't forgotten it in this one. . . . [T]he obituaries are, at the least, premature.[5]

An American revolutionary socialist movement must comprehend both analytically and programmatically the diverse and common problems, needs, and aspirations of the many groups that have been raised to consciousness and anger and effort in recent years and serve to encourage many others; it must understand both the strengths and the weaknesses of the existing system; it must have an analysis of power that tells it where and how and when to move or to hold back (for "action" can be counter-productive, as recent years have shown); it must move toward the liberation, the well-being, and the power of wage-earners, of women, of the nonwhite, of the young—but also of those who in their different yet serious ways are unfree and crippled: the middle-aged, middle-class whites, men and women alike. The revolution we need is one that at least removes the fangs of America in the world and that seeks to make the United States liveable for its own people and a force for cooperative constructive change in the world.

All that is asking a lot. But it is no more, as a perspective, than is necessary if there is to be hope for an effective socialist movement in this society, or if such a movement is to deserve the effort and the sacrifices it will entail. A socialist movement will have to learn, and act upon its knowledge, of the inherent possibilities of all human beings; see itself as comprising not morally or intellectually superior creatures, but men and women privileged to understand the plight of society and to have the energy to spread that privilege until the plight is replaced by what society can make possible for people.

Those who are angry can build such a movement; those who hate cannot. Committed men and women are essential; zealots are a hindrance. Thought, analysis, and reflection are indispensable; dogmatism is poison.

"America," the midwestern poet Carl Sandburg wrote long ago, "was promises." Decency, sanity, and safety require that those promises be redeemed; with effort, patience and impatience, and love, they can be.

---

[5]Kirkpatrick Sale, "The New Left: What is Left?" in the magazine *WIN* (June 28, 1973).

Index of Subjects

(Note: The intent of this index is not to locate all subjects mentioned in the text or, for example, to identify all those pages where "capitalism," "imperialism," or other such central concerns of the book are discussed. Instead, the index seeks first of all to locate passages where critical relationships and processes are discussed; second, it identifies pages where matters deemed likely to be either especially interesting (e.g., alienation) or puzzling (e.g., enclosures) are discussed).

Corn Laws, 13
Corporate liberalism, 267–68, 270, 279–80
Council on Foreign Relations, 212–13
Country town mentality, 160–61
Creditor nation status. *See* Debtor/creditor nation status
Cycles, business, 79–80. *See also* Fluctuations, economic and Growth, economic

Debtor/creditor nation status: immature and mature, 206; U.S. changes in, 208–209
Dehumanization, 140–41
Depression: and Malthus, 11–13; in U.S. and Germany, 21; and economics, 21–25; of the late 19th century, 64, 87; and farm exports, 159; of the 1930's, 21–25, 87; described and analyzed, 96–100; and dual economy, 91–96; and Veblen, 80–82; and the New Deal, 100–105; and political unrest of the 1930's, 103–104; as dominating fear, 106
Development, economic: contrasted with growth and fluctuations, 78; major trends of, 81
Diminishing returns, principle of, 13
Dual economy: and Depression of 1930's, 91–96; and income and wealth distribution, 144, and world economy, 208
Duplex Printing v. *Deering*, 133

Earth Day, 178, 182
Ecology: and economic growth, 33n; and conventional economics, 150–51; and agriculture, 163–64; and speculation, 165–66; crisis of, 175–76; early problems of, 176; dimensions of problem, 176–82
Economics: *classical*, 3–5; and economic development, 15; and expansion, 79; *neoclassical*, 3–5, 15–17; and hedonism, 17–18; and choice, 21; and depression and Keynes, 21–25; and current needs, 25–27; and expansion and depression, 79; inadequacies for ecological and urban problems, 150–52; and agriculture, 164–65; and underdevelopment, 230; and the State, 245
Effective demand, 12–13, 23–24
Enclosures: and creation of working class, 39–40; and distribution of income and wealth, 42–43
Energy crisis. *See* Oil
Executives' compensation, 126–27

Expansion: *economic,* as basic to capitalism, 2–3; and Adam Smith, 10; and population growth, 12; and investment, 24; role and nature in capitalism summarized, 33–34; relation to exploitation, 34–35; aid to early U.S. development, 47; and geographic expansion, 55–58; necessity for, 78–79; and contraction, 82; 19th and 20th centuries contrasted, 85–86; and income distribution, 125; and agriculture, 164–65; changing conditions at present, 296–97; *geographic,* 12; persistence of in and by the U.S., 48–49; nature and role in U.S. economic development, 55–58; and agriculture, 153–54; and changing power relationships, 187; in early mercantilist period, 190–91; in 19th and 20th century, and of U.S. after World War II, 191–92; and imperialism, 194–95; and medieval and early capitalist development, 196–98
Exploitation: as basic for capitalism, 2–3; and Adam Smith, 8, 10–11; and propertylessness, 37–38; and profitability, 125; and inequality of income and wealth, 155; of labor and the land, 165; and imperialism, 194–95; changing conditions of at present, 294–96
Export-Import Bank, 211
Exports. *See* Foreign economic relationships
EXXON, 70–71, 223, 231–32, 277

Farmers. *See* Agriculture
Fascism: beginnings of in Germany, 261–62; and self-management in industry, 265n; as feared by Hoover, 270; and the military, 276; possibilities of in U.S., 296–97, 300
Federal Reserve System, 86, 102, 250–51, 266
Fluctuations, economic: contrasted with growth and development, 78; analyzed, 83–84; record of in U.S., 84–85
Foreign economic relationships of U.S.: and farmers, 156–60; dependence of U.S. upon, 186–87; after Civil War, 205–206; compared to Great Britain, 209–211, 218–20; recent U.S. trade and payments changes, 219–20; and multinational corporation, 224–26; and underdeveloped countries, 231–35; exports and imports, 205n, 207, 216–17, 233; investment, 231–

232. *See also* Free trade and Debtor/creditor nation status

Fortune 500. *See* Business, big

Free trade: and Ricardo, 13; in late 19th century, 194; and North/South conflicts, 204–205; Great Britain and U.S. compared, 209–210; difficulties of for U.S., 219

General Motors, 53, 70–71, 113, 222–24, 232, 277

Geography: advantages of for U.S., 45, *See also* Expansion, geographic

Gross national product (GNP): and big business, 70; and State expenditures, 95; defined, 95n; fall of in 1929–33, 96; components since 1929, 98–100; stability of since World War II, 105; in 1973, 173; and foreign trade, 206–208

Growth, economic: and ecology, 33n; contrasted with fluctuations and development, 78; and "growthmania," 164

Hanseatic League, 189

Hegemony: geographic of the U.S., 191–92; of U.S. after World War II, 202; social, as used by Gramsci, 299–300

Homestead Act of 1862: intent, 156n; as misused, 162n

Immigration, 46; and U.S. development, 56; and class attitudes in U.S., 131–32, 137–38; and urban development, 169, 172

Imports. *See* Foreign economic relationships

Indentured labor, or servants. *See* Workers

Industrial Workers of the World (IWW, Wobblies), 130–31, 138

Industrialism; and economics, 4, 11; spread of in 19th century, 14; in U.S., 19th century, 47; and expansion, 56–59; and falling prices in late 19th century, 156

Inequality of income and wealth: and expansion, 115; and structural change, 116–17; dispute over constancy, 119–120; between rich and poor nations, 121; views toward, 124–25; in world, 227

Investment: and expansion, 24; and tax policies, 110–11; U.S. foreign, 231–33

Irish workers, 129–30

Japanese-American Treaty, 214–15

Just wages and prices, 189

Keynesian economics. *See* Economics, *neoclassical*

Knights of Labor, 130

Labor. *See* Workers or Trade unions

Labor movement: contrasted with trade union movement, 135–37

Laissez-faire, 7–8; and medieval thought, 11; and property and power, 36–37; as social philosophy, 41, 43–44; and the State, 244; in the 1920's, 269

Land policy, 154

Legitimation, 252–55

Lorenz Curve, 121–22

Los Angeles, 150; as model for U.S., 170–171

Mainstream economics. *See* Economics, *neoclassical*

Marshall Plan, 158, 214

Mercantilism: and the State and classical political economy, 5–9; private, 9, 42, 61, 135; and colonialism, 5, 6; and obstacles to development, 8; nature and evolution of, 188–89; compared with imperialism, 190–91; and American colonies, 203–204; in early U.S. development, 204

Mergers: in 19th century, 64–65; in 20th century, 65–69; horizontal, vertical, conglomerate, 68; and concentration and centralization of power, 69

Middle East Treaty Organization, 215

Military in the U.S.: and industrial complex, 62, 75, 272–76; production of since 1941, 82; and internationalization of American economy, 107; growing suspicion of, 107; and concealed unemployment, 112; nature and dimensions of abroad, 219–20; and shift of U.S. to right, 289–90; declining production as percent of GNP, 295

Monopoly: and technology, 36; and property, 37; "natural" and "temporary," 62; and large-scale production, 63–64; rise of in past century, 64–69; as dynamic sector in 1920's, 92–94

Monroe Doctrine, 205

Multinational corporations (MNC): evolution and general nature of, 73–74; characteristics, functions, and consequences of, 221–27

National Industrial Recovery Act (NIRA), 102–103; and Nazi patterns, 265n
National Security Act, 213
Neoclassical economics. *See* Economics, *neoclassical*
Neocolonialism, 191
New Deal: and conservatism, continuity, and periods, 100–101; Second New Deal, 103–104; and power-broking, 104; and impact on post-World War II, 105–106; delayed structural effects, 106–107, 270–71
Non-decisions: and power, 245, 264
North Atlantic Treaty Organization (NATO), 214

Oil: offshore sales by LBJ, 109; and ecological and energy problems, 178–82; and international monetary problems, 226; and foreign investment and politics, 231–34; reserves in Middle East, 234; and Chase Manhattan Bank, 238n
Oligopoly, 21; MNC as form of, 224
Organization of American States (OAS), 214
Organization of Petroleum Exporting Countries, 217

Paley Report, 217
Panics: in U.S. history, 84–85; causes of, 86–87
Pax Britannica, 201–202
Pentagon. *See* Military in the U.S.
Pentagon Papers, 241, 254
Phillips Curve, 108–109
Pluralism: assumptions of, 243; as theory of the State, 244–45
Point Four Program, 214, 230
Political economy. *See* Economics, *classical*
Population growth: and Malthus, 11–12; 1890–1920, 131–32
Populism: and racism, 155n; and falling farm prices, 156; as a movement, 158; as a failed movement, 259–60
Poverty: absolute and relative, 121; recognition of in U.S., 141; definition by government, 142–43; nature and uses of 143–44; causes of, 144–45; and education, 145
Power: and property, 10, 36, 62–63; and exploitation, 37–38; centralization and concentration of, 48; distinguished from prestige and authority, 58; and mergers,

69; and big business, 69–73; and wealth, 123, 127; and social mobility, 128–29; and racism and sexism, 129–30; and geographic expansion, 187; and the State, 242–44, 249–52; and non-decisions, 245; patterns of in the medieval and early modern world, 246–48; sources of, 249; and possibilities of socialism, 301–302
Power élite, 272–73
Proclamation Line of 1763, 154
Progressives (urban), 151; and centralization of power, 261–63
Property, private: as basic to capitalism, 2; and power, 8–11, 62–63; and J. S. Mill, 14; evolution on the land, 38–40; and class, and power, 127–28
Prosperity: and viewpoint, 90–91; and the dual economy, 91–95; and the State sector since World War II, 95–96; and affluence, 145
Protection, privilege, and provisioning, 188–90, 202
Protection rents and costs, 202n, 219

Racism: and U.S. development, 50; and class consciousness, 129; and Irish/British workers, 129–30; and U.S. labor history, 138; and the Populist period, 138; and income differences, 139; compared with sexism, 139n; and farmers, 155
Rationalization: in Germany, 261–62; in U.S., 261–63
Raw materials: dependency of U.S. on, 216–17
Reciprocal Trade Agreements Act, 211–12
Red Scare (of 1920's), 268
Reforms: of New Deal, 102–104; of early 20th century, 266–67
Robber barons, 266
Rockefeller Report, 217

Sacco-Vanzetti case, 268
San Francisco area; deterioration of, 171
Say's Law, 22, 24
Scarcity: and economics, 15–16, 21
Second Bank of the United States, 155, 255–58
Securities legislation, 102
Selective Service Act, 214
"Seven Sisters," 232
Sexism: and class consciousness, 129; and labor, 137–38; and income differences, 139–40; compared with racism, 139n

Slavery: beginnings in U.S., 46; role in U.S. history, 48; role in North's development, 56

Social Security Act, 103

Social-industrial complex, 279–80, 283–85

Socialism: and the Socialist Party, 103; and World War I, 268; possibilities of, in U.S., 298–303

Socialization. *See* Legitimation

Southeast Asia Treaty Organization (SEATO) 215

Speculation: in land, 154–55; in urban real estate, 166; and urban transport, 169

Stagnation, economic: in Great Britain, 21; signs of, 1909–1914, 87–89; as current possibility, 11; and dual economy, 92

State system, 249–52

Stationary state, 14

Structural change: since World War II, 106–107, 110; and tax policies, 110; and income distribution, 115–17; between Great Britain and the U.S., 203

Subversive Activities Control Board, 214

Surplus, economic, 276–77; of capital and labor, 278–79

Taft-Hartley Act, 104n

Taxation: and exploitation, 35; and income and wealth distribution, 118; and 16th amendment, 267; and social tensions, 283–87; and GNP, 285; as percent of income, 286

Technology: and economic growth, 14; and expansion 34n; and monopoly, 36; and competition, 42–45; and mergers, 65; and the MNC, 73

Trade Expansion Act of 1962, 218

Trade Unions: history of in U.S., 130–35; and ethnic and racial antagonisms, 131–32; in 1920's and 1930's, 133–34; contrasted with labor movement, 135–37; and the Cold War, 215; and the MNC, 225

Truman Doctrine, 213

Underdevelopment: causes and consequences of, 227 ff; and economics, 230; characteristics of, 235–37; and aid and trade, 237–39

Unemployment: in 19th century, 87; 1908–15, 88; 1920–29, 91; and understatement today, 91; in the 1930's, 98; substantial degree of since 1930's, and relationship to military production, 111–12;

Union for Radical Political Economics (URPE), 16n, 29, 30, 92n

Urban problems. *See* Cities

Urban renewal, 174–75

Utility, 16; and hedonism, 17

Wagner (National Labor Relations) Act, 103–104, 134

Walker Tariff, 204

Watergate, 2, 76n, 127, 180, 182n, 288, 290, 291

Webb-Pomerene Act, 267

Wobblies. *See* Industrial Workers of the World

Workers: as alienated, 18–19, 40–41; and competition, 35–36; and exploitation, 37–38; and racial and sex discrimination, 137–38; indentured, 46, 152

Index of Names

Aaron, Benjamin, 135n
Abramowitz, Jack, 259n
Acheson, Dean, 212, 288
Ackerman, Frank, 119n, 220n
Adamic, Louis, 137n
Adams, Walter, 76, 77, 93n
Adelman, M. A., 233n
Agnew, Spiro, 128, 254n
Alapatt, Cyril, 196n
Albion, Robert G., 168n
Alexander, Floyce, 150
Allen, F. L., 113, 269
Allen, Robert L., 147
Anderson, Martin, 174n
Arnold, Thurman, 76
Aronson, James, 254n
Ash, Roy, 142
Ashworth, William, 240
Aston, Trevor, 8n
Averitt, Robert T., 70n, 71
Avineri, Shlomo, 51, 240, 290n

Bachrach, Peter, 244n
Bain, Joe S., Jr., 76
Ball, George, 212
Ballard, Hoyt B., 271n
Baran, Paul, 60n, 83, 88–89, 97n, 228, 230n, 276–77
Baratz, Morton S., 244n
Barraclough, G., 247n
Barton, Bruce, 269
Bator, Francis M., 110n
Bell, Daniel, 271n
Benedict, Murray, 162n
Bennett, Roy, 196n
Benston, Margaret, 148
Berle, A. A., 76, 212
Bernstein, Barton, 114
Biddle, Anthony, 257
Blair, John M., 68n, 70n
Bloch, Marc, 39n, 247n

Bluestone, Barry, 92n, 93, 144n, 145, 283n
Boggs, Carl, 299n
Bonn, M. J., 261n
Bonnen, James T., 162n
Bookchin, Murray, 175–76
Borch, Fred J., 126
Bottomore, T. B., 19n, 41n, 148
Bowles, Samuel, 144n
Boxer, C. R., 199n
Boyle, Kay, 1
Brady, Robert A., 59n, 60n, 261n, 262, 265n, 277n, 279n, 292
Brennan, Peter, 136
Bridges, Harry, 136n
Brown, Dee, 148
Bryan, William Jennings, 260
Buchanan, James, 269
Budd, Edward C., 123
Bukharin, Nikolai, 228n
Bundy brothers, 288
Burnham, D. C., 127
Burns, Arthur F., 251
Burns, Arthur R., 61n

Cahan, A., 58n
Cahn, Edgar S., 148
Cammett, John M., 299n, 300n
Carnegie, Andrew, 167n
Carr, Gregg, 174n
Carson, Robert B., 291
Carswell, Harold, 113n
Chandler, Alfred Jr., 77
Chandler, Lester V., 114
Chomsky, Noam, 241
Churchill, Winston, 213
Cirino, Robert, 254n
Clapham, J. H., 39n
Clark, G. N., 8n
Clark, J. M., 31, 79–80
Clay, Henry, 204
Clayton, James L., 273n

60, 78, 80, 82–83, 107n, 121, 127, 129, 149, 165, 198, 240, 249, 271, 283, 290, 293–94

Mattingly, Garrett, 198
Mayer, Arno J., 297n
Means, Gardiner, 76
Meany, George, 136, 215
Melman, Seymour, 272–76
Meszaros, Istvan, 40n
Meyer, John R., 116n
Miliband, Ralph, 245, 249n, 250–52
Mill, John Stuart, 4, 5, 13–15, 17, 37, 79
Miller, Herman P., 118, 120
Miller, S. M., 196n
Mills, C. Wright, 30, 51, 127, 137n, 148, 255n, 271–72, 287, 292
Mintz, Morton, 291
Mishan, E. J., 164
Mitchell, Broadus, 52, 101n, 211n
Mitchell, Wesley Clair, 79–80
Moody, William Vaughn, 242
Moore, Barrington Jr., 51, 248n
Moore, Stanley, 292
Morgan, Robin, 148
Morse, Chandler, 240
Morton, Peggy, 148
Moynihan, Daniel, 175
Mumford, Lewis, 167n, 170, 180, 185
Mussolini, Benito, 299n

Napoleon I, 201
Napoleon III, 290
Nettels, Curtis P., 52, 57n
Neumann, Franz, 292
Nixon, Richard M., 2, 30, 69n, 104, 108, 110, 111, 113n, 126, 136, 160, 172, 175, 216, 220n, 226, 251, 254n, 275, 283, 288, 289, 299
Nordholt, J. W. Schulte, 46n
Nossiter, Bernard, 77
Novack, David, 240

O'Connor, James, 92, 96, 145, 188n, 193, 272, 276n, 277–83, 284n, 292
O'Farrell, James, 58n, 172
Oglesby, Carl, 217n, 287
Osofsky, G., 147, 168n

Palmer, A. Mitchell, 268n
Papandreou, Andreas G., 70n, 127
Parker, Richard, 286
Parrington, Vernon, 48
Parry, J. H., 199n

Pechman, Joseph, 119, 286
Pell, Eve, 55
Perlo, Victor, 114
Perrow, Charles, 77
Phillips, Joseph D., 276n, 291
Pitkin, Walter B., 278–9
Piven, F., 149
Polanyi, Karl, 51
Power, Eileen, 39n, 51
Prothro, James W., 269n

Radosh, Ronald, 114, 215n
Reagan, Ronald, 283
Reich, Michael, 51
Reid, Samuel Richardson, 68n, 70n
Renshaw, Patrick, 147
Resnik, Solomon, 147
Rhodes, Robert J., 188n, 229n
Ricardo, David, 4, 5, 11–14, 44, 79, 209
Ridge, Lola, 53
Ridgeway, James, 151n, 176n, 181
Riis, Jacob, 168n
Robbins, Lionel, 15n
Robinson, Joan, 23, 29
Rockefeller, David, 279–80
Rockefeller, John D., 65n
Rogin, Leo, 29
Roll, Eric, 29
Rolvaag, O. E., 58n
Roosevelt, Franklin Delano, 23, 100–104, 128, 152n, 211, 213, 275n
Roosevelt, Theodore, 264, 267
Rostow, W. W., 230, 288
Rothbard, Murray, 114
Roundtree, M. and J., 148
Royko, Mike, 185
Rusk, Dean, 212, 288
Ryan, William, 148

Sacco, Nicola, 268
Sale, Kirkpatrick, 182n, 303n
Samuelson, Paul, 23, 96
Sandburg, Carl, 115, 303
Say, Jean-Baptiste, 22, 24
Scheiber, Harry, 131n, 162n
Schick, Allen, 281
Schiller, Herbert I., 240, 291
Schlesinger, Arthur Jr., 257n
Schoeffler, Sidney, 30
Schucter, Jerome, 112n
Schultze, Charles L., 281
Schumpeter, Joseph A., 52, 79–80, 193–94, 239

Seligman, Ben, 11n, 147
Selsam, Howard, 52, 130n
Sennett, Richard, 149, 184
Sexton, Patricia Cayo, 147
Shannon, Fred, 52, 57n, 156n
Shaull, Richard, 217n
Shonfield, Andrew, 24n, 277n
Sigal, Clancy, 113
Sinclair, Upton, 58n, 103, 113, 172, 267
Smedley, Agnes, 58n
Smith, Adam, 2–11, 13, 14, 17, 36, 37, 41–
  45, 47, 59–61, 63, 78, 79, 201
Smith, G. N., 299n
Smith, James D., 124
Soule, George, 52, 89n, 94–95, 268n
Steffens, Lincoln, 168
Steinbeck, John, 114, 162n
Stephenson, Hugh, 222n, 223n, 225n, 226
Stern, Philip M., 123n, 285n
Stevenson, Adlai, 104
Stocking, George W., 77
Stone, I. F., 254–55n, 287
Streever, Donald, 97n
Stribling, T. S., 58n
Svennilson, Ingvar, 208n
Swados, Harvey, 114, 185
Sward, Keith, 77, 93n
Sweezy, Paul M., 30, 60n, 83, 88–89, 94n,
  97n, 112, 170n, 193n, 219, 276–77, 287,
  292

Tabb, William K., 147
Taft, Robert A., 215
Taft, William Howard, 264
Tanzer, Michael, 233n, 234n
Tawney, R. H., 11, 40n, 43, 44, 52, 148, 199
Taylor, George R., 52, 57n, 168n
Taylor, Maxwell, 288
Terkel, Studs, 114
Thales, 63
Thompson, E. P., 52
Townsend, Lynn, 127
Truman, Harry S., 104, 108, 160, 213–14,
  230, 275, 290
Twain, Mark, 48

Uphoff, Norman, 241
Upton, Letitia, 118n, 119, 123

Van Alstyne, Richard W., 49n
Vanzetti, Bartolomeo, 268
Vatter, Harold G., 147
Veblen, Thorstein, 4, 17–20, 24, 25, 27, 30,
  31, 43n, 50, 52, 56, 59–61, 75, 79–82, 83,
  90, 93, 107, 127, 129, 149, 154, 155, 160,
  183, 188, 195, 249, 251, 271, 283, 293
Von Horn, General, 43

Wachtel, Howard, 144
Wallace, George, 160, 283
Wallerstein, Immanuel, 240
Walzer, Michael, 248n
Ward, Benjamin, 29
Wasserman, Muriel, 144n, 185
Watkins, Myron W., 77
Weaver, James, 30, 144n
Webster, Daniel, 204
Wecter, Dixon, 114
Weidenbaum, Murray L., 282
Weinstein, James, 86n, 103n, 129n, 261n,
  266n, 268n
Weisberg, Barry, 93n, 178, 179n
Weiss, Leonard W., 76
Weisskopf, Thomas E., 51, 227n, 231n
West, Nathaniel, 170n
Wiebe, Robert, 261n
Wilcox, Clair, 141–2
Will, Robert E., 147
Williams, Gwynn, 299n
Williams, William Appleman, 30, 49n,
  155n, 157, 158, 159n, 187n, 212n, 240,
  270, 287
Wilson, Charles (historian), 204n
Wilson, Charles (Sec. of Defense), 53
Wilson, Thomas, 52
Wilson, Woodrow, 48, 104, 260, 264
Wolff, Robert Paul, 292
Woodward, C. Vann, 155n, 259n

Young, Marilyn Blatt, 159n

Zaretsky, Eli, 148

Index of Periodicals